Geistiges Eigentum und Wettbewerbsrecht

edited by

Peter Heermann, Diethelm Klippel †,
Ansgar Ohly und Olaf Sosnitza

176

Anna Marion Bieri

Patents and Professors

The Interdependence between Patent Law, Science, and Research Universities in the United States of America

Mohr Siebeck

Anna Marion Bieri, born 1975; LL.B. (hons) Durham University (UK); LL.M. Munich Intellectual Property Law Centre; Ph.D. University of Bayreuth; Assistant Professor of Practice and Founding Director of the Science, Technology and Law Program at Virginia Tech, Blacksburg (USA); currently freelance consultant and researcher.

ISBN 978-3-16-161269-5 / eISBN 978-3-16-161270-1
DOI 10.1628/978-3-16-161270-1

ISSN 1860-7306 / eISSN 2569-3956 (Geistiges Eigentum und Wettbewerbsrecht)

The Deutsche Nationalbibliothek lists this publication in the Deutsche Nationalbibliographie; detailed bibliographic data are available at *http://dnb.dnb.de*.

The book was typeset by epline in Böblingen using Times New Roman typeface. It was printed on non-aging paper and bound by Laupp & Göbel in Gomaringen.

Printed in Germany.

To my parents

Preface

This work was accepted as a doctoral thesis by the University of Bayreuth in the winter semester 2020/2021.

Over several years this project accompanied me on the side of my teaching and research appointment at a research university in the US. Its completion would not have been possible with the support and encouragement of many people.

First and foremost, my deepest gratitude is owed to my esteemed advisor Professor Dr. Diethelm Klippel. Most importantly, he helped rescue my work from a temporary slumber and instilled in me the confidence that the work was of value. Throughout the whole process, his guidance, suggestions, and patience were instrumental in bringing the project to fruition.

I am also indebted to Professor Dr. Michael Grünberger for the speedy preparation of the second evaluation and to him, to my advisor, and to Professor Dr. Robert Magnus for a very memorable – pandemic-induced – online but yet intimidate and comfortable colloquium. I am also thankful to Professor Dr. Ansgar Ohly, whose path I crossed multiple times, for his support. I am very grateful to him, my advisor, Professor Dr. Peter Heermann, and Professor Dr. Olaf Sosnitza and, last but not least, to Mohr Siebeck for the acceptance of my work into the series 'Geistiges Eigentum und Wettbewerbsrecht'.

Finally, I am indebted to many friends, colleagues, and my family who have supported me on this journey. I would like to especially mention my parents who have instilled in me the values and discipline necessary to complete such an endeavor and who never stopped encouraging me. I would also like to mention my brother who revealed to me the inner workings of academia and who helped me crystalise my point of view. Above all, I thank my husband who has been my biggest supporter of all and my constant interlocutor. He believed in me when I most needed it and is the reason that I successfully completed this work.

Blacksburg, February 2022 Anna Marion Bieri

Table of Contents

Abbreviations

AAU	Association of American Universities
AAUP	Association of American University Professors
AAAS	American Association for the Advancement of Science
AEA	Atomic Energy Act
ArbnErfG	Arbeitnehmererfindergesetz
AUTM	Association of University Technology Managers
BDA	Bayh-Dole Act
BLK	Bund-Länder-Kommission für Bildungsplanung und Forschungsförderung
BMBF	Bundesministerium für Bildung und Forschung
CAFC	Court of Appeals for the Federal Circuit
CFR	Code of Federal Regulations
CPA	Copyright and Patent Agreement
DOD	Department of Defence
EPO	European Patent Office
EPFL	École Polytechnique Fédérale de Lausanne
ETH	Eidgenössische Technische Hochschule
FCST	Federal Council for Science and Technology
FIFG	Bundesgesetz über die Förderung der Forschung und der Innovation
GAO	US General Accounting Office
HERD	Higher Education Research Expenditures
HEW	Department of Health, Education, and Welfare
HFKG	Bundesgesetz über die Förderung der Hochschulen und die Koordination im schweizerischen Hochschulbereich
HHMI	Howard Hughes Medical Institute
HHS	Department of Health and Human Services
IPA	Institutional Patent Agreement
IPI	Swiss Federal Institute of Intellectual Property
NACU	National Association of College and University Attorneys
NAS Act	National Aeronautics and Space Act
NCES	National Center for Education Statistics
NIH	National Institute of Health
NIST	National Institute of Standards and Technology
NLRB	National Labor Relations Board
NRC	National Research Council
NSF	National Science Foundation
NZZ	Neue Zürcher Zeitung
MPEP	Patent Office Manual of Patent Examination Procedure
OECD	Organisation for Economic Co-operation and Development
PAE	Patent Assertion Entity
PatG	Patentgesetz

PCR	Polymerase Chain Reaction
PCT	Patent Cooperation Treaty
PGO	Patent Grant Opposition
PVA	Patentverwertungsagenturen
R&D	research and development
STEM	Science, Technology, Engineering, Math
SWITT	Swiss Technology Transfer Association
TTO	Technology Transfer Office(s)
USC	United States Code
USPTO	United States Patent and Trademark Office
VCA	Visitor Confidentiality Agreement
WARF	Wisconsin Alumni Research Foundation

Introduction

A Research Questions

America's research universities[1] often receive the highest praise in policy discussions: They are considered to be the cornerstone of the 'nation's intellectual infrastructure'[2], the guarantor of 'the high American standard of living'[3], and a 'miracle machine', which has produced 'a torrent of discoveries and trained generations of scientific talent'[4]. While there are numerous accounts of this miracle machine laying the foundation for successful commercial products and business ventures, it also is generally undisputed that one of research universities' key contribution to society remains the search for and dissemination of knowledge – whether commerciable or not.

The transfer of such knowledge from universities to society has historically occurred via traditional transfer channels, such as publications, conferences, by educating and training students, and via consultations, collaborations, and informal exchanges with industry. For a long time, the use of patents (and other intellectual property rights) to transfer knowledge to the outside world has generally not been considered appropriate, mainly because the legal protection and commercialisation of university-developed research results was viewed to be in conflict with the academic mission and its commitment to open science.

The resistance to patents in academia has continuously crumbled over the course of the past century – first very slowly and cautiously but in the past four decades ever more vigorously. In this sense, the 1980 Bayh-Dole Act (BDA)[5] – which allowed universities to retain title to federally funded inventions in order to facilitate their commercialisation – represents the legislative culmination of a gradual process during which the production of scientific knowledge and its

[1] For simplicity, in this work 'research university' refers to institutions in the R1 category of the Carnegie Classification, which stands for doctoral universities with a 'very high research activity', also see infra n. 85.

[2] American Academy of Arts and Sciences, *Public Research Universities* (2017) 5.

[3] NRC, *Research Universities* (2012) ix.

[4] Lander and Schmidt, 'Miracle Machine' (*Washington Post*). It should be noted that in this description the authors include federally funded 'research centers' and point out that federal investment in science and technology is essential as well.

[5] Officially called Universities and Small Business Patent Procedures Act, Public Law 96–517, 94 Stat. 3015 (1980) (codified at 35 United States Code [USC] §§200–212).

legal protection have become increasingly intertwined. In doing so, the BDA has ushered in a new era for the strategic importance which patent considerations play in higher education. Influenced by continuous reduction in government spending in higher education, a pro-patent environment, and increasing (global) competition for students and faculty, research universities rely more heavily than ever on patents as a means of protecting and commercialising university research results.

This intertwinement of the institutions of the university and of patents raises two fundamental questions this work attempts to answer: Firstly, who owns federally and non-federally funded university inventions and who benefits from the current ownership regime? Secondly, who should benefit from university inventions and what does this infer for the ownership and the management of university inventions?

The ownership question is of significance in the discussions of the use of patents in academia for two distinct reasons. Firstly, the BDA's key policy assumption is that university ownership (rather than ownership of the government or private contractors) – coupled with patenting – is essential to the successful commercialisation of federally funded inventions. Secondly, in the past decades, universities have extended this logic to *all* university-generated inventions, and today claim ownership of inventions which are derived from federally funded and non-federally funded research.

This implies that the ownership combined with the use of patents is essential to the successful transfer of university inventions, but it also suggests that greatest benefit from university research is derived if such research will be developed into commercially marketable products. The two questions this raises is whether the BDA and universities' technology transfer practices undermine the larger value of university research as a public good to society and whether – in following these ownership- and patent-centred technology transfer practices – universities negate the importance of strategic considerations relating to the dissemination of university research through different transfer channels.

It should be noted that not included in this inquiry will be inventions which result from industry-sponsored research. From universities' earliest involvement with patents, universities have traditionally excluded the application of their policies to industry contracts. This is still common practice today and universities usually negotiate such contracts – including the ownership of related inventions – on a case by case basis.

B Current State of Research

Extensive literature has been published on the topic of the BDA and on universities' patenting and licensing activities. At the most basic level, the literature may be divided in two large pools: on the one hand, there are the legal scholars who have critiqued and analysed the Act's provisions, its implementation, and its impact on and correlation with aspects of US patent law.[6] On the other hand, there are the economists, policy and business scholars who have studied the Act's policy environment, its impact and the impact of universities' patenting and commercialisation activities' on the academic mission and the US economy.[7]

Despite this comprehensive discussion of the legal, economic, and policy aspects of the BDA and universities' patenting activities – and perhaps due to the wide-spread conception that the BDA was the cause of universities' engagement with patents – the large majority of the literature is concerned with universities' patenting activities as they relate to federally funded research only.[8] What is missing is a comprehensive discussion of universities' technology transfer practices (including their patent policies and assignment practices) as they relate to university research in general. Universities receive financial support and tax subsidies from federal and state governments beyond the receipt of federal grants for certain research projects. It thus seems important to assess the effect of university patenting in the context of this broader understanding of 'public funding' and against the background of universities' public role in society.

The focus on the totality of university research is vital as – prompted by the 2011 Supreme Court decision of *Stanford v. Roche*[9] – today universities' technology transfer practices generally do not distinguish between federally funded and non-federally funded inventions. While there has been a considerable amount of coverage of the legal implications of *Stanford*,[10] the history of universities' technology transfer practices against the backdrop of the BDA and *Stanford* and the consequences of the extension of the BDA-regime to all university inventions has not yet been addressed in detail by the literature.

Finally, several notable publications discuss universities' patenting activities and their increasingly business-minded and litigious behaviour and its effect on universities' open science culture and on society.[11] While scholars have proposed changes to the BDA (including enhancing the authority of the feder-

---

6 See e. g. Eisenberg (1996) 82 Va. L. Rev. 1663; Heller and Eisenberg (1998) 280 Science 698; Pulsinelli (2005) 7 Minn. J. L Sci. & Tech. 393; de Larena (2006) 43 Hous. L. Rev. 1373; Locke (2003) 8 Va. J. L. & Tech. 1; Gotkin, *Bayh-Dole Act* (2012).

7 See e. g. Mowery and others, *Ivory Tower* (2004); Shane (2004) 19 J. Bus. Ventur. 127; Popp Berman (2008) 38 Soc. Stud. Sci. 835; Schacht, *Bayh-Dole Act* (2010); Thursby and Thursby (2003) 301 Science 1052.

8 Notable exceptions are e. g. Chew (1992) 1 Wis. L. Rev. 259; Smith (1997) 1 Va. J. Law & Tech. 1; Luppino (2009) 78 UMKC L. Rev. 367.

9 *Board of Trustees of the Leland Stanford Junior University v. Roche Molecular Systems*, 131 S. Ct. 2188, 2192 (S. Ct. 2011).

10 See e. g. O'Connor (2011) 6 Intell. Prop. J. 29; Takenaka (2011) 44 Tex. Intell. Prop. L. J. 281; Hagelin (2011) 39 AIPLA Q. J. 335.

11 See e. g. David and Hall, 'Property and the Pursuit of Knowledge: IPR Issues Affecting Scientific Research (2006) 35 Research Policy 767; R. Nelson (2001) 26 J. Tech. Transfer 13;

al government in overseeing universities[12]) and have suggested alternatives to the way universities' technology transfer operations are organised (including changes to the legal ownership of inventions[13]) to mitigate some of the issues that the current ownership regime and universities' patent-centred practices have caused, all proposals suggest a general solution to be applied comprehensively to all institutions.

In contrast, this work develops the perspective that a one-size-fits-all solution will not produce optimal results in terms of the protection of the scientific commons and in terms of the protection of the public interest. Instead, the view is developed that universities ought to approach their involvement with patents and the management of their research on a strategic level.

C Course of the Inquiry

Universities supply the public with the fundamental societal need of knowledge, and in turn have been accorded a special place in society. This special place is rewarded by universities receiving financial support, being exposed to reduced regulatory scrutiny and being exempt from certain taxes. By actively participating in patenting and licensing and other market-oriented activities, however, this special position universities maintain in society may be in peril. To develop an understanding of this seeming disparity between universities' public role and their increasingly business-minded behaviours, *Part I, Chapter 1* reviews the history of the US research university and assesses its regulatory and financial framework.

While research universities initially rejected any engagement with patents, some started to explore the use of patents in the first quarter of the 20th century. To appreciate why universities changed their approach to patents, additionally to the institution of the research university and its role in society, the institution of patents will also have to be examined. *Chapter 2* therefore studies the history of the protection of inventive activity and of US patent law and investigates the theories that underpin US patent law. Particular attention will be paid to the question of why research universities gradually let go of their objections to patents and to the policy arguments for and against university patenting.

Part II places emphasis on the discussion of the legal parameters of the ownership of university inventions. *Chapter 3* defines fundamental concepts, such

---

Mowery and others (2001) 30 Research Policy 99; Eisenberg and Cook-Deegan (2018) 147 Daedalus 76.

[12] See e. g. Nelson (2004) 33 Research Policy 455; Rai and Eisenberg (2001) Proc. Conf. on Pub. Domain 157; de Larena (2006) 43 Hous. L. Rev. 1373.

[13] Kenney and Patton (2009) 38 Research Policy 1407; Phan and Siegel (2006) 2 Found. Trends Entrep. 77.

as inventorship and ownership, and describes the inventor's central role in US patent law, while also pointing to the actual lack of protection of the inventor by the law. *Chapter 4* then investigates the legal parameters of the ownership of employee inventions under common law and under contract law and develops how these principles apply to university inventors. The discussion highlights universities' current practice of having researchers assign their inventions to the university in pre-invention assignment agreements on the outset of the employment. Finally, *Chapter 5* analyses the history and provisions of the BDA and studies the landmark Supreme Court decision of *Stanford v. Roche*. *Stanford* is of relevance because it emphasised – over 30 years after the passage of the BDA – that universities' interpretation of the Act and their technology transfer practices were not in accordance with the Act.

Part III attempts to analyse the impact the BDA and university patenting had on society and universities and attempts to define an approach to university patenting which is in alignment with research universities' public role. *Chapter 6* thus investigates the BDA's policy goals and its effect on the US economy and the academic research mission. But the analysis goes beyond the Act. Indeed, a distinction this work attempts to draw, is the one between the framework which the BDA attempted to establish, and the way universities interpreted and implemented the Act. This work will thus try to elaborate in what ways universities' patenting practices align or deviate from the Act's intent. In order to so, *Chapter 7* studies universities' past and current intellectual property policies and analyses universities' technology transfer practices. It also investigates the question of how important university ownership is to the successful transfer of university research and compares ownership regimes by examining – amongst other things – Germany's and Switzerland's approach to university patenting.

Finally, *Chapter 7* concludes by proposing a three-pronged solution to the problems the university ownership regime and universities' current technology transfer practices pose, which includes amendments to the BDA, a call for universities to become strategic in regard to how they 'manage' their university inventions and university research in general, and last but not least, a suggestion for state governments to hold universities accountable for how they manage university research.

Part I

University Inventions in History

Chapter 1

The Rise of the Modern Research University

While US research universities today are often associated with the generation of commerciable knowledge, research universities' fundamental role in society goes beyond this. Their important function as the key supplier of scientific knowledge[1] will be examined in detail in this chapter. In order to do so, firstly, the historic origin of the modern research university in Europe – which provided the basis upon which the US research university was built – will be reviewed. Secondly, it will be studied how the US landscape of higher education evolved. Thirdly, the modern US research university including its regulatory and financial framework and its contemporary challenges will be analysed.

A The Research University's Continental European Origin

In Europe, the 19th century was marked by the resurrection of the modern research and teaching university as an institution. In this process, the university transitioned from its role as the steward and disseminator of a predominately stagnant body of knowledge to its new role as the generator of new knowledge through research.[2] The new ideal of a scientific interpenetration of the world and a quickly expanding scientific knowledge base generally presented a fundamental challenge to the often rigidly organised curricula and institutional structure of universities. As a consequence, the scientific revolution frequently took place outside academia and – with a few exceptions – universities continued to teach their existing curricula in the arts, theology, law, and medicine and only gradually caught up with the new knowledge base.[3]

While in many countries the 'old universities' eventually managed to integrate the new material, this happened in different ways and at different speeds

---

[1] While there is often a distinction made between the production of new *scientific* knowledge (referring to a discovery) versus new *technical* knowledge (referring to an invention), for the purpose of this work this specific distinction will be ignored and scientific research, scientific knowledge, and university research are all understood to refer to scientific and technical knowledge developed at universities.

[2] See e.g. Asche and Gerber, in *Enzyklopädie der Neuzeit Online* (2012) 10; Perkin, in *Higher Education* (2007) 159, 172–173.

[3] Asche and Gerber, in *Enzyklopädie der Neuzeit Online* (2012) 9–10; Perkin, in *Higher Education* (2007) 159, 173–175.

in different countries. In many instances, the initial inability to respond to the changes also led to the founding of technical schools, which would teach relevant applied science and technology.[4] The examples of France and Germany will be discussed in more detail below before the discussion will turn to developments in the US. France's solution focused on the founding of specialised schools, while in Germany a new idea of the university which centred on the unity of the social and natural sciences emerged.

In 1794 in France, universities – which increasingly were perceived as pillars of the old regime – were replaced with a single school: the *École Polytechnique*. The main purpose of the *École Polytechnique* was to educate senior members of the state's technical services. Technical schools which were already in existence (e. g. *École des Mines, École des Ponts et Chaussées, and the École de Génie Maritime*) were eventually linked to the *École Polytechnique* and became the so-called *Écoles d'Application*. These schools provided practical training in individual engineering disciplines and could only be entered into once the general education at the *École Polytechnique* was completed.[5]

In 1929, the French system of higher education was supplemented with the *École Centrale des Arts et Manufactures* in Paris, which was founded on the initiative of a private entrepreneur as a response to demands in industry for trained engineers.[6] During the early 19th century, the French '*Grandes Écoles*' were highly regarded and Paris became the centre of science, attracting scientists from around the world.[7] The French model was not only exported to the French colonies but also inspired *Hautes Écoles* in Belgium and served as a model for other similar institutions, such as the *Technische Hochschulen* in Germany, as will be discussed below.

France also re-introduced universities and yet again, the solution was a nationally unified approach. Accordingly, in 1808 *Napoleon* created the *Université de France* (also called *Université Impériale* or simply *l'Université*): a single, unified organisation with faculties in medicine, law, letters, and science which would serve the whole nation.[8] The landscape of higher education in France continued to be subject to political and intellectual changes throughout the 19th century, which explains its fragmentation and specialisation which remained a characteristic feature until today.[9]

Similarly, in Germany towards the end of 18th century and the beginning of the 19th century, ever more voices also demanded the abolishment of exist-

---

4 Perkin, in *Higher Education* (2007) 159, 174–175.

5 Grelon, in *Industrial Performance* (1993) 42, 42; Weber, *Geschichte der Europäischen Universität* (2002) 154; Charle, in *A History of the University in Europe* (2004) 33, 34.

6 Grelon, in *Industrial Performance* (1993) 42, 43.

7 See e. g. Moraw, *Universität Giessen* (1990) 136; one such German scientist was the chemist *Justus Liebig*, see ibid. Also see infra n. 27–31/I and accompanying discussion.

8 Clark, *Places of Inquiry* (1995) 92.

9 Charle, in *A History of the University in Europe* (2004) 33, 34.

ing universities.[10] The discussions on the future of German universities which followed and which ultimately led to the inception of the University of Berlin should certainly be considered in the context and thus as a response to these above developments.[11] But they also need to be understood against the larger context of France's dominance and thus as a rejection of France's approach to higher education.[12]

The proposals for the University of Berlin, which was founded in 1810 under *Wilhelm von Humboldt*, were not driven by the desire to reform the existing universities but by the desire to create an entirely new type of institution for a new intellectuality.[13] It is elements of this 'new idea of the university' which would eventually serve as a model to other countries in Europe and around the world, including the US.[14] Inspired by neo humanism and German idealism, at the core of the 'Humboldt University' was the relentless search for knowledge (*Wissenschaft*) which is pursued for its own sake. The continuous pursuit of knowledge from the depth of an individual's intellect was considered necessary because knowledge could never actually be found and discovered completely.[15] In this understanding, the mere collection of existing knowledge is distinct from the active search for knowledge; only the latter is able to transform the character and lead to informed, well-rounded personalities who would positively impact society (*Bildung*).[16] It is this understanding of *Wissenschaft* that constituted the foundation of the three cornerstone principles for which Humboldt University today is still known and which – due to their elegance and simplicity – are responsible for the widespread appeal *Humboldt*'s ideals have to this day.

The first principle, the unity of research and teaching (*Einheit von Forschung und Lehre*), manifests the central position of the scholar and the importance of their research at the 'frontiers of knowledge'.[17] The second principle, the protection of academic freedom, comprises the freedom for students to pur-

---

[10] Schelsky, *Einsamkeit und Freiheit* (1963) 37.

[11] See e. g. Fichte, *Deduzierter Plan* (1807); Schleiermacher, *Gelegentliche Gedanken* (1808); Steffens, in *Fichte, Schleiermacher, Steffens – Über das Wesen der Universität* (1810) 205; von Humboldt, *Organisation* (1810/2010) 229.

[12] Schelsky, *Einsamkeit und Freiheit* (1963) 37, 40.

[13] Ibid. 49–57.

[14] See e. g. Höflechner, in *Humboldt international* (2001) 263, 269, concluding that among European countries, Austria adopted the German university model in the most deliberate and comprehensive way.

[15] 'Es ist ferner eine Eigenthümlichkeit der höheren wissenschaftlichen Anstalten, dass sie die Wissenschaft immer als ein noch nicht ganz aufgelöstes Problem behandeln und daher immer im Forschen bleiben, da die Schule es nur mit fertigen und abgemachten Kenntnissen zu thun hat und lernt.' von Humboldt, *Organisation* (1810/2010) 230; '[...] sieht man leicht, dass bei der inneren Organisation der höheren wissenschaftlichen Anstalten alles darauf beruht, das Princip zu erhalten, die Wissenschaft als etwas noch nicht ganz Gefundenes und nie ganz Aufzufindendes zu betrachten, und unablässig sie als solche zu suchen.' ibid. 231.

[16] Ibid. 232.

[17] Fallon, *German University* (1980) 27–28.

sue the curriculum of their choice (*Lernfreiheit*) and the teachers' freedom to teach and by extension the freedom of inquiry (*Lehrfreiheit*).[18] The third principle evolved around the central importance of the arts and sciences (*Philosophische Fakultät*). The arts and sciences – having formed part of the university since its medieval origin – acquired a new meaning under *Humboldt* and were no longer considered to be subordinate to the more specialised faculties. Quite to the contrary, the arts and sciences moved into the centre of the new university.[19] The reversal of this understanding has been said to be one of the key moments of university reform at the beginning of the 19th century.[20]

While the relevance of *Humboldt*'s ideals in the context of the modern university are undisputed,[21] it appears that the extent of their actual influence in Germany and elsewhere is often misunderstood and possibly overstated.[22] To this effect, *Paletschek* argues that the Humboldt University was never a reality but a thought construct of the 20th century.[23] While it is beyond the scope of this work to assess whether this is indeed so, there seems to be consensus that academic freedom and unity of research and teaching – which are generally considered responsible for the success of the modern German university – cannot be exclusively attributed to *Humboldt*. On the contrary, these ideals had evolved and been implemented at other universities in parallel, such as at the University of Göttingen for example.[24] But while *Humboldt*'s concisely formulated principles seem to have coincided with an already existing sentiment, it seems reasonable to infer that at the very least, *Humboldt*'s achievement was to demonstrate how essential these principles were to the survival of the university as an institution.[25]

Humboldt's idealist concept of *Wissenschaft* was limited in the sense that it focused on philosophy, mathematics, and the humanities, but put little emphasis on laboratory research and empirical science.[26] The first who actualised what *Einheit von Forschung und Lehre* was to mean in practice was *Justus Liebig* at the University of Giessen.[27] What distinguished *Liebig*'s laboratory from other researchers[28] during his time was that his laboratory organically grew out of

[18] Ibid. 28.

[19] Ibid. 29–30.

[20] Ibid. 30.

[21] See generally Schwinges (ed.), *Humboldt international* (2001).

[22] See e.g. Schwinges, in *Humboldt international* (2001) 1, 8–9; Keck, in *National Innovation Systems* (1993) 115, 118; Weber, *Geschichte der Europäischen Universität* (2002) 156–157.

[23] Paletschek, in *Humboldt international* (2001) 75, 76–104.

[24] Moraw, *Universität Giessen* (1990) 105; Patschek (2001) 99.

[25] Fallon, *German University* (1980) 28–29.

[26] Keck, in *National Innovation Systems* (1993) 115, 118.

[27] Moraw, *Universität Giessen* (1990) 142.

[28] In this work the terms of *professor* and *researcher* will be used interchangeably. As such, they will be used to refer to individuals that are employed by a research university in the US as

his own experience and practice. It was the 'unplanned outcome of a series of small innovative moves' which would transform chemistry into a teachable university science.[29] *Liebig*'s laboratory was remarkable in other ways too: Liebig was one of the first to successfully combine academic curiosity with industrial applicability.[30] While professors in the first half of the 19th century increasingly engaged in scientific discovery, it was not until the second half of the 19th century when laboratory research and empirical science became entrenched in the institutional set-up of universities and professors recognised it as part of their mission.[31]

Alongside the founding of the modern German university, a system of polytechnical schools emerged. The main purpose of these polytechnical schools was to train technicians for private industry. The first and most influential one was founded in Karlsruhe in 1825 and was – at least in part – inspired by the *École Polytechnique* in France.[32] In the decade to follow other technical schools were established in almost all German states.[33] The emergence of the polytechnical schools initiated a century long debate over their status and of how they should compare and relate to universities. The fundamental difference between the universities' neohumanistic ideals and the polytechnical schools' focus on technology and industry created an uneasy relationship full of tensions. There was considerable worry that the university's ideal of *Bildung* could not be achieved where technical and material concern dominated the academic discourse and that academic freedom would be jeopardised.[34] Indeed, university professors often were averse to commercial exploitation of their research.[35]

But it was increasingly also recognised that pure *Wissenschaft* without the concern for its applicability would not only isolate the university from society but would impede public welfare and industrial and technical development.[36] During the second half of the 19th century the academic status of polytechnical schools was raised: They now required similar entrance qualifications as universities and were called *Technische Hochschulen*.[37] Probably the most distinc-

---

either assistant professor, associate professor, full professor (both tenure-track and non-tenure track) as well assistant research professor, associate research professor, full research professor. Occasionally, the term researcher may also include PhD students and post-doctoral students.

29 Ibid. 142; Clark, *Places of Inquiry* (1995) 24.

30 Moraw, *Universität Giessen* (1990) 141.

31 See Cahan (1985) 15 Hist. Stud. Phys. Sci. 1, 6–7, 9.

32 Other influences were derived from Prag and Wien, where similar technical schools had been founded, see Manegold, *Universität* (1970) 34–38, providing a detailed description on how these institutions differed from the *École Polytechnique*.

33 Manegold, *Universität* (1970) 43–44.

34 Ibid. 44–50.

35 Keck, in *National Innovation Systems* (1993) 115, 123.

36 Manegold, *Universität* (1970) 44–50.

37 Keck, in *National Innovation Systems* (1993) 115, 120; Manegold, *Universität* (1970) 53–54.

tive element of German landscape of higher education was its high standard of research, which was present at both universities and *Technische Hochschulen*. This pioneering role in research was manifested by comparatively high student enrolments (from domestic and foreign students) and by other countries' use of the German university as a model for their own reforms, as will be discussed below.[38]

Similar technical schools also evolved, for instance, in Britain and Switzerland. The Swiss Federal Institute of Technology (ETH) which was founded in Zürich in 1855, and was modelled after Karlsruhe, also considerably shaped the standing of the technical sciences and the continued development of the landscape of technical schools in Germany.[39] ETH Zürich is a good example of the strength such technical schools were able to develop by extending the idea of *Bildung* to the technical and natural sciences. In doing so, technical universities generated a distinct form of knowledge production which was closely related to industrialisation and technical progress. In this context the Humboldtian ideal not only functioned as an academic self-understanding but favoured new scientific methods and disciplines, linking academic excellence with professional usefulness. As a result, disciplinary specialisation and economic importance were – and partly still are – growing.[40]

B A Short History of Higher Education in the US

I From Colleges to Universities

The history of the US higher education can broadly be divided into two general segments of development. The first segment was the so-called 'age of the colleges' which lasted from the early 17th century until the second half of the 19th century and was strongly shaped by patterns and traditions from England.[41] Because American colleges did not have to conform to a specific organisation, administration, or type of support and due to the existence of a large private sector which was immune to government interreference, colleges of great variety and numbers were founded throughout the whole country.[42] These early colleges were often more akin to a secondary school (or a *Gymnasium* in Germany) than to a university.[43] Although colleges became gradually willing to accommodate

38 Keck, in *National Innovation Systems* (1993) 115, 123; Perkin, in *Higher Education* (2007) 159, 177.

39 Manegold, *Universität* (1970) 58.

40 See S. Bieri, in *Engagement gehört zum Lebenssinn* (2017) 161, 162–163.

41 Clark, *Places of Inquiry* (1995) 116; Brubacher and Rudy, *Higher Education in Transition* (1997) 3–5, 143.

42 Brubacher and Rudy, *Higher Education in Transition* (1997) 59.

43 Ibid. 143.

emerging scientific fields in the early to mid 19th century, their curricula was ultimately oriented towards the education of the generalist rather than the specialist and their mode of instruction was often not suitable for inquiry.[44]

A general movement towards a more elaborate educational and ultimately more research-centred structure gave rise to the 'age of the university' – the second segment of development – which became fully realised with the founding of the Johns Hopkins University in 1876.[45] Perhaps the most influential force that moulded the landscape of American higher education was the appeal that the ideals of the German university had. Johns Hopkins was the first university which managed to assimilate the Germanic conceptions of scholarship into the American context and to crystallise them into a viable institution. In doing so, it carved out universities' research role and created new possibilities for American institutions of higher education.[46]

Other colleges followed suit – such as Harvard, Yale and Princeton for instance – and introduced reforms modelled after Johns Hopkins. In other instances, completely new institutions were founded with the Johns Hopkins model in mind, such as Cornell University, the University of Chicago, and the University of Michigan.[47] What distinguished Johns Hopkins from other colleges[48] was not the focus on research per se but original inquiry combined with a commitment to academic freedom and advanced instruction of a standard comparable to that held at German universities.[49]

But there were other social, political, and economic factors which underpinned the change and the growth of American institutions of higher education, such as the French and American revolutions and accelerating industrialisation and urbanisation. Moreover, the new fields of scientific and technical knowledge upon which industry progressively relied, and which reflected the need of an expanding and secular society, also influenced this development. Discussions often centred on the practicality or utility of knowledge and how it could be integrated into the curriculum.[50] The conviction emerged that higher education should be democratised: The 'common sense of most' should dictate what universities would teach and to whom they should teach it.[51]

---

44 Clark, *Places of Inquiry* (1995) 121.

45 Ibid. 116; Brubacher and Rudy, *Higher Education in Transition* (1997) 143.

46 Geiger, *American Research Universities* (1986) 7–9; Clark, *Places of Inquiry* (1995) 121.

47 Brubacher and Rudy, *Higher Education in Transition* (1997) 143; Geiger, *American Research Universities* (1986) 58.

48 Note, unless otherwise indicated, going forward the two terms *college* and *university* will be used interchangeably to refer to private and public institutions of postsecondary education in the US.

49 Geiger, *American Research Universities* (1986) 8; Kerr, *University* (1963) 13–14.

50 Lucas, *American Higher Education* (2006) 148; Brubacher and Rudy, *Higher Education in Transition* (1997) 143.

51 Lucas, *American Higher Education* (2006) 148–152.

Finally, there were elements which directly related to the organisation of universities that also aided the continued growth of the American research university as an institution. The first one was the introduction of an elective system which allowed students to choose their own courses. The second one was the increasingly specialised scholarship and the institutional reorganisation of faculties within separate discipline-based academic departments that would ultimately lead to a fundamentally different organisation of knowledge.[52] This also meant that the university was no longer primarily concerned with the holistic ideal of *Bildung* and its focus on the education of the whole person but acquired a more vocational focus with a commitment to especially answering society's economic needs instead.[53]

II State and Land-grant Universities

One of the most powerful force of innovation, which simultaneously also mirrors developments in American intellectual and social life at the time when it evolved, was the land-grant college movement.[54] The idea of state universities was first discussed in the late 18th century and was born out of the demand that colleges' curricula should be expanded to include newer subjects such as the natural sciences. None of the established colleges adequately responded to these demands, making it apparent that state intervention would be necessary should the void be filled.[55] While some institutions were founded in the years to come (predominately in southern states), they typically lacked the characteristics to qualify as state universities: The level of instruction was not advanced enough and most of them were in reality mostly under private control.[56]

The first truly public, state university was the University of Virginia which was established in 1825 by *Thomas Jefferson* in Charlottesville, Virginia: It gave advanced instruction, it was a thoroughly public enterprise, and it was a secular and non-denominational institution.[57] Other state schools were founded thereafter, especially in the South and increasingly also in the West. Many institutions were (at least in part) modelled after the University of Virginia, but universities in the West were also often strongly influenced by the French and later by the German university models respectively.[58]

Finally, the most important stimulus to the establishment of state universities was the granting of public lands by the federal government: 4'000'000 acres of

[52] Ibid. 171–176, 181.
[53] Kerr, *University* (1963) 4–5; Delanty, *Challenging Knowledge* (2001) 23–24.
[54] Rudolph, *American College and University* (1991) 264.
[55] Brubacher and Rudy, *Higher Education in Transition* (1997) 144–145.
[56] Ibid. 145–147.
[57] Ibid. 147–148; Lucas, *American Higher Education* (2006) 152.
[58] Brubacher and Rudy, *Higher Education in Transition* (1997) 152–153.

land were given to fifteen states before the 1850s.[59] But these land grants rarely generated enough revenue to keep especially the smaller and more newly established state universities in the West solvent and in business. Many turned to private support and often fell under sectarian control. Enrolments also typically remained small and their respective academic reputations mediocre.[60] What finally turned the decline of these universities around was the passage of the Morrill Acts of 1862 and 1890. Under the Morrill Acts, each state senator and representative received a donation equal to 30'000 acres of federal land. Proceeds from the sale of a specified portion of this land was meant to support at least one 'land-grant college' in each state.[61]

The stimulus of the Morrill Acts together with the social and economic changes which took place towards the end of the 19th century ultimately saved the cause of state universities. Suddenly, there was a strong public demand for the kind of broadly inclusive, all-purpose training which they were generally able to offer.[62] The land-grant colleges were the first institutions of higher education to include agriculture, engineering, economics, and business administration in their curricula and opened their doors to 'the children of farmers and workers as well as to the middle and upper classes'.[63]

Over time, and especially in the Midwest and far West, land-grant colleges also provided services which extended beyond professional and vocational training.[64] The public service these colleges provided included teaching agricultural techniques to farmers, helping communities with the drafting of legal codes, advising state officials on labour and social legislation, and helping engage communities with a vast range of career-related and intellectual topics.[65] State universities played an incredibly important part in the growth which American universities experienced at the turn of the century: Four of the eight universities which had enrolments exceeding 2'500 students by 1900 were state institutions.[66]

---

59 Ibid. 153–154.

60 Lucas, *American Higher Education* (2006) 153.

61 See e. g. ibid. 152.

62 Ibid. 152–153; Brubacher and Rudy, *Higher Education in Transition* (1997) 158–159.

63 Kerr, *University* (1963) 15; Lucas, *American Higher Education* (2006) 152; also see Morrill Act of 1862, 7 USC § 304: 'Without excluding other scientific and classical studies and including military tactic, to teach such branches of learning as are related to agriculture and the mechanic arts, in such manner as the legislatures of the states may respectively prescribe, in order to promote the liberal and practical education of the industrial classes in the several pursuits and professions in life.'

64 Bok, *Beyond the Ivory Tower* (1982) 62.

65 Ibid. For an account of the beginnings of state universities' public service component, see Brubacher and Rudy, *Higher Education in Transition* (1997) 164–170.

66 Ibid. 158.

III The Hegemony of the US Research University in the 20th Century

The structure of the landscape of higher education in the US, which had evolved in the previous decades, proved beneficial for the emergent hegemony of the American research university in the early 20th century. Discussions on academic ideals and goals became markedly less heated and research universities' institutional priorities of research, the graduate school, and a large array of utilitarian undergraduate programs increasingly were accepted as a new standard.[67] Competition between institutions was an important aspect of this process of standardisation: the competitive bidding for faculty (and students)[68] resulted in a productive interchange of personnel among institutions which brought with it emulations of practices.[69] But there were also many colleges which were not able to participate in this process. They lacked the ability and the necessary resources to dedicate themselves to research and to establish a graduate school and as a consequence redefined themselves as teaching institutions.[70]

For those institutions which made the leap, the transformation from a relatively simple college organisation to an institution of structural complexity and great scope, was often not an easy one.[71] Research universities would often replace the old-time professor with a trained specialist, would greatly expand their curricular offerings, would establish new areas of administration, would introduce a steeply hierarchical structure which comprised of a board of trustees or regents, the president, deans, department chairs, and faculty members of several different ranks and, above all, would require extensive sources of financing.[72] In fact, the intellectual organisation and financial structure which was carved out during these early years is still recognisable today.[73]

Decentralisation and compartmentalisation brought increasing distance between faculty and the university administration. Presidents progressively lost touch with academic concerns as they became preoccupied with administrative and, above all, with new financial duties.[74] Critics of this transition of the uni-

---

[67] Lucas, *American Higher Education* (2006) 193.

[68] See e. g. Bok, *Universities in the Marketplace* (2009) 2, stating that as early as 1900 University of Chicago regularly ran advertisements which were aimed at attracting new students.

[69] Clark, *Places of Inquiry* (1995) 123. Emulations of practices among universities would also become a formative aspect of the history of university patenting and are the main explanation for why today universities have virtually identical intellectual property policies, see infra n. 61/III, n. 168/III, n. 199–200/III and accompanying discussions respectively.

[70] Lucas, *American Higher Education* (2006) 195.

[71] Ibid.; Rudolph, *American College and University* (1991) 417.

[72] See e. g. ibid. 417; Veblen, *Conduct of Universities by Business Men* (2015) 8; Geiger, *American Research Universities* (1986) 2.

[73] Rudolph, *American College and University* (1991) 417; Geiger, *American Research Universities* (1986) 2.

[74] Rudolph, *American College and University* (1991) 421, 424–427; Geiger, *American Research Universities* (1986) 16–17.

versity as an institution were concerned that universities 'were becoming too many things' and that ultimately the modern university was ceasing to exist.[75] It is also during this time when the seedling of universities' business-like mentality may be found. Indeed, this new mentality, which was driven by a 'love for money and power' and dominated many aspects of the university, was criticised already then.[76]

Throughout the first half of the 20th century, numbers of colleges and universities continued to grow and student enrolments expanded exponentially well beyond the increase in population for the same time period.[77] The growth rate was especially pronounced for research universities.[78] While the commitment to research continued to be a key aspect of all leading universities, the financial means to sustain the commitment were often not secured. Research was but one of several institutional goals. To facilitate research, universities had to make hard choices: Commit to low teaching loads, invest in libraries, dedicate space for faculty laboratories, invest in state of the art equipment (which progressively became costly, especially in the natural sciences), all of which required the availability of ample resources.[79] The feasibility of research therefore often depended upon the support of philanthropic donors and later additionally on support from industry.[80]

American higher education continued to grow extensively during the era after World War II. The most important factor in shaping academic research in this growth was a greatly expanded role of the federal government and a widening array of federal funding sources for university scientists and scholars.[81] Outside of the context of research, there were other factors which additionally spurred the growth of American higher education and helped American research universities on their rise to national and international prominence, such as general economic prosperity, the baby boom, and last but not least the pass-

[75] Kerr, *University* (1963) 5, referring to Harvard President *Flexner* who in 1930 complained that universities had lost sight of their main mission and had become 'secondary schools, vocational schools, teacher-training schools, research centres, 'uplift' agencies, businesses – these and other things simultaneously'.

[76] See e. g. Lucas, *American Higher Education* (2006) 200; Geiger, *American Research Universities* (1986) 16–17, Kerr, *University* (1963) 5.

[77] Lucas, *American Higher Education* (2006) 247, stating that in 1900 higher education institutions collectively awarded 29'000 degrees, and in 1950 the number had risen to half a million degrees. The numbers of institutions also grew considerably: in 1940 there were already around 1700 colleges and universities, see Graham and Diamond, *American Research Universities* (1997) 24.

[78] See e. g. Geiger, *American Research Universities* (1986) 12, 270–271.

[79] Ibid. 2, 58, 67.

[80] For an overview of the extent and organisation of university philanthropy, see ibid. 44–46. For details on university-industry cooperation, see ibid. 174–191.

[81] Lucas, *American Higher Education* (2006) 252. For a detailed account on the referenced federal science policy, see e. g. Graham and Diamond, *American Research Universities* (1997) 25–50.

ing of the Servicemen's Readjustment Act of 1944 (G. I. Bill), which helped underwrite the cost of college education for millions of returning war veterans.[82]

C US Research Universities in the 21st Century

I Research Universities' Contemporary Challenges and Issues

Today, American colleges and universities are often praised for being the greatest in the world and US research universities are regularly placed at the top of the worldwide rankings.[83] The landscape of higher education in the US continues to be distinguished by a remarkable diversity of institutions of different nature, mission, and of uneven quality. In 2018, there were around 19.8 million students enrolled in 4'300 degree-granting colleges and universities, 14.6 million students were enrolled in public, and 5.2 million students were enrolled in private institutions.[84]

Universities and colleges that have a comparatively high focus on research only account for as little as 3 % of the total of degree granting institutions.[85] Despite this small number, research universities have been and continue to be considered the guarantor of the 'intellectual, cultural, and commercial health'[86] of the nation and are thus considered to be essential to the US economy and society.[87] But in this quest of supplying the nation with scientific and technological

---

82 Lucas, *American Higher Education* (2006) 252; Graham and Diamond, *American Research Universities* (1997) 1, 11.

83 See e. g. Times Higher Education, 'World University Rankings 2020' (*Times Higher Education*). But aside from global rankings, the percentage of Nobel prize winners, the number of international students, impact indicators such as publications and patent citations as well as emulations from universities around the globe, are other indicators of relative success and quality in which American research universities rank highly (individually and collectively compared to their global peers), see NRC, *Research Universities* (2012) 43–53.

84 NCES, 'Educational institutions 1980–2017' (*NCES*); and 'Projected Number of Participants 2018' (*NCES*).

85 According to the Carnegie Classification there are 131 universities in the R1 category (doctoral universities with a 'very high research activity'), see Carnegie Classification of Institutions of Higher Education, 'Doctoral Universities' (*Carnegie Classification*).

86 American Academy of Arts and Sciences, *Public Research Universities* (2017) 4.

87 See supra n. 1–4/Intro. and accompanying discussion; also see e. g. NRC, *Research Universities* (2012) 2; Owen-Smith, *Research Universities* (2018) 4–8. Basic research expenditures are a comparatively small percentage of overall R&D expenditures. Nevertheless, many important advances in science and technology are associated with basic research, see e. g. R. Nelson (1959) 67 J. of Pol. Econ. 297, 301. While it is not easy to appropriate economic and commercial value to basic research, it is estimated that in the absence of academic research more than 10 % of industrial innovation could not have been developed, see e. g. Mansfield (1991) 20 Research Policy 1, 11.

knowledge, research universities are increasingly confronted with an array of critical challenges.

An important side-effect of a densely populated landscape of educational institutions and the resulting frequent and numerous points of contact between the institutions is a heightened sense of competition. To a large extent competition amongst universities is driven by prestige, as the rise and dominance of intercollegiate athletics illustrates, for instance.[88] But beyond sports, competitiveness has also seeped into the academic existence on almost all levels. Accordingly, the success of faculty, laboratories, departments, and institutions as a whole are measured by who can attract the best faculty, the best students, and by various 'outputs', including publications, student satisfaction ratings, grants, start-up companies created, and patents issued and licensed. With regard to patenting this has at least a twofold effect: Firstly, there is growing pressure to make knowledge useful and 'ready to sell'; secondly, the autonomy of the institution and the freedom of the single inventor are affected. The success of the university model, one could say, fires back on its architecture. This phenomenon will be discussed in detail in Part III.

But underneath the competition which is driven by prestige lies the need to raise the resources necessary to keep the enterprise of the university going. Indeed, the continuous dwindling of universities' major founding sources is one of the biggest challenges research universities face today. One of the most important sources which has been declining in the past couple of decades is federal funding.[89] This is especially disconcerting when one considers that in the same time period other countries have increased governmental funding of research and development (R&D).[90] Public universities suffer additionally from a long-term erosion of state support.[91] And, finally, universities' financial situation has been exacerbated by the most recent recession in which universities' endowments have deteriorated; since then only the endowments of the wealthiest institutions have typically recovered.[92]

What makes today's financial crisis more acute to earlier crises that the American system of higher education had to overcome is the degree to which money has to be invested into the happiness of students and the breadth of their campus 'experience' as well as into attracting and retaining (especially high-

---

[88] Geiger, *American Research Universities* (1986) 10; Bok, *Universities in the Marketplace* (2009) 4–5.

[89] See NSF, 'Federally Financed Higher Education R&D Expenditures FYs 2009–18' (*NSF*).

[90] See e. g. NRC, *Research Universities* (2012) 56, 59.

[91] See e. g. American Academy of Arts and Sciences, *Public Research Universities* (2017) 3–7.

[92] There is a big divergence between the wealthiest institutions whose endowments have been growing rapidly and all others, see NRC, *Research Universities* (2012) 55–56; Seltzer, 'Endowment Returns Slow' (*Inside Higher Ed*).

profile) faculty members. Accordingly, universities need to offer and invest in a broad variety of new degree programs, experience-based learning options, libraries and class-rooms equipped with the most modern technology and interactive learning spaces, non-instructional student related services such as admissions, counselling and mental health services, career counselling, financial aid support, student organisations, athletics, and state-of-the art laboratories, dual hire programs, and day care offerings.[93]

The decline in funding is also in sharp contrast to a continuous increase of federal and state regulations and reporting requirements which have become an administrative burden to universities and sometimes pose a challenge to academic freedom and integrity.[94] Finally, US universities also face growing competition from universities abroad. In light of the increasing excellence of research institutions in Europe and Asia, it has become more difficult to continuously attract the world's best scholars and students to US research universities.[95]

In order to close the financial gap, research universities employ different strategies. The largest potential source of additional revenue for universities are tuition fees.[96] But increasing tuitions and raising the percentage of out-of-state students (who pay higher tuition than in-state students at public universities) are a double-edged sword. Tuition has reached a level where college education without financial aid has become unsustainable for many American families.[97] Focusing admission efforts on higher paying out-of-state students is also frowned upon as it is in sharp contrast to the public service mission of state and land-grant universities. On top of raising tuitions, universities also increasingly rely on contributions from private donors.[98] In order to do so, universities will hold fund-raising campaigns, which not only require extensive administrative resources but typically also depend on the participation of faculty. Last but not least, universities progressively focus on the development of an entrepreneurial campus culture and on increasing collaborations with industry. Patenting and licensing activities in the hopes of generating income therefrom have become vital in this pursuit.[99]

---

[93] For instance, between 1999 and 2009 spending on non-instructional student related services increased by 19.4 % at public research universities and 35.3 % at private research universities, see National Science Board, *Trends and Challenges for Public Universities* (2012) 17; also see Bok, *Universities in the Marketplace* (2009) 8–10.

[94] See NRC, *Research Universities* (2012) 129.

[95] See e. g. Bok, *Universities in the Marketplace* (2009) 4.

[96] See e. g. Vedder, *Higher Education in America* (2019) 115; American Academy of Arts and Sciences, *Public Research Universities* (2017) 9.

[97] In 2014, only 17 % of first year students in AY 2013–2014 paid full tuition without any type of financial aid, see ibid.

[98] At public universities on average 7.5 % of the core budget is supported by private gifts, see ibid.

[99] See Part III for a detailed discussion.

II Research Universities' Regulatory and Financial Framework

1 The Roles of the Federal and State Governments in Higher Education

Under the US Constitution, general responsibility over matters regarding education falls to the states.[100] But the states do not have authority over *all* matters concerning education. Many federal constitutional powers, including the spending power, the taxing power, the commerce power, and the civil rights enforcement power are so broad that they may extend to education matters and thus limit states' discretion. This means that in situations where an education activity falls within the scope of such a power, the federal government has the authority to regulate it.[101] This is how – despite its secondary responsibility in matters of education – the federal government has influenced the development of higher education in the US and does increasingly so.[102]

Historically, states' most important function was to provide the legal framework within which public and private universities operated.[103] Beyond this, typically states did not get involved in higher education. Today, states have broad legal authority over matters of higher education, but the extent to which individual states use this authority varies substantially.[104] States' most important contribution is the financing of higher education through direct subsidy to public institutions.[105] In this regard, the state has a dual function: it operates as overseer of the public interest and at the same time as provider of higher education services.[106] States further provide financial aid to students, but the extent of such programs vastly differs between states. Beyond this, states are involved in the planning and coordination of higher education (e. g. in terms of types of degrees or classes an institution may offer) and supporting assessment and accountability initiatives as will be discussed in more detail below.

In the early days, states also served as intermediaries between the federal government and universities as federal support was channelled through the states to institutions.[107] Today, the federal government no longer gives gener-

---

[100] The 10th amendment of the US Constitution divides the powers between the federal and the state government. The federal government is a government of limited powers: it only has powers expressly conferred to it or that can be implied from those conferred. The remaining powers are reserved to the states or to the people, see Kaplin and Lee, *The Law of Higher Education* (2006) 1247, 1297.

[101] Ibid. 1297.

[102] For a detailed account on how federal assistance to higher education evolved, see Brubacher and Rudy, *Higher Education in Transition* (1997) 227–233.

[103] McGuinness, in *American Higher Education* (2011) 139, 141.

[104] Kaplin and Lee, *The Law of Higher Education* (2006) 1247.

[105] Only a few states provide institutional subsidy to private not-for-profit universities and the ones who do continue to limit the funding of these programs, see McGuinness, in *American Higher Education* (2011) 139, 142.

[106] Ibid.

[107] Mumper and others, in *American Higher Education* (2011) 113, 117.

al purpose aid to institutions and support will be directly distributed to the recipient – whether that is a specific institution or a student. This means that – in contrast to the states – federal support may be received by public, private, and proprietary institutions alike, as long as the requirements of the specific subsidy are met. In doing so, the federal government strictly separates between the role of overseeing the public interest and the one of providing higher education services.[108] As a result, there is virtually no coordination between the federal and the state government in terms of direction and funding.

On top of supporting university-based research, the federal government also supports higher education with substantial financial aid to college students (including student loans and veterans' educational benefits) and with tax benefits for students and institutions.[109] The total of the federal government's expenditures towards higher education has continuously increased since World War II and has reached a peak in the early 2000s. Ever since, federal expenditures have flattened and in terms of research expenditure even decreased.[110]

What is distinctively different to the other categories of federal support is that federal research funding is not distributed evenly among institutions but is highly concentrated on a relatively small number of research universities.[111] This uneven distribution has – at least in part – led to a rapid growth in the portion of federal research funding which is allocated through congressional earmarking in the late 1990s and 2000s. Earmarks allow individual congressmen to direct funds to specific projects, which – in the case of research projects – allows for the bypassing of the competitive process and peer-review.[112] Concern over corrupt behaviour has led to more stringent transparency rules and finally to the effective abolishment of earmarking in 2011. But it appears that the practice may soon be resuscitated.[113] The rapid increase in earmarking and the renewed interest in the practice are ultimately an expression of the ever-growing breadth of funding needs and requests which compete for a decreasing share of federal funding.

---

108 Ibid.

109 See e. g. McGuinness, in *American Higher Education* (2011) 139, 142; Mumper and others, in *American Higher Education* (2011) 113, 117–119. Due to the nature of the federal government's powers, support for higher education is largely decentralised and intermixed with other policy goals. This makes it difficult to identify all activities, programs and investments that are geared towards higher education, see e. g. Mumper and others, in *American Higher Education* (2011) 113, 118.

110 See e. g. ibid. 129.

111 Ibid. 128; Owen-Smith, *Research Universities* (2018) 2.

112 Mumper and others, in *American Higher Education* (2011) 113, 130.

113 Hudak, 'Bring Back Earmarks' (*Brookings*); Mutnick and Emma, 'New Earmarks Plan' (*Politico*).

2 Public Accountability

The increasing use of tax funds and the growing involvement by states in higher education has given rise to a general debate about the appropriate balance between university autonomy and public accountability.[114] On the one hand, it is generally agreed that universities ought to be able to govern themselves without or with only minimal outside control. On the other hand, it is expected that the use of tax funds ought to be justified by demonstrating 'responsible actions' to the states and the public.[115] The probably biggest challenge in accountability discussions has been to define what these 'responsible actions' should be: what are the public needs which universities and colleges should meet? The dissonance in these debates is driven by the tension between the 'civic', 'collegiate' and more recently the 'entrepreneurial' or 'commercial' interests and cultures which are inherent to the academic pursuit.[116] Another challenge is how institutions' actions should be assessed: who determines the form and content of the reporting, and what are the consequences where performance is inadequate?[117]

Up until after World War II, states' involvement was generally grounded on a social contract which existed between American society and higher education. According to this contract universities largely assumed a public role and access to higher education, basic research, and public service was understood to be a public good for society.[118] Part of the social contract was that the state taxpayer would adequately fund public colleges and universities which in turn would provide education and training and keep tuition reasonably low.[119] But with the changing economy, recession, and failing revenues, the social compact was increasingly burdened with more specific rights and responsibilities and institutions became subjects of increased accountability.[120] Over time states and the public reduced their support but demanded more and more services from institutions of higher education. Conversely, universities and colleges demanded more funding and started to increase tuitions. Assessment shifted from centralised state regulation which was primarily focused on legality and efficiency of actions to the effectiveness, especially in regard to undergraduate student

---

[114] For a good overview of the literature, see McLendon, in *Higher Education* (2003) 57, 62–70; also see e. g. Carnegie Foundation, *Governance of Higher Education* (1982) 72; Newman, *Choosing Quality* (1987).

[115] Berdahl (1990) 15 Stud. in High. Educ. 169, 172.

[116] Ibid. 172–173; Burke, in *Achieving Accountability* (2005) 1, 9–10.

[117] Berdahl (1990) 15 Stud. in High. Educ. 169, 173; McLendon, in *Higher Education* (2003) 57, 84.

[118] Burke, in *Achieving Accountability* (2005) 1, 5; Zemsky, 'Have we Lost the 'Public' in Higher Education?' (*Chronicle of Higher Education*).

[119] Burke, in *Achieving Accountability* (2005) 1, 5.

[120] Ibid. 6; Zemsky, 'Have we Lost the 'Public' in Higher Education?' (*Chronicle of Higher Education*).

learning. States also increasingly developed an interest in linking state funding to performance.[121]

Today, public higher education faces unprecedented external demands, while state support is at a record low. The demands go beyond access to education and are no longer predominantly driven by the states representing the voice of the public but reflect educational needs and demands on research outputs by students, parents, government agencies, businesses, non-profit organisations, foundations, and communities. A vigorous debate has emerged on how market forces should be balanced with procedural controls in assuring that universities respond to these changed demands.[122] Market accountability leaves the setting of public priorities to the customer and the market. Its supporters are of the opinion that the market is more effective and efficient in allocating resources. Conversely, its critics point to the fact that the market does not reflect the interest of society as a whole but represents private interests of certain industry segments.[123]

Academia's infiltration by market forces has been reinforced by two developments. Firstly, by the changed perception that higher education is not a public good yielding benefits to society but that it is a private good which primarily benefits the student who receives the education. In this view, the enhanced economic return individuals may expect from their education justifies that a greater share of the costs (i. e. higher tuition) is paid by those receiving the education.[124] Secondly, since the 1980s, there has been a trend of states adopting measures to deregulate and decentralise higher education. To this effect, states have implemented different measures which involve a mix of increased institutional autonomy and management flexibility.[125]

Universities' progressive dependence on the market not only results in universities distancing themselves from their role as the steward of the public interest. But universities' 'search for truth', which used to be so inextricably linked with universities' purpose, today is competed by a 'search for revenues'.[126] This has two fundamental implications: Firstly, universities' autonomy is jeopardised. As *Burke* correctly observed, it seems clear then that the strongest threat to universities' autonomy does not come from the state or federal governments but

[121] Burke, in *Achieving Accountability* (2005) 1, 6–9; McGuinness, in *American Higher Education* (2011) 139, 154–155.

[122] See e. g. Burke, in *Achieving Accountability* (2005) 1, 14–17; Zemsky, 'Have we Lost the 'Public' in Higher Education?' (*Chronicle of Higher Education*); Schmidtlein and Berdahl, in *American Higher Education* (2011) 69, 72.

[123] See e. g. Burke, in *Achieving Accountability* (2005) 1, 17; Zemsky, 'Have we Lost the 'Public' in Higher Education?' (*Chronicle of Higher Education*).

[124] See e. g. Ehrenberg (2006) 38 Change 46, 48.

[125] For a good overview, see McLendon, in *Higher Education* (2003) 57, 82–84; also see McGuinness, in *American Higher Education* (2011) 139, 150–151; Burke, in *Achieving Accountability* (2005) 1, 8.

[126] Newman and others, *Future of Higher Education* (2010) 4.

from the market.[127] Secondly, the special place which universities have been accorded in society because of the benefits the public receives in turn, is under threat.[128]

This is not to say that universities should completely distance themselves from the market. But it is to say that universities ought to be reminded that a market for public purposes does not necessarily exist.[129] Accordingly, they ought to find a sensible balance between attempting to satisfy market demands and remaining responsive to the needs of the public and the values that represent academia.[130] No one interest should prevail over the other and both private and public universities should be accountable to these three forces.[131]

Private universities' accountability warrants a special mention. States' authority to oversee private universities is established on the basis of private universities' need to seek governmental license in order to operate.[132] As such, private universities are accountable to the government for their actions as employers, occupants of land, operators of physical plants, for fiscal probity and basic integrity and quality in terms of their services to students and other customers.[133] Historically, state oversight over private universities has been light touch and has generally been limited to ensuring that there was integrity of purpose and fiscal stability of the operation at the initial stage of incorporation.[134] The substantial amount of financial support (student financial support and tax exemptions) private universities receive and the increasing recognition of their concerns in policy discussions on higher education has led to mounting pressure to hold private universities more accountable.[135]

3 The Uneasy Distinction Between Public and Private Universities

Unlike most European countries which rely on a single university sector which is overwhelmingly financed by the state, the US has a large private sector of higher education. In fact, in its early history US higher education was exclusively private, despite the fact that many colonial colleges accepted federal grants.[136] From the beginning, there was hence no neat distinction between private and

[127] Burke, in *Achieving Accountability* (2005) 1, 16–17.
[128] Newman and others, *Future of Higher Education* (2010) 4.
[129] Ibid.
[130] The conflicting demands between state priorities, academic concerns, and market forces have been termed as the 'accountability triangle', see Burke, in *Achieving Accountability* (2005) 1, 21–24. It serves to assess the responsiveness of accountability programs to the three main interest groups which affect higher education in the US, see ibid.
[131] See ibid. 23.
[132] Zumeta, in *Achieving Accountability* (2005) 25, 25.
[133] Ibid. 25–26.
[134] Ibid. 26.
[135] Ibid. 27.
[136] Brubacher and Rudy, *Higher Education in Transition* (1997) 35.

public financing for one or the other sector. While the distinction became more pronounced during the course of the 19th century, up until today it never has been as strict as it is in other countries.[137] Today, private universities in the US receive more public support than private universities in other (especially non-European) countries and public universities in the US typically receive less public support than public universities in European and non-European countries.[138]

In the US, whether a university is considered 'public' or 'private' – apart from the funding sources – also depends on its legal status and governance. Public universities or colleges receive direct state funding, they are owned by the taxpayers and their operation is governed by a myriad of state regulations and laws.[139] Public universities are also often referred to as 'state universities' – which also includes the category of 'land-grant universities' established under the Morrill Acts.[140] 'Community colleges' are also included in the category of public institutions. Community colleges confer associate degrees – a two-year undergraduate qualification which allows an individual to transfer into universities that offer a bachelor degree in the subject area chosen. Private (non-profit and for-profit) universities or colleges do generally not receive direct financial support from the state government but are financed and owned by private stakeholders. Because the most distinct feature of public and private universities is their respective ties to government, private universities are often referred to as 'independent' universities.[141]

It is sometimes said that there are other points of distinction between public and private institutions, especially in terms of their respective missions and their responsibilities. Accordingly, public universities are expected to be more oriented towards the public good than their private counterparts.[142] Public universities are also generally expected to provide a variety of services on top of educational services, such as economic development, health care, continuing education, and agricultural extension that private universities are typically not expected to provide.[143] While these characterisations may historically have been true and today still reflect people's perceptions, in most instances, they are not accurate.

To the contrary, it appears that the differences between the two types of universities are increasingly diminishing as public universities need to progres-

---

137 The two events which were most formative in this regard were the 1819 Supreme Court decision of *Trustees of Dartmouth College v. Woodward*, 17 U. S. 518 (1819) and the passage of the two Morrill Acts in 1862 and 1890, see Brubacher and Rudy, *Higher Education in Transition* (1997) 30–38 for a detailed discussion.

138 Levy (1982) 11 High. Educ. 607, 622.

139 See Duderstadt and Womack, *Beyond the Crossroads* (2004) 12.

140 See supra n. 61–63/I and accompanying discussion.

141 Duderstadt and Womack, *Beyond the Crossroads* (2004) 13.

142 See e. g. Lach and Schankerman (2008) 39 RAND J. Econ. 403, 415.

143 Duderstadt and Womack, *Beyond the Crossroads* (2004) 12–13.

sively rely on alternative funding sources and are forced to emulate their private counterparts in their more business-oriented behaviours. This fundamental shift has not only given rise to a debate on whether public universities are in fact becoming private but has in fact encouraged some universities to actually become private or to at least contemplate such a move.[144] An important and unfortunate sub-current of this development is that, increasingly, the value and appreciation of scientific knowledge as a public good is disappearing.

III Research Universities as Instrument of National Policy

Research universities are essential to the production of new scientific knowledge and, as such, contribute extensively to technical progress, economic development, and the welfare of society. There are numerous accounts of university research which led to successful commercial products or provided the basis for flourishing businesses.[145] It also has been shown that universities have been essential to the development and growth of new industries by generating knowledge of relevance and economic value to these industries.[146] In doing so, universities fulfil the crucial role of stimulating and enhancing the R&D which is undertaken by industry.[147] The interrelation and complementary cooperation between universities and industry was substantiated during the postwar era when the US federal government heavily invested in the building of a strong US scientific enterprise which focused on national security, public health, and economic growth.[148] Due to the surge in federal funding, universities – which up to that point had largely been funded by state governments – and federal R&D laboratories were able to build a large reservoir of scientific and technological knowledge and resources.[149]

In the 1970s, changes in the global political and economic environment and growing concern about the decline of US global competitiveness in many technology fields (particularly in regard to Japanese firms) led to a thorough re-ex-

---

144 See e. g. Vedder, 'There Are Really Almost No Truly Private Universities' (*Forbes*), to illustrate this point the author has calculated that the various government benefits which Princeton University (private university) receives are vastly greater (at least 10 times as much per student) than those conferred to the College of New Jersey (public university). Also see e. g. Ehrenberg (2006) 38 Change 46, 49–52; NPR, 'Are Public Universities Still Public?' (*NPR*); Duderstadt and Womack, *Beyond the Crossroads* (2004) 5; Ebersole, 'Going Private' (*EvoLLLution*); Vedder, 'Is the University of Virginia Going Private?' (*Minding the Campus*).

145 See infra accompanying text to n. 2/III.

146 See e. g. Rosenberg and Nelson (1994) 23 Research Policy 323, 327–333.

147 Ibid. 340.

148 To this effect see e. g. Bush (1945) 48 Trans. Kan. Acad. Sci. 231, 235–242, 245.

149 See e. g. Mowery and others, *Ivory Tower* (2004) 23, stating that federal funding for university research grew from an estimated level of less than USD 150 million in 1935–1936 to USD 2.1 billion in 1960 and USD 14 billion in 1995; Lee (1996) 25 Research Rolicy 843, 843.

amination of the existing science and technology policy. It was recognised that research universities and federal R&D laboratories were an essential asset to the US economy. As a result, the goal to accelerate transfer from universities to industry and more closely link research universities to industry emerged. In order to achieve this, US Congress passed over a dozen pieces of legislation, including the 1980 Bayh-Dole Act (BDA) which will be discussed in detail in Part II.[150]

This 'new' science and technology policy reflected a fundamental shift in the perception of universities' role in and their contribution to society. No longer were universities perceived to be the main producer of knowledge, but they were now considered to be the key producer of *commercialisable* knowledge and, as such, became a strategic asset in the quest for accelerated growth and innovation. Ever since, policy discussions have centred on how economically valuable and industrially relevant knowledge could be extracted from universities and transferred to industry.[151] Patents have become an essential component in this pursuit as will be discussed in detail in the next chapter.[152] Governments across the globe have launched initiatives and programmes like the US, aiming to bring universities closer to industrial innovation.[153] Amplified by the previously described external pressures in the US (i. e. decreasing financial support, increasing competition and steady increase in research costs), the policy shift has prompted universities to adjust their focus to the generation of industrially relevant, commercially marketable, and overall financially lucrative research projects.

The orientation towards industry and market forces can be considered the birth of a new idea of the modern research university: the 'entrepreneurial university'. The entrepreneurial university is not predominately concerned with the supply of knowledge (which may or may not be relevant to industry) but actively participates in economic development by pushing commercially valuable knowledge to the outside world. The existing traditional missions of research and teaching are thus complemented by new and more outwardly focused activities which are understood to be universities' 'third mission'.[154] At the core of

[150] See e. g. Grimaldi and others (2011) 40 Research Policy 1045, 1046; Lee (1996) 25 Research Rolicy 843, 843–844; Popp Berman (2008) 38 Soc. Stud. Sci. 835, 837.

[151] For a good overview of such initiatives and programmes, see Mowery and Sampat, in *Oxford Handbook* (2005) 210, 224–227.

[152] See infra 2. B. I.

[153] For a good overview see e. g. Mowery and Sampat, in *Oxford Handbook* (2005) 210.

[154] It should be added that – especially when it comes to public and land-grant universities – in the US, it has been accepted throughout the history of universites that there is a mission or a purpose beyond teaching and research which consists of 'public service'. The role and the function of this service component in higher education is very much debated and the type of service which insitutions render differes from institution to institution. Nevertheless, most universities will refer to their mission as 'teaching, research, and service' and professors' promotion and tenure evaluations will also reflect these three components. For a good discus-

these third mission activities is the commercialisation of university-knowledge with the use of patents and other intellectual property rights.[155]

Despite the fact that the entrepreneurial university has been widely discussed by scholars and policymakers over the course of the last couple of decades, no universally accepted definition of the entrepreneurial university or its third mission activities has evolved. Part of the difficulty is that there is a great deal of overlap between third mission activities and the traditional two missions of universities. Indeed, most activities which relate to the third mission could be categorised under the existing two missions of research and teaching and arguably have evolved out of research and teaching activities.[156] It has thus been argued that the third mission activities are something akin to the 'emperor's new clothes' since they are not altogether new activities but mainly represent a shift in analysis.[157]

It is certainly true that universities' patenting and commercialisation activities has its roots in the early 20th century, long before the above-discussed policy changes were introduced.[158] But while these activities are not entirely new, what certainly is new, is the intensity with which universities pursue them and the weight that is given to these activities by policymakers, university administrators, and other stakeholders alike. As a result, universities are no longer predominately concerned with conducting research for research's sake and thus for the benefit of the public but are concerned increasingly with research with a view of deriving private returns from it.

sion of the service mission in higher education, see e. g. Crosson, *Public Service in Higher Education* (1983).

[155] For a good description and overview of the different dimensions of the third mission, see e. g. Nedeva (2006) 66 Geogr. of Knowledge, Geom. of Power 85, 85–91; Laredo (2007) 20 High. Educ. Policy 441, 447–448; also see Slaughter and Leslie, *Academic Capitalism* (1997); Etzkowitz (2004) 1 Int'l J. Tech. Glob. 64. The entrepereneurial university has become a global phenomenon, but the ways in which it is promoted and implemented varies from country to country, see e. g. Nedeva (2006) 66 Geogr. of Knoweldge, Geom. of Power 85, 86–89.

[156] For example, a university that offers continued education courses is engaged in teaching in its most basic form. Similarly, technology transfer in the form of patenting and licensing of university-generated research is linked to research in its most basic form, see Jongbloed and others (2008) 56 High. Educ. Research 303, 312.

[157] See e. g. ibid.; Laredo (2007) 20 High. Educ. Policy 441, 442; Nedeva (2006) 66 Geogr. of Knoweldge, Geom. of Power 85, 94.

[158] See infra 2. B. I.

Chapter 2

Patents and Research Universities

The above discussion not only illustrates the fundamental role US research universities play as producers of scientific knowledge in the knowledge-based society in America, but it also demonstrates that from its early beginnings American institutes of higher education had a strong focus on practicality and on the utility of the generated knowledge. It was inevitable, then, that practically focused research would eventually lead to inventions, to patentable inventions, and that – despite the traditionally negative reputation patents had in academia – universities would slowly explore their engagement with patents. This chapter will examine how the institutions of the research university and of patents increasingly became intertwined during the course of the 20th century. It will do so in two steps. Firstly, the origins of the protection of inventive activity, the origins of US patent law, and the theories underpinning patent protection will be analysed. Secondly, the historic account of universities' involvement with patents and the shifting policy arguments for and against university patenting will be discussed.

A History of Inventions and Patent Law in the US: An Outline

I The History of Privileges in Continental Europe and England

In early modern times across Europe, rulers granted different types of subjective exclusive rights to individuals over trade in specified areas with the purpose of raising revenues, fostering the development of certain industries or technologies, or simply rewarding favourites.[159] While inventions and literary works were often protected by privileges, the assumption that privileges constituted the predecessor of today's patent and copyright systems needs to be dismissed. To the contrary, patents and copyrights generally evolved out of the confrontation with and the rejection of the use of privileges.[160] Privileges were not generally aimed at rewarding inventive activity and originality nor were they granted to whomever met certain requirements. Instead, they were based on entirely

159 See e. g. Bugbee, *American Patent and Copyright Law* (1967) 14–15.

160 See e. g. Klippel (2015) 7 ZGE 49, 55–56; Dölemeyer und Klippel, in *Gewerblicher Rechtsschutz und Urheberrecht* (1991) 185, 192–194.

subjective criteria by the sovereign grantor who awarded them.[161] Indeed, the term patent is derived from the Latin *patere* (to be open) and simply referred to an open letter of privilege from the sovereign.[162]

It is often suggested that the first formal patent code originated in 1474 when the Republic of Venice codified a general promise of granting exclusive rights to inventors of workable and useful inventions.[163] The patent code did not permit imitation of inventions for ten years without express permission from the inventor. But the Republic retained the right to use the invention for its own purposes and the general practice included compulsory licensing and the revocation of patents which were not used commercially.[164] It is therefore probably more accurate to think of the 1474 Patent Code as an instrument designed to attract foreign skilled persons who would bring locally unfamiliar processes or devices to the Republic – a practice which had been well established during the 14th and 15th century – and not an instrument which had the purpose of stimulating inventive activity.[165] The opening of trade in Europe allowed for the grant of privileges to spread through craftsmen and artisans to Germany, France, the Netherlands, and England.[166]

In England – that at the time was technologically laggard compared to other countries on the continent – the granting of privileges had widely been established during the 16th and 17th century.[167] The public resentment against this practice eventually culminated in the enactment of the Statute of Monopolies in 1624, which – in contrast to what its name suggests – neither opposed monopolies nor encouraged competition per se but formulated constitutional objections to the Crown's power of arbitrarily granting monopolies.[168] Under the Statute 'privileges' could only be awarded for new manufacture 'to the first and true Inventor' (i. e. 'patents of invention').[169]

---

161 Klippel (2015) 7 ZGE 49, 56.

162 See e. g. David, in *Global Dimensions* (1993) 19, 44. The literature distinguishes between two types of patents: 1) 'Letters patents' (literal translation from Latin *litterae patentes* thus simply meaning 'open letter') generally refer to documents with which the grantor conferred and publicly announced special privileges to individuals. 2) 'Patents for invention' refer to what we typically understand today as patents and in the US as utility patents, i. e. the exclusive right to a novel and useful invention, see e. g. MacLeod, *Inventing the Industrial Revolution* (1988) 10.

163 See e. g. Walterscheid (1996) 78 J. Pat. Off. Soc'y 615, 708–709; Machlup, *Economic Review* (1958) 2.

164 Kaufer, *Patent System* (1989) 5–6.

165 David, in *Global Dimensions* (1993) 47; Kaufer, *Patent System* (1989) 3.

166 Walterscheid (1996) 78 J. Pat. Off. Soc'y 615, 706; Kaufer, *Patent System* (1989) 6.

167 See Hill (1923) 6 J. Pat. Off. Soc'y 405, 406–407; David, in *Global Dimensions* (1993) 19, 44–45; Merges and others, *Intellectual Property* (2012) 126.

168 For a detailed account on the history of patents in England, see MacLeod, *Inventing the Industrial Revolution* (1988) 10–39; also see Letwin (1954) 21 U. Chi. L. Rev. 355, 366.

169 MacLeod, *Inventing the Industrial Revolution* (1988) 18.

The main contribution of the Statute was that it codified the law the courts had established in preceding years regarding patents for inventions, clearly distinguishing them from other privileges. It did not, however, address enforcement of patents or lay out a process by which patents could be obtained.[170] Moreover, importers of manufactures and of technical devices which had been developed by someone in a different country (so called 'importation franchises') continued to be considered 'inventors' under the statute. Consequently, after the enactment of the Statute of Monopolies not much changed in how privileges were awarded, and they generally continued to be considered subjective rewards of the Crown.[171]

Despite these shortcomings, the Statute of Monopolies served as a model for similar efforts and statutes which were later enacted in North American colonies and that ultimately framed the formulation of the 1789 US Constitution's intellectual property clause.[172] In fact, due to this influence on the American patent system, it is sometimes believed that patents are a chiefly English creation.[173] This is not the case. The institution of patents – with or without an element of invention – developed in countries across the continent at around the same time. What was different was the speed at which patents were adopted and the extent to which they were granted.[174] Like in England, often it was the confrontation with the practice of granting privileges by sovereigns and the question of their legitimacy and legality which led to the protection of inventors, authors and publishers.[175]

During the colonial period in the US, much in the spirit of the developments in Europe, privileges in the form of importation franchises and other benefits such as subsidies, bounties, and premiums were provided to encourage the establishment or the stimulation of new or certain existing industries in the 13 colonies. Patents for inventions were awarded as well but the number compared to other privileges were small.[176] American privileges and patents differed to their English counterparts insofar as they were not issued by royal grace and favour but were based almost entirely on private colonial legislative enactments. As a result, they displayed a great variety of provisions and terms of effectiveness.[177] The Massachusetts Bay colony was the first to enact an anti-monopoly clause in 1641 which was directly inspired by the English Statute of Monopolies and

---

170 Ibid. 20, 38–39.

171 Ibid. 18–20, 38–39.

172 See Machlup, *Economic Review* (1958) 3.

173 See e. g. Machlup and Penrose (1950) 10 J. Econ. Hist. 2.

174 See e. g. Kaufer, *Patent System* (1989) 6–9.

175 See e. g. Klippel (2015) 7 ZGE 49, 57–58; Kaufer, *Patent System* (1989) 7.

176 Bugbee, *American Patent and Copyright Law* (1967) 57; Vaughan, *United States Patent System* (1977) 15–16.

177 Bugbee, *American Patent and Copyright Law* (1967) 57.

other colonies later followed.[178] The general impact the practice of awarding privileges had on colonial manufacturers was comparatively small and had almost completely subsided by the 1750s. Only privileges to inventors continued to be issued and, as such, mark the transition to the modern US patent system.[179]

II The History of Patent Law in the US

After the American Revolution – and as was permitted under the Articles of Confederation of 1781 – individual states continued to grant patents independently.[180] However, conflicts between the states (most notably a high-profile dispute over steamboat patents which had been issued to two different inventors) would soon arise and prompt the Constitutional Convention of 1789 to propose the creation of a national patent system as will be detailed below.[181]

But before discussion turns to the US national patent system, brief mention deserves South Carolina which enacted the first general patent provision in 1784. Entitled 'An Act for the Encouragement of Arts and Sciences' the positive phrasing of the Act compared to the English Statute of Monopolies and other 17th century anti-monopoly provisions like the one enacted in Massachusetts, constituted a big step forward in the history of US patent law.[182] The Act offered 14 years of protection for literary works and for 'useful machines'.[183] Although South Carolina continued to issue private grants after the Act's enactment, these grants were clearly influenced by the new Act and its influence extended to other states as well.[184]

---

[178] See ibid. 61: 'No monopolies shall be granted or allowed amongst us, but of such new Inventions yt are pfitable to ye Countrie, & yt for a short time.'

[179] Vaughan, *United States Patent System* (1977) 17–18. South Carolina sometimes is credited for enacting the first general patent law in 1691, see e. g. Machlup, *Economic Review* (1958) 3. However, the 1691 law was not a general patent provision but merely a private grant which was applicable to one inventor alone. It expressed general encouragement to other inventors, but the encouragement had no legal effect, see Bugbee, *American Patent and Copyright Law* (1967) 75.

[180] Vaughan, *United States Patent System* (1977) 18.

[181] For details on the steamboat-patent-dispute, see Bugbee, *American Patent and Copyright Law* (1967) 95–97. A noteworthy detail is that one of the steamship inventors presented his case for patent protection in front of the Virginia House of Delegates in November 1784, where at the time *James Madison* was a member of the House. It is assumed that was the first direct contact of *Madison* with the institution of patents, see ibid. Also see Merges and others, *Intellectual Property* (2012) 127.

[182] Bugbee, *American Patent and Copyright Law* (1967) 92–93.

[183] The statute's purpose was the protection literary property for fourteen years but included the following patent clause: 'The inventors of useful machines shall have a like exclusive privilege of making or vending their machines for the like term of 14 years, under the same privileges and restrictions hereby granted to, and imposed on, the authors of books.', as quoted from Bugbee, *American Patent and Copyright Law* (1967) 93.

[184] Ibid. 93.

At first blush, it may be surprising that South Carolina would be the first state to enact a systematised patent clause. Colonial South Carolina focused on the promotion of its agriculture, and especially on commodities such as rice and indigo. The production of these commodities was achieved through the use of plantations which heavily relied on slaves.[185] This economic environment would not seem easily associable with a spirit of encouragement and reward of the 'inventive genius' as today is understood to be the key principle underpinning US patent law. Indeed, from the late 17th century onward South Carolina employed many 'encouragements' in private and public statutes in order to attract foreign craftsmen with the main purpose of improving industrial (rice) practices.[186]

A logical hypothesis could be that the 1784 South Carolina patent provision was not a pure patent provision in the modern sense after all. This could be explained by the fact that back then, the word *to invent* had a broader meaning than is generally accepted today. An English patent that was issued 1618 illustrates this point: its claim refers to 'bring into use, find, establish or institute manufacture'.[187] When contrasted with the contemporary definition of *to invent*, which means 'to produce something for the first time through the use of the imagination or ingenious thinking'[188], it becomes apparent that the old meaning did not require original inventive activity or (in today's understanding of patent law) 'absolute novelty'.

This broader definition of 'invention', which also informed the 1624 Statute of Monopolies, was likely transplanted to North America's colonies and also continued to live on in its successor states.[189] After all, it is well documented that the practice of awarding privileges for foreign inventions and technologies, which had been relied upon by many countries in Europe, including England and Germany, was relied upon by American colonies as well.[190] It thus seems logical to assume that the South Carolina patent clause principally encouraged

[185] Ibid. 77; Jeremy, *Transatlantic Industrial Revolution* (1981) 12.

[186] Bugbee, *American Patent and Copyright Law* (1967) 77–83.

[187] See e. g. Hill (1923) 6 J. Pat. Off. Soc'y 405, 416.

[188] Merriam-Webster Dictionary definition for 'to invent'.

[189] Also see Hill (1923) 6 J. Pat. Off. Soc'y 405, 416.

[190] For a detailed account on how British technology and skilled labourers influenced and shaped the American textile industry, see e. g. Jeremy, *Technology and Power* (1990), detailing the life and achievements of *James Montgomery*, a Glasgow cotton mill manager who emigrated to New England and later moved to South Carolina. Indeed, it was such a widespread phenomenon that by the end of the 18th century Great Britain, who had very much benefited from the same practice a couple of centuries earlier, showed considerable concern over the reverse problem: the leakage of its technical knowledge by emigrants to its rivals, including the North American colonies, see Merges and others, *Intellectual Property* (2012) 126. For a detailed account, including a detailed description of measures that Britain tried to pass, such as paying return travel expenses in an effort to reverse the tide of emigration, see Jeremy, *Transatlantic Industrial Revolution* (1981) 36–49.

the introduction of new manufacture, and that whether this occurred through transferring the technology from elsewhere or through original inventive activity was secondary.

President *George Washington*'s remark to Congress in January of 1790 contextualises this assumption: 'The advancement of agriculture, commerce, and manufactures, by all proper means, will not I trust, need recommendation; but I cannot forbear intimating to you the expediency of giving effectual encouragement, as well to the introduction of new and useful inventions from abroad, as to the exertions of skill and genius in producing them at home'.[191] Thus, when the foundation of the US patent system was laid, while there was widespread willingness to embrace the encouragement of local inventive activity, the use of patents to attract the importation of foreign technologies was still appealing as well.[192]

States' practice of continuing to grant patents separately increasingly led to conflict, confusion, and legal uncertainty in the young nation, making the desirability of a national patent system ever more pronounced.[193] Finally, the 1789 US Constitution empowered Congress to 'promote the progress of science and the useful arts by securing for limited times, to authors and inventors the exclusive right to their respective writings and discoveries'[194]. Following *George Washington*'s above referenced remarks, in 1790 the US Senate charged a committee to draft a single act addressing the importation franchise, patents and copyrights. During congressional deliberations, the importation franchise was dropped and the protection of patents and copyrights were separated, and in April 10 and May 31 of 1790 respectively, the patent and copyright bills were signed into law.[195]

Despite this, several states continued to award exclusive grants into the early 19th century.[196] Federal grants were not in conflict with state awards per se, as long as the provisions of the respective grants did not contradict each other.[197] Ultimately, however, the national patent system presented too many advantages over the state awards, which eventually led to the complete disappearance of state patents.[198]

---

[191] As quoted from Bugbee, *American Patent and Copyright Law* (1967) 137.

[192] See Hill (1923) 6 J. Pat. Off. Soc'y 405, 420.

[193] See Vaughan, *United States Patent System* (1977) 18.

[194] US Constitution Article 1, Section 8, Clause 8, commonly referred to as 'intellectual property clause' or 'progress clause'. On the meaning of 'science' in this context it has been observed that 'science' comes from the Latin scire 'to know' and meant learning in general at the time when the constitution was written, see Lutz (1949) 18 Geo. Wash. L. Rev. 50, 51.

[195] Bugbee, *American Patent and Copyright Law* (1967) 137–144, David, in *Global Dimensions* (1993) 19, 50.

[196] Bugbee, *American Patent and Copyright Law* (1967) 102.

[197] Ibid., suggesting that it is generally understood that today states could still legally grant patents under the same conditions.

[198] Ibid. 102.

The US Patent Act of 1790 provided up to a 14 year protection for the 'invention or discovery of any useful art, manufacture, engine, machine, or device, or any improvement thereon not before know or used'.[199] In this early form, a so-called Patent Board consisting of the Secretary of State, *Thomas Jefferson*, Secretary of War, *Henry Knox*, and Attorney General, *Edmund Randolph* issued the patents if they deemed the 'invention or discovery sufficiently useful or important'.[200] Only 57 patents were granted under the original 1790 Act. It is not difficult to imagine that the high-level government officials in charge for the scrutiny of the patent applications could not spend the time necessary to do so.[201] To address this, a new Act was passed in 1793 which no longer required inventions to be 'sufficiently useful or important' and allowed inventors to receive a patent if they registered it and made an oath to be the true inventor.[202]

By late 1835, over 9'000 patents had been issued and perhaps unsurprisingly, the lack of examination gave rise to fraud and duplication. Calls to introduce a formal patent examination were finally answered and resulted in the 1836 Patent Act, which also established the patent office in its modern form.[203] Since then, the US patent system has grown dramatically and – with increasing demands placed on it – has continuously developed new procedural and substantive rules.[204] On its path to an ever more effective and refined patent system, it generally is perceived that the US patent system was and continuous to be (at least in part) responsible for the successful economic development in the US.[205]

III The Theory of Patents and its Economic Underpinnings

Today, there are different recognised legal, philosophical, and economic justifications for the protection of inventions with patents in the US.[206] But these theories only evolved over time and generally extend to the protection of intellectual property as an area of law. In the beginning of the history of patent law, there was no generally accepted or even prevailing theory to justify patents or

---

199 Hill (1923) 6 J. Pat. Off. Soc'y 405, 421.

200 Bugbee, *American Patent and Copyright Law* (1967) 149.

201 Ibid. 150.

202 Hill (1923) 6 J. Pat. Off. Soc'y 405, 421; Bugbee, *American Patent and Copyright Law* (1967) 150.

203 Lubar (1990) 6 Am. Heritage Invent. Tech. 8, 10; Bugbee, *American Patent and Copyright Law* (1967) 151. It should be noted that patent examinations were not a US invention, as is sometimes perceived. In France, novelty examinations were undertaken in the 17th century, albeit only if prompted by the King, see Walterscheid (1996) 78 J. Pat. Off. Soc'y 615, 712–713.

204 In 2019 the United States Patent and Trademark Office (USPTO) granted 352'008 patents, see USPTO, 'Calendar Year Patent Statistics 2020' (*USPTO*); also see Eaton, '2019 USPTO Patent Statistics (*ANAQUA*).

205 Also see e. g. Merges and others, *Intellectual Property* (2012) 128.

206 For an overview of the different justifications see, ibid. 2–24.

intellectual property but a multitude of different – sometimes even contradictory – theories.[207]

It was not until the end of the 18th century and the beginning of the 19th century, in Europe, when especially economic and utilitarian arguments, which were generally founded in natural law principles and tested as part of the different national debates on the introduction of national patent laws, were introduced.[208] The different national debates in Europe also framed theories on patents and intellectual property in the US. Arguments against patents were often rooted in the objections to privileges, and thus questioned patents' economic legitimacy and criticised their adverse effect on free trade.[209] Some recognised patents as a 'necessary evil', such as *Adam Smith* for instance, who viewed the existence of monopolies as 'necessarily hurtful to society' but considered their use justified, as they allowed a monopoly period during which the inventor could appropriate a sufficient return for his ingenuity and effort.[210]

In Germany, during the 19th century, discussions on the abolishment of privileges shaped the debate on the justification of patents. While it was generally recognised that intellectual creations should be distinguished from privileges and that they were worthy of protection, a dilemma was that there was no existing legal construct which easily allowed for the protection of such creations.[211] Three arguments emerged in favour of the protection of authors, inventors and publishers, all of which still form the basis of generally accepted justifications of intellectual property rights today: 1) The legitimacy of the protection of intellectual property is justified based on *John Locke*'s labour theory of property. Labour which an individual puts forth is a means by which ownership of property may be assumed as labour combines property with the self of the person; 2) The creator of products of intellectual origin has a right to be rewarded for his labour; 3) The creator has a right to this reward as he or she depends on it for his or her daily subsistence.[212]

While discussions about the introduction of a German national patent legislation in the 1870s still referred to *Locke's* labour theory, they also increasingly focused on the positive impact patents would have on German industry and the economy. Proponents of a national patent law were not only convinced

---

207 Dölemeyer and Klippel, in *Gewerblicher Rechtsschutz und Urheberrecht* (1991) 185, 188, 201–202; Machlup, *Economic Review* (1958) 20.

208 See e.g. Dölemeyer and Klippel, in *Gewerblicher Rechtsschutz und Urheberrecht* (1991) 187–188.

209 See e.g. Klippel (2015) 7 ZGE 49, 57–58; Dölemeyer and Klippel, in *Gewerblicher Rechtsschutz und Urheberrecht* (1991) 185, 192–193.

210 As quoted from Machlup, *Economic Review* (1958) 19–20; also see e.g. Dutton, *The Patent System* (1984) 19.

211 For a detailed history and analysis, see Klippel (2015) 7 ZGE 49, 57–62; also see Klippel (1982) 4 ZNR 132, 137.

212 Klippel (2015) 7 ZGE 49, 61–62.

that patents would encourage the process of discovery and research but that the element of disclosure was crucial and would have a positive effect on technological progress (up to that point the different states had separate patent laws which required secrecy).[213] Aided by a general international pro-patent sentiment (which would culminate in the adoption of the 1883 Paris Convention for the Protection of Industrial Property), the first German national patent legislation was enacted in 1877.[214]

Economic and utilitarian arguments were also key to the introduction of a national patent law in Switzerland towards the end of the 19th century. Switzerland is sometimes referred to as the one industrial country in Europe which failed to adopt a patent system until the late 19th century.[215] This is not entirely accurate: The Helvetic Republic enacted a patent law in 1801, which not only rewarded the introduction of technology from abroad but also encouraged inventive activity.[216] While the law disappeared with the fall of the Republic in 1803, several cantons enacted separate laws which encouraged inventive activity.[217]

Throughout the 19th century, the high level of quality and productivity of Swiss industries which had been achieved without a national patent law, was successfully invoked by opponents of a national patent legislation to argue that patents were not necessary to stimulate inventive activity.[218] Indeed, many firms benefited from the unfettered use of foreign technology.[219] Critics further argued that patents would hinder free trade and present unnecessary work for the government.[220] Perhaps the biggest objection to patents was the emerging conviction that inventions were the creation of industrial progress, not the creation of an individual. As such, extending monopoly power to an individual through a patent was considered unjustified.[221] Nevertheless – and very much influenced by a declining industrial performance towards the end of the 19th century and increasing international pro-patent pressure – Switzerland adopted a federal patent law in 1888.[222]

The arguments in favour of patent protection, which evolved in the 19th century in Europe, also shaped the dominant economic and utilitarian perspective under which patent protection has and continues to be justified in the US. And like in Europe, the justifications typically overlap with the generally accepted

[213] Schmidt, *Erfinderprinzip* (2009) 9–11; Mächtel, *Patentrecht* (2009) 17–21.

[214] See Schmidt, *Erfinderprinzip* (2009) 10–11.

[215] See e. g. Machlup and Penrose (1950) 10 J. Econ. Hist. 4–5; Schiff, *Industrialization* (1971) 2.

[216] Morand, in *Kernprobleme des Patentrechts* (1988) 3, 7.

[217] Ibid. 9–11.

[218] Ibid. 14; Bracher, *Entstehung und Bedeutung des schweizerischen Patentwesens* (1923) 13.

[219] Bracher, *Entstehung und Bedeutung des schweizerischen Patentwesens* (1923) 14.

[220] Ibid. 13–14.

[221] Ibid. 17.

[222] Ibid. 19–25.

justifications for intellectual property protection.[223] The justifications for the use of patents have been integrated by *Machlup* and *Penrose* into four lines of arguments or theories and they will be discussed below.[224] While the four theories are independent of one another, they do not exclude but rather complement each other.[225] While there is one theory that is termed natural law, this is misleading as the intellectual property justifications which emerged in the 19th century are all based on natural law norms.[226]

Natural law theory: The natural law theory is fundamentally based on *Locke*'s above described labour theory of property.[227] According to *Locke* 'every man has a property in his own person' and thus in the 'labour of his body and the work of his hands'.[228] By using body and hands and thus mixing his labour with existing goods, a person may legitimately acquire property rights in the new creation.[229] Although *Locke* had in mind physical property, the theory has been widely applied to intellectual property as well.[230] Whether this is justified, and if so to what extent, is the subject of a larger debate.[231] Justifying the use of patents with the natural law theory has always been controversial at best. Despite this, the theory has been widely relied upon by patent proponents in the early history of patent law and has experienced something of a Renaissance more recently.[232]

The natural law theory is central to patent protection in the US: it is at the core of US patent law which recognises the inventor's property right in his invention.[233] The practice of universities (and employers in general) to have faculty, staff, and students assign their inventions to them is at odds with the natural law theory.[234] Objections to universities' practice of claiming ownership of uni-

---

223 See e. g. Kitch (1977) 20 J. L. Econ. 265, 266; Merges and others, *Intellectual Property* (2012) 2; Machlup and Penrose (1950) 10 J. Econ. Hist. 1, 9–10.

224 See Machlup and Penrose (1950) 10 J. Econ. Hist. 1, 10; Machlup, *Economic Review* (1958) 21.

225 Machlup and Penrose (1950) 10 J. Econ. Hist. 1, 11; Schmidt, *Erfinderprinzip* (2009) 17.

226 See Dölemeyer and Klippel, in *Gewerblicher Rechtsschutz und Urheberrecht* (1991) 185, 196–197.

227 See supra n. 212/I and accompanying discussion.

228 Locke, *Two Treatises* (1999) 116.

229 See ibid. 116; also see Fisher, in *New Essays* (2001) 170.

230 Spinello and Tavani, in *Intellectual Property Rights* (2005) 1, 8–9; Lemley (2015) 62 UCLA L. Rev. 1328, 1339; Goldhammer, *Geistiges Eigentum* (2012) 189.

231 See e. g. Tavani (2005) 7 Ethics Inf. Tech. 87, 89–90; Merges, *Justifying Intellectual Proeprty* (2011) 31–67; Lemley (2015) 62 UCLA L. Rev. 1328, 1338–1344.

232 See e. g. Machlup, *Economic Review* (1958) 22–23, explaining that the French Constitutional Assembly which adopted the French patent law of 1971 heavily relied on the natural law theory: 'It is interesting that some French lawyers conceded that they preferred to speak of 'natural property rights' chiefly for propaganda purposes', ibid. 23; Stierle, *Das nicht-praktizierte Patent* (2018) 192–193.

233 See USC 261: 'Patents shall have the attributes of personal property'.

234 Also see infra 4.B and 7.A.3.

versity-generated inventions are typically (knowingly or not) based on this theory. Accordingly, the American Association of University Professors (AAUP) states: 'Inventions […] are a natural out-growth of scholarly activities. […] the fundamental rights of faculty members to direct and control their own research do not terminate when they make an invention or other research discovery; these rights properly extend to decisions involving invention management, intellectual property licensing, commercialization, dissemination, and public use.'[235]

Reward by monopoly theory: Under the reward theory, the patent is considered a compensation and reward for the inventor's contribution to society. The reward enables the inventor to capture the returns from the investment in the invention and to prevent the appropriation of the same by others.[236] The reward theory was often favoured by those who rejected monopolies but believed that a temporary monopoly was justified.[237] The theory found many supporters in the 19th century discussions in Germany and was also popular in 19th century England, especially with economists such as *John Stuart Mill*.[238] It is a widely accepted theory for the use of patents in the US today and lies at the foundation of the patent system.[239] It is often combined with other theories.[240] Despite or perhaps due to its dominance, the debate over the reward theory's merits and flaws has been repeated and expanded in modern times.[241]

Universities' practice of having inventors assign ownership of their inventions to them is in opposition to the reward theory. By assigning their inventions, inventors forfeit the ability to control the exclusive right awarded to them and thus forfeit the reward they would be entitled to. The problem is arguably diminished if inventors receive a percentage of royalty income or if they develop publicly financed inventions respectively, as will discussed in detail below.[242]

Monopoly profit incentive theory: The incentive theory rests on the assumption that patents present an incentive to inventors to engage in inventive activity

---

[235] AAUP (2014) Bulletin AAUP 35, 36.

[236] Machlup and Penrose (1950) 10 J. Econ. Hist. 1, 10, 17; Kitch (1977) 20 J. L. Econ. 265, 266.

[237] Machlup and Penrose (1950) 10 J. Econ. Hist. 1, 17; Machlup, *Economic Review* (1958) 19, 22–23; also see supra n. 210/I and accompanying discussion.

[238] Schmidt, *Erfinderprinzip* (2009) 19–20; Machlup and Penrose (1950) 10 J. Econ. Hist. 1, 17.

[239] See e. g. Grady and Alexander (1992) 78 Va. L. Rev. 305, 310; S. Cohen (1998–1999) 5 Mich. Telecomm. & Tech. L. Rev. 1, 4.

[240] Hughes (1988) 77 Geo. L. J. 287, 303; Stierle, *Das nicht-praktizierte Patent* (2018) 196.

[241] See Grady and Alexander (1992) 78 Va. L. Rev. 305, 310–313, for a good overview of different arguments in the debate; also see Kitch (1977) 20 J. L. Econ. 265, 266, arguing that the reward theory is an 'incomplete view of the functions of the patent system'. *Kitch*'s critical position towards the reward theory led him to formulate the 'prospect theory', according to which patents allow inventors to develop and commercialise their inventions efficiently, see ibid. 266–271.

[242] See infra 2. B. I. 1.

and to develop inventions which are valuable to society. Without effective incentives, not enough inventions would be generated to support industrial progress.[243] In more recent times, the incentive theory has become the most cited justification for the use of patents.[244]

The incentive theory is closely linked to what is sometimes called the 'appropriability' or 'public goods' problem of intellectual creations.[245] Inventions (and other intellectual creations) display the same characteristics to public goods: once an invention or an idea is developed, it is difficult to exclude others from the benefits of it – it can easily be shared, copied or imitated.[246] Moreover, one individual's use does not detract from another person's use. In the words of *Thomas Jefferson*: 'He who receives an idea from me, receives instruction himself without lessening mine; as he who lights his taper at mine, receives light without darkening me.'[247] In the absence of protection or other incentives, because inventors cannot charge prices necessary to recoup their investments, inventions would be under-produced. Patents (and other intellectual property rights for other intellectual creations) solve this problem as they allow inventors to recover investments which were necessary to develop the invention. In doing so, patents encourage inventors to develop inventions in the first place.[248]

The incentive function of patents has been subject to intense scrutiny and increasingly has been questioned. The main problem is that it has been notoriously difficult to measure patents' positive impact on inventive activity and innovation.[249] At the very least, the incentive function has been criticised for not adequately capturing the cumulative nature of research.[250] According to this view, patents may promote the efficient use of *existing* inventions but not necessarily the development of new ones.[251] This 'new' ex-post justification of patents is at the core of the 'commercialisation argument' which has been used by

---

243 Machlup and Penrose (1950) 10 J. Econ. Hist. 1, 10, 21, in this context citing the 1858 lecture *Abraham Lincoln* gave on 'Discoveries and Inventions' in which he famously stated: 'The patent system [...] added the fuel of interest to the fire of genius.', see ibid. 22.

244 See e. g. Lemley (2004) 71 U. Chi. L. Rev. 129, 129; Note (2005) 118 Harv. L. Rev. 2007, 2007; Boldrin and Levine (2013) 27 J. Econ. Persp. 3, 3.

245 See e. g. *Arrow* and *Nelson*, who have framed this debate in the 1950s and 1960s: Arrow, in *The Rate and Direction of Inventive Activity* (1962) 609; R. Nelson (1959) 67 J. of Pol. Econ. 297.

246 For a more detailed explanation of the characteristics of public goods, see 2. B. II. 1.

247 Foner, *Basic Writings of Thomas Jefferson* (1944) 708, 712.

248 See e. g. Demsetz (1967) 57 Am. Econ. Rev. 347, 359; Landes and Posner, *Intellectual Property Law* (2003) 11, 13; Stierle, *Das nicht-praktizierte Patent* (2018) 199; also see A. Bieri, in *SAGE Encyclopedia* (2015).

249 See e. g. Moser (2013) 27 J. Econ. Persp. 23, 24; Machlup, *Economic Review* (1958) 80; Lemley (2004) 71 U. Chi. L. Rev. 129, 129–130; Granstrand, in *Oxford Handbook* (2005) 266, 280; Burk (2012) 8 Ann. Rev. L. Soc. Sci. 397, 398.

250 See e. g. Kitch (1977) 20 J. L. Econ. 265, 266; Scotchmer (1991) 5 J. Econ. Persp. 29, 29–30.

251 Kitch (1977) 20 J. L. Econ. 265, 271–276; for this reason *Kitch* advocates broad patent

the proponents of the BDA to advocate the use of patents in the context of universities. According to the commercialisation argument, patents are necessary to encourage commercialisation of university inventions.[252]

Assigning ownership of inventions to the university is not consistent with the incentive theory as the assignment removes the very incentive the patent is supposed to create. The same criticism is made by the opponents of the practice used by employers in industry, under which employees are asked to assign ownership rights to inventions to their respective employer.[253] The dampening effect of invention-assignments may arguably be even more pronounced in the case of university inventors as they may simply choose alternative outputs for a given research result.[254]

Exchange for secrets theory: Similarly to the incentive theory, the exchange for secrets theory – which is commonly referred to as the disclosure theory – focuses on political expediency.[255] At its core is the assumption that, as a matter of principle, inventors attempt to keep their inventions secret.[256] According to the disclosure theory, patents counteract this inclination by encouraging the disclosure of inventions and the dissemination of related technical information. As a result, information which would otherwise be kept secret is added to the general pool of knowledge and serves as the basis for new inventions. The social cost, which would be incurred if inventors sought to keep their inventions secret, is thus minimised.[257] The disclosure theory is at the heart of the US patent system and is frequently referenced by courts and scholars.[258] Nevertheless, the disclosure function of the patent system has been criticised for underperforming and ultimately not helping to promote the progress of science.[259]

The disclosure theory is the least effective justification for the use of patents in the context of universities due to universities' open science culture. The open science culture is at the very core of the academic pursuit and ensures that important research and inventions are shared through publications, teaching, con-

---

rights which create an incentive to further develop the technology and to allow investments to be efficiently managed, see ibid. 275–280; also see Lemley (2012) 110 Mich. L. Rev. 709, 738.

[252] For a more detailed discussion, see infra 2. B. I.

[253] For a detailed analysis on the incentive function of patents in the context of employees and university inventors, see infra n 452–468 and accompanying discussion.

[254] In the context of industry-sponsored research where an upfront fee is negotiated for all intellectual property produced under a specific contract, the incentive to produce any valuable inventions may be substantially diminished, see TTO Review (n. 288/III).

[255] Machlup and Penrose (1950) 10 J. Econ. Hist. 1, 11.

[256] Stierle, *Das nicht-praktizierte Patent* (2018) 206.

[257] Machlup and Penrose (1950) 10 J. Econ. Hist. 1, 11; Landes and Posner, *Intellectual Property Law* (2003) 328–329; Note (2005) 118 Harv. L. Rev. 2008.

[258] See e. g. Machlup, *Economic Review* (1958) 76; Note (2005) 118 Harv. L. Rev. 2007–2013; Lemley (2012) 110 Mich. L. Rev. 709, 745.

[259] See e. g. Note (2005) 118 Harv. L. Rev. 2013–2026; Fromer (2009) 94 Iowa L. Rev. 539, 563–594.

ferences, and collaborations with industry. Reverting to patent protection under this rationale thus seems obsolete. To the contrary, one of the biggest criticisms of university patenting is its possible obstruction of the open science culture.[260]

B Patenting of University Research

I Why Universities Started Patenting: A Brief History before the Bayh-Dole Act

For most of the 19th and the early 20th century, the institutions of patents and the university had separate existences in the US. And even when a selected few universities started to explore their involvement with patents in the early 20th century, the vast majority of universities continued to ignore the 'patent problem'.[261] On a practical level, inventions were believed to be the private property of faculty and patents hence the private concern of the respective faculty member.[262] On a more strategic level, an involvement with patents was considered inconsistent with the academic mission and its commitment to open science. Moreover, it was feared that the appearance of profiting at the expense of the public would undermine public trust and support of academia.[263]

Despite this reluctance towards patenting, in the early 20th century, a couple of universities started to engage with patents. These (mainly positive) examples would later not only encourage other universities to also explore the use of patents but also shaped how universities would manage their patenting and licensing activities for decades to come. The key aspect of these early patent management solutions was that universities would not manage the activities themselves but would outsource them to legally separate entities. Indeed, even as universities' patenting activities increased, universities would follow these early tested models and refrain from engaging directly with patents.[264]

Under the first model, the administration of patents and licenses was contracted to a third-party management agent (typically the 'Research Corporation'). The Research Corporation originated from the research conducted by University of California Professor *Fredrick Garner Cottrell*.[265] In 1905 *Cot-*

---

260 For a detailed discussion, see infra 6.A.III.1.

261 See McKusick (1948) 245 J. Franklin Inst. 193, 197, referring to the fact that until the 1930, universities generally ignored the question of what to do about patents and decided against adopting a formal patent policy.

262 Ibid. 207.

263 See e.g. Weiner (1987) 12 Sci. Tech. Hum. Values 50, 50; Mowery and others, *Ivory Tower* (2004) 4.

264 See Mowery and Sampat (2001) 10 Ind. and Corp. Change 781, 781; Mowery and others, *Ivory Tower* (2004) 36–38.

265 Cottrell (1912) J. Ind. and Eng. Chem. 864, 864.

trell's research uncovered promising improvements in the electrostatic collection of smoke and fumes from chemical and metallurgical plants.[266] *Cottrell* was an early advocate of the commercialisation argument: in his view a 'minimum amount of protection' was necessary in order to attract possible investors who would bring an invention to market.[267] He objected to the common practice of placing inventions in the public domain or of licensing patents 'freely' as he believed that this would hinder commercialisation efforts.[268]

Cottrell filed for patent applications on his inventions and while he initially offered the respective rights to the University of California (which refused them based on the grounds that its charter did not allow commercial endeavours) he came to understand that the involvement with patents might grow 'commercialism and competition between institutions' and that it might jeopardise the open science culture.[269] In 1912, *Cottrell* therefore established the Research Corporation, a non-profit organisation which was legally separate from the University of California, and which was charged to administer patents which were transferred to it.[270] The income generated from the management of the patents and licences was to be assigned to university research and institutions dedicated to scientific research.[271] But beyond the hope to generate additional resources towards research from the administration of the patents, *Cottrell*'s main motivation was to provide a 'laboratory experiment in the public administration of patents' as he understood the administration of patents for public purposes to be complex and difficult.[272] *Cottrell*'s vision was that the Research Corporation would administer patents for academic inventors from different fields and institutions.[273] This vision indeed materialised: Between 1937 and 1980 most major universities eventually ended up signing an invention administration agreement with the Research Corporation.[274]

The second strategy, which a minority of universities followed in order to deal with the management of university patents, was to establish university-affiliated but legally separate foundations.[275] The most prominent example of this strategy is the Wisconsin Alumni Research Foundation (WARF), which was

---

[266] Ibid. 864.

[267] Ibid. 865.

[268] Ibid.

[269] Cottrell (1932) 26 Trans. Am. Inst. Chem. Eng. 222, 222–223; Weiner (1987) 12 Sci. Tech. Hum. Values 50, 51; Cottrell (1912) J. Ind. and Eng. Chem. 864, 864.

[270] Cottrell (1912) J. Ind. and Eng. Chem. 864, 865.

[271] Ibid.

[272] Cottrell (1932) 26 Trans. Am. Inst. Chem. Eng. 222, 224.

[273] Cottrell (1912) J. Ind. and Eng. Chem. 864, 865. While the initial purpose was for the Research Corporation to administer exclusively 'academic' patents, *Cottrell* soon realised that private individuals and large business corporations also were interested in having (some of) their patents managed by the Research Corporation, see ibid.

[274] See Sampat (2006) 35 Research Policy 772, 775.

[275] Ibid. 775.

founded in 1924 by members of the University of Wisconsin. Similarly, to the Research Corporation, the main motivation to get involved with patenting was not driven by predominantly economic arguments but considerations about the protection of the public interest.

The invention which triggered the establishment of WARF was a process which enhanced the concentration of vitamin D in food and pharmaceutical products developed by Professor *Harry Steenbock*.[276] *Steenbock* filed a patent on his invention out of the conviction that a patent would allow him to most optimally protect the public.[277] He was concerned that in the absence of patent protection, his process would be exploited in a harmful way and in a way that might hurt the dairy industry (which had been a long-time supporter of the University of Wisconsin).[278] While some of his colleagues saw the need to protect the public from 'unwise or fraudulent use' of university research, they generally objected to the use of patents.[279] The university's reluctance finally eased when *Steenbock* managed to convince the university that the patents should be administered by a legally separate entity and that this could potentially also financially benefit future research at the university. Accordingly, in 1925 WARF was founded.[280]

A number of additional universities started to patent inventions in the 1920s, however, there was typically no strategic element to such involvements. Most universities had neither a formal patent policy nor a 'generally accepted practice' on how to handle patentable inventions.[281] It was not until the early years of the depression in the 1930s, when several more universities would turn their attention to figuring out how to deal with patents on a more strategic level.

Different factors influenced this change in attitude. Firstly, and arguably most importantly, the growth in research collaborations between US universities and industry during the 1920s and 1930s and the resulting increase in the likelihood of patentable inventions demanded that universities would formulate a generalised policy toward patents.[282] Secondly, financial pressure engendered by the depression resulted in universities seeking alternative sources of income.[283] Positive examples such as WARF, which managed to generate prof-

---

[276] Weiner (1986) 89 Tech. Rev. 1, 2.

[277] Apple, *Vitamania* (1996) 34–35.

[278] Ibid. 36–37.

[279] Ibid. 37–38.

[280] Ibid. 41–42. Other universities such as Purdue University and Cornell University would follow the example of the University of Wisconsin in the 1930s and also establish affiliated but legally separate foundations, see Mowery and Sampat (2001) 10 Ind. and Corp. Change 781, 788.

[281] For a detailed account on the history of universities' patent policies, see infra 7.A.I.1.

[282] McKusick (1948) 245 J. Franklin Inst. 193, 214.

[283] Ibid. 213, referring to how universities considered this option for revenue generation before but typically distanced themselves from it for a fear that the resulting bad publicity would harm their endowments. Consequently, focus was placed on finding the type of patent management solutions which would not be detrimental to their public relations.

it from the University of Wisconsin's patent portfolio, encouraged universities to attempt to do the same.[284] Not surprisingly, perhaps, land-grant universities, whose research typically focused on applied research for industry and agriculture, were generally the first universities to get involved in patenting activities.[285] Thirdly, there was a growing belief that the public should benefit from university-generated inventions through the use of patents. This was particularly true for state and land-grant universities which were predominately funded through public funds.[286]

Indeed, in the 1930s debate on the desirability of patenting the results of research, the commercialisation argument for the use of patents progressively gained traction. Accordingly, it was commonly believed that research which would merely be published and 'thus thrown open equally to all' would typically not be adopted by industry unless it was of 'great importance'.[287] A patent would thus serve to raise the funds necessary to develop on a commercial scale new products or processes out of scientific inventions.[288] This is still the key argument made today in favour of university patenting and will be discussed in more detail below.

What distinguishes the 1930s debate from the debate leading up to the BDA (and arguments which continue to be made in favour of university patenting ever since) is that in the 1930s the only real concern was the protection of the public interest.[289] This concern was reflected in three arguments which were typically made in support of the use of patents. Firstly, the common conviction emerged that patents were justified where they prevented commercial firms from wrongfully appropriating university inventions (piracy argument). These patent pirates would search scientific publications and file patent applications on the most evident practical applications of the discoveries, thereby reducing the public availability of publicly funded inventions.[290] Secondly, it was commonly believed that the use of patents was necessary where they allowed the university to control the development and future use of the invention and thus the quality of the product or process derived from an invention. The 'quality control argument' for the use of patents was especially stressed in the context of chemical, pharmaceutical, and public health inventions.[291] Thirdly, it was gen-

[284] Ibid. 213; Mowery and others, *Ivory Tower* (2004) 40.

[285] Mowery and others, *Ivory Tower* (2004) 38, 40.

[286] McKusick (1948) 245 J. Franklin Inst. 193, 213.

[287] AAAS, *Protection by Patents of Scientific Discoveries* (1934) 9; also see McKusick (1948) 245 J. Franklin Inst. 193, 294.

[288] McKusick (1948) 245 J. Franklin Inst. 193, 294–295; AAAS, *Protection by Patents of Scientific Discoveries* (1934) 10.

[289] Also see infra 6. B.

[290] See e. g. McKusick (1948) 245 J. Franklin Inst. 193, 295; also see AAAS, *Protection by Patents of Scientific Discoveries* (1934) 10.

[291] See e. g. McKusick (1948) 245 J. Franklin Inst. 193, 295; also see infra accompanying discussion to n. 188–190/III.

erally recognised that patents could place restrictions on follow-on research and that therefore patents needed to be used in 'liberal terms' in order to make them available to the 'entire public'.[292]

Despite the engagement with patents by more and more institutions, before World War II, most universities still lacked a formal patent policy and continued to be sceptical of patents. Indeed, some universities even enacted 'antipatent' policies which discouraged or prohibited faculty to patent their research in general or in certain fields. Many universities were especially critical of patenting of health-related research and either forbade or restricted it. It was not until after World War II that due to the surge of federal funding universities motives for patenting got further strengthened and their involvement with patents grew.[293]

As was the case in the 1930s, the increased funds and the resulting increase in the quantity of university research led to an increased likelihood of the advent of patentable inventions. Many federal agencies also started to demand that universities adopt formal patent policies.[294] During this time, however, governments' main concern was its own access to the vast amount of research it funded.[295] Due to this pressure universities continued to enact patent policies and by the early to mid 1950s most of the major US research universities had a patent policy in place. This, however, did not mean that universities readily turned to patents – to the contrary, many universities' position towards patents remained ambivalent and to the extent that they would engage with patents, they would only do so on a case by case basis well into the 1960s.[296]

Throughout the 1950s and 1960s, federal support of academic research continued to increase and by 1968 US universities share of total basic research performance amounted to 50%.[297] The expansion of universities' research operations and their exposure to new fields would eventually lead to the final change in universities' attitudes towards patents and patent related policies and practices. And finally, during the 1970s and the early 1980s, with the growth of biomedical research and the ground-breaking advances in this field (and with its potential for commercial application) and with the passage of the BDA, the last bastion fell, and universities increasingly got directly involved into the management of patents and licenses, which up until then they had refused to do.[298]

---

292 AAAS, *Protection by Patents of Scientific Discoveries* (1934) 12.

293 See infra 7.A.I.1; also see e. g. Mowery and others, *Ivory Tower* (2004) 41.

294 See e. g. Mowery and others, *Ivory Tower* (2004) 41.

295 For details on the debate regarding the ownership of federally funded research, see infra 5.B.

296 For more details on the history of universities' patent policies, see infra 7.A.I.1.

297 See e. g. Mowery and others, *Ivory Tower* (2004) 43–44.

298 See e. g. Weiner (1986) 89 Tech. Rev. 1, 6; Mowery and others, *Ivory Tower* (2004) 43–44.

II Objections to the Commercialisation Argument as a Default Justification for the Use of Patents

While the commercialisation argument for the use of patents in the context of universities has not been introduced by the proponents of the BDA, what has changed in the debates leading up to the BDA and in discussions on university patenting ever since, is the dominance of the commercialisation argument. In other words, while the commercialisation argument formed part of the patent debate in the 1930s, equal weight was given to the quality control and the piracy argument.[299] Moreover, it was well understood that if an invention was patented it should be made available to the 'entire public'.[300] In general, the key concern was how the public could derive the biggest benefit from university research and hence from the use of patents in academia.

But perhaps most important of all, implied in the different arguments and considerations which were made during the early debate on the use of patents was that a balanced approach was necessary. Accordingly, the use of patents was never considered the default approach to the dissemination of university research. The piracy and the quality control arguments disappeared over time and with them the concern for the protection of the public. Today, patents are predominately seen as the preferred mean by which university research is transferred from universities to industry. The details of this shift, including how the BDA has enabled it, its implications to academia, and how universities have contributed to it, will be discussed in detail in Part III. The main objections to the commercialisation argument from a point of view of policy will be discussed below.

1 Public Good Objection

The most common argument for policy intervention on the enforcement of intellectual property rights is that there is a 'market failure'. The argument is that due to the public good characteristic of scientific knowledge, in competitive markets, there is not enough incentive for individuals and organisations to produce a socially optimal amount of such knowledge.[301] The public good properties of ideas and knowledge have long been noted and ultimately relate to the question of the usefulness of (basic) research and the question of how much government should invest in the production of the same.[302]

---

299 See supra n. 290–291/I and accompanying discussion.

300 See supra n. 292/I and accompanying discussion.

301 See e. g. David, in *Global Dimensions* (1993) 19, 25; also see e. g. Bator (1958) 72 Q. J. Econ. 351, 370–371; Stiglitz, in *Global Public Goods* (1999) 308, 308–310.

302 These are questions which have been discussed for over half a century, see e. g. David in *Global Dimensions* (1993) 19; R. Nelson (1959) 67 J. of Pol. Econ. 297; Arrow, in *The Rate*

A public good has two main qualities: it is non-rivalrous and non-excludable. If a good is non-rival, it is not diminished by use and it is non-excludable if it is freely available to all.[303] Applied to knowledge this means that once knowledge has been developed, it can be used by a multitude of people, without the use by one person hindering the use by someone else.[304] But there is no consensus that the best remedy for market failure is the creation of private rights in the knowledge.[305]

There are different institutions which governments use to address the incentive problem which arises due to the non-rivalrous and non-excludable nature of knowledge. *David* classifies these institutions under the categories of procurement, patronage, and property rights. Procurement refers to the situation where the government is contracting specific intellectual work to a contractor. This is typically done where the government is interested in a certain outcome i. e. in the development of specific knowledge as part of a sensitive defence research project for instance.[306] Public patronage refers to a system in which the government directly finances scientific research and inquiry.[307] It is a common solution to the 'public goods' problem of scientific knowledge and publicly supported universities and government laboratories are examples of this institution. Importantly, the so produced knowledge should be made available freely or at nominal charge to the public since it was financed through taxes.[308] Finally, property rights refer to the granting of exclusive rights to private producers of new knowledge.[309]

Patenting of federally funded research falls under two of these institutions, property rights and patronage. This is problematic as the two institutions are considered alternatives to each other and should thus not be simultaneously used to address the same incentive problem.[310] As a result of the overlapping of the two institutions, the public will end up paying twice: The first time for financing the research which lead to the invention through paying taxes and the second time in form of higher (monopoly) prices on the patented invention once it enters the market.[311]

---

and Direction of Inventive Activity (1962) 609; Pavitt (1991) 20 Research Policy 109; Salter and Martin (2001) 30 Research Policy 509.

303 The classic example is a lighthouse: the enjoyment of a person or a group of people does not distract from the enjoyment of another group of the population, nor can the enjoyment be reserved for only a special group of the population.

304 See e. g. Verspagen (2006) 20 J. Econ. Surv. 607, 609.

305 See e. g. David, in *Global Dimensions* (1993) 19, 25.

306 Ibid.

307 Ibid. 27.

308 Ibid. 27, 29.

309 Ibid. 29.

310 See e. g. Verspagen (2006) 20 J. Econ. Surv. 607, 610.

311 For a detailed discussion on the issue of double paying, see infra n. 301/II and n. 147–160/III and accompanying discussions respectively.

From this point of view the commercialisation argument for the use of patents, i. e. to use patents to induce private investments to further develop research, may be justified if the research is funded through private sources. But the logic should not be extended to publicly funded research. Restrictions on the use of publicly funded research (which the patent imposes) reduce the social returns for such public investments. Unfortunately, the BDA ignores this logic as it does exactly that: It encourages the application of patents on publicly funded research. In doing so, it calls into question the very reason for the government to invest in the production of scientific research.[312]

2 The Innovation-is-not-linear Objection

The linear model of innovation was one of the first theoretical frameworks to understand science and technology and their relation to the economy.[313] The model describes a linear process according to which innovation follows a straightforward progression, starting with basic research, moving to applied research and further development, and ending with production and diffusion. Only at the last step true innovation, in the form of new products and processes, is introduced.[314] In this linear model, the funding of basic research is both necessary and sufficient to promote innovation. Accordingly, governments support basic research as a form of public goods production, from there basic research flows into applied research, and private firms bring the benefit of these research results to the market through commercialisation.[315] Overall, the process is characterised by a 'laissez-faire' mentality, where neither universities nor the government stipulate the direction of the research or specific research topics. As a consequence of this separation of functions, the linear model assumes a strict separation between basic and applied research.[316]

The linear innovation model has been an influential conceptualisation, especially regarding the role of academic research within a national system of innovation.[317] The linear innovation model has been criticised for being inaccurate and overly simplistic: the distinction between basic and applied research is often artificial and does not reflect the more appropriate distinction between the different ends to which research is directed (i. e. is the research commercial or

---

312 See Mowery and others (2001) 30 Research Policy 99, 103; Verspagen (2006) 20 J. Econ. Surv. 607, 612; Eisenberg (1996) 82 Va. L. Rev. 1663, 1663, 1667.

313 The exact origins of this model are not quite clear, however, many credit *Vannevar Bush* for it, see Bush (1945) 48 Trans. Kan. Acad. Sci. 231. For a detailed account on the historic development of the linear model, see e. g. Godin (2006) 31 Sci. Tech. Hum. Values 639.

314 See ibid. 639; OECD, *Knowledge Management* (2000) 22.

315 See e. g. R. Nelson (2004) 33 Research Policy 455, 458; Frischmann (1999) 24 Vt. L. Rev. 350; Mowery and Sampat, in *Oxford Handbook* (2005) 210, 212.

316 Vest, in *University Research for Innovation* (2010) 51, 54.

317 Mowery and Sampat, in *Oxford Handbook* (2005) 210, 212.

not).[318] Despite wide-spread criticism, the model still forms the basis of the US' science policy and continues to feed public discourses, policy discussions, and academic analyses.[319]

The BDA (and in extension university patenting as an institutional imperative – as will be discussed in Part III) is built on a linear understanding of innovation: faculty generate research, the technology transfer office (TTO) protects and licences commercial valuable research to industry, and industry develops the research into commercial products and processes. Implied in this logic is thus the view that with strong research, technological advances and innovation may be planned and that competition in the development of the technology is not necessary.[320] The model further assumes that the inventor's participation is not necessary in the final two stages of the innovation process.[321] Instead, it is assumed that once research is developed and transferred to industry by virtue of a patent, the technology will be developed successfully. This 'technology push' theory, however, has been refuted. Studies have shown that the process of technological advancement is an evolutionary one which depends on competition and on feedback loops between the different stakeholders in the innovation process.[322]

The more modern understanding of the innovation process thus moves away from a linear progression and the strict separation between basic and applied research. It describes a more complex and interactive process which involves indeterminate feedback loops between basic and applied research and is driven by its stakeholders and their interrelations. The feedback loops sometimes lead to unexpected but important spillover effects.[323] As a consequence, basic research is not always the starting point but can also be the consequence of a practical application.[324] In the more modern conception of innovation, 'market pull' – i. e. the feedback, experiences, and knowledge which are channelled back from industry to the researchers – is as important as 'technology push'. Rather than the process moving from academic research to the market, there is a two-way

[318] See e. g. Frischmann (1999) 24 Vt. L. Rev. 347, 351; Godin (2006) 31 Sci. Tech. Hum. Values 639, 659. For a comprehensive rebuttal of the linear model, also see Kline and Rosenberg, in *Positive Sum Strategy* (1986) 275.

[319] See e. g. Frischmann (1999) 24 Vt. L. Rev. 347, 350–351; Godin (2006) 31 Sci. Tech. Hum. Values 639, 659.

[320] See e. g. R. Nelson (2004) 33 Research Policy 455, 458; See e. g. Lee and Gaertner, in *Technology Transfer* (1997) 110, 114–116.

[321] Also see Kenney and Patton (2009) 38 Research Policy 1407, 1419.

[322] See e. g. R. Nelson (2004) 33 Research Policy 455, 458.

[323] Spillover effects are recognised as being socially beneficial: they describe situations where research in a certain sector leads to beneficial progress in another, unrelated or only remotely related sector.

[324] Lundvall, in *Technical Change* (1988) 349, 349; Kline and Rosenberg, in *Positive Sum Strategy* (1986) 275; Frischmann (1999) 24 Vt. L. Rev. 347, 350; R. Nelson (2004) 33 Research Policy 455, 458.

stream of knowledge flowing in both directions: from the university to industry and from industry back to the university. It is this two-way communication which allows for successful research.[325] In this view, innovation is understood as a learning process where information flows between researchers in the public and private sphere. The process works like a flow-chart, running in continuous iteration with continuous feedback from the market.[326]

For universities this would mean that focus should not predominately be placed on the patenting of university research but on the establishment and fostering of transversal connections between universities and industry. This seems especially important if one considers that most industries do not in fact consider patents to be the most important transfer channel as the discussion in the next section will illustrate.

3 The Knowledge Flows Objection

There are many ways through which university knowledge is transferred to the outside world: through the publication of research results, participation of faculty and students in conferences and workshops, consulting arrangements, various forms of cooperation between universities and industry, such as firm sponsored research projects for instance, informal exchanges via social networks, and different entrepreneurial activities by faculty and students.[327] A source of knowledge transfer which has been underestimated for a long time but today is considered a key transfer channel is mobility. It occurs when faculty transfer from one university to another, when faculty work part-time jobs in industry or when educated and trained students move to private or public employment.[328]

The different transfer mechanisms operate in a complementary fashion to one another and in their totality contribute significantly to the economy.[329] The knowledge flow between university and industry has been studied in detail in the last few decades and it has been shown that the importance of the different transfer channels is assessed differently by firms active in different industries. In contrast to this reality, however, the commercialisation argument suggest

---

[325] There are two important ways how the feedback loops have to be in place: 1) between basic and applied research (e. g. patients die from side effects of a drug: this information needs to be fed back to basic research); and 2) between industrial application and a university (e. g. technical specialist who may assess information on what works and what does not from a technical point of view). Because the university may not be able to do certain things in a) a cost-efficient way; and/or b) from a procedural point of view, these feedback loops are crucial.

[326] See e. g. Verspagen (2006) 20 J. Econ. Surv. 607; Lee and Gaertner, in *Technology Transfer* (1997) 110, 114–116.

[327] For a comprehensive overview and analysis of different knowledge transfer channels, see e. g. NRC, *University Intellectual Property* (2011) 1.

[328] See e. g. Verspagen (2006) 20 J. Econ. Surv. 607, 612; NRC, *University Intellectual Property* (2011) 2.

[329] NRC, *University Intellectual Property* (2011) 2.

that patents are the generally preferred means by which technology transfer happens. This leads to universities employing patents where not only they may not be necessary but where industry does not consider them useful and is increasingly weary of paying a patent premium. This is therefore perhaps the most damaging objection to the commercialisation argument.[330]

[330] For additional discussion on the flow of knowledge between university and industry and industry's general preference of 'traditional' transfer channels also, see infra accompanying discussion to n. 12–20/III.

Part II

The Ownership of University Inventions: Legal Parameters

Chapter 3

General Inventorship and Ownership Issues

A The Inventor, the Owner, and the Applicant

I The Central Role of the Inventor in US Patent Law

US patent law historically has been centred on the notion of the inventor, who has a constitutionally based right to his invention. More specifically, Article 1, Section 8, Clause 8 of the US Constitution provides the authority for Congress to 'promote the progress of science and useful arts, by securing for limited times to authors and inventors the exclusive rights to their respective writings and discoveries'.[1] But despite this central role inventors play in progressing science and the arts, the Constitution does not further elaborate the term of the inventor. Moreover, in its role as a guardian and interpreter of the Constitution, the US Supreme Court has refrained from defining the constitutional meaning of inventorship to date.[2]

The narrative of the 'inventor' in US patent law has been shaped by the 'heroic inventor motif', the origin of which can be traced back to the mid 19th century.[3] This motif describes the typical 'garage inventor', who tinkers about in his free time, attempting to perfect an idea and eventually stumbles across a breakthrough invention that turns out to be beneficial to society. He typically works by himself and is not constrained by the traditional thinking prevalent in a field or profession or by the bureaucracy of a large organisational setting.[4] What drives him is his own curiosity and ingenuity. The narrative of the heroic, in-

---

1 This provision of the US Constitution is also known as the 'progress clause'.

2 This is especially noteworthy since the Supreme Court has addressed the constitutional meaning of other terms of the progress clause multiple times: 'authorship' (see e. g. *Feist Publications, Inc. v. Rural Telephone Service Co., Inc.*, 499 U. S. 340 [1991]) and more recently the interpretation of 'limited times' (*Eldred v. Ashcroft,* 537 U. S. 186 [2002]); *Golan v. Holder*, 565 U. S. [2012]). For an in-depth analysis of the terms, see e. g. Cherensky (1993) 81 Cal. L. Rev. 595, 602.

3 See e. g. Burlingame, *Inventors Behind the Inventor* (1947) 4. For a detailed discussion on the 'heroic inventor motif' and its British origins, see Janis (2002) 17 Berkeley Tech. L. J. 899, 908. Sometimes the literature also refers to the 'individual inventor motif', see e. g. Cotropia (2009) 12 Yale J. L. & Tech. 52, 57–58. While *Cotropia* offers a slight distinction between the 'heroic' and the 'individual inventor motif', going forward the two terms will be used interchangeably.

4 See e. g. Cotropia (2009) 12 Yale J. L. & Tech. 52, 54.

dependent inventor is deeply rooted in the American culture and in many ways depicts the American dream: Anyone can become successful through perseverance and ingenuity, irrespective of their background.[5]

Despite its historic origins, the heroic inventor motif is still firmly entrenched in the logic of US patent law and has continuously been relied upon in patent discourse.[6] After all, at the very core of patent law is the idea that an independent inventor, if given the proper incentive, will and can solve problems that perplex experts. Indeed, patents are denied on inventions that are 'obvious' to such experts. It is the goal of the patent law to encourage the development of unpredictable and extraordinary inventions.[7] In reality, however, there is very little evidence that the independent inventor is actually helped or protected by any legislation, the patent law, or even the Constitution.[8] In spite of this void in the law, as documented by *Janis*, all three government branches continued to make clear reference to the heroic inventor motif throughout the late 1990s and early 2000s.[9]

Janis predicted that policy debates would continue to revert to narratives about the heroic inventor.[10] It appears he was correct: *Cotropia* conducted a thorough analysis of the continued use of the individual inventor narrative by the three government branches and of major patent law changes and their impact on small inventors and concluded that, up until 2009, Congress and the USPTO (but not the courts) continued to heavily rely on the individual inventor motif, but that there was a lack of substance behind the motif.[11] He pointed out that it appeared as though Congress tried at least to avoid laws that *hurt* individual inventors, but that on balance, most of the patent law changes either proposed or made, came out against individual inventors.[12]

---

[5] Examples of such celebrated individuals include *James Watt*, *Thomas Edison*, the *Wright* brothers, *Steve Jobs*, to name just a few.

[6] See Janis (2002) 17 Berkeley Tech. L. J. 899, 910; Cotropia (2009) 12 Yale J. L. & Tech. 52, 57; Lemley (2012) 110 Mich. L. Rev. 709, 710.

[7] Lemley (2012) 110 Mich. L. Rev. 709, 710.

[8] As noted above, the Constitution specifically refers to 'inventors', which suggests that the addressee is an individual and not a corporation, however, more specific provisions are lacking. Also see Meurer (2008) 45 Hous. L. Rev. 1201, noting that there are only few patent law doctrines which target small businesses, see ibid. 1203–1204, also noting that it is far from clear whether patents actually help independent inventors, see ibid. 1230–1235.

[9] Janis (2002) 17 Berkeley Tech. L. J. 899, 911–921. A good example is quoted by *Janis*, who is referring to an old version of the USPTO website: 'To paraphrase our Declaration of Independence, America is the land of the free, home of the brave, and haven for the independent inventor. Nowhere else in the world does a government exist that supports its independent inventors to the extent that we do. The independent inventor is America's natural resource.', see ibid. 911. For a comprehensive discussion of *Janis*' catalogue of the usage of the motif, see Cotropia (2009) 12 Yale J. L. & Tech. 52, 57–61.

[10] Janis (2002) 17 Berkeley Tech. L. J. 899, 922.

[11] Cotropia (2009) 12 Yale J. L. & Tech. 52, 64–79.

[12] Ibid. 79–81.

This trend continued with the most recent change to the US patent law, the Leahy-Smith America Invents Act (AIA).[13] A little more than a month before signing it into law, President *Obama* stated: 'Through patent reform, we can cut the red tape that stops too many inventors and entrepreneurs from quickly turning new ideas into thriving businesses, which holds our whole economy back.'[14] Despite this clear reference to the individual inventor motif, the main focus of the reform was in reality not placed on inventors or entrepreneurs.[15] On the contrary, substantial concern has emerged that changes introduced by the AIA negatively impact independent inventors and small businesses and benefit corporations instead.[16] It is not within the scope of this work to analyse in detail to what degree the AIA has or has not harmed inventors. What can be concluded, however, is that the AIA is consistent with the history of US patent law on two seemingly contradictory levels: The heroic inventor motif lives on in patent discourse while the substantive changes introduced to the patent law mostly work to the detriment of individual inventors.[17] The perseverance of the narrative of the individual inventor can thus not be constructed from the workings of the patent system – as the patent system in actuality does not support it. Rather, it appears to be the loyal collective belief in the independent inventor and his importance to the American economy that is responsible that the narrative continues to live on.

Considering the prominence of the individual inventor motif in patent discourse, it may not be surprising that the individual inventor also plays a crucial role in the broader context of innovation theory. It has generally been acknowledged that independent inventors were one if not the major driver of innovation

[13] The AIA (125 Stat. 284–341) is arguably the most substantial revision of the US patent law since the 1952 Patent Act.

[14] Obama, 'Transcript' (*Washington Post*).

[15] For an overview of the wide-ranging issues the AIA tried to address, see e. g. Matal (2011) 21 Fed. Cir. B. J. 435; Thomas, *Leahy-Smith America Invents Act* (2014) 1. An exception is the newly created category of 'microentities': The Patent Act previously benefited small entities from a fee reduction of 50 % and the AIA increased this fee reduction to 75 % for microentities. An inventor can qualify for this status if he is an independent inventor or if he is affiliated with an institution of higher education. For a detailed discussion, see e. g. Cutaia and Kadle, 'Micro-Entity Status' (*Hudgson Russ*). This continues an existing tradition of the USPTO to adjust filing fees based on the size of the filing entity, see e. g. Cotropia (2009) 12 Yale J. L. & Tech. 52, 70.

[16] See e. g. Becker, 'Patent Reform' (*Washington Post*); Lohr, 'Inventor Challenges' (*New York Times*); Abrams and Wagner (2013) 65 Stan. L. Rev. 517, 563, suggesting that the overall change of the patent system from first-to-invent to first-to-file will likely result in a reduction of numbers of individual inventors seeking and receiving patents. Nash-Hoff, 'Has the AIA Been Benefical or Harmful? (*Industry Week*), arguing that the 'first-to-file' system and the new 'Patent Grant Opposition' (PGO) are especially detrimental to independent inventors.

[17] See Cotropia (2009) 12 Yale J. L. & Tech. 52, 57, arguing that up to 2009 every amendment to the patent law was to the detriment of small inventors, while the narrative of the individual inventor continued to be adhered to.

in the 19th and early 20th centuries.[18] Whether this role continued throughout the 20th century up until today and whether independent inventors indeed contribute more profoundly to technological progress than corporate research teams is highly controversial.[19] Increasingly, studies point to the importance of a team approach in creativity and in the development of breakthrough inventions.[20] Especially in science research, where scientists from different disciplines work together in order to solve societal, environmental, and public health problems, the team based approach has gained momentum.[21] Nevertheless, it still seems to be commonly believed that inventors, entrepreneurs and small businesses are disproportionally responsible for revolutionary innovations and job creation in the US.[22]

This logic has carried over to universities, where many efforts are undertaken to not only support faculty in start-up efforts, but to also engage graduates and undergraduates in entrepreneurship and start-up activities.[23] The fundamental belief is that students have the ingenuity and perseverance necessary to succeed and that it is the universities' responsibility to enable them in their pursuit by teaching the necessary skills and giving them the infrastructure and space (both physically and mentally) to succeed. The logic is that in doing so, not only students, but society at large will benefit through the creation of jobs and a growing economy.[24] But like the individual inventor narrative, the narrative of the student entrepreneur seems to be predominately fed by the belief in the narrative itself. It is controversial to what extent young entrepreneurs and start-ups positively impact the economy and studies suggest that most young and small businesses are not in fact primary creators of jobs.[25]

---

[18] See Schumpeter, *Entwicklung* (1912), identifying the independent entrepreneur as the primary agent of economic change. Also see e. g. Singh and Fleming (2010) 56 Mgmt. Sci. 41; Lamoreaux and Sokoloff (1996) 93 Proc. Nat'l Acad. Sci. USA 12686, concluding that – contrary to common belief – well into the 20th century productive inventors were 'free agents' for the most part.

[19] See e. g. Janis (2001) 17 Berkeley Tech. L. J. 899, 915, pointing to the concern that the tendency to attribute important technological inventions to individual inventors – where in reality they were generated by collective teams – causes mischief in historical records.

[20] Singh and Fleming (2010) 56 Mgmt. Sci. 41, arguing that individuals working alone, especially those without affiliation to organisations, are less likely to achieve breakthroughs and more likely to invent poor outcomes. Also see Paulus and Nijstad, in *Group Creativity* (2003) 1, 3–5.

[21] See e. g. Stokols and others (2008) 35 Am. J. Prev. Med. 77, describing the emerging 'science of team science' which analyses and promotes multidisciplinary collaboration between scientists in research in order to solve today's sticky problems.

[22] See e. g. Meurer (2008) 45 Hous. L. Rev. 1201, 1203.

[23] See e. g. Narea, 'How to Teach Entrepreneurship' (*Forbes*).

[24] See e. g. Januta, 'Job Growth' (*Reuters*), referring to *Eric Barron*, President of Pennsylvania State University, who suggested that 'entrepreneurship is critical not only to benefit students, but also to serve society by creating jobs and driving economic growth'.

[25] See e. g. Decker and others (2014) 28 J. Econ. Persp. 3, 21.

Whether independent inventors are more prone to develop breakthroughs and whether they do or do not contribute more profoundly to innovation than their corporate counterparts will not be answered conclusively here. What can be conclusively observed is that the share of independent inventors who own patents has been continuously decreasing and that corporate inventorship is responsible for the overall increase in the volume of patent applications.[26] To put this in perspective: In 1888 around 12 % of patents were issued to corporations, in 2015 around 93 % were issued to corporations and only around 6 % to individual inventors.[27]

From the above numbers it can be clearly inferred that employee-inventors working in an organisational setting play a key role in the US innovation ecosystem. As will be discussed in more detail further below, the legal problems surrounding employee-inventors are numerous and complex and often evolve around the question of inventorship and ownership of the respective invention. In spite of this complexity and the huge numbers of corporate employee-inventors, the US Patent Act is of only limited relevance to determining the ownership employee-inventions.[28] This is in contrast to other major industrialised jurisdictions which address the ownership of employee-inventions in their respective statutes (e. g. UK, Switzerland, France, Japan) or even have enacted specific laws (e. g. Germany, Denmark, Norway).[29] While more recent patent policy discussions and patent law changes in the US have shown increasing concern for corporations, the employee inventor who appears to be the backbone of American innovation is treated like the unloved stepchild and is left out of the debate.[30]

---

[26] See e. g. Shane, 'Patents Granted' (*Small Business Trends*), stating that the share of patents filed by independent inventors and small entities fell to 20 % in 2009; Crouch, 'Independent Inventors' (*Patently-O*), suggesting that the percentage of inventor-owned patents is only relative: The actual number of inventor-owned patents has stayed relatively stable over the past decades but there has been a clear rise in the number of patents granted to corporate owners. Also see Merges (2000) 88 Cal. L. Rev. 2187, 2215–2216.

[27] Merges (2000) 88 Cal. L. Rev. 2187, 2216. In 2020 the total number of utility patents granted in the US was 352'008, the total number of patents granted to independent inventors was 14'413, and the total number of patents granted to organisations was 330'528 (not including patents issued to US and foreign governments), see USPTO, 'Calendar Year Patent Statistics 2020' (*USPTO*).

[28] The only two provisions which are relevant are 35 USC § 261 (Assignments) and § 262 (Joint ownership).

[29] Also see e. g. Takenaka (2011) 44 Tex. Intell. Prop. L. J.284. For an overview over the different European approaches, see Peberdy and Strowel (2009) Cross-border Life Sci. Handbook 63.

[30] Regarding the increased concern for corporations in policy debates, see e. g. Nash-Hoff 'Has the AIA Been Benefical or Harmful? (*Industry Week*), quoting members of Congress and supporters of the AIA bill saying: 'We need to make it easier for companies to innovate and make things here at home'. The AIA's introduction of 'the applicant' (which will be discussed in more detail under 3.A.IV.) is also a good example of this focus on corporations: Pre-AIA a patent application could only be filed in the inventor's name and by the inventor himself. With

II The Difficulty of Determining Inventorship

In the US, patents are granted to the inventor who invents an invention and claims the respective subject matter in a patent application.[31] This tie between the inventor and the patent is a reflection of the aforementioned individual inventor narrative. The inventorship standard is exclusively based on federal law and is implemented by USC Title 35.[32] Moreover, only patents which list the true inventor(s) are valid and enforceable.[33] This is especially relevant in situations where there are multiple inventors as a result of collaborative research, which is commonplace in academia. Here, errors in patent inventorship can arise easily. If such errors arose pre-AIA it was not always easy to correct them, as corrections required an absence of 'deceptive intent'.[34] But the AIA reduced

the AIA's introduction of 'the applicant' this has changed, and with it, an important shift away from the inventor to the corporate employer and/or owner has taken place.

[31] 35 USC §101 provides that 'whoever invents or discovers' patentable subject matter 'may obtain a patent'; see also 35 USC §111: 'An application for patent shall be made, or authorized to be made, by the inventor, except as otherwise provided in this title [...]'. Section USC 35 §102(f) also used to be relevant but was eliminated by the AIA. It provided that a person is 'entitled to a patent unless he did not himself invent the subject matter sought to be patented'. In the discussions leading up to the AIA, the intended elimination of §102(f) raised the concern that the existing inventorship standard could not be maintained without it. However, Congress was assured that the inventorship standard was sufficiently protected by the constitutional reference of 'inventors' as well as §101 and that, therefore, even without §102(f) the grant of patents would continue to be restricted to inventors. It was pointed out that many years earlier the perhaps superfluous nature of the paragraph had been discussed: Commentary on the 1952 Patent Act had alluded to the fact that §102(f) might be altogether unnecessary. For a more detailed discussion, see Matal (2011) 21 Fed. Cir. B. J. 435. While many scholars and professionals agree with this reading, the final word on the matter may not have been spoken as *MadStad & Mark Stadnyk v. USPTO* 12-cv-1589 (M. D. Florida 2012) illustrates. In *MadStad* Shadnyk, a 'garage inventor' of motorcycle windshields, sued the US challenging the AIA as an unconstitutional modification of US patent law. The district court dismissed the case for lack of standing, but in its response, the USPTO highlighted that the AIA retained the requirement that patents would only be awarded to actual inventors and that the 'AIA's deletion of the redundant requirement in 35 USC §102(f) (was) irrelevant', see Kappos, 'Memorandum' (*USPTO*).

[32] *University of Colorado v. American Cynamid Company* 196 F.3d 1366, 1372 (Fed. Cir. 1999): 'The federal patent act leaves no room for states to supplement the national standard for inventorship'.

[33] *Amax Fly Ash Corporation v. United States*, 514 F. 2d 1041, 1050 (Court of Claims 1975): 'Where more or less than the true inventors are named, the patent is void'; *Ethicon, Inc. v. United States Surgical Corp*., 135 F. 3d 1456, 1460 (Fed. Cir. 1998): 'Patent issuance creates a presumption that the named inventors are the true and only inventors'; *Trovan Ltd. v. Sokymat SA, Irori,* 299 F. 3d 1292, 1301 (Fed. Cir. 2002): 'A patent is invalid if more or less than the true inventors are named'. Finally, it does not matter whether all or just one individual acted with a deceptive intent, see *Stark v. Advanced Magnetics, Inc., 119 F. 3d 1551,* 1556 (*Fed. Cir. 1997*): 'One bad apple spoils the entire barrel.'

[34] USC 35 §256: 'Whenever through error a person is named in an issued patent as the inventor, or through error an inventor is not named in an issued patent and such error arose without any deceptive intention on his part, the Director may, on application of all the parties

the severity of incorrectly listing inventors and the obstacles of correcting inventorship by removing all inquiries into the subjective issues of intent.[35] As a consequence, in essentially every situation it should now be possible to correct the inventorship of an application or a patent and avoid that a given patent be found invalid or unenforceable based on incorrectly listed inventor(s).[36]

The inventor's central role in US patent law is also reflected by the fact that inventorship cannot be stipulated or negotiated. After all, granting an exclusive right to the inventor of a patent is at the core of patent law's utilitarian justification and is anchored in the US Constitution.[37] Allowing parties to negotiate or stipulate inventorship would be in breach with this policy.[38] Accordingly, the question of inventorship is a question of law which requires corroborative evidence by any putative inventor of any asserted contributions.[39]

As one might imagine, determination of inventorship can be a tricky and dispute-prone issue.[40] This is especially so, where multiple i. e. 'joint' inventors are involved. In academia, where research projects have become increasingly complex and usually involve multiple researchers, joint inventorship has become the rule rather than the exception. In many instances, it can be extremely challenging to keep track of the different contributors in a given project and consequently to correctly determine the inventors of an invention. This is especially the case, where different types of researchers (students, post-doctoral students, professors, industry experts) are working on a long-term project. Not surprisingly, perhaps, what constitutes (joint) inventorship has historically been considered one of the more difficult areas of patent law and has aptly been de-

---

and assignees, with proof of the facts and such other requirements as may be imposed, issue a certificate correcting such error.'

[35] In an effort to reduce litigation burdens, the explicit mention of 'deceptive intention' has been removed under the AIA throughout the statute, see 35 USC §§116 (Inventors), 184 (Filing of application in foreign country), 251 (Reissue of defective patents), 253 (Disclaimer), 256 (Correction of named inventor), and 288 (Action for infringement of a patent containing an invalid claim). Prior to these changes, 'deceptive intent' was often asserted by litigants, at which point inventorship could not be corrected and the patent would be held invalid and/or unenforceable. For a detailed discussion, see Armitage (2012) 40 AIPLA Q. J. 1, 123–128.

[36] See 35 USC §§116 and 256.

[37] US Constitution Article 1, Section 8, Clause 8.

[38] Okuley (2003) 18 Ohio St. J. on Disp. Resol. 915, 932.

[39] *Sewall v. Walters*, 21 F. 3d 411, 415 (Fed. Cir. 1994): 'Conception, and consequently inventorship, are questions of law that this court reviews de novo; of course, any facts found by the Board in reaching an inventorship holding are reviewed for clear error.'; *Ethicon, Inc. v. United States Surgical Corp.*, 135 F. 3d 1456, 1456 (Fed. Cir. 1998): 'Inventorship is a question of law, which this court reviews without deference'. Also see, *Eli Lilly and Co. v. Aradigm Corp.*, 376 F. 3d 1352, 1362 (Fed. Cir. 2004): 'Inventorship is a mixed question of law and fact: The overall inventorship determination is a question of law, but it is premised on underlying questions of fact.'

[40] *See e. g. Chou v. University of Chicago*, 254 F. 3d 1347 (Fed. Cir. 2001); *Shukh v. Seagate Technology*, LLC, 803 F.3d 659 (Fed. Cir. 2015).

scribed as 'one of the muddiest concepts in the muddy metaphysics of the patent law'.[41]

As a matter of principle, if more than one individual were involved in developing a particular invention, the inventors will have to apply for the patent together and will be named as joint inventors on the patent.[42] In order to determine the inventorship in a given situation, the process of making an invention has to be considered. It involves two distinct and independent steps: the 'conception' and the 'reduction to practice'. 'Conception' is the touchstone of inventorship and refers to the mental part of the inventive activity.[43] Conception is complete when an inventor has developed an idea in his mind which is definite and permanent, so that only ordinary skills and no further inventive steps are needed to reduce it to practice.[44] The 'reduction to practice' is thus the step beyond the conception that is undertaken once the idea is developed. It involves the actual construction of the invention in a physical form to the point that all the steps and tests which are necessary to do so have been undertaken.[45] An individual is considered an inventor under patent law if he has conceived or contributed to the conception of the invention; whether or not the individual also contributed to the reduction to practice is not relevant for the determination of inventorship.[46] That is the case, even where the reduction to practice is the most time consuming, costly, and difficult part of developing the invention.[47]

It follows that an individual which merely implements a completely conceived idea will not be considered an inventor.[48] Having an idea about the results which need to be accomplished (rather than knowing the means of accomplishing them) will not suffice.[49] From a practical point of view, determining the inventorship will not be possible unless there is a full understanding of the

[41] *Mueller Brass v. Reading Industries, Inc.*, 325 F. Supp. 1357, 1372 (Dist. Court, ED PA 1972).

[42] 35 USC §116.

[43] *Fina Oil and Chemical Co. v. Ewen*, 123 F. 3d 1466, 1473 (Fed. Cir. 1997); Rooklidge and von Hoffmann (1988) 63 St. John's L. Rev. 1, 7.

[44] *Burroughs Wellcome Co. v. Barr Laboratories, Inc.*, 40 F. 3d 1223, 1228 (Fed. Cir. 1994).

[45] See e. g. Rooklidge and von Hoffmann (1988) 63 St. John's L. Rev. 1, 7; Hunter, *Intellectual Property* (2012) 96. Note that the reduction to practice can be 'actual' or 'constructive': Actual reduction to practice exists when the invention or the process is successfully made or performed and tested. Constructive reduction to practice occurs when a patent application is filed that contains sufficient disclosure under the 'how to use' and 'how to make' requirements. See MPEP 2138.05 'Reduction to Practice'.

[46] *C. R. Bard, Inc. v. M3 Systems, Inc.*, 157 F.3d 1340, 1352 (Fed. Cir. 1998): 'The 'inventor' in patent law, is the person or persons who conceived the patented invention'; *Ethicon, Inc. v. United States Surgical Corp.*, 135 F. 3d 1456 (Fed. Cir. 1998); *StoneEagle Services, Inc. v. Gillman*, 746 F. 3d 1059 (Fed. Cir. 2014).

[47] Gattari (2005) 17 Intell. Prop. & Tech. L. J. 16, 17.

[48] *Sewall* 414–415.

[49] *Garrett Corporation v. United States*, 422 F. 2d 874, 881 (Court of Claims 1970).

precise definition of the invention. More often than not, such an understanding cannot be gained until the drafting of the claims takes place, and until they have to be submitted as part of the application.[50] Thus, practically, the determination of inventorship will often coincide with the drafting of the application.

In the case of joint inventorship, it is not necessary for co-inventors to contribute equally nor do they have to contribute to all claims of the invention.[51] It is possible for a co-inventor to only have contributed to one claim and still be considered an inventor.[52] What matters is not so much the amount or level of contribution but that – aside from contributing to the conception of the invention – the individual also participated in some 'collaboration or concerted effort' towards the invention.[53] In other words, there has to be some element of collaboration, joint behaviour or contact between the respective individuals which makes them aware of the other's work.[54] Hence, although the individuals do not have to work together physically or work at the same time at the invention, they nevertheless need to have 'some open line of communication during or in temporal proximity to their inventive efforts'.[55]

This raises the question whether employers may qualify as inventors. The short answer is yes, but only if the employer is a natural person.[56] Legal entities such as corporations or non-profit organisations cannot be named as inventors on a patent. Hence, even though employers may contribute to their employees' inventions by providing the infrastructure and the financial resources and may even instruct their employees to conduct their research in a certain way, they will not qualify as inventors. Only if the employer is a natural person, they may be named, but of course only if they contributed sufficiently to the conception.

This is a unique feature of patent law, as normally, whatever workers produce as part of their employment is owned by the employer.[57] Even copyright law

---

[50] Nash and Rawicz, *Intellectual Property* (2008) 72.

[51] See USC 35 §116: 'Inventors may apply for a patent jointly even though, 1) they did not physically work together or at the same time, 2) each did not make the same type or amount of contribution, or 3) each did not contribute to the subject matter of every claim of the patent.' Before 1984 named inventors had to be contributors to all claims of an invention. This meant that claims and inventors had to be listed and segregated from each other depending on the claims they contributed to. Multiple applications needed to be filed so that a proper listing of inventors could be ensured. This was cumbersome and negatively impacted team-based research, which is the reason why the rule was amended. For a more detailed account, see Nash and Rawicz, *Intellectual Property* (2008) 72.

[52] *SmithKline Diagnostics, Inc. v. Helena Lab. Corp.* 859 F.2d 878, 888–889 (Fed. Cir. 1988).

[53] *Eli Lilly* 1359.

[54] *Kimberly-Clark v. Procter & Gamble* 973 F. 2d 911, 916 (Fed. Cir. 1992).

[55] *Eli Lilly* 1359 (Fed. Cir. 2004).

[56] *University of Utah v. Max Planck Gesellschaft zur Förderung der Wissenschaft E.V*, 734 F.3d 1315, 1323 (Fed. Cir. 2013).

[57] The Supreme Court most recently addressed this in *Board of Trustees of the Leland*

addresses this problem differently under the 'work made for hire' doctrine.[58] Under the doctrine, the employer will be considered the author and the work which is created by an employee will directly be owned by the employer.[59] Under patent law, however, employers will not be considered inventors nor will they normally own the patent which has been developed by their employees unless the rights are assigned to them.

State common law provides some protection for employers, especially where an employee was specifically hired to invent a specific invention or where the job description requires employees to pursue inventive activities quite generally. The protection that common law provides, however, is limited – which is why employers typically have employees contractually transfer ownership of employee-inventions to the employer.

The above also applies to universities: As legal entities they cannot be named inventors or co-inventors of inventions which were developed by their faculty, staff, or students. Universities' position is arguably even more difficult as common law doctrine will rarely be of service at all. Universities therefore have become accustomed as well to rely on contractual assignment of faculty and researchers' inventions. Both the common law and the contractual assignment of employee-inventions will be discussed in detail in the next chapter.

III Inventorship versus Ownership

While ownership and inventorship are closely related, they are strictly distinct concepts under patent law. The question of inventorship determines who invented the subject matter of the invention claimed in the patent. In contrast, the question of ownership addresses who owns the property rights to the subject matter claimed in the patent.[60] Nevertheless, the two concepts are intrinsically linked as the inventorship also determines the initial ownership: The ownership of a patent or patent application initially vests in the inventor(s) of the invention disclosed in the patent.[61] Accordingly, the inventor is considered the presumptive owner of a claimed invention unless or until he assigns his ownership interest to someone else. Any ownership analysis will thus have to begin with

---

Stanford Junior University v. Roche Molecular Systems, 563 US 776 (S. Ct. 2011). For a detailed discussion of the case, see infra 5.D.

58 See 17 USC §§101 (Definition work made for hire) and 201 (Ownership works made for hire).

59 Also see n. 100–101/II.

60 *Beech Aircraft Corp. v. Edo Corp.*, 990 F. 2d 1237, 1248 (Fed. Cir. 1993): 'It is elementary that inventorship and ownership are separate issues [...] inventorship is a question of who actually invented the subject matter claimed in a patent. Ownership, however, is a question of who owns legal title to the subject matter claimed in a patent, patents having the attributes of personal property.'

61 *Gayler v. Wilder,* 51 US 477, 493 (S. Ct. 1851); *Stanford v. Roche* 2195.

first establishing the inventorship. It is clear, then, that a wrong designation of inventor(s) could potentially lead to complex ownership problems.

Despite the close link of the two concepts, more often than not inventorship and ownership will deviate from each other. Patents have the attributes of personal property and may thus be transferred to someone else by written agreement.[62] If an inventor assigns his rights in the invention, the application or the patent, ownership will vest in the assignee. Assignments may be filed with the USPTO where the new ownership rights will be recorded.[63] Once this is the case, the assignee is entitled to move the patent application through prosecution in the name of the inventor. In fact, the assignee will be able to do so even if the inventor refuses to cooperate but has an obligation to assign the invention.[64] If an inventor assigns his interest in a patent that has yet to be issued, the patent may be issued directly to the assignee.[65]

Employers rely heavily on the assignability of patents and inventions. This is why employers generally put in place written contractual agreements (most of the time as part of the employment agreement) which have employees assign ownership interests in inventions and patents to the employer. While these 'pre-invention assignment agreements' are often viewed critically, as they are generally broad and do not leave any room for bargaining, courts have historically upheld them.[66]

An important change which the AIA introduced, and which will be discussed in more detail below, is the new definition of the 'patent applicant'. Under the AIA a patent owner, such as an employer, who succeeds to establish himself as an 'assignee', 'obligated assignee' or 'person showing sufficient proprietary interest', may file a patent application on an invention which has been developed by his employee.[67] Despite this new power an owner (such as an employer) has, the AIA did not change the ownership presumption, which means that the initial ownership will still vest in the inventor. This implies that the importance of the determination of inventorship, as well as the likely occurrence of inventorship disputes, will remain unchanged.[68]

---

[62] USC 35 § 261: '[…] (P)atents shall have the attributes of personal property, […] (a)pplications for patent, patents, or any interest therein, shall be assignable in law by an instrument in writing'. Also see *United States v. Dubilier Condenser Corp.,* 289 US 178, 187 (S. Ct. 1933): 'A patent is property and title to it can pass only by assignment.'

[63] USC 35 § 261.

[64] USC 35 § 115(d), providing that in lieu of an oath or declaration by the original inventor – as is necessary for the application – a 'substitute statement' can be made if the inventor 'is under an obligation to assign the invention but has refused to make the oath or declaration'.

[65] 35 USC § 152.

[66] See infra 4.D.

[67] 37 Code of Federal Regulations (CFR) § 1.42(b). For a more detailed discussion, see infra 3.A.IV.

[68] For a discussion of examples of such disputes in an academic research context, and the difficulty of asserting ownership based on them, see infra 3.B. I.

The determination of ownership of patent rights and rights in pre-inventions can be confusing as it involves a mixture of federal patent law, state laws of contracts, employment, and trade secrets.[69] As stated above, the inventorship standard is determined based on federal patent law.[70] It also seems to be generally accepted that federal law applies to assignments of patent applications and patents which have been issued.[71] Conversely, where the patent application has not actually been filed yet, it used to be generally accepted that the question of who owns the invention is determined by state law.[72] However, in more recent history, a few decisions by the Federal Circuit and the Supreme Court have cast doubt whether state law and not federal law should govern pre-invention assignment agreements. But to this date there has not been any conclusive answer on the matter.[73]

IV Post America Invents Act: Enter the Applicant

As pointed out above, the US patent law is centred on the inventor and, as a logical consequence, the inventor also plays a central role in 'patent prosecution'.[74] Hitherto absent exceptional circumstances, the inventor of a claimed invention was normally also the applicant and as such a natural person. Post AIA, however, the applicant does not have to be (and most of the time will not be) the inventor.[75] According to the AIA, assignees of an inventor will be able to file a patent application themselves, with the simple requirement on the assignee-applicant to properly name the inventor.[76] An applicant can be any natural person or 'juristic entity' (i. e. a corporation or any other legally created organisation) as long as the inventor has assigned the invention to them, is under an obligation to assign the invention to them, or any person or legal entity that shows sufficient proprietary interest in the invention.[77]

---

[69] See e. g. Crouch, 'Inventors Can Retain Rights' (*Patently-O*); LaFrance (2003) Nevada L. J. 88, 90.

[70] 35 USC §101.

[71] For a detailed analysis of the question whether state or federal law applies to post- and pre-invention transfers, see e. g. Hovell (1982) 58 Notre Dame L. Rev. 863, 865–866.

[72] Ibid. 865; LaFrance (2003) Nevada L. J. 88, 90.

[73] For a more detailed analysis see infra n. 219/II.

[74] 'Patent prosecution' refers to the process of navigating the legal and administrative requirements of the USPTO while pursuing protection for a patentable invention. It also encompasses interchanges with the USPTO after the patent has been granted, see e. g. Hunter, *Intellectual Property* (2012) 108; also see 35 USC §115 (Naming the Inventor; Inventor's Oath or Declaration).

[75] Armitage (2012) 40 AIPLA Q. J. 1, 20.

[76] Ibid. 20; see 35 USC §118: 'A person to whom the inventor has assigned or is under an obligation to assign the invention may make an application for patent.'

[77] See CFR §1.42(b); for a detailed explanation of the rule, see e. g. Jordan and Kaiser, 'Inventor Challenges' (*Mondaq*).

While the term 'applicant' already existed in the pre-AIA world, it did not bear much meaning as it was essentially synonymous with the inventor. In the post-AIA world, the 'applicant' has a meaning distinct from the inventor and the owner. This new definition of the term and the added flexibility for assignee-applicants that the new rule introduced make good business sense: They simplify the application process and remove obstacles for employers to obtain ownership over employee-inventions where employee-inventors do not cooperate or cannot be found. The flipside is that the change is a continuation of the general neglect of the employee-inventor in the actual protection by the law and, as such, further weakens the already weak position of employee-inventors.

Moreover, and perhaps more importantly, the change also ignores the realities of how inventive activity actually happens. One of the biggest challenges in the patenting process remains the translating of the technical details of an invention into the patent claims.[78] Isolating the employee-inventor from the application process will only exacerbate this problem. In this context, it seems rather fitting that it has been pointed out that the AIA did not in fact introduce a 'first-to-file' or a 'first-inventor-to-file' system but a 'first-owner-to-file' system instead.[79]

B Inventorship and Ownership Issues in an Academic Research Context

I Determining Inventorship and Ownership in an Academic Setting

Research groups in academia often are more complex than research groups in industry, which makes the determination of inventorship and ownership especially challenging for universities. There are two reasons for this complexity. Firstly, a typical academic research group consists of many different types of researchers: faculty, laboratory specialists, administrative staff, graduate, undergraduate, post-doctoral students, and visiting researchers (from other academic or non-profit institutions as well as industry). These groups of researchers will typically have different types of contractual relationships with the specific laboratory, department, and/or the university. Secondly, a typical university research group is a dynamic construct, where new people join, and existing ones leave on a regular basis. Most often there is an especially high fluctuation of graduate, undergraduate, and post-doctoral students.[80] Due to these layers of complexity, it often proves especially

[78] Also see infra 7.A.II.4.
[79] See e. g. Crouch, 'AIA Shifts USPTO Focus' (*Patently-O*).
[80] For a good discussion of the inner workings of an academic research group, see e. g. Seymore (2006) 16 Alb. L. J. Sci. & Tech. 125, 130–132.

challenging for universities to identify inventors and ownership interests in a given research project.

For the determination of ownership, the contractual relationship between the university and the respective researcher will be of essence. Faculty, staff, graduate students, and post-doctoral students will typically be in an employment relationship with the university which will determine the ownership rights of inventions generated under said employment. In most cases, inventions will be assigned to the university by way of an invention assignment clause in the employment contract or by having employees sign a special assignment agreement.[81]

In contrast, undergraduate students and external researchers will typically not be in a formal employment relationship with the university.[82] Despite this, universities will typically assert ownership claims of inventions generated by external researchers (from industry or another academic institution) and have them contractually transfer their rights to the university. Conversely, where faculty conduct research with another university or a partner in industry, they will generally also be asked to sign an invention assignment agreement. It is not difficult to imagine that this will inevitably lead to situations where ownership claims on certain research results will overlap.

For instance, a faculty member may be employed by a university but may choose to work on a research project with a firm in industry during a summer or a sabbatical. As a consequence, if an invention results from the research conducted, it will most likely be claimed by both the university and the firm. As a matter of fact, the landmark *Stanford v. Roche* Supreme Court case is exactly an example of a situation where a researcher signed two competing assignment clauses which both covered the same research project.[83] In general, working out the ownership rights based on different (contractual) arrangements increasingly presents a challenge to universities.[84]

In the context of such collaborative research environments, an additional challenge will often be to correctly identify the researchers who have contributed to an invention's conception. What adds to the difficulty is that researchers often are uneducated about general intellectual property questions, including when an invention might be patentable and when someone might qualify as an inventor.[85] This will inevitably lead to situations where a patentable subject-matter will be developed, and a given researcher may believe that his con-

[81] See infra 4.D.III.

[82] For a detailed discussion on universities' treatment of student inventions, see infra 7.A.I.3.

[83] For a detailed discussion of the case and its facts, see infra 5.D.

[84] Also see e. g. Reder (2011) 44 Bus. L. Rev. 211, 212.

[85] See infra n. 291/III and accompanying text; also see e. g. Villasenor, 'Intellectual Property Awareness at Universities' (*Forbes*); Okuley (2003) Ohio St. J. on Disp. Resol. 915, 923.

tribution was substantial enough for him to be named as an inventor. What may add to the confusion is that someone who normally qualifies as an 'author' in an academic publication will not necessarily also qualify as an 'inventor'.[86]

Many challenges in determining inventorship arise out of the technology transfer process which generally stipulates that faculty, staff, and students ought to disclose university-generated inventions to the TTO. While the disclosure may be made by anyone involved in the research project, and perhaps ideally should be made by the leader of the research group or the director of the respective research laboratory, in reality, disclosure forms will often be prepared and submitted by graduate students.[87]

The disclosure is a crucial step in the technology transfer process, as it not only informs the TTO's decision whether or not to file a patent, but it also identifies the inventors of the respective invention. It may easily occur that whoever is in charge of preparing the disclosure, is not willing to identify everyone who has contributed to the invention, or is simply not aware or has not been made aware of all the inventors who were involved in the research which resulted in the invention. While the determination of inventorship will not always be solely based on the disclosure, but may also be informed by subsequent conversations between the TTO and the research group, often the person who prepares and submits the disclosure will lead the conversation with the TTO and thus bares a huge responsibility in correctly identifying all inventors.

II The Difference between Authorship and Inventorship

As mentioned above, while authorship and inventorship are two distinct concepts, in academia the concepts are often used interchangeably. This may occur because authorship and inventorship are intrinsically related to the nature of the academic work. Accordingly, a given research project may yield a publication as well as a patentable invention. But researchers often do not distinguish between an involvement in the research which is sufficient to warrant authorship and a contribution to the conception of the invention which qualifies for inventorship.[88] This may be especially pronounced where research activities are conducted by larger teams, as is typically the case in the sciences and in engineering. In fact, in the past decades, the average number of authors per publication and the average number of inventors per patent has continued to increase.[89] The

---

[86] Also see 3.B.II.

[87] In a 2015 Interview, the President of Virginia Tech's TTO mentioned that up to 80% of invention disclosures would typically be prepared and submitted by graduate students.

[88] Also see Okuley (2003) Ohio St. J. on Disp. Resol. 915, 923–924.

[89] Lissoni and others (2013) 95 J. Econ. Behav. & Org. 49, 50.

inability to correctly differentiate the two concepts has given rise to many inventorship disputes.[90]

Perhaps not surprisingly, it is more likely for an inventor to also be named as an author than for an author to be named as an inventor. Or put differently, in cases where an article and a patent are the output of a research project, the number of authors is typically higher than the number of inventors.[91] The most obvious explanation for the higher number of authors is that authors may simply have been excluded by their colleagues and not have been named as inventors in the invention disclosure.[92] This would make sense, especially in fields such as the life sciences or engineering, where patents have progressively gained in importance. Especially where inventors hope to commercialise the invention in question, they may be inclined to not list additional inventors in the invention disclosure as – in contrast to additional authors listed in publications – every additional inventor would diminish the potential future pay-out of the invention.

Another explanation for the discrepancy could be that the inventorship standard is more restrictive than the authorship standard. Indeed, in many instances academic authors' involvement does not qualify as a contribution towards the conception of the invention.[93] To this effect, the court in *In re Katz* determined that 'authorship of an article does not raise a *presumption* of inventorship with respect to the subject-matter disclosed in the article' and that 'the content and nature of the printed publication, as well as the circumstances surrounding its publication, not merely its authorship, must be considered' when determining inventorship.[94]

Finally, it should be mentioned that when it comes to the attribution of authorship and inventorship in academia an important factor appears to be academic tradition.[95] Being named on a publication of a particular research project is central to the career structure in academia and is often determined by subjective rather than objective criteria. There may be situations where students and young academics do the majority of the work and a senior faculty member or project leader 'lends' his or her name. Conversely, in other instances, authorship may be conferred as an honorarium or some sort of gift where the student's or

---

[90] See e. g. *In re Katz*, 687 F. 2d 450 (Ct. of Customs and Patent Appeals 1982); *University of Colorado Found. v. American Cyanamid,* 196 F. 3d 1366 (Fed. Cir. 1999); *Chou v. University of Chicago*, 254 F. 3d 1347 (Fed. Cir. 2001); *Meng v. Chu,* No. 14–1746 (Fed. Cir. 2016); *Arefolov. v. Presidents and Fellows of Harvard College et al*, 1:17-cv-10785 (Dist. Ct. Massachusetts).

[91] See e. g. Ducor (2000) 289 Science 873.

[92] See e. g. Benderly, 'Who Counts as an Inventor?' (*Science*).

[93] See *In re Katz* 455; also see Seymore (2006) 16 Alb. L. J. Sci. & Tech. 125, 140; Okuley (2003) Ohio St. J. on Disp. Resol. 915, 924; Lissoni and others (2013) 95 J. Econ. Behav. & Org. 49, 52.

[94] *In re Katz* 455.

[95] TTO Review (n. 288/III); also see e. g. Lissoni and others (2013) 95 J. Econ. Behav. & Org. 49, 52.

young academic's contribution would not be sufficient to warrant authorship.[96] In this context, the focus of authorship is about visibility and thus ultimately about being published and cited. In an effort to eliminate such practices, scientific organisations and journals in certain academic fields (such as e. g. the medical sciences) have attempted to adopt stricter authorship standards. However, the success of this has been limited as these standards are generally self-enforced and, as a result, they are often ignored.[97]

In many academic fields, the situation may be similar in regard to the determination of inventorship. After all, most academics are fairly inexperienced with patents and related concepts such as inventorship. Hence, while a minimal level of contribution would technically not suffice to meet the necessary contribution to the conception of an invention and thus to qualify as an inventor, it appears that the legal norms are often rejected in favour of individual, arbitrary judgment.[98]

As academics gain more exposure to patents and attain a greater understanding of them and related concepts, this may change. In time, this may lead to an even greater discrepancy between named authors and inventors, and it may also evoke ever more legal disputes surrounding inventorship (as well as other) issues. It is for this reason, that it makes sense for universities to educate faculty and students on the basics of patent law.[99]

---

[96] Ducor (2000) 289 Science 873, 873; Okuley (2003) Ohio St. J. on Disp. Resol. 915, 924.

[97] See Okuley (2003) Ohio St. J. on Disp. Resol. 915, 923 n. 39; Dreyfuss (2000) 53 Vand. L. Rev. 1159, 1183–1184.

[98] Lissoni and others (2013) 95 J. Econ. Behav. & Org. 49, 52; Colyvas (2007) 36 Research Policy 456, 461–462.

[99] Also see infra 7.C.III.3.

Chapter 4

Legal Conditions of the Ownership of University Inventions

A The Law on Employee Inventions

It is generally accepted that in most instances employers own the work products of their employees. Whatever an 'autoworker' produces as part of his or her job, will be owned by his employer. Similarly, under copyright law's 'work made for hire' doctrine, whenever an employee prepares a work 'within the scope of his or her employment'[100], 'the employer [...] is considered the author for purposes of this title, and [...] owns all of the rights comprised in the copyright'[101]. Patent law is different in this regard: Employment is not enough to vest title to an employee's invention in the employer.[102] Instead, the ownership of an invention developed by an employee-inventor is initially vested in the employee-inventor.[103]

Despite this, today, most employee-inventions will not be owned by the employees but are owned by the respective (corporate) employer. Indeed, a very high percentage of all patents issued by the United States Patent and Trademark Office (USPTO) are assigned to corporations at the time of their issuance.[104] In some instances, the duty to assign employee-inventions will be inferred by certain default rules under state common law.[105] But most commonly, obligations to transfer ownership title to the employer arise under contractual assignments between the employee and the employer.[106]

The practice of having ownership rights of employee-inventions rest with employers has been generally criticised, mainly on the basis of it being un-

[100] 17 USC § 101 (Definition).

[101] 17 USC § 201 (Ownership).

[102] This has been confirmed by *Stanford v. Roche* 2196: 'It is often the case that whatever an employee produces in the course of his employment belongs to his employer. No one would claim that an autoworker who builds a car while working in a factory owns that car. But, as noted, patent law has always been different: We have rejected the idea that mere employment is sufficient to vest title to an employee's invention in the employer.'

[103] Ibid. 2199: '[...] the basic principle of patent law that inventors own their inventions.'

[104] In 2020, of a total of 352'008 patents issued, 336'695 (i. e. 95.6 %) were owned by US and foreign corporations and governments, see USPTO, 'Calendar Year Patent Statistics 2020' (*USPTO*).

[105] See infra 4.C.

[106] See infra 4.D.

fair.[107] It is generally accepted that the general skills, knowledge, and experience an employee gained in the course of his employment will belong to the employee.[108] However, if the employee applies the same knowledge or skills within the job and a patentable invention results, under the generally accepted assignment practice, the respective ownership rights in the invention vest in the employer. Intuitively, this seems contradictory and unjust.[109]

The rationale for employer-ownership appears to be a direct inference of the traditional, linear understanding of the process of innovation that has been discussed above.[110] A positive outcome (i. e. patentable inventions) is assumed where investments in terms of resources (such as time, facilities, materials) and in the employment of technically trained or skilled employees are made. The central role that employee-inventors play in this process is disregarded. Instead, it is assumed that an employee-inventor's output is not different to an autoworker's output. Autoworkers work towards a predictable output: They are expected to produce a certain number of products within a given timeframe. Similarly, employee-inventors are also expected to work towards a predictable output, only that they are not expected to produce pre-defined products but inventions. This logic ignores that inventions cannot be planned, and that innovation is not a linear process. Accordingly, it is impossible to foresee whether a new idea can be developed into a viable and economically realisable product or process and whether it may ultimately be patented.[111]

The distinction which thus needs to be made is not between the autoworker and the inventor per se, but between how the different outputs – i. e. cars versus inventions – are achieved. While an autoworker will follow strict specifications and perform assigned tasks, ultimately following a linear process, an employee-inventor's generation of an invention predominantly depends on his inventive genius.[112] It is this special trait which allows an idea to be developed to the point where it becomes a patentable invention. Depriving an employee-inventor of his

---

[107] See e.g. Merges (1999) 13 Harv. J.L. & Tech. 1, 2; Lobel, 'My Ideas' (*New York Times*); Dratler (1979) 16 Harv. J. on Legis. 129, 155–158.

[108] *Hallmark Personnel of Texas, Inc. v. Franks*, 562 SW 2d 933, 936 (Texas Ct. of Civil Appeals 1978): 'The efficiency and skills which an employee develops through his work belong to him and not to his former employer, and the employee is not obligated to forego the exercise of his inventive powers even if his expertise was gained in the performance of his contractual duties.'; *Reading & Bates Const. Co. v. O'Donnell*, 627 SW 2d 239, 243 (Texas Ct. of Appeals 1982): '(A) former employee may use in later employment or venture the general skills, knowledge and experience which he has acquired. […] This is true even if the former employment has acted to increase his skills and if such training is complex and extensive.'

[109] Also see e.g. van Slyke and Friedman (1990) 18 AIPLA Q.J. 127, 134; Hershovitz (1995) 3 J. Intell. Prop. L. 187, 197; Bartow (1997) 37 Santa Clara L. Rev. 673, 674.

[110] See supra 2.B.II.2.

[111] Ibid.; also see e.g. Dratler (1979) 16 Harv. J. on Legis. 129, 137.

[112] Cherensky (1993) 81 Cal. L. Rev. 595, 648–649, referring to a letter *Thomas Jefferson* wrote to *Isaac McPherson* in which he defined inventions as 'the fugitive fermentation of an individual brain'.

legal rights to his invention, removes the incentive function which is intrinsic to patent law and, as such, runs counter to the constitutional purpose of encouraging disclosure and innovation in the interest of the general public.[113]

As a consequence, inventors may decide to hold back their inventions – by not disclosing inventions to their employers or by leaving their employment and pursuing their inventions in a more supportive environment or by themselves.[114] Indeed, *Merges* suggested that the latter provides a necessary counterbalance to the powerful position of employers.[115] The employee-inventor's ability to leave his employer with an inchoate concept thus provides him with the necessary bargaining power to adequately be compensated by his current or a prospective employer. To *Merges*, this bargaining leverage and the firm-internal reward systems, which some employers have established, represents adequate compensation for inventive employees.[116]

There are different solutions which have been proposed to compensate employee-inventors beyond this. The most obvious one proposes that employee-inventors should retain ownership rights in their patentable inventions.[117] Others support a variation thereof, such as *Dratler* for instance, who suggests dividing ownership rights between the inventor, his supervisors, and middle management within the corporation, on the basis of their relative contributions.[118] *Cherensky* proposes a legal framework similar to copyright's moral and economic rights according to which inventor-employees have inalienable personality interests in their pre-inventions.[119]

A more practicable and widely supported solution is to equitably compensate employee-inventors for the assignment of their respective inventions to their employers.[120] In contrast to other countries which have a robust patent system and a comparatively high patent activity, such as Germany for instance, the US has no federal provisions to compensate inventors beyond the regular salary they are getting paid as part of their employment.[121] Mandatory finan-

[113] See e. g. Dratler (1979) 16 Harv. J. on Legis. 129, 140, 158; Neumeyer and Stedman, *Employed Inventor* (1971) 56.

[114] Hershovitz (1995) 3 J. Intell. Prop. L. 187, 211; Cherensky (1993) 81 Cal. L. Rev. 595, 668.

[115] Merges (1999) 13 Harv. J. L. & Tech. 1, 3.

[116] See ibid. 3; also see e. g. Overly, 'How Ford Turned Thousands of Employees into Inventors' (*Washington Post*), illustrating that some companies take matters into their own hands and financially compensate inventors who develop inventions.

[117] See e. g. Chew (1992) 1 Wis. L. Rev. 259, 304–310; Bartow (1997) 37 Santa Clara L. Rev. 673.

[118] Dratler (1979) 16 Harv. J. on Legis. 129, 191.

[119] See Cherensky (1993) 81 Cal. L. Rev. 595, 657–664.

[120] See e. g. Hershovitz (1995) 3 J. Intell. Prop. L. 187, 211.

[121] Germany has a separate Act which addresses employee-inventions and stipulates reasonable compensation if an employer claimed an employee-inventor's invention, see *ArbnErfG* § 9; also see infra 7.B.II.1. Other countries which have similar laws include Denmark, Finland, and Norway. The Netherlands and France, for instance, include employee inventor compen-

cial compensation has been discussed in the US on several occasions starting in 1961, with the most recent effort occurring in the 1980s. While it has generally been acknowledged that compensating employee-inventors in proportion to the economic value of their inventions could increase the quantity and quality of patentable inventions, all proposed bills have ultimately been rejected or never even reached a vote.[122] Due to the ever-mounting focus in patent policy debates on corporations, it seems unlikely that such legislation will be passed in the foreseeable future.

B University Faculty as Employee-Inventors

The question of the allocation of ownership rights in employee-inventions is also relevant in the context of universities; however, here it is a much more recent issue. As late as the 1960s and early 1970s, many universities were not concerned with inventions made by their faculty, students or staff and did not claim the respective ownership thereof.[123] With universities' increasing involvement with patents and with the enactment of the BDA, universities progressively claimed ownership of inventions generated by their faculty, staff, and students. But the legal bases on which the ownership was claimed were often murky and associated processes not refined.[124] Today – like employers in industry – universities rely on pre-invention assignment agreements which faculty, staff, and graduate students have to sign upon their employment.[125]

Universities' ownership claims to employee-inventions have been criticised on similar grounds as the allocation of ownership rights of employee-inventions in industry.[126] At its core, it raises the question whether, from a policy perspective, it is reasonable to treat academic researchers like corporate employees. In many respects, the description of the typical academic inventor is similar to the one of the typical employee-inventor: both conduct research as part of their

sation provisions in their national patent laws, see Peberdy and Strowel (2009) Cross-border Life Sci. Handbook 63. Switzerland only compensates employees for their inventions if they are created in the course of work, but not ones created in performance of contractual obligations, see e. g. Benhamou and Rieder, in *Employees' Intellectual Property Rights* (2015) 367, 380.

122 Parker (1984) 57 Cal. L. Rev. 603, 605. For a detailed overview, also see Hovell (1982) 58 Notre Dame L. Rev. 863, 883–888.

123 See infra 7.A. I.1.

124 It appears that the justifications for the broad ownership claims were predominately based on emotional and not legal reasons, see e. g. Chew (1992) 1 Wis. L. Rev. 259, 281, noting that the main justifications universities referenced for their ownership claims were: 1) All universities follow same policy; 2) policy is consistent with business practices; 3) policy is legally enforceable; 4) federal government requires this policy; 5) policy reflects common law. Also see infra 7.A. I.2.

125 For a detailed discussion of universities' practice in this regard, see infra 4.D.III.

126 See e. g. Scott (1998) 84 Acad. 22, 22; Chew (1992) 1 Wis. L. Rev. 259, 305–307.

jobs, in a 'corporate' environment,[127] both often conduct their research as part of a larger group or team, and both depend on the infrastructure and resources provided by their respective employer. Indeed, university administrators increasingly work with the assumption that there is no substantial difference between university researchers and corporate employees.[128]

But there are important differences between the two. The most obvious difference is that treating academic researchers like employee-inventors is not easily reconcilable with the core academic principle of academic freedom. The very essence of the university's function and the professor's related role of sharing his independent expert scholarly investigations with students and the general public is defeated if academic researchers are treated like corporate researchers.[129]

The American Association of University Professors' (AAUP) '1915 Declaration of Principles on Academic Freedom and Academic Tenure'[130], has been the generally accepted non-legal understanding of academic freedom to this date.[131] The 1915 Declaration adapted the German concept of academic freedom to the American context. But in contrast to the German model, the 1915 Declaration does not address *Lernfreiheit* but is limited to *Lehrfreiheit*.[132] Accordingly, professor's academic freedom comprises three elements: freedom of inquiry and research, freedom of teaching within the university or college, and freedom of extramural utterance and action.[133]

One of the core distinctions the 1915 Declaration draws is the one between a university and its 'appointees' and 'ordinary business ventures' and its employees.[134] In order to be able to impart knowledge to students and to the general public 'without fear or favour', professors need to be able to act as independent experts and scholars.[135] The nature of the social function discharged by the professor lies at the heart of this distinction: Professors will only be able to successfully fulfil their public duty if their academic freedom is warranted. Like other figures in the public service, such as judges for instance, they need to be able to perform their research and scholarly activities independently from their employers' opinions and motivations. Here, the central element is the public: A professor's research and teaching is conducted for the benefit of society and the public as a whole. This is in contrast to corporate employees, whose work is dedicated to the benefit of the company and of the company's shareholders. As

[127] In contrast to the 'lone garage inventor'.
[128] See e. g. AAUP (2014) Bulletin AAUP 38, 44.
[129] See ibid. 44.
[130] AAUP, in *Academic Freedom and Tenure* (1967) 291.
[131] Rabban (1990) 53 L. & Contemp. Probs. 227, 232.
[132] See supra n. 18/I and accompanying discussion.
[133] AAUP, in *Academic Freedom and Tenure* (1967) 292.
[134] Ibid. 294.
[135] Ibid.

the AAUP puts forth, it thus would seem more fitting to consider professors as 'appointees' rather than employees.[136]

If one accepts that professors are distinct from corporate employees due to the principle of academic freedom, which enables their public duty of unbiased discovery and research, the question is how academic freedom should be applied to inventions and professors' involvement with commercial activities. On the one hand, it seems inconsistent to only apply academic freedom to traditional scholarly outputs but not to inventions. In other words, if academic freedom implies that professors should have ownership of their scholarly outputs, they also should own their inventions. Making a distinction which is purely based on how the research is classified under intellectual property laws seems arbitrary.[137]

On the other hand, universities' active engagement with market forces, raises the question to what extent universities continue to be committed to the public interest and hence to what extent the reliance on the principle of academic freedom is justified. If the chief role of the university continues to be understood as one of public duty, it would appear logical that academic freedom should indeed extend to all outputs and activities professors engage in and that thus professors should own the rights to all academic outputs. However, if it is not, it seems that a more differentiated understanding of ownership of the outputs of academic activities could be justified.

This is not to say that, from a policy perspective, it is justified that employees do not own their inventions. But it is to say that if professors should be treated differently to employees due to the principle of academic freedom, which is derived from universities' public function, then, if the professors operate in a context that is removed from the public function, it seems justified to treat them like corporate employees.

Another aspect which is often overlooked or downplayed in the emotional discussion on the allocation of ownership rights in university inventions, and which clearly distinguishes universities from employers in private industry, is special compensation. In contrast to most employers in industry, from the earliest involvement with patents, universities shared royalties with their inventors on a fairly generous basis.[138] Today, most if not all universities compensate their employee-inventors through royalty payments, some with shares as high as 50 percent. While this does not negate the discussion on the allocation of ownership rights in the inventions created, it needs to be acknowledged that sharing royalties is a form of stimulus or compensation for inventors' contribution and, as

---

136 Ibid. 294–295; AAUP (2014) Bulletin AAUP 38, 44; also see Rabban (1990) 53 L. & Contemp. Probs. 227, 233, for a more detailed discussion on academic freedom as it relates to the first amendment.

137 AAUP (2014) Bulletin AAUP 38, 44.

138 See infra 7.A. I.1.

such, may function on a similar basis as promotions, bonuses, or simple curiosity or a desire for prestige, which encourage inventors to pursue inventive activity.[139]

As briefly mentioned above, there are two strands of the law which control the allocation of rights between employee-inventors and the employer: default rules under a branch of state common law and the law of contracts – both will be discussed in detail in the next two sections of this chapter. While invention assignment agreements prevail for the most part today, state common law rules still may be of relevance in situations where there is no explicit contract in place. This may occur due to simple inadvertence on behalf of employers, but it may also result in an academic setting or any other R&D setting where researchers with different backgrounds work on a research project.[140] Despite the fact that the law has been settled since the late 19th century and is fairly simple, complex and controversial cases have emerged over the years and the distinction between the different common law rights continues to be obscure.[141]

C Common Law Rules on Ownership regarding Employee-Inventors

I Description of the Common Law Doctrine

The legal basis of the common law doctrine stems from early concepts of what is considered fair and equitable between the employer and his employees.[142] Under the doctrine, the rights to an invention developed by an employee are divided in three ways, depending on the nature and scope of employment, including the field of the employer's business and surrounding circumstances (e. g. resources used). They move along a spectrum from the employee working on an invention completely independently to an employee being directed to invent something specific.[143]

On one side of the spectrum is an inventor who invents independently from his job duties, in his own time, without using the employer's resources, and without instructions from the employer or assistance by anyone related to the employer. These 'independent inventions' are typically owned by the employee.[144]

On the other side of the spectrum is an employee who is 'hired to invent'. This employee is directed to work on something specific, for instance towards a

---

139 Also see Neumeyer and Stedman, *Employed Inventor* (1971) 65–67.

140 See supra 3.B.1; also see e. g. Merges (1999) 13 Harv. J. L. & Tech. 1, 5.

141 See Stedman (1970) 45 Ind. L. J. 254, 256.

142 Neumeyer and Stedman, *Employed Inventor* (1971) 43.

143 Stedman (1970) 45 Ind. L. J. 254, 256; Gullette (1980) 62 J. Pat. Off. Soc'y 732, 733–734; Parker (1984) 57 Cal. L. Rev. 603, 607–608.

144 This is generally referred to as 'non-inventive employment', see Gullette (1980) 62 J. Pat. Off. Soc'y 732, 733; Merges (1999) 13 Harv. J. L. & Tech. 1, 6.

specific solution of a technical problem or an improvement to an existing technology. If his efforts result in an invention, the employer owns the invention.[145]

In between the two extremes are situations which would give rise to a 'shop right'. Here, an employee develops an invention during work hours and/or using resources from his employer but outside of his employment contract. In other words, the employee was not hired specifically to find the specific solution and thus to invent the invention. Because such inventions generally depend on substantial contributions by the employer, the employer will have a limited right to use the invention. Ownership will thus vest in the employee, but the employer will have a royalty-free, non-exclusive licence to use them (a so-called 'shop right').[146]

Where ownership rights are determined under the common law doctrine, the results appear mostly fair and reasonable on the opposite ends of the spectrum. A completely independently developed invention and the resulting patent rights should be owned by an employee. Similarly, an employer who hires an employee to dedicate his time towards a specific, defined inventive activity should own the results of this effort. Arguably, the allocation of rights in these cases is often similar to what the parties would have negotiated if they have had the opportunity to do so.[147] This is typically not so with cases in the middle of the spectrum – it is here where the doctrine can result in considerable arbitrariness.[148] It is often especially difficult to establish a clear line between the hired to invent doctrine and general employment which may lead to a shop right.[149] The result of such cases will ultimately depend on the specific terms of the contract, the circumstances of the inventive activity, and the use and value of the invention as assessed by a court.[150] When making these assessments, the courts today still rely on the Supreme Court's last ruling on the topic, the 1933 decision in *United States v. Dubilier Condenser*[151]. Perhaps not surprisingly, the many cases that have applied and confirmed the *Dubilier* principles also resulted in different interpretations of the opinion.[152]

[145] This is generally referred to as 'specific inventive employment', see Gullette (1980) 62 J. Pat. Off. Soc'y 732, 733.

[146] This is generally referred to as 'general inventive employment', see Gullette (1980) 62 J. Pat. Off. Soc'y 732, 733, Stedman (1970) 45 Ind. L. J. 254, 256.

[147] Neumeyer and Stedman, *Employed Inventor* (1971) 43; Stedman (1970) 45 Ind. L. J. 254, 256–257.

[148] Neumeyer and Stedman, *Employed Inventor* (1971) 43.

[149] See e. g. Wright (2000) Nat'l L. J. 1, 1.

[150] Ibid. 43; Stedman (1970) 45 Ind. L. J. 254, 257.

[151] *United States v. Dubilier Condenser Corp.*, 289 US 178 (S. Ct. 1933).

[152] See e. g. Gullette (1980) 62 J. Pat. Off. Soc'y 732, 737; Parker (1984) 57 Cal. L. Rev. 603, 607; for an example of a different, in fact erroneous interpretation in the context of university inventions, see the discussion on *Speck v. North Carolina* infra 4.C.III.

II Historical Development of the Common Law Doctrine

The earliest opinions in the early to mid-19th century on the rights of employers in their employees' inventions were simple infringement cases between the employer and third parties. In these cases, an infringer would typically argue that the employee-inventor was the actual inventor and not the employer. The courts' main concern was thus to establish who the 'true' inventor was.[153] The courts' analysis often involved the assessment of the character and abilities of the employee in order to determine whether the employee was 'inventive' enough to come up with the invention. Employees were often seen as servants or simple machinists who followed instructions of their employers. The use of expressly class-biased terms was not uncommon.[154] While these cases did not address disputes between employers and their employees over an idea, they nevertheless laid the seed for the later developed principle that whoever has the idea for an invention should be treated as its inventor.[155]

The first case addressing an employee-employer dispute over an invention was the Supreme Court's *McClurg v. Kingsland*[156] decision in 1843. The employee in question had developed improvements to a work process which he got patented. The employer used the new method continuously but refused to pay for a transfer of ownership rights once the patent was issued. Based on the reasoning that the employee allowed the employer's use of the invention, the court held there to be a licence for the continued use of the invention by the employer.[157]

Similarly, the Supreme Court in *Hapgood v. Hewitt*[158] found there to be the presumption of a personal, non-transferrable licence to the employer to use the

[153] Fisk (1998) 65 U. Chi. L. Rev. 1127, 1132, 1165–1166.

[154] For a detailed analysis, see ibid. 1165–1167; 1170–1179; while assessing whether employees were inventive, courts would describe the respective employees as 'merely a workman or a mechanic' or as a 'servant with manual dexterity' or 'an instrument through which the employer realises his idea', ibid. 1165.

[155] Fisk (1998) 65 U. Chi. L. Rev. 1127, 1142–1143.

[156] *McClurg v. Kingsland,* 42 US 202 (S. Ct. 1843).

[157] Ibid. 208. While *McClurg* was concerned with an employee-employer dispute, the decision did not rest on the employment relationship but on the fact that the (employee) inventor had given consent to someone else's (his employer's) use of the invention before the patent was filed. The court thus applied the established equity doctrine of estoppel: Because the employee had knowingly allowed this use, he could not later sue the user for infringement, see Fisk (1998) 65 U. Chi. L. Rev. 1127, 1144–1146. In the next 40 years, courts continued to give licenses to employers based on the fact that the employee had permitted the use and did not base their opinions on the employee-employer relationship, ibid. 1148–1150.

[158] *Hapgood v. Hewitt,* 119 US 226 (S. Ct. 1886). *Hapgood* involved a similar fact pattern to *McClurg*: *Hewitt*, who was an employee of Hapgood & Company, a plough manufacturer, worked on improvements to a plough during the course of his employment and obtained a patent protection for his improvements. The company manufactured the improvements and required *Hewitt* to transfer the ownership rights in the patent.

invention.[159] Adding to the rationale in *McClurg*, in *Hapgood*, the court not only emphasised that the employee consented to the manufacture of the invention but also that the employer financed the development of it.[160] Following *Hapgood*, courts increasingly shifted their focus from the employee's conduct in permitting the use of the invention to the employer's conduct in supporting the development of the invention.[161]

While courts grew more favourable of employers, they were initially still reluctant to meddle with the allocation of the ownership rights associated with employee-inventions. In *Hapgood*, the Supreme Court addressed the ownership claim of the employer but rejected it. Central to the decision was the question whether the employee was expressly required 'to exercise his inventive faculties for the benefit of his employer'.[162] The court answered this in the negative, holding that – based on the employment contract – such an obligation could not be inferred. The contract only gave rise to a 'naked licence' to make and sell the invention to the employer.[163]

A similar reluctance can be sensed in the Supreme Court decision *Solomons v. United States*.[164] Referring to *McClurg*, the court held that the principles previously established did not change only because the employer was the government.[165] The court also attempted to clarify the distinction between employer ownership and a shop right. According to the court, if an inventor performed the duties he was hired to do, but in the process used his inventive faculties and developed an invention, the invention would belong to the employee.[166] Conversely, if an employee was hired to invent something particular, the employer would be the owner.[167]

---

159 Ibid. 233: 'Whatever right the employer had to the invention by the terms of *Hewitt*'s contract of employment, was a naked licence to make and sell the patented improvement as a part of its business, which right, if it existed, was a mere personal one, and not transferable, and was extinguished with the dissolution of the corporation.'

160 Ibid. 230: 'The time during which he was so engaged was the regular working hours in the factory. The men who did the manual labor on the new plough were all employés of, and paid by, the corporation; and all the materials used in its construction were bought and paid for by the corporation.'

161 Fisk (1998) 65 U. Chi. L. Rev. 1127, 1151–1154.

162 *Hapgood* 233.

163 Ibid. 226, 229, 233.

164 *Solomons v. United States*, 137 US 342 (1890).

165 Ibid. 346: 'The government has no more power to appropriate a man's property invested in a patent than it has to take his property invested in real estate; nor does the mere fact that an inventor is at the time of his invention in the employ of the government transfer to it any title to, or interest in it. […] There is no difference between the government and any other employer in this respect.'

166 Ibid.: 'An employé, performing all the duties assigned to him in his department of service, may exercise his inventive faculties in any direction he chooses, with the assurance that whatever invention he may thus conceive and perfect is his individual property.'

167 Ibid.: 'That which he has been employed and paid to accomplish becomes, when accomplished, the property of his employer.'

In contrast to previous decisions, the Supreme Court in *Standard Parts v. Peck*[168] focused its analysis on the terms of the employment contract. Peck's contract required him 'to devote his time to the development of a process and machinery for the production of the front spring now used on the product of the Ford Motor Company'.[169] The court in his analysis made it clear that Peck was specifically employed to devote his time to the development of the stated process and machinery and that, in return for the said development, he would receive compensation in the form of a salary. Because this was expressly stated in the contract, the court concluded that the process and machinery, once developed, were the property of the employer.[170]

Going forward courts increasingly focused their analysis on defining the terms of the respective employment contracts, thereby moving away from presumptions of employee ownership as they had done before. This development was underpinned by the progressive use of contractual pre-invention assignments by employers, which – as will be discussed below – were also seen favourably by courts.[171] *Standard Parts* thus marks the turning point from a comparatively pro-employee to a pro-employer legal standard. Remarkably, this shift was not prompted by a change in the law, but merely reflected a change in application due to a changed perception by the courts of the notion of the inventor (from the hero inventor to the corporate team-based inventor).[172]

In its most recent ruling in 1933 in *United States v. Dubilier*[173], the Supreme Court attempted to clarify the principles to be applied in determining the ownership of employee-inventions.[174] The court confirmed that the ownership rights in employee-inventions needed to be assessed based on the employment contract and the resulting job responsibilities. Concluding that general inventive employment did not yield assignable inventions, the court explained: 'One employed to make an invention […] is bound to assign to his employer any patent obtained. The reason is that he has only produced that which he was employed

---

[168] *Standard Parts v. Peck,* 264 US 52 (1924).

[169] Ibid. 59.

[170] Ibid. 59–60: 'Whose property was the 'process and machinery' to be when developed? The answer would seem to be inevitable and resistless – of him who engaged the services and paid for them, they being his inducement and compensation, they being not for temporary use but perpetual use, a provision for a business, a facility in it and an asset of it […].'

[171] Also see Fisk (1998) 65 U. Chi. L. Rev. 1127, 1180.

[172] Ibid. 1161–1162, 1165; Merges (1999) 13 Harv. J. L. & Tech. 1, 5. This is to be understood against the backdrop of the above discussed shift in patent law away from the individual inventor to corporations and corporate team-based research, see supra 3.A. I.

[173] *Dubilier* 178.

[174] The case involved two government employees who were hired to conduct research on airplane radio technology. While completing their regular tasks, the employees experimented with different things and developed the inventions in question. The employer was aware of this, including the fact that government resources were used to perfect the inventions. Later, the employer claimed the ownership of the patents covering the inventions.

to invent. His invention is the precise subject to the contract of employment.' Conversely, '[…] if the employment be general, albeit it cover a field of labor and effort in the performance of which the employee conceived the invention for which he obtained a patent, the contract is not so broadly construed as to require an assignment of the patent.'[175]

The Supreme Court also drew a distinction between research and inventive activity.[176] This distinction and the special nature of inventions called for caution in finding ownership of employee inventions by an employer. Unless the employee was specifically hired to invent and inventive activity was stipulated by the employment contract, assignment of ownership should not be inferred or implied.[177] The Supreme Court also used these assertions to make clear the distinction to the shop right, confirming that the justification for an employer's right to use his employee's invention was based in equity. The employer is thus allowed to use and multiply 'that which embodies his own property' because the employer contributed to the 'concrete result' by allowing the employee to use 'his master's time, facilities, and materials'.[178]

III The Application of the Common Law Doctrine to Faculty

Among the many cases which applied and reconfirmed *Dubilier*, there is only one which applies the common law principles in a university setting and it will be discussed further below.[179] However, there have been several cases which

[175] *Dubilier* 187.

[176] Ibid. 188: 'The reluctance of courts to imply or infer an agreement by the employee to assign his patent is due to a recognition of the peculiar nature of the act of invention, which consists neither in finding out the laws of nature, nor in fruitful research as to the operation of natural laws, but in discovering how those laws may be utilized or applied for some beneficial purpose, by a process, a device or a machine. It is the result of an inventive act, the birth of an idea and its reduction to practice; the product of original thought; a concept demonstrated to be true by practical application or embodiment in tangible form.'

[177] Ibid.

[178] Ibid. 188–189. On the particular facts of the case the Supreme Court found that the two employees were neither employed to invent nor had been assigned the task of inventing and thus, that they owned the rights in the patents, see ibid. 194–196: 'In no proper sense may it be said that the contract of employment contemplated invention; everything that *Dunmore* and *Lowell* knew negatived the theory that they were employed to invent they knew, on the contrary, that the past and then present practice was that the employees of the Bureau were allowed to take patents on their inventions and have the benefits thereby conferred save as to use by the United States. The circumstances preclude the implication of any agreement to assign their inventions or patents.'

[179] *Speck v. North Carolina Dairy Foundation*, 319 S.E.2d 139 (NC S. Ct. 1984). The analysis in this section will focus on typical tenure-track and tenured teaching and research faculty. University staff will be excluded from the analysis as the large majority of their work is of administrative nature and does not involve research or design. While focus is placed on 'faculty' the analysis would also apply to graduate students who are employed by the university as 'research assistants' (in contrast to 'graduate teaching assistants').

deal with ownership interests between employers and employees who conduct institutional research and present analogous fact patterns to a university research environment.[180] These cases lend themselves to infer how *Dubilier* and the common law doctrines should be applied in an academic context.[181] In fact, *Dubilier* dealt with institutional researchers who were employed by the federal government, and the Supreme Court stressed that the same principles which apply to 'normal' employers as regards ownership of employee inventions should also apply to the government.[182] It would thus appear that no distinction should be made either if the employer is a university.

Moreover, the job content of institutional researchers and the one of university researchers is often similar indeed: They both are usually employed with the expectation to pursue research within a general field, but they are generally not directed towards the solving of a specific problem.[183] Both typically use resources provided by their employer and dedicate work time to the pursuit of their research. There are also notable differences between the two. For instance, in contrast to researchers in industry, most faculty have substantial additional teaching and administrative duties next to their research obligations. This, however, typically should work in favour of the argument that faculty, even more so than industrial researchers, should not fall under the hired to invent doctrine.

Indeed, this last argument was an important factor in *Kaplan v. Corcoran*[184], where the court found that the hired to invent doctrine would not apply. *Dr.*

[180] See e. g. *Kaplan v. Johnson*, 409 F. Supp. 190 (Dist. Ct ND Illinois 1976); *Kaplan v. Corcoran*, 545 F.2d 1073 (7th Cir. 1976); *State v. Neal*, 12 So. 2d 590 (LA S. Ct. 1943); *Ingersoll-Rand Co. v. Ciavatta*, 542 A.2d 879 (NJ S.Ct. 1988); *Banks v. Unisys Corp.*, 228 F.3d 1357 (Fed. Cir. 2000); *Peregrine Semiconductor Crop. v. RF Micro Devices Inc.* No. 3:2012cv00911 (Dist. Ct. S. D. CA 2014).

[181] Also see e. g. Browning (1985) N. C. L. Rev. 1248, 1254–1256; Chew (1992) 1 Wis. L. Rev. 259, 265–266.

[182] *Dubilier* 189: 'The title of a patentee is subject to no superior right of the government. The grant of letters patent is not, as in England, a matter of grace or favour, so that conditions may be annexed at the pleasure of the executive.' Although patent infringement is governed by federal statute, state contract and property law generally govern an inventor's employment status and related ownership rights in patents, see Hovell (1982) 58 Notre Dame L. Rev. 863, 865–866; Chisum (1971) 46 Wash. L. Rev. 633, 647. Also see *New Marshall Engine Co. v. Marshall Engine Co.*, 223 U. S. 473, 477 (S. Ct. 1912): 'The Federal courts have exclusive jurisdiction of all cases arising under the patent laws, but not of all questions in which a patent may be the subject-matter of the controversy. For courts of a state may try questions of title and may construe and enforce contracts relating to patents.' States are thus not bound to apply above common law doctrine but could make their own common law. See e. g. *Standard Brands Inc. v. US Partition & Packaging Corp.*, 199 F. Supp. 161, 176 (Dist. Ct. ED Wis. 1961): 'The substantive rights of the parties in this action must be determined in accordance with applicable state law. Cases from other jurisdictions granting the employer greater rights in comparable situations are not controlling.' Despite this, state courts have overwhelmingly adopted the common law doctrine, see e. g. Chew (1992) 1 Wis. L. Rev. 259, 265.

[183] Also see 4.B.

[184] *Kaplan v. Corcoran*, 545 F.2d 1073 (Ct. of Appeals, 7th Cir. 1976); *Kaplan v. Johnson*, 409 F. Supp. 190 (Dist. Ct. ND Ill. 1976).

Ervin Kaplan was employed for 20 years by the US Veterans Administration, 15 years of which he served as Chief of the Nuclear Medicine Service at the Veterans Administration Hospital in Hines, Illinois. His main duties were of an administrative nature, but his job also encompassed clinical, teaching, and research responsibilities, which resulted in him developing a camera for whole body imaging.[185] The trial court referred to the distinction the *Dubilier* court had made between employment which involves general research work, and employment which has the specific objective of invention.[186] The *Kaplan* court recognised that – like the employees in *Dubilier* – *Kaplan* performed and supervised research and, more importantly, that *Kaplan*'s duties went beyond the performance and the supervision of research and that therefore he was not hired to invent the invention in question.[187] The court also held that the fact that 'the government provided facilities, equipment, materials and the efforts of other employees' did not tip the balance in favour of government ownership.[188]

The one case that directly addressed ownership of university inventions based on the *Dubilier* principles is *Speck v. North Carolina North Carolina Dairy Foundation*.[189] *Dr. Marvin Speck* was a professor of food science and microbiology at North Carolina State University. As a result of extensive research and experimentation during the 1960s and 1970s, and with the assistance of *Dr. Stanley Gilliland*, who also was a professor at the university, *Speck* developed a method by which the microorganism lactobacillus acidophilus could be added to the milk without the milk turning sour.[190]

In 1972, *Speck* informed his department head of the discovery and suggested that – while the process was not sufficiently novel to warrant the filing of a patent application – the registration of a trademark and subsequent licensing should be pursued by the university. At the recommendation of his department head, *Speck* submitted a proposal to the university patent committee, asking that the North Carolina Dairy Foundation (a non-profit corporation with close ties to the university) would register the trademark and handle subsequent licensing.[191] Within a year, a company was hired to market 'Sweet Acidophilus' and

---

185 *Kaplan v. Corcoran* 1074.

186 *Kaplan v. Johnson* 200.

187 Ibid. 202: 'One significant difference between the two cases is that plaintiff has many duties other than research, including clinical work and teaching, whereas *Dunmore* and *Lowell* worked solely in the area of research.'

188 Ibid. While the district court agreed with this part of the reasoning of the lower court, it ultimately found that *Kaplan* had to assign his rights under the employer's 'Executive Order 10'006', which applied to federally employed workers and provided that inventions needed to be assigned to the employer.

189 *Speck v. North Carolina Dairy Foundation*, 319 SE 2d 139 (S. Ct. NC 1984) (hereinafter *Speck II*); *Speck v. North Carolina Dairy Foundation*, 307 SE 2d 785 (NC Ct. of Appeals 1983) (hereinafter *Speck I*).

190 *Speck II* 141.

191 Ibid.

a producer of the lactobacillus acidophilus cultures was found. In early 1975, the university announced the successful development of Sweet Acidophilus and claimed credit for the scientific and commercial success.[192] By 1980, royalty income from the product exceeded half a million dollars.[193]

In 1975, *Speck* inquired about royalty payments, suggesting that the payment of his share must have been 'overlooked'.[194] The president of the patent committee proposed honouring the request by awarding *Speck* a one-time payment of USD 30'000, in order to avoid any 'hard feelings and tensions within the faculty'.[195] However, the legal counsel of the university denied that *Speck* had any rights in the royalty income, and accordingly, the university never made any payments to *Speck*. In 1981, *Speck* and *Gilliland* brought suit against the university and the Dairy Foundation.[196]

Without going into the details of the procedural history of the case, the main question the trial court and the appellate court were concerned with was whether the university was in breach of their fiduciary duty towards the plaintiffs. *Speck* had entrusted the university with his secret process, believing that the university would find the best use for it and be able to develop and market it accordingly.[197] While *Speck* realised that the discovered process was not patentable, he still assumed that the university's patent policy would apply to it.[198] This was evidenced by his decision to disclose the process to the university pursuant to the patent policy and by the general behaviour both plaintiffs displayed, as they continued working closely with the university long after the disclosure was made.[199]

While the trial court and the appellate court found there to be a fiduciary duty, the North Carolina Supreme Court disagreed and focused its analysis on the ownership question.[200] The court argued that if the plaintiffs did not have

---

192 Ibid.; *Speck I* 789.

193 *Speck I* 790.

194 *Speck II* 142.

195 Ibid. 143; *Speck I* 790.

196 *Speck II* 143–144.

197 *Speck I* 789.

198 Under the university's patent policy inventors would receive a 15% share of royalties, see *Speck I* 790, 793.

199 Ibid. 789: 'Acting pursuant to the university's patent policy, *Dr. Speck* presented his secret process to the Patent Committee. He reasonably assumed that the university had ownership rights to his invention but that he would be equitably compensated as specified in the patent policy.' 'Plaintiffs turned their secret process over to their employer without asking for anything. Their primary concern was for the university to make the best use of acidophilus; they relied on the superior business and legal skills of the defendants for marketing acidophilus milk. Yet they understood from the patent policy that surrendering their legal ownership rights did not deprive them of an equitable or beneficial interest in their invention.'

200 The ownership question had previously not been addressed; however, the question had been raised by *Speck* in 1973 and 1974, when he inquired whether the university or the foundation would own the trademark and was subsequently told that the Foundation owned the

any rights to the process, the university did not have a fiduciary duty towards the plaintiffs with regard to the process.[201] Relying on *Dubilier* the court continued to reason that since the plaintiffs were hired to invent, the process was owned by the university.[202] The court based its conclusion on the plaintiffs' use of the defendant's resources and on the fact that they were employed as teachers and researchers and were expected 'to engage *inter alia* in just such R&D'.[203]

With this the North Carolina Supreme Court put its own spin on the common law doctrine and contradicted cases like *Dubilier* and *Kaplan* where similar facts did not result in employer ownership.[204] It seems apparent that the court was under the same miscomprehension as most universities were in the 1980s, namely that, as a general rule, universities would own research developed by their professors. Indeed, the court held: 'Under these facts, the secret process developed through the research of the plaintiffs belonged to the university absent a written contract by the university to assign'.[205] This turns on the head the general rule that the inventor owns his invention *unless* he assigns it to someone else. While *Dubilier* is an exception to this rule, it is not a general default rule for ownership of employee inventions. Put differently, the *Speck* ruling would imply that faculty who conduct research would generally be considered persons hired to invent. On a policy level, such an outcome would run counter to the spirit of the academic mission, as was discussed above.

Lastly, the court also seemed to ignore the distinction *Dubilier* had established between research and inventive activity: 'Regrettably, the plaintiffs in the instant case were not employed pursuant to a written contract detailing their duties as professors and researchers. It is clear, however, that the plaintiffs were permitted and encouraged by their employer the university to conduct the precise research which led to the discovery and perfection of the secret process.'[206] Referring to *Houghton v. United States*[207], a case that predates *Dubilier*, the court then concluded that *Speck* was hired to invent the acidophilus process.[208]

trademark. In 1976, *Speck* was advised by a legal advisor of the university that since the process was not patentable it would not fall under the patent policy and all rights would be returned to him. The advisor then assumed that *Speck* had waived his rights 'in favor of the Foundation'. See *Speck II* 142.

201 Ibid. 143.

202 Ibid.: 'The fruit of the labor of one who is hired to invent, accomplish a prescribed result, or aid in the development of products belongs to the employer absent a written contract to assign'.

203 Ibid. 143–144.

204 Also see Browning (1985) N. C. L. Rev. 1248, 1251; Chew (1992) 1 Wis. L. Rev. 259, 301; Smith (1997) 1 Va. J. Law & Tech. 1, 14.

205 *Speck II* 143.

206 Ibid. 143–144.

207 *Houghton v. United States*, 23 F. 2d 386 (Circuit Ct. of Appeals, 4th Circuit 1928).

208 *Speck II* 144: 'It matters not in what capacity the employee may originally have been hired, if he be set to experimenting with the view of making an invention, and accepts pay for

This reasoning not only ignores that *Speck* pursued the discovery out of his own passion and interest, but it also reflects a clear misunderstanding of the process of research and discovery.

In conclusion, it seems clear that faculty members' duty to conduct research could not be construed as being specific enough to consider them as persons hired to invent. Even in situations where faculty are hired to work on a specific research project, it is unlikely that it could be inferred that they were hired to invent. As cases like *Kaplan* illustrate, job responsibilities which go beyond mere research are typically construed against the application of the hired to invent doctrine. Lastly, there is no recorded case which would support the application of the doctrine based on the use of university time and resources, however, a shop right may possibly be inferred on this basis.

Indeed, a faculty's general research responsibility fits more neatly with the definition of a shop right. If an employee uses the employer's 'time, facilities, and materials' the employer is entitled, based on equity, to a non-exclusive licence to use the employee-invention in his business.[209] Thus, it is not the existence of an employment relationship alone which gives rise to a shop right, but the existence of an implied contract – which would be given where time, facilities, and materials are used.[210] Nevertheless, it is questionable, how relevant a shop right is to a university. Universities are generally not in the business of commercially developing, marketing, and selling products to third parties.[211] This is important, as a shop right does not allow the employer to sell articles outside its normal range of business. A shop right is also not transferrable, which altogether makes it not useful to universities.[212]

A separate mention deserves federally funded research. The BDA is silent on the common law doctrine – which is not surprising, as it does not address the allocation of ownership interests between universities and their inventors but regulates ownership between the government and universities. If research is funded by the government, it may also be possible to infer that the government would be entitled to a shop right based on it providing the necessary resources for the development of a given invention. But, as in the instance of universities, a shop right would probably also be of little practical relevance to the government, as the government does not typically commercially develop and sell products either.

---

such work, it is his duty to disclose to his employer what he discovers in making the experiments, and what he accomplishes by the experiments belongs to the employer.'

[209] See supra n. 178/II and accompanying text.

[210] Also see Hovell (1982) 58 Notre Dame L. Rev. 863, 873.

[211] Also see Chew (1992) 1 Wis. L. Rev. 259, 270.

[212] Hovell (1982) 58 Notre Dame L. Rev. 863, 875.

D Contract Law

I Pre-Invention Assignment Agreements

Employers have become conscious of employees spending time and resources on inventions which they might not be able to claim due to the limited scope and the uncertainty of the common law. But luckily for employers, not only patents but inventions are freely assignable, even before they are conceived.[213] Employers have taken advantage of this fact, and today, most employers require their employees to assign inventions made during the employment to the employer as a condition of employment. The standard employment contract, including employment contracts at most research universities, provides for an immediate assignment of future inventions in exchange for salary and other benefits.[214] These contractual pre-invention assignments supersede the common law.[215]

In general, the scope of these pre-invention assignment agreements are broad and can go beyond the assignment of all inventions made during the employment. Accordingly, they may include inventions created before and after the duration of the employment as well as inventions which do not relate to the employer's business or research interests.[216] Aside from the duty to assign ownership interests to inventions made, pre-invention assignment agreements often impose related duties, such as a duty to cooperate in disclosing inventive activities, in assisting in the patent prosecution process and in the further development and perfection of the invention in question.[217] They often also include an obligation to retain in confidence trade secrets and other confidential information.[218]

The law imposes few restrictions on pre-invention assignment agreements and courts have traditionally upheld and enforced them.[219] Accordingly, courts

[213] 35 USC § 261: 'Applications for patent, patents, or any interest therein, shall be assignable in law by an instrument in writing.'

[214] See Reichman (1992) 51 Colum.-VLA J. L. & Arts 51, 57.

[215] See e. g. Hovell (1982) 58 Notre Dame L. Rev. 863, 875.

[216] See ibid. 876; Stedman (1970) 45 N. Y. U. L. Rev. 1, 4; Dratler (1979) 16 Harv. J. on Legis. 129, 141–142; Cherensky (1993) 81 Cal. L. Rev. 595, 618–619. Sometimes employers even claim the rights to their employee's thoughts, see e. g. *Alcatel USA, Inc. v. Brown*, No. 199–00596–97 (Tex. Dist. Ct. 2002): *Evan Brown*, a software engineer at Alcatel/DSC, worked on an idea over the course of several years. He had not written down the idea or documented it anywhere and he had developed it in his own time. The idea was too abstract and incomplete to be patented. *Brown* eventually mentioned the idea – a software algorithm – to his employer who claimed ownership rights to the invention. *Brown* refused to fully disclose the algorithm and eventually was let go and a lawsuit was brought against him. The employer based its ownership claim on an agreement which *Brown* had signed upon his employment. The agreement granted the employer rights to any invention *Brown* developed and which was related to the employer's business or that was 'suggested by his (the employee's) work'. The district court in Texas ordered *Brown* to turn over the algorithm to Alcatel.

[217] Neumeyer and Stedman, *Employed Inventor* (1971) 44; Merges (1999) 13 Harv. J. L. & Tech. 1, 8.

[218] Neumeyer and Stedman, *Employed Inventor* (1971) 44.

[219] Hovell (1982) 58 Notre Dame L. Rev. 863, 876; Dratler (1979) 16 Harv. J. on Legis.

have found that an inventor's continued employment is adequate consideration for the assignment of all future inventions.[220] The courts' reluctance to invalidate contracts is rooted in the freedom-of-contract principle, which was particularly pronounced during the 19th century, which is when the first pre-invention assignment agreements reached the courts.[221] Indeed, even in instances where an employers' approach was found to be overbroad, courts would usually try to find ways to invalidate only parts of the contract or to re-interpret the contract in a way that the employer's overreaching could be avoided.[222] Similarly, courts have found binding contracts where consideration was as low as USD 1, where a contract was signed only after the invention was made, or where the contract was signed once the employee had already started with his job duties.[223] Only in rare instances, if contracts seriously offend public policy or if an agreement stipulates unconscionable conditions, are courts likely to negate them.[224]

As mentioned above, the idea of employers owning the rights to their employees' inventions is generally seen critically, and the criticism is especially pronounced where employers ask employees to sign pre-invention assignment agreements. Pre-invention assignment agreements usually form part of a standard employment contract and, as such, are signed upon the beginning of the em-

129, 142. When the validity of pre-invention agreements is determined, an important question is whether federal or state law applies. While patent law is regulated on a federal level, state law is not pre-empted only because a patent is at issue: 'The patent laws do not create a federal common law concerning the pre-invention title to patents.', see Hovell (1982) 58 Notre Dame L. Rev. 863, 865. Also see *Aronson v. Quick Point Pencil* 440 U. S. 257, 262 (1979): 'Commercial agreements traditionally are the domain of state law. State law is not displaced merely because the contract relates to intellectual property which may or may not be patentable; the states are free to regulate the use of such intellectual property in any manner not inconsistent with federal law.' Also see *University Patents, Inc. v. Kligman,* 762 F. Supp. 1212, 1219 (Dist. Court, ED PA 1991): 'Since contracts to assign patent rights do not have a statutory basis, but rather have a basis in common law or in equity, they need not be in writing, and they may be implied as well as express.' This needs to be contrasted with more recent cases: In *FilmTec Corporation v. Allied-Signal Inc. and UOP Inc.* 939 F.2d 1568 (1991) the Federal Circuit did not state whether it based its decision regarding a pre-invention assignment agreement on state law or federal law and in *DDB Technologies v. MLB Advanced Media* 517 F. 3d 1284, 1296 (Fed. Cir. 2008) the Federal Circuit held that invention assignment agreements are governed by federal common law. Specifically, the Federal Circuit held that because pre-invention assignment agreements are integral to the question of patent standing this was the logical consequence. Finally, in *Stanford v. Roche* the Supreme Court would have had an opportunity to clarify this question but it chose not to do so.

220 Hovell (1982) 58 Notre Dame L. Rev. 863, 876; Cherensky (1993) 81 Cal. L. Rev. 595, 623.

221 Dratler (1979) 16 Harv. J. on Legis. 129, 142; Stedman (1970) 45 N. Y. U. L. Rev. 1, 13–15.

222 Dratler (1979) 16 Harv. J. on Legis. 129, 142.

223 See e. g. Merges (1999) 13 Harv. J. L. & Tech. 1, 8; also see infra 4.D.II.

224 Stedman (1970) 45 N. Y. U. L. Rev. 1, 4; Dratler (1979) 16 Harv. J. on Legis. 129, 144–146; Hovell (1982) 58 Notre Dame L. Rev. 863, 877.

ployment relationship. Because they are signed before an invention might be developed, the parties enter into the agreement without knowing what they are bargaining for and what they are potentially giving up.[225] Indeed, an invention may never be conceived at all. Or the employee may sign away the most valuable invention ever made for that employer.[226] The root cause of this problem is the inherent uncertainty and unpredictability of the inventive process coupled with the intangible nature of inventions.

Because a prospective employee does not know what the eventuality or the value of a potential invention is, in the vast majority of cases, fair negotiations are not possible. There may be exceptions to this, for instance, if an inventor has a special reputation and can negotiate more desirable terms, but in most instances, prospective employees will not be in a position which allows them to bargain. As a result, there is generally no 'meeting of the minds' which would ordinarily be required for the existence of a binding contract. Because of this, pre-invention assignment agreements have been categorised as so-called 'contracts of adhesion' – but they are rarely held invalid for that reason alone.[227]

Beyond the (limited) restrictions which are imposed by courts on employers in regard to pre-invention agreements, some states have enacted separate statutes which address employers' powers to negotiate pre-invention agreements.[228] While the rules typically mitigate the harshness of 'all inclusive' assignment agreements, they usually also limit the established common law rules which may benefit employees.[229] The solution, which the majority of the states which have implemented such statutes have followed, allows employees to retain ownership if an invention was made in the employee's own time and without the employer's resources.[230] However, in any other instance – and essentially in most instances where an overreaching would typically occur – the states in question eliminated any scenario under which the employee retains the ownership right and the employer receives a shop right. Thus, in the most likely instance, where an employee develops an invention which is either related to the employer's business or results from the work the employee was expected to

---

225 Also see e. g. Pisegna-Cook (1994) 2 U. Balt. Intell. Prop. L. J. 163, 163; Cherensky (1993) 81 Cal. L. Rev. 595, 598.

226 See e. g. *Roberts v. Sears, Roebuck & Co.*, 697 F. 2d 796 (Ct. of Appeals, 7th Circuit 1983).

227 A contract of adhesion is a 'standardized contract written entirely by a party with superior bargaining power, leaving the weaker party in a 'take-it-or-leave-it' position', see *Cubic Corp. v. Marty*, 185 Cal. App. 3d 438, 449 (CA Ct. of Appeal 1986). Also see infra accompanying discussion to n. 248–249/II.

228 For a detailed overview of state statutes governing employment agreements, see Howell (2012) 8 Wash. J. L. Tech. & Arts 80, 88–91.

229 Smith (1997) 1 Va. J. Law & Tech. 1, 27.

230 States following this approach are: California, Illinois, North Carolina, Washington State, Delaware, Kansas and their statutes are modelled on Minnesota's statute (Minnesota Statute §181.78), see Howell (2012) 8 Wash. J. L. Tech. & Arts 80, 88.

do, an assignment to the employer is supported.[231] Employees thus receive even less protection than they would under common law.[232]

There are two states which provide even more power to the employer: Nevada and Utah. Utah supports pre-invention assignment of employee inventions even if an invention was created entirely in an employee's own time.[233] Nevada, has implemented a statute which allows ownership of inventions to be transferred from the employee to the employer in the complete absence of an assignment agreement and without any actual notice to the employee. It is the only state which follows this remarkable approach.[234] Perhaps unsurprisingly, Nevada's motivation for enacting such provisions was to attract high-technology businesses to the state. This approach has been criticised and it is unclear whether the statute was able to produce the expected positive effect on Nevada's technology business landscape.[235]

In the context of research conducted at a university, it is difficult to imagine a situation where an invention does not relate to a universities' 'business' or where no university resources are used to develop an invention. It appears that any university invention which evolves out of research conducted by a faculty or a graduate student would typically be directly related to the university missions of research and teaching and moreover, would also likely have been created with resources provided by the university.[236] Consequently, under the 'majority approach', university-generated inventions would not be exempt from the stipulated statutory assignment.

The majority of states have chosen not to specifically address assignment of employee-inventions, but some states nevertheless stipulate limited requirements for state supported institutions, such as the implementation of an intellectual property policy. This will be discussed in more detail in the final chapter.

II Requirements to Transfer Title Under Pre-Invention Assignment Agreements

The basic requirements of an enforceable contract are offer, acceptance, and consideration.[237] While it would go beyond the scope of this work to discuss the details of these requirements, there a few aspects of pre-invention assignment agreements which deserve a special mention.

---

[231] See Smith (1997) 1 Va. J. Law & Tech. 1, 27; Howell (2012) 8 Wash. J. L. Tech. & Arts 80, 88–91.

[232] Also see Smith (1997) 1 Va. J. Law & Tech. 1, 27.

[233] See e. g. Howell (2012) 8 Wash. J. L. Tech. & Arts 80, 91.

[234] See e. g. LaFrance (2003) Nevada L. J. 88, 88.

[235] See e. g. ibid. 90, predicting that the volume of litigation would increase due to the enactment of the statute. Also see Howell (2012) 8 Wash. J. L. Tech. & Arts 80, 92.

[236] Also see Smith (1997) 1 Va. J. Law & Tech. 1, 27.

[237] See e. g. Bix, *Contract Law* (2012) 18.

Firstly, a contractual agreement to transfer ownership of an invention, a patent application, or a patent has to be made in writing.[238] Additionally, the writing should 'show a clear and unmistakable intent' of the inventor to transfer ownership of the invention to the employer.[239] While most employers will choose to integrate such agreements in their employment contracts, what is of great relevance is the wording which is used for the agreements. For instance, 'does hereby assign' is considered to be stronger than 'agrees to assign', as will be discussed in the next chapter.[240]

Secondly, the doctrine of consideration is especially important to the formation of a valid pre-invention assignment agreement. Consideration is a unique feature of US contract law and has its roots in the English common law.[241] It stands for the idea that there has to be some level of reciprocity (i. e. A gives X to B, B gives Y to A) for a promise to be enforceable. In other words, consideration separates an exchange which is based on a bargain from other sorts of one-sided promises or gifts.[242] There are two modern tests which are used to establish consideration. The first one is the 'benefit-detriment' test under which something is considered consideration if it is a benefit to the promisor (here the inventor) and a detriment to the promisee (here the employer).[243] In contrast, the 'bargained-for-exchange' test establishes whether there was an exchange of something for something else.[244] In most instances, commercial contracts will pass both tests.[245]

Applied to the context of pre-invention assignment agreement, this implies that an employee must receive something in return for the transfer of the ownership of his inventions to the employer. But it appears that this 'something' may be very little. Indeed, often employers get away with paying as little as USD 1 or not giving anything at all – in which case the payment of the salary would be viewed as consideration.[246] In regard to the assignment of inventions generated by undergraduate students, consideration is the biggest hurdle to the formation of a valid contract, as undergraduate students are generally not employed by the university.[247]

Thirdly, while consideration presupposes that there is an element of bargaining or negotiation between the parties, there is often no bargaining in the con-

---

238 35 USC § 261.

239 See e. g. *University Patents v. Kligman* 1219.

240 The difference of these two wordings will be discussed in the context of *Stanford v. Roche*, see infra 5.D.

241 Bix, *Contract Law* (2012) 32–33.

242 See ibid. 34–35; M. Eisenberg (1982) 67 Cornell L. Rev. 640, 640.

243 See e. g. Bix, *Contract Law* (2012) 33; Knapp and others, *Contract Law* (2019) 102.

244 Knapp and others, *Contract Law* (2019) 102.

245 Ibid. 113.

246 Sutton, in *Chemists and Engineers* (1977) 45, 46; also see supra accompanying text to n. 223/II.

247 For a detailed discussion, see infra 7.A. I.3.

text of pre-invention assignment agreements. This is why pre-invention assignment agreements are commonly considered to be 'contracts of adhesion'.[248] But while courts are generally sceptical of adhesion contracts, they are not necessarily unenforceable.[249] Indeed, courts have traditionally enforced pre-invention assignment agreements and they yet have to invalidate a contract based on the fact that an employee allegedly lacked bargaining power.[250]

Finally, a controversial issue regarding pre-invention assignment agreements, which has received considerable attention since *Stanford v. Roche*, is whether an assignment of ownership rights in future inventions will result in the transfer of legal or equitable title to that specific invention.[251] In *Stanford*, the Supreme Court confirmed that the BDA did not re-order ownership rights and that thus initial ownership in an invention would vest in the inventor unless these rights were transferred. Interpreting the pre-invention assignment agreements in the case, the Supreme Court based its analysis entirely on contract law principles and on the Federal Circuit's distinction between transfer of equitable and legal title in *FilmTec v. Allied-Signal*.[252]

The facts of *FilmTec* were as follows: John *Cadotte* was employed with a not-for-profit research organisation called North Star Division of Midwest Research Institute (MRI). MRI conducted research for the US government in the area of reverse osmosis membranes. The research that *Cadotte* conducted was based on a contract between MRI and the government, which stipulated that MRI 'agrees to grant and does hereby grant to the government the full and entire domestic right, title, and interest in any invention […] made in the course of or under this contract or any subcontract […]'.[253] *Cadotte* left his employer and filed a patent application for an invention which was related to his work at MRI. He assigned the rights in the application and any subsequently issuing patent to FilmTec, a new company of which he was a co-founder. When Allied-Signal manufactured a reverse osmosis membrane, FilmTec sued Allied-Signal for patent infringement. Allied-Signal contested the assignment, claiming that the government had title to the patent at issue.[254]

On appeal, the Federal Circuit confirmed that patents could be assigned and that ownership rights in an invention may also be assigned 'between the time

---

[248] Also see supra n. 227/II and accompanying discussion.

[249] See *Cubic Corp. v. Marty* 449: 'a contract of adhesion can be fully enforced according to its terms unless some other factors exist, such as the oppressive or 'unconscionable' provision.'

[250] See e. g. Machi, in *Intellectual Property in Academia* (2011) 235, 269.

[251] The case and the larger context of the BDA will be discussed in more detail in Chapter 5, here the discussion will be limited to the question of whether pre-invention assignment agreements are capable of transferring legal and equitable title to future inventions.

[252] *FilmTec v. Allied-Signal Inc. and UOP Inc.*, 939 F.2d 1568 (1991).

[253] Ibid. 1570.

[254] Ibid. 1570–1571.

of the development of an invention and the issuance of a patent'.[255] The court further held that where an assignment was made 'prior to the existence of the invention' this was considered 'an assignment of an expectant interest' and that this could be a valid assignment.[256] The court clarified that while such an assignment would only grant equitable title to the invention at first, once the invention was conceived and an application was filed, legal title would immediately be transferred to the assignee and that thus no further action was required.[257] At the same time, the court distinguished such an assignment of expectant interest from an obligation to grant rights in the future to a third party, in which case the transfer of title only occurs once the invention exists.[258] The court went on to conclude that 'does hereby grant' was sufficient to create an assignment of an expectant interest and that – under the contract between MRI and the government – once the invention was conceived, the transfer of title occurred by operation of law.[259]

While the Supreme Court in *Stanford* relied on this distinction between an assignment of a future interest, which is capable of immediately transferring title to a future invention, and an obligation to assign rights in the future, which is not, three Justices did not agree with this interpretation of the law.[260] It was especially questioned why the wording of 'does hereby grant' should have a different legal meaning to 'agree to assign'.[261] This concern is shared by several scholars.[262] Indeed, by stating that '(a)pplications for patent, patents, or any interest therein, shall be assignable in law', 35 USC § 261 seems to be clear that a transfer of legal title to a patent application or a patent may not occur before a patent application has been filed or a patent issued respectively.[263] This reading of the law is reinforced by the fact that under chapter 300 of the Patent Office Manual of Patent Examination Procedure (MPEP), only assignments of patent applications and issued patents may be recorded in the USPTO.[264] Thus, even if employees sign an employment contract in which they agree to immediately assign rights in future inventions, legal title to such inventions should not be

---

[255] Ibid. 1572.

[256] Ibid.

[257] Ibid.

[258] Ibid. 1573.

[259] Ibid.

[260] See *Stanford v. Roche* 2199–2205, dissenting opinion by *Justice Breyer*, who was joined by Justice *Ginsburg* as well as Justice *Sotomayor* who shared this specific concern.

[261] Justice *Breyer* noted that '(g)iven what seem only slight linguistic differences in the contractual language, this reasoning seems to make too much of too little.', see ibid. 2203–2204.

[262] See e. g. Hagelin (2011) 39 AIPLA Q. J. 335, 346–350; Sandrik (2014) 66 Rutgers L. Rev. 299, 302–305; O'Connor (2011) 6 Intell. Prop. J. 29, 36–40.

[263] Also see Hagelin (2011) 39 AIPLA Q. J. 335, 346–347.

[264] See e. g. MPEP 301 'Ownership/Assignability of Patents and Applications'.

transferred until an assignment document is executed after a patent application has been filed or a patent has issued.[265]

III Universities' Approach to Pre-Invention Assignments

While most employers in industry include standard pre-invention assignment agreements in the employment contract, thus requiring an employee to sign the agreement as condition of employment, universities have taken this practice one step further. Accordingly, it has become common practice that appointment or offer letters, which are sent out by universities to prospective faculty and which are signed by faculty upon accepting the conditions stated therein, make reference to a university's respective faculty handbook. The faculty handbook contains a university's different policies and procedures and typically includes a university's intellectual property policy. By referring to the handbook in the offer letter and by faculty accepting the letter, faculty implicitly also accept the terms and conditions of the intellectual property policy as part of the employment relationship. In effect, a university's intellectual property policy thus functions as a pre-invention assignment agreement.[266]

Courts seem to be comfortable with this assignment practice. To this effect, the Federal Circuit in *Chou v. University of Chicago*[267] confirmed that the referencing of the faculty handbook in the letter of appointment sufficed to assign a graduate student's invention to the university. While the handbook contained the statement '(t)he contents of this handbook do not create a contract or agreement between an individual and the university', what the court considered important was that the handbook also read that 'the basic terms and conditions of the employment agreement (were) set out in the letter of appointment'.[268] Since the letter of appointment referred to 'the administrative policies of the university', the court found there to be an effective assignment of the student's invention.[269]

---

[265] Also see Hagelin (2011) 39 AIPLA Q. J. 335, 348–350.

[266] Also see Luppino (2009) 78 UMKC L. Rev. 367, 370; Reichman (1992) 51 Colum.-VLA J. L. & Arts 51, 69; Chew (1992) 1 Wis. L. Rev. 259, 286–289.

[267] *Chou v. University of Chicago*, 254 F. 3d 1347 (Fed. Cir. 2001).

[268] Ibid. 1357.

[269] Ibid.

Chapter 5

The Special Case of Federally Funded University Inventions

A Federal Statutes and Regulations on Ownership Issues

There are a number of federal statutes which influence the determination of ownership and the subsequent use of inventions in a university setting, depending on the type of funding which has been used to develop the invention and/or the type of invention which has been developed.[270]

For instance, the Invention Secrecy Act of 1951[271] allows the federal government to keep secret inventions if 'the publication or the disclosure by the grant of the patent' are deemed to be 'detrimental to the national security'.[272] There is a slight variation in procedure, depending on whether the 'government has a property interest' in the invention or not.[273] If the government does not have a property interest in the invention, the invention cannot simply be kept secret but will have to be made 'available for inspection to the Atomic Energy Commission (AEC), the Secretary of Defense, and the chief officer of any other department or agency of the government designated by the President as a defence agency of the United States'.[274] If either considers the invention to be detrimental to national security, the invention will be kept secret and the granting of a patent will be withheld 'for such period as the national interest requires'.[275] Thus, while the ownership of such inventions are not assigned to the government, the inventor will not be able to use his invention but merely has the right to apply to be compensated for the damage caused by the order of secrecy and/or the government use of the invention.[276]

270 For an analysis of how the Atomic Energy Act (AEA) and the National Aeronautics and Space Act (NAS Act) secure government ownership over federally funded inventions that fall in the respective subject-matter categories, see Takenaka (2011) 44 Tex. Intell. Prop. L. J. 307–309. *Takenaka* acknowledges that such an automatic transfer mechanism would not work for the BDA mainly because the AEA and the NAS Act both rely on the screening by the USPTO, a task that – considering the volume of inventions that would need to be scrutinised under the BDA – could not feasibly be expanded to the BDA, see ibid. 310.

271 35 USC §§181–188.

272 35 USC §181.

273 Ibid.

274 Ibid.

275 Ibid.

276 35 USC §183.

Under the Atomic Energy Act (AEA) of 1954[277], the federal government exerts control over inventions related to the use of special nuclear material or atomic energy in an atomic weapon. Generally, the government will own such inventions if the work resulting in the invention has been conducted under some sort of research contract or arrangement for the AEC.[278] But even if an invention related to the use of special nuclear material or atomic energy has been developed without federal funds, and if a patent application is filed, the USPTO will either not grant a patent for the respective invention or the scope of the rights will be limited to non-military uses.[279] Special mention deserves the fact that in this latter case, the government does not actually own the inventions either; nevertheless, it can stop the USPTO from issuing a patent or have it modify the scope of the specific patent.[280]

Similarly, the National Aeronautics and Space Act (NAS Act) of 1958[281] allows for a transfer of ownership of federally funded inventions which result from aeronautical and space activities to the federal government.[282] If the government was not involved in the funding of or linked contractually to the development of an invention, but the invention is found to have 'significant utility in the conduct of aeronautical and space activities', no patent will be granted to the inventor.[283] Further, the federal government has the authority to request that the USPTO issue a patent directly to the National Aeronautics and Space Administration (NASA).[284]

The 1980 Universities and Small Business Patent Procedures Act, colloquially called the Bayh-Dole Act (BDA)[285], is the most comprehensive statute on the specific topic of the ownership of federally funded research. As such, and given the large amounts of federal research dollars universities annually receive, it is the most important federal statute in the context of university generated inventions. In fact, over the years, it has received considerable international attention, to the point where it has inspired governments in different countries

---

277 42 USC §§2011–2021.

278 42 USC §2182: 'Any invention or discovery, useful in the production or utilization of special nuclear material or atomic energy, made or conceived in the course of or under any contract, subcontract, or arrangement entered into with or for the benefit of the (Atomic Energy) Commission, regardless of whether the contract, subcontract, or arrangement involved the expenditure of funds by the Commission, shall be vested in, and be the property of, the Commission [...]'.

279 42 USC §2181.

280 See Takenaka (2011) 44 Tex. Intell. Prop. L. J. 308. For a detailed analysis of the patent provisions in the AEA, see Riesenfeld (1958) 46 Cal. L. Rev. 40.

281 Codified as amended in scattered sections of 42 USC.

282 42 USC §305(a): '[...] such invention shall be the exclusive property of the United States, and if such invention is patentable a patent therefor shall be issued to the United States [...]'.

283 42 USC §305(c).

284 42 USC §305(d).

285 Public Law 96–517, 94 Stat. 3015 (1980) (codified at 35 USC §§200–212).

around the globe to enact similar legislation.[286] But before the discussion turns to the legislative history and the provisions of the BDA, it is important to understand the BDA's scope and how it relates to the relevant ownership provisions in the Patent Act and the law of employee-inventions in general.

As will be discussed in detail below, the BDA's main objective was to promote the commercialisation of inventions that result from federally funded R&D at non-profit organisations, including universities, and small businesses ('contractors'). But contrary to what was widely believed after the BDA was enacted, the BDA does not achieve this goal by automatically transferring ownership of federally funded inventions to the recipient of the federal funds. To the contrary, it leaves untouched the supremacy of the ownership of the inventor.[287] In other words, the mere fact that federal funding is involved does not change the cornerstone rule of the US patent law that the ownership of an invention originally vests with the inventor. Only if there is a contractual assignment to the contrary, the ownership may be changed. As a result, ownership questions at universities essentially boil down to the question of whether there is an enforceable agreement which transfers the ownership rights from the inventor to the university or a third party in place. In the absence of such a contractual assignment, the ownership of federally funded inventions vests with the inventor.

The BDA does thus *not* address the allocation of ownership rights to inventions between universities (or other contractors) and their inventors but is only concerned with the relationship between the contractor and the government.[288] Of course, the allocation of rights between the contractor and the inventor will also be relevant in order to determine the ownership of a specific invention, however, it does not fall in the scope of the BDA. As such, the discussion in the previous chapter on the ownership of employee-inventions – while related – is distinct. Indeed, it is this very distinction which was often simply overlooked or confused to the point where universities assumed that the BDA vested ownership of federally funded university inventions in them.

Finally, in certain limited situations, federal regulations may apply and have a bearing on the determination of ownership of inventions which are developed at universities. This can be the case where a researcher is an employee of a federal agency but conducts his research at a university. Here, the government does

---

[286] See e. g. The Economist, 'Golden Goose' (*Economist*), calling the BDA 'possibly the most inspired piece of legislation to be enacted in America over the past half-century'; also see infra n. 23/III and accompanying discussion.

[287] This has most famously been confirmed in *Stanford v. Roche*, see infra 5.D.

[288] This was acknowledged by the Federal Circuit in *Board of Trustees of Leland Stanford v. Roche*, 583 F. 3d 832 (Fed. Cir. 2009): 'The primary purpose of the BDA is to regulate relationships of small business and non-profit grantees with the government, not between grantees and the inventors who work for them.' This also explains why the BDA is silent on the common law shop right and hired-to-invent doctrines, see supra n. 212/II and accompanying discussion.

not provide the funds for a research project to the university but pays the salary and other benefits for the researcher. In such instances, if the research results in a patentable invention, the government will obtain the right, title, and interest to the invention in question.[289]

B The History of the Bayh-Dole Act

I The History of Federal Patent Policy and the Public Interest

The passage of the BDA reflected a new vision of government policy relating to federally funded research: In order to successfully develop federally funded research results, they needed to be patented and transferred to the private sector.[290] With this, Congress embraced the earlier discussed commercialisation argument and distanced itself from its earlier view that research should be made widely available through government ownership and dedication to the public domain in order to optimally benefit the public. But the transition to this new government policy was anything but sudden. Indeed, the question of the ownership of government-sponsored inventions had been the subject of heated debates ever since World War II and the early postwar era, during which time the federal government dramatically increased federal spending on R&D. As a consequence, at the time, the government's main concern was to ensure its own access to federally funded research, as will be discussed below.[291]

Considering the long history of legislative discussions surrounding the commercialisation and ownership of research results and inventions produced by employees and contractors of the government, it seems surprising that it took the federal government until 1980 and many failed efforts to finally formulate a uniform policy on the matter (hereinafter 'patent policy').[292] This is especially striking, when one considers that in other complex fields, such as commerce,

---

[289] See e. g. 37 CFR 501.6 (a)(1) (Criteria for the determination of rights in and to inventions), stating that if an invention has been made: i) during working hours; ii) with some contribution of the government such as equipment, facilities or materials; or iii) if the invention bears a direct relation to the inventor's official duties, the government will own it.

[290] As part of this vision, another statute was passed: the Stevenson-Wydler Technology Innovation Act of 1980, Pub. L. No. 96–480, 94 Stat. 2311–2320 (codified as amended at 15 USC §§ 3701–3714 [1994]). The Stevenson-Wydler Innovation Act's purpose was to encourage technology transfer between federal laboratories and other performers of federally funded research and state governments, local governments, and private industries, see 15 USC §§ 3701–3702. For the purpose of making accessible the developed research the Act requires federal laboratories to establish technology transfer offices, see 15 USC § 3710(b).

[291] Also see Eisenberg (1996) 82 Va. L. Rev. 1663, 1663–1664; 1671–1672.

[292] For a comprehensive account of the history of federal patent policy, see Neumeyer and Stedman, *Employed Inventor* (1971) 207–424; Eaton (1967) 45 Harv. Bus. Rev. 101, 105–109; Eisenberg (1996) 82 Va. L. Rev. 1663, 1671–1695.

defence, or public health, unified policies have long been established.[293] There are two explanations for the difficulty in putting in place a unified patent policy.

The first reason – which directly relates to the nature of patent law – is the varying relevance of patent law to the respective fields of the different federal agencies and the benefits which the different agencies derive from the commercial application of their research results. For instance, while the Department of Defense (DOD) may have little need for commercial application of its research, the Department of Health and Human Services (HHS, as it is called today) or the Department of Agriculture (USDA), may have a much bigger interest in the commercial application of their research respectively. This divergence of needs could much better be served by having agencies formulate their own policy – based on an agency's respective mission, the kind of technical activities it was involved in and other factors.[294]

The second reason for the difficulty in formulating a uniform patent policy follows from the first one but is predominately a political one. Due to the lack of guidelines provided by the executive branch on a consistent overall policy, a hodgepodge of different policies emerged, ranging between two extremes of the so-called 'licence' and the 'title' policies.[295] The advocates of these two opposed schools of thinking dominated Congress on the issue of patent policy during the postwar years and provided for an on-going, but fruitless debate on the path to a unified federal patent policy, stretching over several decades until the 1970s.[296] While both sides cited their belief in the free private enterprise economy, the supporters of the title policy advocated uncompromising and total government ownership of all inventions made under publicly financed research, while the supporters of the licence policy advocated that the inventor and teams who developed the invention should own it.[297]

The debate between the two groups not only grew increasingly heated and emotional over the years but also often provided for a chaotic result: The inconsistencies meant that at times, the same contractor was presented with vastly differing patent clauses from different agencies for similar types of work in the same field.[298] Nevertheless, at the core of the debate was the concern about how to best serve the public interest. To that effect, both positions reflected broader arguments regarding the overall merit of the patent system.[299]

---

293 See Neumeyer and Stedman, *Employed Inventor* (1971) 209.

294 See ibid.; also see Eaton (1967) 45 Harv. Bus. Rev. 101, 103; Dratler (1979) 16 Harv. J. on Legis. 129, 149.

295 Eaton (1967) 45 Harv. Bus. Rev. 101, 103.

296 Ibid.

297 Neumeyer and Stedman, *Employed Inventor* (1971) 209–210; Eaton (1967) 101, 103–104.

298 Eaton (1967) 45 Harv. Bus. Rev. 101, 104.

299 R. Eisenberg (1996) 82 Va. L. Rev. 1663, 1674.

The proponents of a licence policy did not believe that government ownership of inventions was equitable. Since the government did not contract for inventions but for specific research, inventions were incidental to the performance of the contract. In their view, the government was also not as well-positioned as commercial firms to develop and market such inventions. Thus, if exclusivity was required to attract the investment necessary to commercialise an invention, the contractor should own the invention and the government would only maintain the possibility of a royalty-free, non-exclusive license in order to be able to use the invention for a public purpose.[300]

By contrast, advocates of a title policy acknowledged that inventions were incidental to most contracts, but they also maintained that such inventions still constituted government property as the government financed the research. The title policy proponents were concerned that not making such inventions freely available to the public would result in the public having to pay twice: once through the publicly funded government contract and again through the monopoly pricing of the patented product.[301] The title policy advocates also feared that contractor-ownership would lead to favouritism towards private firms and to a concentration of economic power in the hand of large companies, which also would be to the detriment of the public.[302]

It seems worth pointing out that while the title policy advocates expressed mistrust of the patent system, they still believed in patenting as a mechanism of ensuring public access to publicly funded research results. Thus, in their view, government ownership combined with patents did not serve to exclude others from using the inventions but to place federally funded research in the public domain for the benefit of the public. The position that such inventions should simply be dedicated to the public and not patented at all, however, was absent to the debate at the time.[303]

This can most likely be explained with the fact that in the beginning of the history of federal patent policy, inventions developed with federal funds were not treated differently to other employee-inventions. Until after World War I, most government agencies followed a 'laissez-faire' policy in regard to ownership of government-sponsored research and inventions.[304] There were usually no express contracts which allocated patent rights and sometimes agencies even compensated their employees voluntarily for the use of an invention. Nevertheless, if disputes arose, courts typically did not consider the govern-

[300] See Eaton (1967) 45 Harv. Bus. Rev. 101, 103–104; R. Eisenberg (1996) 82 Va. L. Rev. 1663, 1674; Popp Berman (2008) 38 Soc. Stud. Sci. 835, 842.

[301] Eaton (1967) 45 Harv. Bus. Rev. 101, 103–104; also see infra n. 147–160/III and accompanying discussion on 'double paying'.

[302] R. Eisenberg (1996) 82 Va. L. Rev. 1663, 1673–1674.

[303] See ibid. 1675–1676.

[304] Dratler (1979) 16 Harv. J. on Legis. 129, 149.

ment to be significantly different to other employers and generally applied the common law.[305]

In 1910, Congress enacted a statute which allowed patent owners to sue for compensation for the government's use of their invention.[306] Once the number of such suits became more frequent, however, several agencies initiated a new policy (now known as the licence policy) which allowed the agencies to use without royalty payments inventions made with government funds.[307] Using departmental regulations which codified the common law doctrine of shop right, governments became ever more vigorous in attempting to fend off contractors' and inventors' claims for compensation in an effort of protecting their own access to inventions which they funded.[308]

Moreover, due to continuously rising government investments in R&D during and after World War II, it was increasingly questioned whether inventors should have any claim to inventions which were created with government support.[309] These developments ultimately gave rise to the title policy which would allow the government to assert the title to government-financed inventions or patents. While the title policy first appeared as early as 1933, it took some time for it to gain traction.[310] Indeed, the licence policy was continued to be widely

---

305 See e. g. *Solomons*, where the Supreme Court confirmed that the common law principles did not change only because the employer was the government, see supra n. 165/II and accompanying text. Also see Dratler (1979) 16 Harv. J. on Legis. 129, 149–150.

306 Act of June 25, 1910, 36 Stat. 851, see *Dubilier*, 289 US 178, 204–205.

307 Dratler (1979) 16 Harv. J. on Legis. 129, 150–151.

308 Ibid. 151.

309 Ibid. 151.

310 In 1933, in *Dubilier v. United States*, the title policy was unsuccessfully tested. Referring to *Solomons v. United States*, the Supreme Court confirmed that the government – to the same extent as a private employer – was entitled to a shop right in its employees' inventions, see *Dubilier* 192. But what makes *Dubilier* a particularly interesting case and one which is relevant to today's continuing debate, is not the application of the shop rights rule but the discussion around the government's public interest argument; also see Dratler (1979) 16 Harv. J. on Legis. 129, 159. In *Dubilier*, the question was discussed whether a patent policy which allows for the private ownership of federally funded inventions ultimately benefitted the public, see *Dubilier* 198–199: 'Will permission to an employee to enjoy patent rights as against all others than the Government tend to the improvement of the public service by attracting a higher class of employees? Is there in fact greater benefit to the people in a dedication to the public of inventions conceived by officers of government, than in their exploitation under patents by private industry? Should certain classes of invention be treated in one way and other classes differently?' In a dissenting opinion, Justice *Stone* answered these questions by pointing out that a distinction between the government and a private employer should be made since the government's work was not conducted for private gain but for the overall benefit of the public, see ibid. 217: 'The inventors were not only employed to engage in work which unmistakably required them to exercise their inventive genius as occasion arose; they were a part of a public enterprise. It was devoted to the improvement of the art of radio communication for the benefit of the people of the United States, carried on in a government laboratory, maintained by public funds. Considerations which might favor the employee where the interest of the employer is only in private gain are therefore of slight significance [...].' Nonetheless, the *Dubilier* court

used until the 1950s, when the title policy was introduced for the disposition of rights in government employees' inventions (but not in inventions arising from research conducted by a contractor).[311]

But despite increasing pressure from both sides, Congress did not adopt either of the two policies in a uniform manner but adopted a title policy in a limited number of statues that were applicable to certain programs and agencies. All other agencies decided freely whether to adopt a title or a licence policy.[312] Until the mid 1970s, the debate continued and despite numerous Congressional hearings on the issue, no legislation was adopted.[313] What reinforced the deadlock situation were statements by both President *Kennedy* in 1963 and President *Nixon* in 1971 on the issue of federal patent policy, which did not take a stance for either one of the two approaches but underlined that agencies should have considerable discretion to handle patent policy according to their own judgement.[314] Nevertheless, *Kennedy*'s 'Presidential Memorandum and Statement on Government Patent Policy' for the first time established basic criteria to guide departments and agencies (not otherwise governed by statutes) in determining rights to inventions made under government contracts or grants.[315] This was also considered the first attempt to establish a central rationale for allocating such rights in accordance with the public interest.[316]

The public interest concern inherent in this whole debate was also illustrated by the 1974 case of *Public Citizen v. Sampson*[317], which was filed in response to regulations attempting to implement a uniform patent policy. Public Citizen was a non-profit, consumer rights advocacy group which – together with seven members of Congress – challenged provisions of federal regulations which au-

made it clear that this was a question of policy and that whether an assignment to the government should occur and under what circumstances was ultimately a question to be addressed by Congress, see ibid. 208.

311 For a detailed account of how the title policy applied to the different categories of inventions under the *Truman* administration in 1950 and the *Kennedy* administration in 1968, see Dratler (1979) 16 Harv. J. on Legis. 129, 151–154; Neumeyer and Stedman, *Employed Inventor* (1971) 228.

312 Agencies which adopted a title policy: Atomic Energy Commission, Department of Agriculture, Department of Health, Education and Welfare, Department of the Interior, and National Aeronautics and Space Administration. Agencies which adopted a licence policy: DOD and NSF, see R. Eisenberg (1996) 82 Va. L. Rev. 1663, 1676–1677.

313 US Senate Select Committee on Small Business, 1959, 1960, 1963; US Senate Committee on the Judiciary, 1960, 1961, 1965, see Popp Berman (2008) 38 Soc. Stud. Sci. 835, 843.

314 *Kennedy*'s presidential statement attempted to find a middle ground between title and licence policy. *Nixon*'s presidential statement was in essence a revision of Kennedy's 1963 statement, see Walterscheid (1990) 3 Har. J. L. & Tech. 103, 103; also see Kennedy, *Memorandum and Statement of Government Patent Policy* (1963); Nixon, *Memorandum and Statement of Government Patent Policy* (1971).

315 See Harbridge House, *Patent Policy Study* (1968) Preface.

316 Ibid.

317 *Public Citizen v. Sampson*, 379 F. Supp. 662 (Dist. Ct. 1974).

thorised exclusive licensing of federally-owned patents. They claimed that the authorisation for federal agencies to grant rights 'greater than a non-exclusive licence [...] to patents and inventions developed under federally-financed research' lacked congressional approval and harmed the plaintiffs as taxpayers, consumers, and the congressmen as members of Congress.[318] While the case was ultimately dismissed for lack of standing on the part of the plaintiffs, it nevertheless illustrates important concerns regarding the transfer of title to federally funded inventions to contractors, and the legality of achieving the same through administrative regulations instead of new congressional legislation.[319] Central to the case was the question whether federally funded patents and inventions were in fact government property.[320] Although the court did not answer the question, it nevertheless pointed out that if it were to find it was, government agencies would not have the authority to convey such patent rights without proper authorisation.[321]

II University Research as a Topic of Interest

From today's perspective, it seems surprising that universities were largely ignored in most debates about federal patent policy. There are two likely explanations for this. Firstly, universities' overall contribution to federally funded research had historically been comparatively low.[322] Secondly, as was discussed above, for the most part during the postwar era, universities were only engaged on a limited level in patenting and licensing activities.[323] Therefore, during the majority of the debates on federal patent policy, universities were simply not on the radar of most politicians.

This changed, however, in 1968 with the publication of two major studies on federal patent policy: One was released by the consulting firm Harbridge House, Inc., the other by the US General Accounting Office (GAO).[324] Harbridge House was commissioned by the Committee on Government Patent Policy to evaluate the effectiveness of government patent policy in achieving po-

---

318 Ibid. 664.

319 See e. g. R. Eisenberg (1996) 82 Va. L. Rev. 1663, 1688.

320 *Public Citizen* 667.

321 Ibid. 667, quoting *Houghton* 386: 'No official of the government was authorized to give away any interest in it, and no subsequent recognition of a right in defendant, not even a conveyance to defendant, could have conferred any right upon him or been binding upon the government.'

322 In the 1950s and 1960s, less than 10 % of federal funds towards R&D was going to universities, see NSF, 'Federal Funds Survey, FYs 1951–97' (*NCSES*).

323 See supra 2.B. I.; also see e. g. Mowery and others, *Ivory Tower* (2004) 87.

324 See Harbridge House, *Patent Policy Study* (1968); GAO, *Medicinal Chemistry* (1968). The GAO Report focused its analysis exclusively on the National Health Institutes' (NIH) medicinal chemistry program, see ibid. 3.

licy objectives.[325] The Committee was established by the Federal Council for Science and Technology (FCST) to examine the principles established by the patent policy and their effect on the public interest.[326] Both studies brought to light the negative effect National Institute of Health's (NIH) medicinal chemistry program had on collaborations between US pharmaceutical firms and academic researchers in the field of medicinal chemistry.

The importance of these two studies must be understood against the backdrop of the overall federal funding structure pertaining to universities at this time. During the postwar era, the federal funding universities received came disproportionately from a handful of federal agencies. By the 1960s, the Department of Health, Education, and Welfare (HEW) was the largest funder of universities. Its contribution to universities continued to grow rapidly and it administered its grants through the NIH who had become a separate operating agency within the HEW.[327] Moreover, the HEW provided roughly one third of overall R&D funds received by universities.[328]

Consequently, changes in the HEW's patent practices immediately impacted universities' patent practices, as will be detailed below. Simultaneously, these changes – as well as changes in a couple of other federal departments and agencies which contributed to university research – brought federally funded university research generally more into the focus of discussions on a federal patent policy.[329]

When the NIH began to fund research grant programs on a large scale in the mid 1950s, there was a strong bond and a mutually beneficial relationship, which had been developing over the course of the previous 20 years, between the drug industry and the academic community. Indeed, at that time, most of the outside financial support for university research in medicinal chemistry came from industry.[330] At the heart of these contacts was typically a mutual understanding that the specific firm would provide biological testing for the profes-

[325] See Harbridge House, *Patent Policy Study* (1968); the study sought to achieve this by answering the following three questions: '1) How does patent policy affect commercial utilisation of government-sponsored inventions?; 2) how does patent policy affect business competition in commercial markets?; 3) how does patent policy affect participation of contractors in the government's R&D programs?', see ibid. iii.

[326] *President Kennedy* asked the FCST and the Justice Department to prepare annual reports on the policy and to make recommendations for changes based on these reports, see Harbridge House, *Patent Policy Study* (1968) Preface.

[327] See GAO, *Medicinal Chemistry* (1968) 3; also see Popp Berman (2008) 38 Soc. Stud. Sci. 835, 844–846. In early 1960, contributions were around USD 350 million, by the end of the 1960s they rose to USD 677 million, and by 1974 they were USD 1.2 billion, see ibid. Today, the HEW does no longer exist in this form: In 1979, the HEW was divided into the Department of Education and the Department of Health and Human Services (HHS) which houses the NIH.

[328] Popp Berman (2008) 38 Soc. Stud. Sci. 835, 846.

[329] Ibid. 845–846; Mowery and others, *Ivory Tower* (2004) 87.

[330] Harbridge House, *Patent Policy Study* (1968) II-19–20.

sor's compounds in exchange for certain rights in any inventions made or reduced to practice during testing.[331]

But the potential benefits for academia went beyond the testing. If a collaboration proved successful universities often would receive a small grant in support of the research, the professor or researcher would be engaged by the pharmaceutical firm as a consultant, students would be recruited, and new products developed would generally be recognised through royalty agreements and through papers published.[332] Similarly, the pharmaceutical firms received a substantial return on their investment: Most importantly, firms typically received the exclusive rights to develop and market the compounds they tested. They considered exclusive rights necessary in order to recover R&D costs.[333] Moreover, the large-scale testing exposed the firms to new ideas and cutting-edge research in the field of medicinal chemistry, which helped them develop successful products in their own right. Last but not least, the close working relationship with academia gave them valuable access to human capital.[334]

During the 1960s, the NIH greatly increased its support for research in medicine and medicinal chemistry to the extent that it ended supporting virtually all of the established medicinal chemists in the country, most of which were in academia.[335] While the medicinal chemistry program was a relatively small program – with an estimated USD 8 million per year it only accounted for about 1.3% of the NIH budget[336] – it nevertheless had a huge impact on the working relationship between the pharmaceutical industry and academia.[337]

Up until 1962, US pharmaceutical firms had screened compounds for academic institutions free of charge, regardless of who had sponsored the research.[338] In 1962, HEW implemented more stringent procedures for reporting inventions and determining rights in inventions.[339] According to these new procedures, pharmaceutical firms which were screening compounds and universities which obtained funding had to sign a patent agreement, which essentially prevented either party from obtaining patents on inventions resulting from or developed in the course of the work funded by the NIH. Moving forward and in the interest of protecting the public interest, recipients of grants had to refer to

---

331 Ibid. II-20.

332 Ibid.

333 See GAO, *Medicinal Chemistry* (1968) 10.

334 Harbridge House, *Patent Policy Study* (1968) II-16–20, referring to a firm which stated that out of a total of 40'000 new compounds only 6'500 were derived from non-academic sources, see Ibid. II-20.

335 Ibid. II-20–21.

336 Ibid.

337 Ibid.

338 Ibid. II-20–21.

339 Ibid. II-15.

the NIH to determine whether patent protection should be sought and how potential patent rights should be disposed of or administered.[340]

Pharmaceutical firms almost unanimously rejected to sign these patent agreements due to the loss of exclusive patent rights. But they also feared a 'contamination' of the in-house research by the research which was sponsored by the NIH in which the academic investigator was engaged in.[341] The worry essentially was that the HEW would assert ownership claims over compounds and products which had been developed independently by the firm but which would be construed as having evolved through the support of NIH funding.[342] As a result, in most cases, firms declined to collaborate with academia on grants and immediately suspended biological screening under NIH grants.[343]

Different alternative screening sources were tested, none of which proved satisfactory and most of which ended up being more expensive.[344] Overall the lack of availability of industry screening services hampered the academic research by generating a large build-up of untested compounds, by not producing biological data relevant to the potential usefulness of compounds, and last but not least, by encouraging academic researchers to find ways to circumvent the rules.[345] The new patent policy also weakened the general working relationship between the academic community and industry, which resulted in reduced exchange of test data and new ideas and a reduced output of consultation work and publications.[346]

In response to the two reports, and following an investigation by the Controller General of the US, in 1968 the HEW revised the terms of its patent agreements and started to use standard institutional patent agreements (IPA).[347] These IPAs permitted universities with 'approved technology transfer programs' to retain title to federally sponsored inventions.[348] In 1973, the National Science Foundation (NSF) followed the example of HEW and introduced the same IPAs.[349] Indeed, the IPAs were specifically drafted for certain universities which showed a knack for peddling their inventions to industry.[350] The DOD

---

340 Ibid. II-13.

341 Ibid. II-16, 20.

342 Ibid.

343 Ibid. II-14.

344 Ibid. II-14, 18–19.

345 Ibid. II-23–25.

346 Ibid. II-29–40.

347 See R. Eisenberg (1996) 82 Va. L. Rev. 1663, 1683. The Committee on Government Patent Policy conducted a thorough review of the Harbridge House study and concluded that the results did not provide enough basis to change the basic principles of the presidential policy, and that neither a single licence nor a title policy would be in the public interest, see ibid. 1683–1684.

348 US Senate, *University and Small Business Patent Procedures Act* (1979) 37.

349 Ibid. 37.

350 Broad (1979) 205 Science 473, 473, noting that by 1979 there were only very few IPAs in place: 72 HEW grantee institutions and out of 1'200 NSF institutions there were only 20.

had already earlier changed their policy to allow universities to retain title to federally sponsored inventions if they had approved the respective university's patent policy. As a consequence to these changes in agencies' patent policies, in the beginning of the 1970s, it had become a lot easier for universities to patent the results of federally funded research.[351]

III The Bayh-Dole Bill

The above-discussed positive developments regarding federal patent policies came to a halt in the mid 1970s. It was universities' frustration with these negative changes which ultimately triggered the introduction of the Bayh-Dole bill. During the mid 1970s, there was growing concern that HEW might limit the ability to negotiate exclusive licences under its IPA programs and that it might revert back to its pre-1968 policies.[352] HEW's major concern and the reason for its scepticism towards university patents, licences, and particularly exclusive licences was that they generally limited the agency's ability to control availability and cost of sponsored inventions.[353] In 1977, the HEW deferred the processing of all petitions for ownership rights pending completion of an overall review of the HEW patent policy, and in 1978, the HEW's Office of General Counsel recommended to reconsider the use of IPAs based on the main concern that IPAs encourage exclusive licensing.[354]

Similar concern was voiced regarding the change which DOD had implemented to its patent policy in 1975.[355] Under the new DOD regulation, in order for universities to obtain title to agency-sponsored inventions, they had to demonstrate that the research was in a field of technology directly related to an area in which the university had an effective technology transfer program or a commercial position.[356] Because of the additional administrative burden, many universities chose not to submit the required information to retain title to such inventions.[357] There was additional concern that administrative costs to the government and universities were unnecessarily increased by the need to prepare, review, and respond to these requests to retain title on a case-by-case basis and that due to the cumbersome administrative process decisions were delayed.[358]

---

351 See Mowery and others, *Ivory Tower* (2004) 88.

352 See e. g. ibid. 88–89; R. Eisenberg (1996) 82 Va. L. Rev. 1663, 1961–1692.

353 See Eskridge (1978) 28 BioScience 605.

354 See R. Eisenberg (1996) 82 Va. L. Rev. 1663, 1692.

355 The reason why the debate focused on HEW and DOD is probably linked to the amount of contribution they each made: Combined R&D funding to colleges and universities amounted to over 60% in 1978, see US Senate, *University and Small Business Patent Procedures Act* (1979) 36.

356 Ibid. 38, 60–62.

357 Ibid. 62.

358 Ibid.

During all this time, the above discussed debate over a unified federal patent policy continued in a heated and emotional manner.[359] What underscored the urgency of the debate was the growing worry that the US was losing its comparative advantage with regard to the manufacturing industry, especially in relation to the Japanese economy that continuously grew stronger.[360] Voices which called for mechanisms enabling private appropriation of the results of government-sponsored research became increasingly loud as time went on.[361] There was growing concern that federal ownership of federally funded research would inhibit the commercialisation of the same: Such technology would lie idle, as federal agencies and the government did not have the processes required, the resources or the incentive to assess the research results and move the successful ones to the market.[362]

In the fall of 1978, Senator *Robert Dole* criticised the HEW for the changes it introduced. He argued that with the new procedures, the HEW 'effectively destroyed the process by which breakthroughs are transferred from the laboratory to the public' and announced that he would introduce a bill to establish a uniform federal patent policy, which would give universities and small businesses the right to patent government-sponsored inventions.[363] A general concern was that the existing framework was not in the interest of the public, as the following example, which was presented in the Senate hearing, illustrates.[364]

Sydney E. Salmon, a biomedical researcher at the University of Arizona, was the co-inventor of a new method to screen the effectiveness of new anticancer drugs. Because the salary of one of the researchers in his lab was paid by the HEW, all rights to the invention reverted to the agency. While industry was very interested in his new method, *Salmon* could not proceed without HEW's agreement. It took him almost 20 months for the HEW to transfer the rights to him.[365] *Salmon* not only shared his negative experiences but also underlined that he believed that the slow process of obtaining HEW approval delayed the availability

[359] According to the General Counsel of the NSF, *Charles Herz*, the debate was 'a thicket a prudent man hesitates to enter' and in which 'reasonable men can and espouse remarkably diverse and divergent approaches, often heatedly, with equal and great conviction. Perhaps the difficulty is that much of the debate has the character of philosophizing in a vacuum.', quoted from Eskridge (1978) 28 BioScience 605, 606.

[360] See supra n. 150/I and accompanying discussion.

[361] See e. g. R. Eisenberg (1996) 82 Va. L. Rev. 1663, 1685–1687, referring to a report issued by the Commission on Government Procurement (established by Congress in 1969 to recommend methods to promote the economy, efficiency, and effectiveness of procurement by the Executive Branch of the federal government) which highlighted the issue of patent rights in government funded inventions. The Commission clearly stated its support of leaving government-supported inventions with contractors and of using exclusive licenses.

[362] See e. g. US Senate, *University and Small Business Patent Procedures Act* (1979).

[363] See e. g. Eskridge (1978) 28 BioScience 605, 606.

[364] See e. g. Broad (1979) 205 Science 473, 473.

[365] See ibid.

of his new method to the public by at least one year.[366] Accounts like this, which illustrated the frustrating and bureaucratic hurdles inventors had to go through in order to set free and transfer their inventions to industry, ultimately provided the fertile ground for the Bayh-Dole bill to take hold.[367]

On 13 September 1978, the University and Small Business Patent Procedures Act was introduced by Senators *Birch Bayh* and *Robert Dole*. The bill did not include provisions which were part of most IPAs, such as the provision that a university must have an 'approved technology transfer' capability.[368] The bill reflected the general conviction that the contractor or rather the inventor would be in a better position to successfully transfer the technology than the agency.[369] The bill also did not impose another IPA restriction, namely that contractors should first try to obtain a non-exclusive license. It was understood that this was too inefficient of a process for contractors to go through.[370] Lastly, and in contrast to previous approaches to introduce a uniform patent policy by statute, which failed, the Bayh-Dole bill did not make any provision for large business contractors but only focused on small businesses and non-profit contractors.[371]

Contrary to the perception that the BDA was the father of university patenting and licensing in the US, universities, which were already active in this area, lobbied for its introduction and actively tried to help its passage.[372] The bill was also favoured by small businesses, which felt that they received discriminatory treatment under the various agency policies. They saw themselves as more innovative than larger firms and believed that patent rights to government-sponsored inventions would strengthen their position so they could better compete with larger firms.[373]

In general, the Bayh-Dole bill did not attract much opposition. Large firms and their representatives pushed for similar types of rights, but despite their many efforts, this was not successful. Indeed, the fact that 'big business' did not benefit from the bill helped its passage, as many members of Congress – out of a fear that this might favour large companies – had been opposed to transfer-

366 See ibid.

367 For other such examples, see e. g. Henig (1979) 29 BioSci. 281, 284.

368 Ibid.

369 Ibid.

370 See ibid.; Mowery and others, *Ivory Tower* (2004) 89.

371 See R. Eisenberg (1996) 82 Va. L. Rev. 1663, 1691. In 1976, the FCST created a draft bill to establish a uniform patent policy by statute, but the bill never was introduced into Congress. A similar bill was introduced in 1977, but no hearings were held on it. Moreover, in 1979, a proposal for a new legislation to establish a uniform government patent policy was announced by *President Carter*'s administration. Such new legislation was part of a wide-ranging effort to promote industrial productivity and innovation, see ibid. 1688–1691 for a more detailed discussion.

372 See supra 2.B. I.; also see Mowery and others, *Ivory Tower* (2004) 90; R. Eisenberg (1996) 82 Va. L. Rev. 1663, 1693.

373 R. Eisenberg (1996) 82 Va. L. Rev. 1663, 1693.

ring patent rights to contractors for a long time.[374] Finally, what also helped the positive reception of the bill was its introduction at a time when the US's global economic competitiveness was of general public concern.[375]

In the winter of 1980, the BDA was passed overwhelmingly in both the House of Representatives and the Senate, was signed into law by *President Jimmy Carter* in December 1980, and came into effect on July 1, 1981

C Key Provisions of the Bayh-Dole Act

I Objective and Operation of the Bayh-Dole Act

The Act is codified in sections 200–212 of Chapter 18, Title 35, of the US Code and implemented by 37 CFR sections 401.1–401.16 and 404.1–404.14. The BDA's objectives are numerous and varied.[376] At the core of its objectives is the use and commercialisation of federally funded inventions through the use of patents and by giving access to such inventions to commercial organisations, and especially to small businesses. Many of the BDA's objectives point to its noble intent.[377] Accordingly, the Act does not only introduce a unified federal patent policy but also attempts to ensure that the public interest be honoured (through the protection of research and discovery, broad dissemination, and the public availability of federally funded inventions) and that small businesses benefit from the commercialisation efforts. Unfortunately, however, many of these objectives have been ignored, as will be discussed in Chapter 7.

The Act further defines its objectives and scope through the definition of certain terms. Only a few will be discussed here briefly. Importantly, the BDA uses the term 'invention' in the standard meaning of the federal patent law. Government sponsored inventions are thus subject to the standard patentability

---

374 Also see infra n. 145–146/III and accompanying discussion. Nevertheless, large business contractors unsurprisingly found a back-door to having their interests met: first by way of an executive order signed by *President Reagan* in 1983 and then in an inconspicuous amendment to the BDA, see Eisenberg and Cook-Deegan (2018) 147 Daedalus 76, 77.

375 See e. g. Mowery and others, *Ivory Tower* (2004) 90.

376 35 USC § 200: 'To use the patent system to promote the utilization of inventions arising from federally supported research or development; to encourage maximum participation of small business firms in federally supported R&D efforts; to promote collaboration between commercial concerns and non-profit organizations, including universities; to ensure that inventions made by non-profit organizations and small business firms are used in a manner to promote free competition and enterprise without unduly encumbering future research and discovery; to promote the commercialization and public availability of inventions made in the US by US industry and labor; to ensure that the Government obtains sufficient rights in federally supported inventions to meet the needs of the Government and protect the public against nonuse or unreasonable use of inventions; and to minimize the costs of administering policies in this area.'

377 Also see e. g. de Larena (2006) 43 Hous. L. Rev. 1373, 1377–1378.

requirements of 35 USC §§101, 102, 103, and 112. A claim that they should be subject to lesser requirements was rejected by the Federal Circuit in 2004.[378] 'Invention' is distinguished from 'subject invention' which refers to a contractor invention which was 'conceived or first actually reduced to practice in the performance of work under a funding agreement'.[379]

'Funding agreement' refers to 'any contract, grant, or cooperative agreement entered into between any federal agency [...] and any contractor for the performance of experimental, developmental, or research work funded in whole or in part by the federal government'.[380] In the federal system, 'grant' and 'contract' have specific technical meanings, however, the BDA does not make such a distinction.[381] Last but not least, the term of 'contractor' is defined as 'any person, small business firm, or non-profit organization that is a party to a funding agreement'.[382]

II Disposition of Rights

Under 35 USC § 202 the disposition of rights is specified. The Act allows for the contractor to 'elect to retain title to any subject invention'.[383] In order to do so, however, the contractor must comply with several procedural steps. Firstly, the contractor must disclose the invention to the respective federal agency 'within a reasonable timeframe'.[384] Failure to do so may result in the federal government receiving title to the subject invention.[385] Thus, the Act does not automatically vest title of inventions in the contractor but merely allows the contractor to elect title to inventions resulting from funded research.[386] Secondly, the contractor must inform the government of its intent to patent the invention and provide the government with updates.[387] Thirdly, the Contractor must make a written election to retain title to the invention within a specified timeframe.[388] Fourthly, the contractor has to agree to file the patent application on the subject inven-

378 Gotkin, *Bayh-Dole Act* (2012) 22.

379 35 USC § 201(e).

380 35 USC § 201(b).

381 In the federal system, contracts are used by the government if – for its own needs and under its own control – a solution to a particular scientific or technical problem is needed. In contrast, grants are used if the government does not look for a specific solution but funds the scientific enterprise more broadly. Here, the government exercises typically less control over the endeavours of the grantee. For a detailed illustration of the distinction, see Pulsinelli (2005) 7 Minn. J. L Sci. & Tech. 393, 405–407.

382 35 USC § 201(c).

383 35 USC § 202(a).

384 35 USC § 202(c)(1).

385 35 USC § 202(c)(1).

386 35 USC § 202(a); § 202(c)(2); this was confirmed by the Supreme Court in *Stanford*, see infra 5.D.

387 35 USC § 202(c)(5).

388 35 USC § 202(c)(2).

tion prior to any expiration of patent rights due to priority in the US and other countries where protection is sought.[389] And fifthly, licensing income must be shared with the inventors and (in the instance of universities) – after subtracting patenting expenses and the inventor share – must be used to support 'scientific research or education'.[390]

III Government Rights

In order to safeguard the government's access to federally sponsored inventions and to ensure the protection of the public interest, the BDA includes several provisions that allow the government to either share certain rights with contractors, to place restrictions on the use of federally funded inventions, or to require that title reverts back to the government.[391]

1 Non-exclusive License

On every invention which is created with federal funds and where the contractor elects title, 'the federal agency shall have a non-exclusive, non-transferrable, irrevocable, paid-up licence'.[392] The licence does not only allow the government to practice the invention but allows the government to have anyone else practice it.[393] In other words, government agencies have the right to use and benefit from federally funded inventions without the risk of infringing upon any patent rights and without having to pay royalties.[394] While the provision is generously phrased and allows for a varied use of such non-exclusive licenses, federal agencies are often not aware of it, and as a consequence, it is rarely used.[395]

There are a couple of factors which may stand in the way of a more frequent use of these government licenses: the absence of a searchable database of federally funded inventions, working practices which are not able to easily identify if a patented invention has been used, and finally, a general unwillingness of federal agencies to invoke the government license.[396] Undoubtedly, the public would benefit if these non-exclusive government licenses would more broadly be used, as they not only could potentially reduce research costs incurred by government agencies and their contractors, but they could also be used by the

389 35 USC § 202(c)(3).

390 35 USC § 202(c)(7)(B) and (C).

391 Also see e. g. de Larena (2006) 43 Hous. L. Rev. 1373, 1391.

392 35 USC § 202(c)(4).

393 Ibid.

394 GAO, *Biomedical Inventions* (2003) 5.

395 Ibid. 5, 12.

396 See de Larena (2006) 43 Hous. L. Rev. 1373, 1395–1396; GAO, *Biomedical Inventions* (2003) 10–12.

government to produce cost-effective alternatives to certain essential products (such as pharmaceuticals, for instance).[397]

2 March-In

Under the 'march-in' provision, the government agency may require a contractor, an assignee or exclusive licensee 'to grant a non-exclusive, partially exclusive, or exclusive license' of a federally funded invention to an interested third party.[398] The Act further qualifies that such licenses will be granted to 'responsible applicants' and 'upon terms that are reasonable under the circumstances'.[399] If such a request is refused, the federal agency may also 'march-in' and grant such a licence itself.[400]

The march-in provision further stipulates that the funding agency must determine that one of the following four circumstances exists in order for a license to be granted: 1) the contractor did not take effective steps to apply the invention to a field of use within a reasonable amount of time;[401] 2) the contractor did not use the invention to alleviate health or safety needs;[402] 3) the contractor did not satisfy a public need that is stipulated by federal regulations;[403] or, 4) there are formal constraints such as a breach of the licensing agreement.[404]

The march-in provision has been highly controversial.[405] While it uses potentially broad language, the determination of whether it can take effect is subject to extensive administrative proceedings and an administrative appeals procedure needs to be established.[406] Additionally, contractors, assignees, exclusive licensees as well as inventors which are adversely affected by a determination under the march-in provision may file a petition in the US Court of Federal Claims in order to reverse the determination.[407]

To this date, no federal agency has ever invoked the march-in provision.[408] Although it functions as a safeguard of the public interest, only the federal government has the authority to use it. This is unfortunate, as the legislative history

---

[397] For a detailed account on how government licenses would benefit the public in the context of pharmaceuticals, see de Larena (2005) 43 Hous. L. Rev. 1373, 1395–1396; also see GAO, *Biomedical Inventions* (2003) 8–12.

[398] 35 USC § 203(a).

[399] Ibid.

[400] Ibid.

[401] 35 USC § 203(a)(1).

[402] 35 USC § 203(a)(2).

[403] 35 USC § 203(a)(3).

[404] 35 USC § 203(a)(4).

[405] See e. g. McGarey and Levey (1999) 14 Berkeley Tech. L. J. 1095; O'Brien (2013) 43 Seton Hall L. Rev. 1403; Treasure and others (2014) 311 JAMA 907; Arno and Davis (2000) 75 Tul. L. Rev. 631, 642–691.

[406] 35 USC § 203(b) and 37 CFR § 401.6 (Exercise of march-in rights).

[407] Ibid.

[408] See e. g. Penman and Quigley (2017) 54 Willamette L. R. 171b 173.

of the Act indicates that it was anticipated for third parties to inform the federal government of possible needs for such action.[409] The only federal agency which has ever been petitioned to 'march-in' is the NIH, and although requests for march-in rights have become more vocal over the years, in all instances, the NIH has declined to act.[410]

3 Receiving Title

If the contractor fails to disclose a federally funded invention to the agency, the agency may receive title to the invention in question.[411] The government may also claim title to an invention if the contractor elected to retain title and agreed to file a patent but failed to file a patent application in the US or in other countries.[412] Additionally, if a contractor chooses not to retain title to a subject invention, the federal agency – after consulting with the contractor – may consider granting the individual inventor's request to retain rights to the invention.[413]

The logic of the BDA's provisions thus implies a bias towards patenting. According to this bias, the contractor (e. g. a university) may choose title of a federally funded invention but if it does not (or if it chooses to retain the title too late or does not file a patent application), the federal agency may receive the title of the invention and finally, if the contractor does not retain title of the invention, an inventor may request to retain rights to the invention and be granted to retain them.[414] In other words, the taking of title of a federally funded invention and its subsequent patenting is preferred above other means of disseminating the research results in question with the outside world.

This bias towards patenting has been reinforced by the 2018 amendment to the regulations which implement the BDA (the so-called 'Bayh-Dole Rule').[415] Under the new regulations, if a contractor fails to disclose or elect title to a federally funded invention within the stipulated timeframe, the government agency now has an indefinite time period (and not only 60 days as under the old regulation) to receive title of such an invention.[416] The change was implemented in an effort to hold universities and other contractors to their reporting require-

---

409 McGarey and Levey (1999) 14 Berkeley Tech. L. J. 1095, 1099; also see 37 CFR § 401.6 (b): 'Whenever an agency receives information that it believes might warrant the exercise of march-in rights, before initiating any march-in proceeding, it shall notify the contractor in writing of the information and request informal written or oral comments from the contractor as well as information relevant to the matter.'

410 Treasure and others (2014) 311 JAMA 907–908; O'Brien (2013) 43 Seton Hall L. Rev. 1403, 1405; Penman and Quigley (2017) 54 Willamette L. R. 171, 200.

411 35 USC § 202(c)(1).

412 35 USC § 202(c)(3).

413 35 USC § 202(d).

414 35 USC § 202(c)(2); § 202 (c)(1); § 202 (c)(3); § 202(d).

415 Regulations implementing the BDA are codified under 37 CFR Part 401.

416 37 CFR § 401.14(d)(1).

ments under the Act, which they have thus far largely neglected, as will be discussed below.

4 Enforcing the Bayh-Dole Act

The arguably biggest problem of the above discussed provisions, which allow the government to receive title in the outlined instances, is their enforcement. The enforcement of the BDA is left to the federal agencies. But the individual agencies are logistically unable to monitor universities and have to rely on universities to self-report patents which they received due to government funding.[417] Universities have systematically and continuously been violating these reporting requirements.[418] By failing to identify inventions which have been funded by the federal government, universities are disregarding their role as stewards of the public interest.[419] The failure to observe the reporting requirements may have profound implications. It may not allow the government to control the pricing of certain essential products which were developed based on federally funded inventions and which should benefit the public.[420]

It remains to be seen whether the changed deadlines and procedures in the above-mentioned amendments to the Bayh-Dole Rule will prompt universities to be more responsive and to observe their self-reporting duties. It also remains to be seen whether agencies will be more aggressive in asserting their rights in taking title to federally funded inventions.[421] It is unquestionable that universities should be held accountable for not complying with provisions stipulated by the BDA. Increasing the administrative hold over universities, however, might not be the optimal path. Instead, universities should overall be held to a stricter standard in the way they manage their federally funded inventions and research outputs in general. This will be discussed in the final chapter.

---

[417] See e. g. GAO, *Administration of the Bayh-Dole Act by Research Universities* (1998) 1, 6–13, detailing that the BDA relies on universities' willingness to 'voluntarily comply' with reporting and notifications requirements. Also see Arno and Davis (2000) 75 Tul. L. Rev. 631, 648–649; de Larena (2006) 43 Hous. L. Rev. 1373, 1396.

[418] Arno and Davis (2001) 75 Tul. L. Rev. 631, 677–679; GAO, *Reporting Requirements* (1999) 2: 'In our review of more than 2'000 patents issued in calendar year 1997 as well as an Inspector General's draft report on 12 large grantees of the NIH, we found that the databases for recording the government's royalty-free licenses are inaccurate, incomplete, and inconsistent and that some inventions are not being recorded at all.' Also see Locke (2003) Va. J. L. & Tech 1; de Larena (2006) 43 Hous. L. Rev. 1373, 1396–1399.

[419] Some go as far as to refer to it as 'theft of government property', see Arno and Davis (2000) 75 Tul. L. Rev. 631, 678.

[420] See ibid. 679.

[421] For a detailed overview of all the changes to the Bayh-Dole Rule, see e. g. Gardner and Haider, 'Practical Advice' (*Quarles & Brady*); also see infra 7.C.II.

D *Stanford v. Roche*: Back to Square One?

I Background and Legal Issue

In *Stanford v. Roche*[422], the Supreme Court addressed the question whether the BDA re-ordered the priority of ownership rights in federally funded inventions and thus whether it vested the ownership of such inventions directly with contractors. The case attracted much attention in academia and beyond. The Association of American Universities (AAU)[423], together with the Association of University Technology Managers (AUTM)[424] and a number of other academic associations[425], as well as the AAUP[426], both filed an amicus brief in support of Stanford.[427] The question whether federally funded inventions were assigned by operation of law to the contractor was especially important to universities, which – over the course of the previous couple of decades – had developed practices that relied on automatic assignment of such inventions.[428]

Indeed, it was this interpretation of the BDA which prompted some research universities to adopt generally liberal patent policies for inventions which did not arise under industry funding agreements. As a matter of fact, Stanford was such an institution and therefore benefitted from its reputation as a faculty friendly institution.[429] Before *Stanford v. Roche*, it was thus not common practice for universities to put pre-invention assignment agreements in place or to pay special attention to how such agreements or university patent policies were worded. *Stanford* changed this. Contrary to common belief, at its very core

---

[422] *Board of Trustees of Leland Stanford v. Roche Sys*., 131 S. Ct. 2188 (S. Ct. 2011) (hereinafter *Stanford III*).

[423] AAU is an association of 62 public and private research universities in the US and Canada. Its membership 'is by invitation and is based on the high quality of programs of academic research and scholarship and undergraduate, graduate, and professional education in a number of fields, as well as general recognition that a university is outstanding by reason of the excellence of its research and education programs.', see AAU website www.aau.edu.

[424] AUTM is a non-profit association with a focus on technology transfer between universities, research institutions, and third parties; it counts around 300 members worldwide, see AUTM website www.autm.net.

[425] See AAU and others (2011) *Stanford v. Roche.*

[426] AAUP is a non-profit association of faculty and other academic professionals. AAUP's mission is to advance academic freedom and shared governance; to define fundamental professional values and standards for higher education; to promote the economic security of faculty, academic professionals, graduate students, post-doctoral fellows, and all those engaged in teaching and research in higher education; to help the higher education community organize to make our goals a reality; and to ensure higher education's contribution to the common good, see AAUP website www.aaup.org.

[427] All amicus briefs are available on the website 'Supreme Court of the United States Blog' under *Board of Trustees of the Leland Stanford Junior University v. Roche Molecular Systems, Inc.*

[428] See e. g. AAU and others (2011) *Stanford v. Roche* 27–37.

[429] See infra n. 432/II and accompanying text.

Stanford was not about an interpretation of the BDA but about contract law and the art of contract drafting.

II The Facts

The facts of the case involve a small research company called Cetus which conducted research relating to methods of quantifying HIV in human blood samples. Cetus had developed the Nobel Prize winning technique 'polymerase chain reaction' (PCR) which was part of this research.[430] In 1988, Cetus started collaborating with researchers at Stanford University. The same year, Dr. *Mark Holodniy* joined Stanford as a research fellow and was asked to sign a Copyright and Patent Agreement (CPA) whereby he 'agree(d) to assign' his 'right, title, and interest in' inventions resulting from his employment to Stanford.[431] At the time, Stanford had a patent policy which allowed 'all rights to remain with the inventor if possible'.[432] In order to gain a better understanding of his research, *Holodniy*'s supervisor arranged for *Holodniy* to work at Cetus in order to learn about PCR.[433] Upon his arrival at Cetus, *Holodniy* was required to sign a Visitor Confidentiality Agreement (VCA) which stated that he 'will assign and do(es) hereby assign' to Cetus his 'right, title, and interest in each of the ideas, inventions, and improvements' made 'as a consequence of (his) access' to Cetus.[434]

In the nine months at Cetus, *Holodniy* conducted research together with other Cetus employees and developed an invention, a PCR-based procedure for calculating the amount of HIV in a patient's blood. It is this invention which is at the heart of the dispute. After his return to Stanford *Holodniy* continued to work on his invention, testing and refining it together with other Stanford researchers.[435] Stanford alleged that it received funding from the NIH in order to test and further refine the invention. In fact, these very funds or rather the origin of the funds provided the basis on which Stanford later claimed ownership rights to the invention under the BDA.[436]

Within the next few years, Stanford obtained written assignment agreements from all Stanford researchers involved in the testing and refining of the inven-

[430] *Board of Trustees of Leland v. Roche Molecular*, 487 F. Supp. 2d 1099 (Dist. Ct. 2007) (hereinafter *Stanford I*) 1105.

[431] *Stanford III* 2192.

[432] Murane and Tyndale, 'Should the Supreme Court Dismiss Certiorari' (*Intellectual Property Today*).

[433] There were two other researchers involved in the Stanford research, *Merigan* and *Katzenstein*, but to simplify the facts, it will be only referred to *Holodniy*, see *Stanford I* 1109.

[434] *Stanford III* 2192.

[435] Ibid.

[436] Ibid. 2193.

tion and filed several patent applications.[437] In 1995, *Holodniy* assigned his interests in the patent application to Stanford and the assignments were recorded at the USPTO.[438]

While Stanford was in the process of filing patent applications and assigning rights to inventions, in 1991, Cetus' PCR assets were acquired by Roche Molecular Systems, Inc. (Roche).[439] After the transaction, Roche started manufacturing HIV. detection kits which involved the invention in question.[440] In 2000, Stanford approached Roche asserting Stanford's ownership of the invention and offering Roche an exclusive licence to all patents descending from the patent application.[441] Negotiations and discussions between the two parties about ownership interests and possible licensing terms continued until spring of 2004.[442] Finally, in 2005, Stanford filed suit against Roche alleging that its HIV kits infringed Stanford's patents.[443] Stanford, basing its ownership claim on the BDA, asserted that *Holodniy* had no interest in the invention, and that therefore he could not have assigned it to Cetus.[444] Roche filed a counterclaim alleging that it possessed ownership, licence, and/or shop rights to the patents through its acquisition of Cetus' PCR assets and *Holodniy*'s assignment to Cetus.[445]

III The Rulings by the Courts

The district court held that *Holodniy*'s purported assignment to Cetus' conflicted with the legal requirements of the BDA.[446] According to the court, the Act mandated that Stanford be given a superior right to retain title to the patents. As a consequence, *Holodniy*'s assignment was superseded by Stanford's election to retain title.[447] In the district Court's reading of the BDA, the government had the 'right of first refusal' regarding the patents in question and, if the government indeed refused, Stanford had the 'right of second refusal'.[448] Because Stanford had elected to retain title, according to the court, 35 USC § 202(d) was never implicated.[449] The court's analysis confirmed the then popular belief that the BDA reordered the normal priority of rights in an invention conceived with

437 *Stanford III* 2192.
438 *Stanford I* 1109.
439 Ibid. 1105, 1109.
440 *Stanford III* 2192; *Board of Trustees of Leland Stanford v. Roche*, 583 F. 3d 832 (Court of Appeals, Federal Circuit) (hereinafter *Stanford II*) 838.
441 *Stanford II* 838.
442 Ibid.
443 Ibid.
444 *Stanford I* 1117–1120.
445 *Stanford II* 838.
446 *Stanford I* 1119.
447 Ibid.
448 Ibid.
449 Ibid.

federal funding.[450] Accordingly, an inventor could only obtain title to a federally funded invention after the government and the contractor had declined to obtain it. Following this reasoning, the court concluded that because Stanford exercised its right and obtained title in the patent, *Holodniy* had no interest to assign to Cetus, thereby rendering void the provision of the VCA.[451]

On appeal, the Federal Circuit reversed the district court's holding and rejected its reading of the BDA. More specifically, the Federal Circuit dismissed the district court's interpretation that the Act implies a 'right of second refusal' for contractors and in this instance for Stanford. It did not agree that 35 USC § 202(d) implied that *Holodniy* could only keep title to his invention if Stanford did not elect to retain title to it.[452] According to the Federal Circuit, the Act did not automatically void *Holodniy*'s assignment to Cetus.[453] The Federal Circuit further pointed out that the BDA regulated the relationship between the government and contractors, and not the relationship between contractors and the inventors who work for them.[454] Lastly, the court stressed that the wording 'do hereby assign' in Cetus' VCA created a present assignment of *Holodniy*'s future inventions to Cetus and that, in contrast, the wording 'agree to assign' used in Stanford's CPA only reflected a mere promise to assign rights in the future.[455] The Federal Circuit thus concluded that Cetus' VCA trumped Stanford's CPA.

The Supreme Court affirmed the Federal Circuit's holding. In its reasoning, the court reaffirmed the general rule it had earlier established that rights in an invention belong to the inventor.[456] The court also confirmed that the inventor could assign his rights in an invention to a third party, and that unless an employee-inventor expressly grants ownership rights to an employer, the employer does not have rights in an invention 'which is the original conception of the employee alone'.[457]

The court underlined that if Congress had intended the BDA to reorder the normal priority of rights in federally funded inventions, there would be unambiguous language to that effect. To illustrate this, the court pointed out that under certain federal contracts, inventors would be divested of their rights in their inventions, such as contracts dealing with nuclear material or atomic energy, or inventions made pursuant to contracts with the National Aeronautics and Space Administration.[458] According to the court, such unambiguous language

450 *Stanford III* 2195.
451 *Stanford I* 1119.
452 *Stanford II* 844.
453 Ibid.
454 Ibid. 845.
455 Ibid. 841–842.
456 *Stanford III* 2195.
457 Ibid.
458 Ibid.; also see 5.A.

was absent from the BDA, which meant that the BDA did not vest title to federally funded inventions in the contractor (and here in Stanford).[459]

The practical consequence of the court's analysis meant that the invention in question initially vested in *Holodniy* and that the ownership rights had to be determined based on contract law. The Court agreed with the Federal Circuit's conclusion that – based on its wording of 'agree to assign' – *Holodniy*'s initial agreement with Stanford in the CPA constituted a mere promise to assign rights in the future. In contrast, *Holodniy*'s agreement with Cetus in the VCA – which included the wording 'does hereby assign' – constituted a present assignment of *Holodniy*'s rights in the invention to Cetus. Therefore, concurring with the Federal Circuit's holding, the Supreme Court concluded that, as a matter of contract law, Cetus had obtained *Holodniy*'s rights.[460]

It is worth to briefly summarise the dissenting opinion of Justice *Breyer* – the main thrust of which was based on public policy and which would have placed title to Stanford.[461] In Justice *Breyer*'s view, the background against which BDA was passed would point to the Act's intent of leaving federally funded inventions in the hands of the recipients of the federal funds. Vesting title to inventions with contractors would encourage institutions to commercialise 'that otherwise might not realize their potentially beneficial public use'.[462] *Breyer* stressed that the consequence of the majority opinion – which allows individual inventors to lawfully assign federally funded inventions to third parties – was inconsistent with the Act's basic purpose.[463] In contrast to the majority opinion, *Breyer*'s understood the BDA to establish a three-tier system for the ownership in federally funded research under which universities have first, government has second, and employee inventors have third priority.[464]

E In Search of the Bayh-Dole Act's Intent

The *Stanford* ruling came as a shock to universities and their TTOs which had become comfortable on relying on the BDA for their ownership claims of federally funded inventions. After *Stanford*, they could no longer do so and had to ensure that they would acquire ownership rights by contractual assignment.

459 *Stanford III* 2195–2196, 2197: 'The Bayh-Dole Act does not confer title to federally funded inventions on contractors or authorize contractors to unilaterally take title to those inventions; it simply assures contractors that they may keep title to whatever it is they already have.'

460 Ibid. 2194.

461 See dissenting opinion by *Justice Breyer*, who was joined by *Justice Ginsburg*, ibid. 2199–2205.

462 Ibid. 2201.

463 Ibid.

464 Ibid. 2200.

Contract drafting suddenly became a crucial aspect to universities and their technology transfer operations. After all, had Stanford used different language in their assignment agreement, it most likely would have won the case. Justice *Ginsburg*'s statement in the case's oral argument sums this up beautifully: 'The whole thing that was wrong here is that Stanford, instead of drafting the agreement 'I agree to assign' should have said 'I hereby assign' and then there would have been no case.[465]

This new reality increased the administrative burden on universities and their TTOs which now had to ensure that assignments were properly worded and executed. As Justice *Breyer* in his dissent pointed out, despite the fact that there is an indication of which words are 'blessed' by the courts, the rule itself amounts to a 'technical drafting trap for the unwary'.[466] Given the often complex structure of a typical research project, which usually consists of a multitude of different types of researchers, in most instances, universities are no longer able to rely on standard employment contracts but will need to develop different contractual solutions for different situations. Coordinating these often overlapping and contradictory assignments which may arise from inter-institutional research projects may prove challenging to the point that universities may need to hire contract specialists.[467] As *Stanford* illustrated, such overlapping claims may often go unnoticed until a dispute arises.[468] Thus, making sure that the ownership assignments are correctly worded and executed is of utmost importance.

Unsurprisingly, universities responded to *Stanford* by rephrasing their intellectual property policies and implementing new clauses into their employment contracts. For instance, under Virginia Tech's old intellectual property policy, employees were merely obliged to assign the rights to the university upon request.[469] As a reaction to *Stanford*, the wording in the intellectual property policy was changed to 'do hereby assign'[470]. Other universities additionally started to require faculty, staff, student employees, graduate students, and postdoctoral fellows to sign separate patent assignment agreements.[471]

---

465 Supreme Court of the United States, '*Stanford v. Roche,* Oral Argument Audio Transcript' (*SCOTUS*) 36; *Stanford III* 2202.

466 *Stanford III* 2203.

467 The author served from 2014–2018 on the Board of Directors of the Technology Transfer Office of Virginia Tech (hereinafter 'TTO Board of Directors').

468 For a good overview of the legal issues surrounding university-industry collaborations, see e. g. Reder. 44 Bus. L. Rev. 225–227.

469 Virginia Tech Policy 13'000, 15 April 2008: 'Ownership of the IP rests with the university and the originator(s) are obliged to sign the appropriate legal assignment documents upon request.'

470 Virginia Tech Policy 13'000, 3 June 2013: 'Ownership of the IP rests with the university and the originator(s) do hereby assign ownership, right, title, and interest in any IP, discovery, or invention to the university.'

471 See e. g. 'Stanford University Patent Agreement', Stanford University Website (doresearch.stanford.edu).

Seen from this perspective – while attempting to move beyond the legal challenges which were created as a result of the different federal agencies' patent policies – the BDA created new legal complexities and uncertainties that perhaps were not intended. But it appears that some of the blame for the ever-increasing legal complexities universities have to deal with is also to be placed on universities themselves, which have continued to expand ownership claims to inventions in their quest to generate income from their patenting activities. Indeed, it often does not appear as if universities had a choice to retain title to federally funded inventions but were under an *obligation* to own patent rights to *all* university inventions instead.

This focus on the ownership of university inventions in conjunction with the default use of patents in an attempt to maximise potential licensing income is ultimately a reflection of the absence of a coherent university intellectual property strategy. An intellectual property strategy, which takes into account a university's research strengths, its characteristics (including its regional environment and existing partnerships with industry), and its institutional objectives and priorities, would allow a university to only employ patents where they are efficient and effective and would promote the use of other transfer channels in other instances. But because the strategic element in universities' technology transfer practices is generally absent, universities squarely focus on the ownership and patenting of inventions, thereby increasing the administrative workload and the legal responsibilities and, in most instances, losing money in the process.[472]

This is unfortunate. Considering the BDA's objectives, its core provisions, and its legislative history, it seems clear that this was not what Congress intended. Certainly, the desire was to find ways to commercialise federally funded inventions for the benefit of the public. But as the majority opinion in *Stanford* correctly observed, if Congress had intended for ownership rights to vest directly with universities, it would have found ways to do so.[473] Instead, it is more likely that the intent was for universities to have the *option* to retain title to inventions in situations where they felt strongly about commercially developing them.

[472] For a detailed discussion of theses aspects, see infra Chapter 7.
[473] See supra 5.D.III.

Part III

Towards a New University Research Transfer Model

Chapter 6

Public Policy and Law

A Universities as Instrument of Public Policy: From Splendid Isolation to Academic Capitalism

I The Bayh-Dole Act's Policy Assumptions

Long before the passage of the BDA, university research contributed to technical progress and economic development.[1] Indeed, there are many historical accounts of university-generated inventions which have ended up as commercial products or led to the founding of new and successful companies, such as GPS technology, MRI body scanning, the seat belt, the atomic force microscope, the technology behind Google's search engine, the vaccine for hepatitis B, the Excel spreadsheets, just to name a few.[2] Despite this positive impact on society, increased focus of policy makers on the role of universities in the innovation ecosystem is a more recent phenomenon, which gained a lot of traction since the 1970s. In these policy discussions, universities' main contribution was seen as the supplier of commercialisable knowledge and it was increasingly believed that patents were essential in facilitating the transfer of such knowledge from universities to industry.[3]

While some universities started to get involved in patenting and licensing activities in the early 20th century, in tendency, universities were reluctant to do so out of a fear that such activities would be in conflict with the academic mission, the commitment to open science and that they would impinge on the public's trust and support of academic researchers. Universities which did start to patent university research despite these concerns, generally did so with the hope that patents would help commercialise inventions for the benefit of the public, but they also employed patents for quality control reasons and to prevent wrongful appropriation of developed inventions. Perhaps most importantly, well into the 1960s, universities did not consider patents a standard solution to the dissemi-

---

[1] See e.g. R. Nelson (2004) 33 Research Policy 455, 467–468; R. Nelson (2001) 26 J. Tech. Transfer 13, 16.

[2] See e.g. Litan and others (2007) 23 Issues Sci. Tech. 57, 63; The Economist, 'Bayhing for Blood' (*Economist*); also see IP Advocate Foundation, 'University Inventions that changed the world (*IP Advocate Foundation*).

[3] See supra 2.B.I.; 5.B.II.; 5.B.III. and infra 6.A.II.

nation of university research and only employed them as they were needed on a case by case basis.[4]

Today, most universities in the US and many universities around the world pursue patenting and licensing activities.[5] This widespread introduction of university patenting is mainly a reflection of the commercialisation argument, which has been pushed on a policy level and has to be understood against the backdrop of a general trend of governments of industrialised nations to implement policies which aim at the enhancing of university-industry linkages. These policies are based on the premise that the exploitation of university research stimulates industrial innovation and economic development. In this very spirit, in the US, the BDA was introduced in the hope that it would encourage patenting of federally funded research and thereby increase the transfer of technology from universities to industry.[6]

The positive expectation was that through the use of patents faster and more effective (compared to other, more traditional channels of transfer) commercial exploitation of university research could be ensured. By the creation of new products and new jobs – through the creation of university spin-offs[7] – the

---

[4] See supra 2. B. I. and infra 7. A. I.

[5] While university patenting has become a global phenomenon, it appears that the top-patenting universities are predominantly in the US, see e. g. Fisch and others (2015) 40 J. Tech. Transfer 318. But there may be an alternative explanation for the top performance by US universities: In contrast to the US, in Europe firms and not universities often file the application on university inventions. Accordingly, about 80 % of patents filed at the EPO, which have at least one academic inventor, are not owned by a university. Thus, what appears to be a lack of university-invented patents may be a lack of university-owned patents, which could potentially translate to numbers of university-invented-owned patents that are similar to the US, see Crespi and others (2010) 19 Econ. Innov. New Tech. 627, 644.

[6] The BDA facilitated university patent and licensing activities in three ways: Firstly, it replaced the web of agencies' patent policies and IPAs which had been negotiated between individual universities and federal agencies with a uniform patent policy, see Mowery and others (2001) 30 Research Policy 99, 102. This generally reduced universities' administrative burden. Secondly, the Act was an expression of the Congressional support for universities to be able to negotiate exclusive licenses, see e. g. Clements (2008) 49 Idea 469, 479; Mowery and others (2001) 30 Research Policy 99, 102. Congress and universities both recognised exclusive licensing as the principal advantage that universities held, see Clements (2008) 49 Idea 469, 479, quoting the Senate Judiciary Committee: 'Universities, on the other hand, which can offer exclusive or partially exclusive licenses on their patents, if necessary, have been able to successfully license 33 % of their patent portfolios.' ibid. Finally, and more generally, in its logic the BDA reflects the view that failure to protect federally funded research with patents limits the commercial exploitation of the same, see e. g. Mowery and others (2001) 30 Research Policy 99, 102.

[7] Geuna and Nesta (2006) 35 Research Policy 790, 794; the underlying logic is that – due to the embryonic nature of the majority of university inventions – it is often difficult to assess their commercial potential. To have a reasonable chance of commercial success, significant additional development by the inventor is typically required – development that is ideally undertaken under the umbrella of a start-up company, see Jensen and Thursby (2001) 91 Am. Econ. Rev. 240, 240–241. Supporters of the BDA used this logic to argue that firms would typically

US economy would be reinvigorated, and society at large would benefit.[8] This would also ensure that research which was sponsored by the US government would be developed by US firms.[9]

Given the severe financial constraints which universities were more and more facing, another factor which made such policies particularly attractive was that they appeared to promise increased financial resources for little additional investment of public funds.[10] Not only was the hope that patents would induce the private funding necessary to develop existing university research into commercial products and bring them to the market, but it was also expected that universities could generate additional financial income to be re-invested in existing or new research endeavours.[11]

It is surprising that during the discussions leading up to the BDA, little focus was placed on understanding the nature of the knowledge flow between university and industry. More recent studies have examined the influence of university research on innovation in various industries and analysed university-industry knowledge flows.[12] These studies confirmed the substantial effects university research has on innovative activity and performance in industry.[13] But in contrast to what is often suggested, this importance is not limited to the generation of new ideas but it also exists in regard to the completion of existing projects.[14] Further, the relationship between university and industry varies greatly across industries, and the relative impact that university research has on industrial innovation also depends on the industry.[15] For instance, university research contributes to innovation across a broad segment of manufacturing sectors and has a direct and significant impact on innovation in the biomedicine sector, and especially in biotechnology and pharmaceuticals.[16]

Notably, the studies indicate that the main channels through which university research reaches industry are the traditional channels of open science: publications, conferences, informal contacts as well as consulting relationships and

---

not invest in these costly development activities unless they could obtain ownership rights to the respective invention, see Mowery and others, *Ivory Tower* (2004) 91.

[8] See e. g. Geuna and Nesta (2006) 35 Research Policy 790, 794; Mowery and others (2001) 30 Research Policy 99, 103.

[9] R. Eisenberg (1996) 82 Va. L. Rev. 1663, 1663–1665; Geuna and Nesta (2006) 35 Research Policy 790, 794.

[10] Mowery and others (2001) 30 Research Policy 99, 102–103.

[11] Indeed, universities financial motivation behind their involvement with patents has taken a life of its own, see infra 7.A.II.3.

[12] See e. g. Mowery and Sampat, in *Oxford Handbook* (2005) 210, 221; for a good review of studies conducted in this area, see Cohen, in *Economics of Innovation* (2010) 129, 179.

[13] Ibid. 180; Mansfield (1998) 26 Research Policy 773, 775, stating that over 10% of products and processes could not have been developed or developed without substantial delay in the absence of academic research.

[14] Cohen and others (2002) 48 Mgmt. Sci. 1, 2.

[15] Ibid. 2; Bekkers and Freitas (2008) 37 Research Policy 1837, 1837–1838.

[16] Ibid.; Mowery and Sampat, in *Oxford Handbook* (2005) 210, 221.

personnel mobility.[17] Indeed, it appears that in most instances, these channels are more important than patenting, licensing, and formal cooperative efforts, and that in general, only a minority of university-industry interactions are motivated by the prospect of directly realised commercial products.[18] The pharmaceutical industry is unusual also here as it assigns more importance to patents and licensing agreements than other industries; however, it still does not assign more meaning to patenting and licensing than to other transfer channels.[19] One explanation for this could be that the pharmaceutical industry – much earlier than other industries – strategically outsourced certain R&D needs and relied on research contributions from universities.[20]

In contrast to this data on the knowledge flows between universities and industry and the relevance of the different transfer channels, the BDA is built on a general assumption that patents are the essential vehicle to aid in the transfer and commercialisation of university research. As such, the Act reflects a narrow, linear understanding of innovation which centres on patents and ignores other channels of transfer. Implicitly, then, it is assumed that innovation can be planned or foreseen: Universities provide the basic input which is transferred through the use of patents to the highest bidder, which will further develop the invention and bring it to the market as commercial product. This contravenes the more modern understanding of the innovation process which assumes a non-linear process that is based on an exchange with feedback loops between university and industry.[21] The above discussed studies confirm this non-linear understanding: Transfer channels such as publications, meetings, and conferences allow for such reciprocal engagement and interaction.

To this day, it is controversial whether patents allow for more effective technology transfer and consequently whether the BDA had a positive effect on technology transfer, university-industry collaboration, and the US economy.[22] Despite this, policy makers and commentators in the US continue to adhere to the view that patents are the key ingredient to universities' technology transfer efforts. The positive expectations related to the effect of patents have also been

---

[17] See e. g. Cohen, in *Economics of Innovation* (2010) 129, 180; Agrawal and Henderson (2002) 48 Mgmt. Sci. 44, 45; D'Este and Patel (2007) 36 Research Policy 1295, 1296.

[18] Cohen, in *Economics of Innovation* (2010) 129, 180; Agrawal and Henderson (2002) 48 Mgmt. Sci. 44, 45: 'Our results suggest that a focus on patenting as a measure of the impact of university research must be carefully qualified by the recognition that patenting may play a relatively small role in the transfer of knowledge out of the university.' Also see D'Este and Patel (2007) 36 Research Policy 1295, 1296.

[19] Cohen, in *Economics of Innovation* (2010) 129, 180; Cohen and others (2002) 48 Mgmt. Sci. 1, 2.

[20] Also see the discussion supra 5. B. II. on the collaboration between university and industry in the field of organic chemistry.

[21] See supra 2. B. II. 2.

[22] See e. g. Mowery and others (2001) 30 Research Policy 103; Lemley (2016) 95 Tex. L. Rev. 1, 36; Backs and Stummer (2015) 65 Mgmt. Rev. Q. 35, 39.

transplanted to other parts of the world, including Europe, where policy discussions have consciously been influenced by the positive perception of the American experience.[23] Indeed, often the benefits of university patenting are presented without conclusive, statistical, empirical evidence.[24] As a result, governments around the world have been inspired to move away from their existing federal government or inventor ownership models and to introduce Bayh-Dole like legislation or at least to consider the introduction of the same.[25]

Such emulations seem misguided. As *Mowery and Sampat* observe, they often only result in a 'selective borrowing from another nation's policies for implementation in an institutional context that differs significantly from that of the nation being emulated'.[26] Important national and regional differences, such as the role of universities in relation to society and the national innovation system, the structure of higher education more generally, universities' different funding models, the relationship between universities and state and federal governments, as well as the structure of private industry and the general legal and policy environments, are often ignored.[27]

II The Bayh-Dole Act's Contribution to Commercialisation and the Economy

An extensive amount of literature has been published on the Act's impact on the US economy, university-industry collaborations and on its effect on universities, including universities' research missions.[28] The reception of the Act has

[23] See e. g. Geuna and Nesta (2006) 35 Research Policy 790, 794; Pavitt (2001) 10 Ind. Corp. Change 761; David (2005) 04–27 SIEPR 9.

[24] Geuna and Nesta (2006) 35 Research Policy 790, 794.

[25] Countries that introduced Bayh-Dole like legislation: South Africa, Brazil, the Philippines. For a more detailed discussion, see e. g. Mowery and Sampat (2005) 30 J. Tech Transfer 233, 241; also see Siepmann (2004) 30 U. Dayton L. Rev. 209, 240.

[26] Mowery and Sampat (2005) J. Tech Transfer 233, 241–242.

[27] Also see ibid. 211, 232–233. These policy efforts are not only questionable due to the lack of conclusive evidence of the effects of the BDA and of the relevance of patents in the technology transfer process but they also ignore the larger context within which technology transfer and industry-university collaboration happens. Accordingly, there are other factors which account for a successful university-industry interaction, such as the motivation of the researchers themselves, see e. g. D'Este and Patel (2007) 36 Research Policy 1295, 1296, illustrating that researchers choose to engage with industry because of potential additional research income, applicability of research, access to industry skills and facilities, and keeping abreast of industry problems. Finally, there are factors linked to effective technology transfer outside of the legal protection framework and the motivation of the researchers, such as the quality of a university's basic research endowments, the university's prestige, the organisational practices and funding surrounding technology transfer ('push factors'), and the existence of functioning regional social networks in which academics are integrated ('pull factor'), see e. g. Casper (2013) 42 Research Policy 1313, 1313–1314, 1322.

[28] For an overview see e. g. Grimaldi and others (2011) 40 Research Policy 1045; Nelson (2001) 13; Gotkin, *Bayh-Dole Act* (2012); Backs and Stummer (2015) 65 Mgmt. Rev. Q. 35.

been mixed. On the one side, the BDA has been touted as 'possibly the most inspired piece of legislation to be enacted in America over the past half-century' which 'helped to reverse America's precipitous slide into industrial irrelevance'[29] and for ultimately achieving its goals.[30] Accordingly, it has been praised for the increase in universities' patenting and licensing activities, which have led to enormous royalty incomes for some institutions, for the increase in collaborative research between university and industry, and in sum, for improved innovation and technology transfer efforts to the benefit of the public.[31]

On the other side, critics have questioned the Act's impact on technology transfer, suggesting that there is only minimal evidence that government ownership retarded the commercialisation of university inventions and that university ownership facilitates and accelerates technology transfer.[32] Moreover, and as was touched upon above, the effectiveness of patents in the technology transfer process has been questioned altogether.[33] According to these views, the BDA was only one of several different factors that contributed to a rise of university patenting and licensing activities.[34] Many critics also point to one of the fundamental arguments raised against the BDA before it was passed, namely, the concern over 'double paying', which will be addressed in detail in the final section of this chapter. Finally, the Act has also received a fair share of criticism for its unintended consequences, especially on aspects of the academic research mission.[35] This aspect will be covered in detail in the next section.

Undoubtedly, the BDA has been successful at establishing a uniform federal patent policy, a benefit which should not be underestimated and is often over-

29 See The Economist, 'Golden Goose' (*Economist*).

30 See e. g. GAO, *Administration of the Bayh-Dole Act by Research Universities* (1998) 2.

31 See e. g. GAO, *Patent Policy* (1987) 3; GAO, *Administration of the Bayh-Dole Act by Research Universities* (1998) 2; Bremer, Presentation (2001), also pointing out that the growth of the technology transfer function can be measured by the continuous growth of the membership in the ATUM; Loise and Stevens (2010) 52 Sci. Transl. Med. 185, 187–188; Schacht, *Bayh-Dole Act* (2010) 9, referring to the President of Yale who complimented the BDA for creating positive public benefits; Gotkin, *Bayh-Dole Act* (2012) 47, concluding that 'the BDA's effects on commercialisation are clear and positive'.

32 In order to illustrate how the government failed to commercialise federally funded inventions, supporters of the BDA presented data indicating that only a small portion of patents held by the government were actually licensed. This is misleading, as the data in question was predominately based on patents from the DOD, an agency that was liberal in giving patent rights to its contractors. It is probable that contractors were predominately interested in inventions that they expected to have commercial potential. By the same token, then, it is likely that the inventions that they did not seek to assert ownership over and remained with the DOD were the ones with little commercial potential, see R. Eisenberg (1997) 82 Va. L. Rev. 1663, 1702–1705, Mowery and others (2001) 30 Research Policy 102.

33 See supra 6. A. I.

34 Mowery and others (2001) 30 Research Policy 101.

35 See e. g. Leaf, 'Unintended Consequences' (*Fortune*), suggesting that 'the Bayh-Dole's impact was not so much in the industry it helped create, but rather in its unintended consequence – a legal frenzy that's diverting scientists from doing science'.

looked in the assessment of the BDA's contributions. By allowing universities to retain title to federally funded inventions, the BDA removed the uncertainties regarding the determination of ownership of federally funded research which were caused by the federal agencies' different policies. While the BDA may have increased universities' legal and administrative burden in other ways, as was illustrated above, this may be overcome by universities if they approach their technology transfer efforts more strategically.

More difficult is the question whether the BDA is the sole, or at least the main factor responsible for universities' positive patenting and licensing record, and to what extent these numbers adequately measure the positive effect the BDA had on the US economy. Since the adoption of the BDA, there has been a continuous increase in the numbers of US patents issued to universities. While in 1979 there were only 264 patents issued to universities, in 2017 the number reached 8'706.[36] Since 1996, academic institutions have accumulated over 380'000 invention disclosures of which more than 80'000 US patents were issued and which have led to the founding of over 11'000 start-ups.[37] A similar increase of licensing income has been reported: Licensing income of AUTM universities increased from USD 222 million in 1991 to USD 3.1 billion in 2017.[38] Finally, AUTM has estimated that academic technology transfer contributed USD 591 billion to the US gross domestic product and supported 4.3 million jobs since 1996.[39]

These figures are impressive. Nevertheless, they have to be read with caution in terms of their economic significance. There is only very little well-documented empirical evidence detailing the actual impact of university patents and licenses and of how the different data points correlate to each other.[40] More generally, it is questionable whether the commonly used measure of number of patents and patent citations is indeed meaningful to evaluate the impact of technology transfer and the effect of the BDA.[41] More significant values would be the rate at which knowledge is disseminated, the rate at which knowledge is applied commercially, or the economic value of patents.[42]

---

36 AUTM, '2020 Licensing Activity Survey' (*AUTM*) 11; Mowery and others (2001) 30 Research Policy 104.

37 AUTM, 'Academic Technology Transfer in Numbers' (*AUTM*) 1.

38 Ibid. 13; Mowery and others (2001) 30 Research Policy 104.

39 AUTM, 'Academic Technology Transfer in Numbers' (*AUTM*) 1–2; for a more detailed estimate of the contribution of university licensing to the US economy, see Roessner and others (2013) 42 Research Policy 23, 31.

40 See Roessner and others (2013) 42 Research Policy 23, 31; A. Nelson (2012) 41 Research Policy 678, 689, pointing out that the AUTM data provides no correlation between disclosures, patents, and licenses such that it is not possible to follow the fate of a given disclosure or a patent.

41 See e. g. Sampat and others (2003) 21 Int'l J. Ind. Org. 1371.

42 Crespi and others (2010) 19 Econ. Innov. New Tech. 627, 628.

The statistics also obscure the fundamental asymmetries among and within universities in relation to patenting and commercialising of university research. For one, most universities do not generate money from their patenting and licensing efforts. As a matter of fact, in recent years, only around 15 universities accounted for 70 % of all university licensing revenue.[43] Similarly, the majority of start-up companies have evolved out of only a few universities.[44] What is more, only universities from among the same group of institutions typically manages to make money from their technology transfer activities. Or stated differently, 85 % of all universities which engaged in technology transfer efforts regularly do not break even and thus operate on an operational loss.[45] Finally, the most successful universities based on licensing numbers or number of start-ups relate their success to a small fraction of their patented inventions (blockbuster patents).[46]

More notably, there are several other factors that may have inspired the described surge of patenting and licensing activities by universities after the 1980s, which makes it almost impossible to separate the effects of these factors to the ones of the Act.[47] At the time of its passage, the BDA was one aspect of a general shift in US policy toward stronger patent rights.[48] During the 1980s, Congress passed fourteen laws with the general purpose of strengthening the protection of intellectual property rights. The Court of Appeals for the Federal Circuit (CAFC), which was established in 1982, also emerged as a strong proponent of patentholders rights.[49]

Not to be missed in the list of factors that may have positively influenced university patenting is the 1980 Supreme Court decision *Diamond v. Chakrabarty*[50]. In this decision, the Supreme Court extended patentable subject matter to 'living things' as long as they were in some way 'modified' by humans. Before the decision, such inventions were excluded from patentability.[51]

---

[43] Valdivia, *University Start-ups* (2013) 1; Merrill and others, 'Billions at Stake' (*Bloomberg*). The same is the case in Europe, see e. g. Geuna and Nesta (2006) 35 Research Policy 790, 795.

[44] Hagelin, *Technology Innovation Law* (2011) 485.

[45] See e. g. Merril and others (2016); Valvida, *University Start-ups* (2013) 6–9.

[46] See e. g. Merril and others (2016); also see GAO, *Administration of the Bayh-Dole Act by Research Universities* (1998) 18, 54, 56; and typically over 90 % are directly federally funded, see ibid. 54, 56, 63; TTO Board of Directors (n. 467/II).

[47] Mowery and others (2001) 30 Research Policy 116; Rafferty (2008) 37 Research Policy 29, 39; making a similar argument for Europe, see Geuna and Nesta (2006) 35 Research Policy 790, 794.

[48] See Mowery and others (2001) 30 Research Policy 103.

[49] Katz and Ordover (1990) Brookings Pap. Micorecon. 137, 142, noting that the CAFC has upheld patent rights in 80 % of the cases it heard, compared to only 30 % pro-patentholder decisions prior to its the establishment in 1982; Henry and Turner (2006) 35 J. Legal Stud. 85, 87, stating that the CAFC has earned the reputation as a 'pro-patent court'; Lemley (2016) 95 Tex. L. Rev. 1, 7.

[50] *Diamond v. Chakrabarty*, 447 U. S. 303 (1980).

[51] Ibid. 313–314. Referring to the type of subject-matter which is excluded from patent-

All these changes led or at least strongly supported the growth of university research in the field of biomedicine and especially biotechnology – fields which were (and still are) of great interest to industry.[52] Biomedicine (including pharmaceuticals) tends to be one of the few industries where patents are regarded as essential to the development of commercially successful products.[53] It is not surprising then, that biomedicine has become an area of extremely high university patent activity.[54] Finally, during this time, university researchers also found new ways to use computers in their research and in the development of software technologies – an area which was equally interesting to industry.[55]

Taking into account these developments and the fact that universities had begun to expand patenting activities before the BDA, it seems all but certain that the increase in numbers is not only a result of a change in policy but represents the acceleration of a trend which was strongly shaped by the growing opportunities in the biomedical sciences and other new research fields, and importantly, which predated the BDA. Consequently, it could be argued that the BDA was as much an effect as it was a cause of an increased patenting effort by universities.[56]

This conclusion also seems to be supported by another observation: the resilience of the patent ecosystem to changes in the law. A recent study by *Lemley* suggests that changes in patent law do not substantially influence the overall operation of and behaviours associated with the patent ecosystem.[57] There is little evidence that 'patent owners and patent challengers actually behave differently

ability the court held: 'The relevant distinction was not between living and inanimate things, but between products of nature, whether living or not, and human-made inventions.', ibid. 313.

52 See e. g. Mowery and others (2001) 30 Research Policy 116.

53 See Levin and others (1987) Brookings Pap. Econ. Act. 783, 796, 817, finding that patent protection of drugs is generally strong and effective; Mansfield (1986) 32 Mgmt. Sci. 173, 174. Also see Bessen and Meurer, *Patent Failure* (2008) 14–15, arguing that pharmaceutical and chemical industries are the ones benefiting from the existence of the patent system. In these industries firms typically earn more from their patents than they lose to litigation.

54 Mowery and others (2001) 30 Research Policy 117, finding that the patent and licensing portfolios of three universities (University of California, Stanford, Columbia) displayed remarkable similarities a decade after the passage of the BDA: A very small share of patent inventions accounted for the majority of licensing income, and more importantly, the big earners were concentrated in the biomedical field. This seems also to be the case in Europe, see Geuna and Nesta (2006) 35 Research Policy 790, 794, concluding that the rapid rise of academic patenting was more likely linked to growing opportunities in biomedical science than to any policy changes implemented.

55 Colyvas and others (2002) 48 Mgmt. Sci. 61, 62.

56 Also see Mowery and others (2001) 30 Research Policy 104; Mowery and others, *Ivory Tower* (2004) 97; Geuna and Nesta (2006) 35 Research Policy 790, 794.

57 Lemley (2016) 95 Tex. L. Rev. 1, arguing that changes in the USPTO, the process of litigation, and the substance of legal rules (continuously oscillating between stronger and weaker patent protection) seem to have little effect on how many applications are filed, how many patents are issued, how many patents are licensed, how many suits are filed, and who wins those suits.

because of changes in the law'.[58] Instead, it appears that patent prosecution and patent litigation have their own internal dynamics and justifications. The reasons why people file patents or pursue patent litigation may not depend very heavily on the strength of the patent rights and the enforceability of patents.[59] Rather, patents seem to be like a trophy – an end in itself.[60] This would suggest that patents and behaviours associated with the patent ecosystem are more of a socio-economic phenomenon than is typically understood or acknowledged.

Applied to the context of universities, this would provide for an alternative explanation for the increase in patenting activities, according to which universities pursue patents not for the benefits they may provide in the commercialisation process but simply because universities believe patents to be valuable. It is not uncommon for universities to mimic each other's approaches, such as the drafting of intellectual property policies, the set-up of TTOs, and more recently, the founding of larger on-campus services, such as so-called business engagement centres or offices.[61] It is likely that the same is happening in regard to patenting and licensing activities, fuelled by a growing presence and awareness of universities' patent statistics and rankings.

Universities' desire to excel at patenting could thus be seen as a continuum of the ever-expanding, publicity-conscious, and commercially active university which *Thorstein Veblen* criticised at the turn of the twenty-first century.[62] The focus that is placed on patents, the desire to do well in patent statistics and to maximise licensing income, appear to be driven much more by the business-minded administration than by the faculty.[63] This would also suggest – in contrast to what the supporters of the BDA argue[64] – that the availability of patents for university research does not per se stimulate the further development of such research but is desirable in itself.

Ultimately, it will be difficult to conclusively establish whether these positive developments in the area of technology transfer would have happened without the passage of the Act. Nor will there probably ever be persuasive evidence

---

[58] Ibid. 2.

[59] Ibid. 40, 53: 'Patent applications may be driven by economic considerations almost entirely independent of the enforceability of the resulting patents.'

[60] Ibid. 53–54, comparing the market of patents to the markets of tulips or gold: 'There is no underlying intrinsic value for which people are paying; the asset is valuable because, and only to the extent that, people think it is valuable.', ibid. 54.

[61] See supra n. 69/I and infra n. 168/III and n. 199–200/III and accompanying discussions respectively. There is anecdotal evidence from Virginia Tech when during the process of the re-writing of the intellectual property policy, the review of the TTO, and the establishment of a new 'business engagement office' direct inspiration was sought from peer institutions.

[62] Veblen, *Conduct of Universities by Business Men* (2015).

[63] This is also in line with a general concern over a growing dominance of university administrators over faculty, according to which administrators tend to view management as an end in itself; to that effect see e. g. Ginsberg, *Faculty* (2011).

[64] See e. g. Pulsinelli (2005) 7 Minn. J. L Sci. & Tech. 393, 435–436.

to establish whether or to what degree patents further research, and whether the patent system actually drives innovation for that matter.[65] More importantly, however, and irrespective of the cause for the increase in patenting and licensing activities, the positive patent and licensing numbers have to be weighed against some of the arguably negative effects of university patenting activities, as will be discussed below.

III The Impact of the Bayh-Dole Act on the Academic Research Mission

1 The Threat to the Scientific Commons: The Emptying of the Research Pipeline

Aside from the arguably positive effects of university patenting activities on university-industry collaboration and technology transfer, an important consideration is the effect of such activities on the academic scientific performance and the long-term effect on the public. As discussed above, there is reason to believe that the BDA triggered something of an arms race where universities rushed into joining or intensifying their patenting and licensing efforts based on reasons beyond desired commercialisation of their research. The consequence is a steady privatisation of the scientific commons which is essentially caused by the use of patents.[66] Patents pose a challenge to the very core of the academic research mission and have a negative impact on alternative channels of knowledge transfer.[67] On the most general level, patenting is clearly at odds with the process of scientific publication: While publication focuses on rapid and free dissemination of the knowledge in question, the patent process requires secrecy before the patent application is filed.

University research tends to be revealed rapidly, disseminated widely and freely.[68] Universities traditionally have been the principal performers of basic 'curiosity-driven' research, the protection of which was typically not a concern. Indeed, and as pointed out above, out of a fear that patenting would compromise the commitment to knowledge dissemination and open science, universities normally refrained from pursuing patent (or any other intellectual property) protection. Free access and dissemination of knowledge is key to the open science model and its incentive structure, which centres on the production of knowledge and the training and teaching of students. Recognition and advancement in academia depend predominately on publication – in this regard, the disclosure of research findings is very much desired. Finally, university research is also key to the larger innovation ecosystem. The process of advancing new

65 See e. g. Lemley (2015) 62 UCLA L. Rev. 1328, 1334.
66 Also see e. g. R. Nelson (2004) 33 Research Policy 455, 457–460.
67 See e. g. Crespi and others (2011) 40 Research Policy 55, 56.
68 David and Hall (2006) 767.

science and technology is evolutionary: Existing research often builds the foundation for further research (both in private and public sectors).[69]

Conversely, in the private sector, research findings are often kept secret or disclosed only selectively and when they are disclosed, the use is typically restricted by one or another form of intellectual property protection.[70] A rapid dissemination of such findings is thus normally not desired in order not to jeopardise the economic value and success of the research in question. Moreover, payment is typically expected in return for sharing those research findings.[71]

Decades ago, there was a more or less clear separation between the two different research schemes. However, this has changed and today, universities participate in both worlds.[72] By exposing universities to patents (and intellectual property rights), universities have been dragged into the realm of organisational and institutional research, and with it, the corresponding mind-set has been impressed upon universities. Of big concern is the restriction this imposes on the free access and dissemination of university research and the impact this inevitably has on the academic autonomy and scientific integrity – elements which are fundamental to the open science culture.

Universities have been encouraged by the BDA to consider commercial and monetary motives over the traditional mission of providing research for the general benefit of the public. The different regimes under which research is conducted in industry and university and the different cultural disclosure norms – while not absolute and different according to area and industry – may not only provide an obstacle to close industry-university collaboration but could impede the free flow of knowledge between university and society and ultimately impoverishes the public domain.[73]

The continuous push to commercialise research, which before the widespread use of patents used to be shared in an unencumbered way, may thus lead to an 'emptying of the research pipeline'.[74] This research pipeline used to be the foundation upon which scientific progress and innovation were built. To that effect, it has been shown that without open access to scientific and technological research other-follow-on research would not have been possible, or at the very least not as quickly as it has.[75] Such 'enabling' knowledge is essential and

[69] See e. g. David and Hall (2006) 767; Dasgupta and David (1994) 23 Research Policy 487, 517; R. Nelson (2004) 33 Research Policy 455, 455.

[70] See e. g. David and Hall (2006) 767.

[71] See e. g. Dasgupta and David (1994) 23 Research Policy 487, 517.

[72] For a detailed analysis of the conflict arising due to the disappearing boundary between research conducted by public institutions and research conducted by the private sector, see David and Hall (2006) 767.

[73] See e. g. Dasgupta and David (1994) 23 Research Policy 487, 517; R. Eisenberg (1996) 82 Va. L. Rev. 1663, 1667, Mowery and Sampat, in *Oxford Handbook* (2005) 210, 213; Schacht, *Bayh-Dole Act* (2010) 19.

[74] Also see infra n. 369/III and n. 396/III and accompanying discussions respectively.

[75] See R. Nelson (2004) 33 Research Policy 455, 463–467, stating that outputs of research

builds the foundation of universities' research enterprise. The use of patents and the continuous push to protect and commercialise such research, however, empties the research pipeline and, in doing so, weakens the foundation upon which future research depends. Ensuring that the scientific commons is protected and that the majority of university research remains freely accessible seems thus essential to the future of scientific and technical progress and finally also to a meaningful future of universities.

Two specific situations in which the use of patents may hinder research, and which have been extensively studied will be discussed below. The first one is the situation where the development of a useful product or technique is inhibited as the science and technology that is necessary for the research is covered by multiple patents. The other one is the problem which arises where 'research tools' are protected by a patent. But before discussion turns to these two specific situations, the impact patents have on publications will first be analysed.

2 Patents and Publications

Since the passage of the BDA, a large body of literature has been published evaluating the potentially negative impact of university patenting on the academic mission. One of the key questions that has emerged is whether there is a negative relationship between patenting and publication. On the whole, it appears that the question may be answered in the negative: At least for top academics there seems to be no substitution effect between patent and publication activities.[76] Indeed, some studies find evidence not only that academic inventors publish more, but also that patenting volume may be positively correlated to research impact.[77] Despite these positive indicators, there is also indication that the increased involvement with patents and collaboration with industry do negatively weigh on publication behaviours and on other aspects of the academic research mission in the following ways.

Firstly, it appears that especially most productive and entrepreneurially spirited faculty have been found to delay or even forego publication in favour of

---

almost never are final products or even close to final products, but that they have their main use in further research directed at advancing science and in doing so enable the development of useful products or processes at a later stage. Also see e. g. Lemley (2005) 58 Stan. L. Rev. 601, 609–611; Scotchmer (1991) 5 J. Econ. Persp. 29, 30–31.

[76] See e. g. Crespi and others (2011) 40 Research Policy 55, 55, but also noting that some evidence is contradictory, ibid. 55.

[77] See e. g. Perkmann and others (2013) 42 Research Policy 423, 428; Agrawal and Henderson (2002) 48 Mgmt. Sci. 44, 46; Azoulay and others (2009) 57 J. Ind. Econ. 637, 638. There is also evidence that the complementarity of the two activities depends on the field of research. Accordingly, the most basic sciences, such as physics and chemistry, for instance, show evidence of a crowding-out effect, i. e. higher levels of patenting are associated with lower levels of publishing, see Crespi and others (2011) 40 Research Policy 55, 56.

patent protection.[78] While not a wide-spread phenomenon, it seems to be especially pronounced in the life sciences and in areas where industry sponsorship is involved in a research project.[79] Some faculty – in an effort to protect the commercial value of their research results – seem to be willing to delay publication out of their own accord. Moreover, universities and industry sponsors generally require, or at least encourage, the delay of publication or the presentation of research results at conferences until after the filing of a patent application is completed.[80]

Secondly, there is indication that academic researchers who are involved in commercialisation activities exercise higher degrees of secrecy than their non-commercialising colleagues.[81] And more worryingly perhaps, there is also evidence that there is a trade-off between academic knowledge accumulation and commercialisation of university based research.[82] In other words, there appears to be an increasing trend among university faculty to pursue commercialisation using employment positions at for-profit firms, such as spin-offs.

This may adversely affect traditional academic outputs, such as the number of journal publications, impact factors-weighted publications, grant research awards, and patents.[83] Research also suggests that increased patenting may result in a reduction in the exploitation by other researchers and, as such, may slow the unencumbered diffusion of academic knowledge.[84] There is also concern that the patenting of basic research findings, particularly where they are primarily valuable as inputs into further research, poses an obstacle to further research.[85] This is in line with research which suggests that, on a more general level, stronger intellectual property rights limit the degree of spillover and may reduce the efficient sharing of research findings.[86]

Thirdly, there is indication that patenting induces a shift in the content of the research undertaken and that resources are increasingly directed away from basic research to more commercially viable areas.[87] This occurs not only be-

---

[78] See e. g. Blumenthal and others (1997) 277 JAMA 1224, 1224; Lemley (2008) 18 Fordham Intell. Prop. Media & Ent. L. J. 610, 620.

[79] See e. g. Kneller (2001) 7 Clinical Cancer Research 761, 768; Blumenthal and others (1997) 277 JAMA 1224, 1224.

[80] See TTO Review (n. 288/III); also see e. g. Blumenthal and others (1997) 1224; Bagley (2005) 47 B. C. L. Rev. 217, 218; also see infra n. 268–273/III and accompanying discussion on universities' practice of filing provisional patent applications.

[81] Perkman and others (2013) 428.

[82] Toole and Czarnitzki (2010) 56 Mgmt. Sci. 1599, 1612.

[83] See Ibid. 1612.

[84] Murray and Stern (2006) 7 Innov. Policy & Econ. 33, 61; Perkmann and others (2013) 42 Research Policy 423, 428.

[85] See infra 6. A. III. 3.

[86] Katz and Ordover (1990) Brookings Pap. Micorecon. 137, 142.

[87] R. Nelson (2001) 26 J. Tech. Transfer 13, 15, Azoulay and others (2009) 57 J. Ind. Econ. 637, 638; Backs and Stummer (2015) 65 Mgmt. Rev. Q. 35, 45, noting that a similar shift in research content due to industry-contributions has been found in research institutes in Germany.

cause an individual researcher might allocate his time to different projects, but also because patenting researchers will gain visibility in industry circles, which will enhance opportunities to collaborate with industry, which in turn is likely to lead to a researcher's increased sensitivity to questions that are of relevance to industry.[88]

Finally, there is ever-growing concern over conflicts of interest among university researchers. There have been increasing accounts where the integrity of university research has been compromised through industry funding.[89] A lot may be at stake: A study may cast doubt on the products or methods of a company or entire industry, and as a result, corporate sponsors may be easily tempted to try to influence the outcome.[90] While perhaps not directly associable with patenting, it nevertheless illustrates the problems and temptations that may arise due to the mixing of the two research environments.

And there are other issues of conflict of interests as well, for instance where a faculty has a financial as well as a scientific interest in a research endeavour. This is often the case in pharmaceutical or biotechnology research where a successful product may yield a big financial pay-off. The more a researcher is involved in entrepreneurial activities, the more it has become a challenge to determine how such a researcher is to split his time between his traditional university duties (such as teaching and administrative duties) and his research driven activities, which may predominately be driven by non-academic i. e. financial interests.[91]

3 Blocking Patents and Experimental Use Exemption

Under US patent law, a patent gives his owner the right to exclude others from making, using, selling, offering to sell, and importing the protected invention.[92] Because patents do not confer an absolute right to practice the invention, patents may 'block' each other. In other words, an invention, although patentable, may infringe on an earlier invention. In order to be able to practice or improve the invention, a licence to the earlier patent will have to be obtained and in instances where multiple patents need to be combined in order to make a product or technology, cross-licences have to be negotiated.[93] A situation with blocking

[88] Azoulay and others (2009) 57 J. Ind. Econ. 637, 643.

[89] This problem seems to be particularly pronounced in the medical and biotech fields, see e. g. Ornstein and Thomas, 'Top Doctors' Ties to Industry' (*New York Times*).

[90] See e. g. Bok, *Commercialization of American Research Universities* (2004) 32, 41: 'Companies endangered in this way may try to cultivate and reward 'friendly' academic experts or actually harass and intimidate scientific experts who threaten to publish results damaging to their products.'

[91] See e. g. R. Nelson (2001) 26 J. Tech. Transfer 13, 17; Clements (2008) 49 Idea 469, 488.

[92] 35 USC § 271.

[93] See e. g. Schechter and Thomas, *Patent Law* (2004) 4–5.

patents normally involves a 'pioneer' and one or multiple 'improver(s)' where one or more refuse to cross-license their respective aspect of the product or technology.[94] Because there is only a limited experimental use exemption available under US common law, problems for universities could potentially arise if a patent is used to block the development of research.

The origin of the common law experimental use exemption can be traced back to the early 19th century. It recognises that a purely 'experimental use' of a patented invention, with no commercial purpose, should be exempt from claims of infringement.[95] The experimental use exemption reflects the idea that patent law is eminently a utilitarian doctrine and that pure research, which is not directed towards profits, should not be deemed an infringement as it does not interfere with the pecuniary interests of the patentee.[96] When the exemption was developed by the courts, the distinction between using patented subject-matter to learn about the patented invention, which should be exempt from patent infringement, versus using patented subject-matter for business or commercial purposes, which should not, seemed relatively straightforward.[97] Accordingly, the originally established distinction between uses of an intellectual character and uses for sale persisted well into this century.[98] Still, there were cases which raised hard questions, for instance, whether the activities necessary for Food and Drug Administration (FDA) approval of generic drugs would be considered infringing or not.[99]

In the context of academia, cases involving the common law experimental use exemption have only rarely arisen. This is not surprising, after all, academic scientists have historically not patented their inventions, nor have they gen-

---

94 Merges (1994) 62 Tenn. L. Rev. 75.

95 Pulsinelli (2005) 7 Minn. J. L Sci. & Tech. 393, 418–419; R. Eisenberg (1989) 56 U. Chi. L. Rev. 1017, 1018–1019.

96 Pulsinelli (2005) 7 Minn. J. L Sci. & Tech. 393, 419–420.

97 See e. g. Dreyfuss (2004) 46 Ariz. L. Rev. 457, 457–458.

98 For a detailed account, see ibid. 458. For a history of the statutory experimental use defence, which will not be addressed in detail, see e. g. ibid. 459–451.

99 *Roche Products v. Bolar Pharmaceutical Co.*, 733 F.2d 858 (Fed. Cir. 1984): The defendant's argument was that if research and testing on a patented drug prior to the expiration of the patent was not considered to fall within the experimental use exemption there would be a delay between patent expiration and the public's access to generic drugs. The court held, however, that such activities would not fall within the common law experimental use defence, see ibid. 863. The decision was soon overturned with the passage of the Hatch-Waxman Act of 1984, in exchange for a new statutory experimental use defence. The statutory defence only applied to 'uses reasonably related to the development and submission of information under a federal law which regulates the manufacture, use, or sale of drugs' (35 USCA §271(e)(1), see Dreyfuss (2004) 46 Ariz. L. Rev. 457, 459; Pulsinelli (2005) 7 Minn. J. L Sci. & Tech. 393, 426. In this case, the Federal Circuit did not address the common law experimental use exemption but several years later, in *Embrex, Inc. v. Service Engineering Corp.*, 216 F.3d 1343 (Fed. Cir. 2000). *Judge Rader* indicated what was later to come when he stated in his concurrence that the experimental use defence no longer existed, see Pulsinelli (2005) 7 Minn. J. L Sci. & Tech. 393, 426.

erally been mindful of patent law as it applies to their research.[100] Moreover, the experimental use exemption has usually operated in an informal manner in the context of academia: University researchers have typically simply ignored patent protection or have assumed that non-profit academic research was excused from patent infringement liability and that they could use patented inventions and technologies without having to pay any royalties.[101] Additionally, firms were often reluctant to enforce their patents against universities because of the low damage awards and bad publicity which suing a university typically would entail.[102]

This interpretation of the experimental use exemption was most recently scrutinised in *Madey v. Duke University*[103]. Professor *Madey*, a physicist, had developed a field electron laser while at Stanford University and obtained patent protection for the invention.[104] He left Stanford for Duke University, where he integrated some of the technology in his new lab.[105] After the employment relationship with Duke unravelled and Duke continued to use his technology, *Madey* sued Duke for patent infringement. Duke in turn asserted a defence based on experimental use.[106]

The Federal Circuit held that university research did typically not fall under the exemption because it was not 'strictly philosophical'[107] in nature or conducted to satisfy 'idle curiosity'.[108] *Madey* narrowed down the experimental use exemption to the point where essentially any patented technology which is used

[100] See e. g. infra n. 291/III and accompanying text.

[101] See e. g. Walsh and others, in *Patents in the Knowledge-based Economy* (2003) 285, 324–325; Pulsinelli (2005) 7 Minn. J. L Sci. & Tech. 393, 425; Strandburg (2004) Wis. L. Rev. 84–85.

[102] Walsh and others, in *Patents in the Knowledge-based Economy* (2003) 285, 325–326; Eisenberg and Cook-Deegan (2018) 147 Daedalus 76, 83.

[103] *Madey v. Duke University,* 307 F.3d 1351 (2002).

[104] Ibid. 1352.

[105] Ibid.

[106] Ibid. 1353.

[107] This reading of the word 'philosophical' has been criticised. It goes back to the 1813 case of *Whittemore v. Cutter*, 29 F. Cas. 1120 (1813), in which *Justice Story* held: 'It could never have been the intention of the legislature to punish a man, who constructed such a machine merely for philosophical experiments, or for the purpose of ascertaining the sufficiency of the machine to produce its described effects.' However, in *Integra Lifesciences I v. Merck* 545 US 193 (S. Ct. 2005), in a dissenting opinion *Judge Newman* noted that back then 'philosophical experiments' referred to what we understand of 'science' today. For a detailed account on the history of the experimental use defence, see e. g. Pulsinelli (2005) 7 Minn. J. L Sci. & Tech. 393, 419–428.

[108] *Madey* 1362: 'In short, regardless of whether a particular institution or entity is engaged in an endeavour for commercial gain, so long as the act is in furtherance of the alleged infringer's legitimate business and is not solely for amusement, to satisfy idle curiosity, or for strictly philosophical inquiry, the act does not qualify for the very narrow and strictly limited experimental use defence. Moreover, the profit or non-profit status of the user is not determinative.'

in the course of university research would not qualify.[109] The effect of the holding is thus that most university researchers would now need to obtain a licence from patentees in order to be able to legally pursue their research.[110]

Many commentators expressed concern over the *Madey* decision because of the significant chilling effect it could potentially have on university research and basic science and have therefore suggested the legislative adoption of an exemption for basic or non-profit research.[111] Certainly, the absence of an effective research exemption may lead to complex legal situations for universities and requires universities and their TTOs to be more on guard. While this is more cumbersome than before *Madey*, it seems to be the logical consequence of universities' increasing commercial behaviour: They now are treated like any institution attempting to advance its business interests.[112]

In *Madey*, the Federal Circuit abandoned the distinction between 'commercial' and 'non-commercial' uses which it had established in *Roche Products v. Bolar Pharmaceuticals, Inc.*[113] and shifted its focus on the core question of whether Duke's conduct was in keeping with the 'legitimate business' of the infringer.[114] The court held that university research projects 'unmistakably further the institution's legitimate business objectives, including educating and enlight-

---

109 See e. g. Walsh and others, in *Patents in the Knowledge-based Economy* (2003) 285, 335. The BDA does not foresee a research exemption for universities either. While there is an effective research exemption for the federal government under which the government is provided with a non-exclusive licence of federally funded inventions (35 USC § 202), there is no such licence for universities.

110 Also see e. g. Dreyfuss (2004) 46 Ariz. L. Rev. 457, 461.

111 See e. g. Walsh and others (2003) 335; Strandburg (2004) Wis. L. Rev. 83–85; R. Eisenberg (2003) 299 Science 1019; Derzko (2003) 20 Santa Clara Computer & High Tech. L. J. 347, 365–366, referring to the appeal of Duke University to the Supreme Court that was largely supported by the academic community. Accordingly, concern was raised that *Madey* would stifle university research and scientific progress and would endanger US leadership in science and technology. The academic community was also concerned about the additional resources they would have to spare in order to cover patent searches, licensing efforts, and litigation expenses, see ibid. 365–366 (quoting Brief of Amicus Curiae Association of American Medical Colleges). Boettiger and Bennett (2006) 24 Nature 320, 321; Rowe (2005) 57 Hastings L. J. 921, 922. Several commentators suggested the adoption of an experimental use defence through legislation, such as through an amendment to the BDA, see e. g. Dreyfuss (2004) 46 Ariz. L. Rev. 457, 461; Pulsinelli (2005) 7 Minn. J. L Sci. & Tech. 393, 425. For the suggestion of an exemption for research intended for the public domain or non-profit research, see e. g. Walsh and others, in *Patents in the Knowledge-based Economy* (2003) 285, 335; Dreyfuss (2003) 59 N. Y. U. L. Sch. Pub. L. 1, 8–11.

112 See *Madey* 1362: '[…] regardless of whether a particular institution or entity is engaged in an endeavour for commercial gain, so long as the act is in furtherance of the alleged infringer's legitimate business and is not solely for amusement […] the act does not qualify for the very narrow and strictly limited experimental use defence.'

113 *Roche Products v. Bolar Pharmaceuticals Co.*, 733 F. 2d 858 (Fed. Cir. 1984).

114 Ibid. 863: 'We cannot construe the experimental use rule so broadly as to allow a violation of the patent laws in the guise of 'scientific inquiry,' when that inquiry has definite, cognizable, and not insubstantial commercial purposes.'; *Madey* 1362.

ening students and faculty participating in these projects'.[115] The court continued to explain that such research projects 'also serve, for example, to increase the status of the institution and lure lucrative research grants, students, and faculty'.[116]

As some of the critics have argued, it is perhaps not easy to imagine what type of research would qualify as being 'solely for amusement, to satisfy idle curiosity, or for strictly philosophical inquiry'[117], especially since research which is aimed at 'enlightening students and faculty' is in the category which is not exempt from infringement liability.[118] While the court did not explain why university research – as a matter of principle – should fall outside of the exemption, it explained that Duke could not rely on its non-profit educational status while pursuing 'an aggressive patent licensing program'.[119]

From a policy perspective, the outcome of the decision seems thus fair. While universities predominately conducted (basic) research for its own sake, it made sense to treat (non-commercial) university research differently to research conducted with a (for-profit) motivation in industry.[120] Today, however, the nature and the motivation of university research is often no longer solely non-commercial.[121] Universities have not only been increasingly engaged in patent prosecution, licensing, and litigation but they also have embraced their participation in general business and entrepreneurial activities, including the setting up of seed funding, entertaining incubators, and increasingly seeking out industry partnerships. Under this aspect, it would be difficult to justify exempting universities' infringement of patents in the pursuit of their research activities while holding their industry counterparts accountable for the same behaviour.

It appears that *Madey* would have presented a great opportunity for universities to realise that the tide might be turning and therefore to evaluate more strategically to what extent they desire to participate in commercial activities. Yet, it appears that the Federal Circuit decision has changed very little. In the 15 years since the decision, the absence of a working experimental use defence does not seem to have adversely affected universities. While some universities have attempted to respond to *Madey* by reserving rights for the use of inven-

---

115 Ibid.

116 Ibid.

117 Ibid.

118 See e.g. Strandburg (2004) Wis. L. Rev. 81, 84–85.

119 *Madey* 1362–1363, including footnote 7: 'The district court attached too great a weight to the nonprofit, educational status of Duke, effectively suppressing the fact that Duke's acts appear to be in accordance with any reasonable interpretation of Duke's legitimate business objectives' and 'Duke's patent and licensing policy may support its primary function as an educational institution […] Duke, however, like other major research institutions of higher learning, is not shy in pursuing an aggressive patent licensing program from which it derives a not insubstantial revenue stream.'

120 See supra 2. B. II. 1.

121 See to this effect Rowe (2005) 57 Hastings L. J. 921, 923.

tions within their own institution and other academic or non-profit institutions in their exclusive licensing agreements, most researchers seem not more prudent or even concerned about the 'patent issue'.[122] Indeed, even in fields characterised by extensive patenting, many academic researchers continue to be either oblivious to the patents they might be infringing or simply unconcerned about potential infringement.[123]

What is more, it appears that despite *Madey*, firms in industry are not more likely to bring an action against an academic institution than they were before the decision.[124] This essentially means that universities have the cake and eat it: They continue to benefit from their 'special status' in society while embracing their new business identify. But it would certainly not be prudent for universities to strategically rely on this state of affairs. The more calculated universities continue to use their de facto research exemption while aggressively pursuing their own patent enforcements and litigations, the less willing businesses might be to give them a pass and not sue them for infringement in the future. It seems obvious that the Federal Circuit attempted to send this message to universities, but universities were simply not willing to receive it.

4 Tragedy of the Anti-commons

Patents can also block innovation in connection with research tools.[125] According to the NIH, a research tool is considered an invention whose primary usefulness is as a tool for discovery rather than as a product or component of a product.[126] A resource is considered a research tool if it is a broad, enabling, technology which may be useful to many scientists (or multiple companies in developing multiple products), rather than a project or product-specific resource.[127] Finally, a resource needs to be readily useable or distributable as a tool rather than needing private sector involvement for its expedient development or distribution.[128] Problems occur where access to such research tools

[122] See e. g. Boettiger and Bennett (2006) 24 Nature 320, 321; Walsh and others (2007) 36 Research Policy 1184, 1189–1190, reporting that in a survey of 381 university, government, and non-profit biomedical researchers in genomics and proteomics only 2 % have begun checking for patents since *Madey*.

[123] See Walsh and others (2007) 36 Research Policy 1184, 1189–1190, noting that only 5 % regularly check for patents and 73 % reported that they did not require access to someone else's intellectual property to conduct their research; see also R. Eisenberg (2008) 45 Hous. L. Rev. 1059, 1061; Villasenor (2012).

[124] See Walsh and others (2007) 36 Research Policy 1184, 1189–1190, indicating that before Madey 3 % of academic respondents said they had received a notification letter making them aware of intellectual property that was relevant to their research, after *Madey* the number only rose to 5 %.

[125] See R. Nelson (2004) 33 Research Policy 455, 464.

[126] See e. g. NIH (1999) 64 FR 72090.

[127] Ibid.

[128] Ibid.

is inhibited, especially due to patenting and/or exclusive licences, and as a consequence, where the advancement of commercial or non-commercial research is hindered. An example of such an 'upstream' technology is the Cohen-Boyer basic recombinant DNA techniques, which enabled the development of an entire industry in the 1980s, and which generated approximately USD 255 million for Stanford University and the University of California.[129]

The negative effects of privatisation of 'upstream' research are particularly strong in the context of biomedical research. The 'tragedy of the commons' describes the phenomenon of people overusing resources they own in common because they have no incentive to conserve.[130] Conversely, the 'tragedy of anticommons' describes the reverse situation where a resource is prone to underuse where multiple owners have a right to exclude others from the use of a scarce resource but no one has the effective privilege of use.[131] The anticommons effect of patenting, referring to the practice of universities to irresponsibly overpatent, has emerged as a widely discussed topic in the past decades. Here the anticommons problem is especially pronounced as universities often patent basic research tools and early-stage findings.[132]

There is concern that follow-on research is frequently hindered as a result and that benefits from scientific progress may ultimately be reduced.[133] Due to its arguable bias towards patenting, the critics maintain that the BDA encourages universities to patent 'upstream' inventions where they would be better left unprotected and dedicated to the public domain. This jeopardised future research that would build on upstream research and, in the long run, might lead to a deterioration in the culture of upstream research.[134]

Especially in the biomedical field, there has been continuous concern over the negative impact of the *Madey* decision combined with the impact of research tool patents on academic science. There are many anecdotal accounts and a number of empirical studies that have sought to shed light on the extent of the adverse effect on biomedical research.[135] While the empirical studies do

---

[129] See e. g. Eisenberg and Cook-Deegan (2018) 147 Daedalus 76, 78.

[130] Hardin (1968) 162 Science 1243; Heller and Eisenberg (1998) 280 Science 698, 698.

[131] Ibid.

[132] See e. g. de Larena (2006) 43 Hous. L. Rev. 1373, 1376; Heller and Eisenberg (1998) 280 Science 698, 698.

[133] Heller and Eisenberg (1998) 280 Science 698, 698.

[134] See supra 5.B.III; Link and others (2018) 34 Issues Sci. Tech. 33; Walsh and others (2005) 309 Science 2002, 2002; Pulsinelli (2005) 7 Minn. J. L Sci. & Tech. 393, 416; also see infra 7. A. II. 2.

[135] See e. g. Walsh and others, in *Patents in the Knowledge-based Economy* (2003) 285; Walsh and others (2005) 309 Science 2002; Walsh and others (2007) 36 Research Policy 1184; Link and others (2018) 34 Issues Sci. Tech. 33. For a perspective of the anti-commons problem in Germany, see e. g. Straus and others, *Genetic Inventions* (2004). For a good overview and analysis of different studies, see Caulfield and others (2000) 24 Nat. Biotech. 1091, 1092; R. Eisenberg (2008) 45 Hous. L. Rev. 1059, 1063–1075.

show that there are a large number of patents associated with genes, they also show that the anti-commons problem presented much fewer impediments to research than was originally expected.[136] Indeed, although some researchers may have been denied access to a particular upstream research tool, others did manage to secure access to the same research tool, indicating that the resulting limitations have more to do with willingness to accept market prices and access terms.[137] Overall, academic research does not seem to be negatively affected as only 1 % of researchers had to modify or delay their research project and none had to abandon a project due to anti-commons restrictions.[138]

B The Missing Piece: The Protection of the Public Interest

Policy discussions on university patenting were always intertwined with the question of how to best protect the public interest. Indeed, during the first wave of university patenting in the 1930s, the patent policy debate among university administrators was not only concerned with the question of whether patenting was necessary for the commercialisation of university inventions but gave much consideration to the question of how the public could benefit most from federally funded university inventions. It was generally agreed that any appearance of profiting at the public expense had to be avoided. But while there was concern over the potentially negative effect of patents on the progress of research and the impact university patenting would have on open science, arguments were also made that patenting could provide a viable solution against wrongful appropriation (piracy argument), non-use of government funded inventions, and a means to ensure quality control, especially in regard to public health inventions.[139]

While some of these discussion points on university patenting resurfaced in the debates leading to the introduction of the BDA in the 1960s and 1970s, many concerns about the effects of patenting in the academic environment were ignored. Instead, deliberations focused on more general issues such as the question whether governments or private contractors should retain title to federally funded inventions and the feasibility and desirability of a uniform federal patent policy across funding agencies.[140] Universities were not more experienced than government in patenting and licensing activities, nor were they less hostile

[136] See Caulfield and others (2000) 24 Nat. Biotech. 1091, 1091; R. Eisenberg (2008) 45 Hous. L. Rev. 1059, 1061.

[137] Caulfield (2000) 24 Nat. Biotech. 1091, 1092.

[138] See e. g. Walsh and others (2005) 309 Science 2002, 2002; Caulfield (2000) 24 Nat. Biotech. 1091, 1092.

[139] See 2. B.I and 5. B. I.

[140] See e. g. Sampat (2006) 35 Research Policy 772, 777; also see supra 5. B. III.

towards it. However, they were believed to be best positioned to enable the collaboration necessary between the academic inventor and potential licensees in industry which was crucial for the effective transfer of (especially early-stage) university inventions. Universities were also considered to be more trustworthy than businesses – it was just generally assumed that they would use their patents for the public benefit rather than private gain.[141]

Possible criticism of how the patenting of federally funded inventions would lead to 'profiteering' at the expense of the public, and general concern about the protection of the public interest, were cleverly anticipated and defused by the proponents of the BDA.[142] Accordingly, the bill's drafters included a recoupment provision under which institutions would have to pay back a share of licensing income or proceeds to funding agencies and provisions which stipulated time limits on exclusive licences.[143]

Another (tactical) precaution was that ownership would only be given to universities and small businesses but not to large firms. Only a few years prior to the Bayh-Dole bill, a similar patent legislation that applied to all businesses was criticised for giving away government property and for encouraging the formation of monopolies so that the bill soon died.[144] Supporters of the BDA understood that it was crucial to leave 'big business' out of the picture from the outset. To that effect, a Senate aide commented that there had been the intention of extending the new default ownership rule to everybody, 'but if we did, the bill would never have a chance of passing.'[145] Unsurprisingly though, only a few years after the bill's passage, the new policy was extended to large firms.[146]

The deliberations prior to the enactment of the BDA also re-visited the 'double paying' issue.[147] Many were concerned for the obvious reasons, namely that it was unfair to expect the public to pay for something that private companies would ultimately benefit from.[148] To them the proposed legislation was considered a 'pure giveaway of rights that properly belong to the people'.[149] But the proponents of the legislation put a new spin on the argument, suggesting that patenting of federally funded research presented the lesser of two evils. Without university patents the public would not derive the benefit from the research it sponsored because the research was laying idle and was wasting funds.

141 See e. g. Eisenberg and Cook-Deegan (2018) 147 Daedalus 76, 77.

142 See e. g. Sampat (2006) 35 Research Policy 772, 779.

143 Ibid.

144 Broad (1979) 205 Science 473, 474.

145 Ibid. 473–474.

146 First by an executive order signed by *President Reagan* in 1983 and then in an inconspicuous amendment to the BDA, see Eisenberg and Cook-Deegan (2018) 147 Daedalus 76, 77.

147 See supra n. 301/II and accompanying discussion.

148 See e. g. de Larena (2006) 43 Hous. L. Rev. 1373, 1383–1384.

149 Brooks and Moffett, 'Views of Representatives Jack Brooks and Toby Moffett on BDA' (*Knowledge Ecology International*).

Conversely, with the aid of patents – so they reasoned – publicly funded research could be commercialised, and the new products and technologies would enrich society at large. Thus, there was ultimately a choice between paying once and getting nothing or paying twice and getting something, which in the view of the BDA proponents was preferable.[150]

This argument misses a very important point, namely, that as producers of scientific knowledge universities fulfil a crucial function in society. It is exactly for this reason that university research has been and should continue to be publicly supported. Accordingly, universities' main purpose is not to produce commercial products, nor should it be their main goal to successfully commercialise their research results, however much this might be a desired auxiliary objective. But importantly and fundamentally, universities which do not succeed at commercialising their research do not waste public funds as the research will be disseminated to the public via other transfer channels.[151]

Indeed, as pointed out earlier, the private appropriation of publicly funded inventions questions the very rationale that basic research should be publicly funded.[152] Not surprisingly, perhaps, this objection to university patenting was entirely absent from the pre-BDA debate.[153] This may explain why the logic of the BDA implies a general bias towards patenting and licensing university research above other transfer channels. According to this bias, the question whether a greater social good might be achieved by transferring a given research result via other transfer channels (including placing them in the public domain) is seemingly absent.[154]

---

150 See e.g. Dreyfuss (2000) 53 Vand. L. Rev. 1159, 1194; R. Eisenberg (1997) 82 Va. L. Rev. 1663, 1666; Pulsinelli (2005) 7 Minn. J. L Sci. & Tech. 393, 410–411. A counterargument to the double paying concern has been made more recently, see Hemel and Ouellette (2017) 4 J.L. Biosci. 282. According to the authors, patents on federally funded inventions allow for a practical way of internalising the positive externalities these inventions confer on consumer in other countries. In other words, if there were no patents on publicly funded inventions consumers in other (especially 'rich-world') countries could avoid paying at all for these inventions. This seems a very academic and neglectable argument – the majority of university patents are filed in the US as national applications. And even where Patent Cooperation Treaty (PCT) applications are filed, most will never enter the national stages, see TTO Board of Directors (n. 467/II). Moreover, the countries which, according to the authors, have benefited from US universities' research, i.e. Germany and Norway, are countries which are innovative in their own right. Chances are that the German and Norwegian taxpayers have equally funded research which now benefits US taxpayers. More importantly, and more troublingly (and as the authors briefly acknowledge) US university patents have been criticised for the negative effect they have on the developing world. See supra n. 157–162/II and accompanying discussion.

151 See 5.B.II.

152 See discussion supra 2.B.II.1.

153 See supra 5.B.; also see R. Eisenberg (1997) 82 Va. L. Rev. 1663, 1666–1667.

154 See supra n. 414/II and accompanying discussion; also see e.g. R. Eisenberg (1997) 82 Va. L. Rev. 1663, 1666–1667; Rai and Eisenberg (2003) 66 L. & Contemp. Probs. 289, 303.

Looking more closely at the 'double paying' issue, it is not only not fair from the point of view of the taxpayer who should pay twice for publicly funded research, but also, it is not desirable that private firms should be able to receive the lion share in profits which result from publicly funded research projects. This creates the wrong incentive for industry. It puts private firms in a position where they can not only outsource their R&D needs to universities, but where they can also outsource the risk which comes with a (basic) research endeavour. Since the outcome of a research project cannot be planned (including whether it will result in a successful commercialisable product or not) the risk is ultimately borne by the university and by extension by society and thus the taxpayer. Conversely, firms in industry are in the comfortable position, by choosing between more or less successful research projects, to ultimately pick the winners.

The effects of university patenting are particularly disconcerting in the area of public health and, more specifically, in the fields of biotechnology and pharmaceuticals where the most obvious problems have arisen. There are many examples of federally funded research projects which resulted in successful commercial pharmaceutical products and medical applications and processes.[155] Not only does this beg the question whether it is appropriate for the respective private companies to profit from such projects in general, as was outlined above, but it is also a question of degree, as the cost associated with the development of such inventions and the potential impact the availability of such inventions has on the (taxpaying) patient are both comparatively high.[156]

In this context, there is also mounting concern over the effect that Bayh-Dole patents have on the developing world.[157] The breakthrough treatment for pros-

[155] Examples include Cleevec, Taxol, Epogen, Myriad Genetics.

[156] An example which illustrates this problem is Myriad Genetics, a spin-off of the University of Utah, which held patents to genes underlying breast cancer and on the process of extracting breast cancer genes. Myriad developed diagnostic tests and generally pursued an aggressive business strategy, such as attempting to eliminate tests which were being developed at competing laboratories (including laboratories at other universities), see Gold and Carbone (2010) 12 Genet. Med. 39. This practice did not even stop after the Supreme Court in *Association for Molecular Pathology v. Myriad Genetics*, 132 S. Ct. 1794 (S. Ct. 2012) invalidated some of Myriad patents. Indeed, Myriad together with the University of Utah Research Foundation continued to sue competitors in spite of the Supreme Court ruling and most recently, it has started to undermine its competitors by stoking fear that other tests are faulty, see e. g. Begley, 'Overblown Claims' (*Stat News*).

[157] See e. g. Kapczynski and others (2005) 20 Berkley Tech. L. J. 1031; Roose-Snyder and Doyle (2009) 35 Am. J. L. & M. 281; So and others (2008) 6 PLoS Biol. 2078; Lee, 'Patent Trolls' (*Washington Post*), detailing that Yale developed the AIDS drug d4T that it licensed to Bristol Myers Squibb (BMS) in 1994. BMS set the price for the drug so high that many people in the developing world could not afford it. Interestingly, the researcher who developed the drug was infuriated about this (he was quoted saying 'we were interested in developing a compound that would be a benefit to society'). With the help of activists, BMS was convinced to lower the price in the developing world in 2001.

tate cancer, which has been developed by research scientists at UCLA, illustrates this. UCLA holds the patent on the chemical compounds which are used to create a drug called Xtandi.[158] UCLA licensed the drug to Medivation Inc., a biotech company, which reported worldwide sales of USD 1.9 billion (1.2 billion in the US market) in 2015, one year before they were acquired by Pfizer for USD 14 billion.[159] While UCLA does not benefit directly from the drug sales, it received USD 520 million under its licensing agreement. UCLA has been particularly criticised for deciding to patent the drug in India and generally for mismanaging its patent rights in a way which allows the pricing of Xtandi to be targeted at high income countries and elites in developing countries.[160]

What is at the very least surprising about such accounts is the extent to which universities have changed their willingness to forfeit their public role for the benefit of profiting from publicly funded inventions. In regard to public health inventions, for the longest time universities were reluctant to not only employ patents but to use them to the detriment of the public and for their own financial benefit. This is especially troubling considering that in doing so universities do not act in the spirit of the BDA. After all, the importance of the public health issue was obviously apparent to the drafters of the Bayh-Dole bill who included the 'march-in rights', which would allow an agency to license Bayh-Dole patents if necessary in order to 'alleviate public health or safety needs'.[161] However, as discussed above, to this day no federal agency has ever relied on the march-in provision and the only federal agency which has ever been petitioned to 'march-in' has declined to act.[162]

158 Feltz, 'UCLA's Patent' (*Los Angeles Times*).
159 Ibid.
160 See e. g. Schlesinger, 'UCLA Students Protest' (*Health Policy*).
161 35 USC 203(a).
162 See supra n. 405–410/II and accompanying discussion.

Chapter 7

Managing University Research in the Public Interest: Results and Perspectives

A Universities' Patent Policies and Technology Transfer Practices

I Universities' Patent Policies

1 A Brief History of Universities' Patent Policies

In the early years of patent activity, US research universities typically did not have a formal patent policy but addressed patent issues as they arose. Universities believed that inventions were private property and thus the concern of the respective faculty member.[163] While the earliest patent policy dates back to 1913 and was implemented by the University of Illinois,[164] most universities did not start adopting a formalised patent policy until after World War II.[165] By the early to mid 1950s, many of the major US research universities had a patent policy, displaying a wide breadth of attitudes towards issues such as ownership of inventions, profit generation, allowance of public health and medical patents, inventor shares, licensing practices, and patent management.[166] Universities which adopted policies later, in the mid to late 1940s, 1950s, and early 1960s, often (partially) copied existing policies, especially the policies of the University of Illinois, Lehigh University, Massachusetts Institute of Technol-

[163] McKusick (1948) 245 J. Franklin Inst. 193, 207.

[164] There are conflicting references regarding the date of the earliest patent policy: Palmer, *Patents and Nonprofit Research* (1957) 6, states that Lehigh University established the first policy in 1924. In contrast, McKusick (1948) 245 J. Franklin Inst. 193, 219, states that University of Illinois' policy was the first and was established in 1913. It appears undisputed that at least the roots of Illinois' policy can be traced back to 1913, when the university's engineering experiment station issued patent regulations; these provisions were then or later extended to the entire university, see Palmer (1934) 16 J. Pat. Off. Soc'y 96, 103.

[165] In 1934, only 2 institutions had a formalised patent policy, Palmer (1934) 16 J. Pat. Off. Soc'y 96, 103; McKusick (1948) 245 J. Franklin Inst. 193, 219; Palmer, *University Research and Patent Policies* (1962) 8.

[166] In 1952, out of a surveyed 811 institutions, 70 had a patent policy, see Palmer, *University Patent Policies* (1952) 9, 11. For the patent policies of these institutions and for details on institutions which had a 'generally accepted practice' on how to handle patentable inventions, see ibid. 27–229. In 1962, out of 945 institutions, 147 had a patent policy, 596 had no policy and conducted 'little or no scientific or technological research', see Palmer, *University Research and Patent Policies* (1962) 6, 4.

ogy (MIT), and Pennsylvania State University.[167] This will not have been the last time universities turn to peer institutions in order to find solutions regarding various patenting issues. Indeed, the emulation of other institutions' practices is a reoccurring phenomenon which can be observed throughout the history of research universities and reaches beyond the copying of patent-related practices.[168]

Amongst universities which actively participated in research, three different approaches to the question of ownership of university-generated inventions may be distinguished. The first group required inventors to assign to the university inventions which resulted from regular university duties. This policy was inspired by the one which governed employee-inventions in industry.[169] While it was the least desirable policy in the beginning, it continued to gain traction over time and is the norm today. In early years, it was predominately followed by land-grant universities, such as the University of Illinois, Pennsylvania State, Purdue, Ohio State, and Colorado State University.[170] Later, it was also adopted by private institutions such as Lehigh, Georgetown University, and MIT.[171]

A modified approach of this policy was implemented by the University of Chicago. It required inventors to directly assign ownership of their inventions to an independent patent management organisation.[172] This approach was prompted by universities' general unease with the direct management of patents.[173] Cornell University had a similar provision for inventions arising from discoveries made by researchers in its medical college.[174]

The second group, which includes Columbia, Syracuse, Northwestern, John Hopkins, and Notre Dame University, left ownership rights with the inventor. This did not necessarily mean that universities remained completely passive. Indeed, some policies still required inventors to disclose their inventions to the university.[175] It was also not uncommon for universities in this group to provide some assistance to inventors who wished to obtain patent protection for their invention. To that effect, some universities would give inventors the option to

---

167 Palmer, *University Research and Patent Policies* (1962) 14.

168 See e. g. supra n. 69/I and infra n. 199–200/III and accompanying discussions respectively.

169 McKusick (1948) 245 J. Franklin Inst. 193, 219.

170 Palmer, *University Research and Patent Policies* (1962) 48–274.

171 McKusick (1948) 245 J. Franklin Inst. 193, 219; Palmer, *University Research and Patent Policies* (1962) 10, 48–274.

172 '(N)either the University nor any members of its staff shall retain ownership, management or licensing responsibilities for patents resulting from research or other activities carried out at the University or with the aid of its facilities.', Palmer, *University Research and Patent Policies* (1962) 97.

173 See supra n. 264/I and accompanying discussion.

174 Palmer, *University Research and Patent Policies* (1962) 177–178.

175 E. g. Northwestern University, see Palmer, *University Research and Patent Policies* (1962) 94.

voluntarily assign their inventions to the university or to a patent management agency.[176] In the event of a successful licensing of the invention, the University of Texas required the inventor to pay a percentage of the income to the university.[177]

The third and last group did not have a formalised patent policy – some as late as 1962 – and handled patenting-related questions on a case by case basis. What these universities typically stipulated was the patent management agency which would handle the patenting process and management for situations where patents were pursued.[178] This group included Harvard, George Washington, Duke, Michigan State University, Georgia Institute of Technology, and the University of Denver.[179]

Most institutions placed little or no restriction on the disposition of an invention if the research was conducted in the inventor's own time and at his own expense, even if institutional facilities and equipment were used. Accordingly, the right to an invention which was not related to the individual inventor's teaching, research or administrative duties typically belonged to the inventor.[180] Most universities also excluded the application of their policy to inventions which stemmed from contracts with industry and generally dealt with them on a case by case basis.[181]

Most institutions shared licensing income derived from the exploitation of patented inventions with inventors. However, there was no uniformity in how income was divided between the institution and the inventor.[182] Only a few exceptional institutions did not share any proceeds with inventors.[183]

Many of these older policies reflected an awareness of and a commitment to universities' mission of discovery and broad dissemination of research results. Some policies specifically accentuated the freedom of publication and the pro-

---

176 E. g. Columbia, Syracuse, Northwestern, Johns Hopkins University, see Palmer, *University Research and Patent Policies* (1962) 176, 194, 94, 124.

177 Palmer, *University Research and Patent Policies* (1962) 254–255.

178 See e. g. Michigan State, George Washington, Duke University, see Palmer, *University Research and Patent Policies* (1962) 139, 82, 199.

179 Palmer, *University Research and Patent Policies* (1962) 48–274. The third group is distinct to a much larger group of 596 institutions that *Palmer* listed in his 1962 study, and which performed 'little or no scientific or technological research' and lacked a patent policy and generally accepted practices for how inventions or patents would be handled, see Palmer, *University Research and Patent Policies* (1962) 275. For a complete list of institutions, see ibid. 275–282.

180 Ibid. 27.

181 See ibid. 48–274.

182 The contributions to inventors ranged from comparatively high shares of 75% (e. g. Wittenberg) or 50% (Lehigh, Northwestern, Notre Dame) to as little as 7% (e. g. Southern California), see Palmer, *University Research and Patent Policies* (1962) 48–274.

183 See e. g. Ohio State University Policy: 'No faculty member, employee, or student […] shall have any rights to or interest in such discoveries or inventions, including income therefrom.', Palmer, *University Research and Patent Policies* (1962) 209.

tection of the public interest. For instance, Columbia University underscored its dedication 'to scholarly activity in the broadest sense' and that 'results of university research should be made public with the greatest possible freedom'.[184] Similarly, the University of Chicago stressed the 'complete freedom of research and the unrestricted dissemination of information'.[185] Likewise, the University of Washington held that the interests of the inventor, the university, and the public interest were best served by 'immediate publication and dissemination of results of research'.[186] The policy also acknowledged that there may be occasions where – in order to be able to control the invention in the public interest – the optimal solution was to obtain a patent.[187]

Another reflection of universities' concern for the protection of the public interest was the treatment of medical research: Columbia, Johns Hopkins, Harvard University, and the University of Notre Dame explicitly forbade the patenting of inventions that related to public or individual health.[188] The University of Pennsylvania, Ohio State, Johns Hopkins, and Mississippi State University only allowed patenting of health-related inventions where it was deemed necessary to protect the public interest.[189] Some universities also forbade making profit from inventions related to public health.[190]

Up until the 1960s, universities' general reluctance towards patents, including a discontent toward the generation of income from university research, was often still detectable in their policies. For instance, Princeton University encouraged 'research and scholarship as such without regard to potential gain from royalties or other such income'.[191] Johns Hopkins University held that the university makes 'no claim to royalties derived from patents'.[192] Finally, the University of Chicago stated that 'research done primarily in anticipation of profit is incompatible with the aims of the university'.[193] Nevertheless, these policy statements were often a subtler version of earlier ones of the respective universities.[194] They point to a sliding scale on which universities moved to-

184 Ibid. 175.

185 Ibid. 97.

186 Ibid. 267.

187 Ibid. For other similar policies, see e.g. Iowa State, ibid. 108; University of Maine, ibid. 122.

188 Ibid. 175–176, 124, 128–129, 104.

189 Ibid. 236, 208–209, 124, 146.

190 See e.g. Northeastern University, Palmer, *University Research and Patent Policies* (1962) 132.

191 Palmer, *University Research and Patent Policies* (1962) 161.

192 Ibid. 124.

193 Ibid. 97.

194 See e.g. McKusick (1948) 245 J. Franklin Inst. 193, 217, referring and partially quoting earlier polices of the University of Pennsylvania, University of Chicago, Harvard, Yale, and Johns Hopkins University, which 'expressed themselves as being vehemently opposed to profits from inventions', ibid. 217.

wards being ever more comfortable with university patenting, generating income therefrom, and sacrificing elements of the academic mission and the protection of the public interest in order to participate in these activities.

2 Universities' Patent Policies since the Bayh-Dole Act

Universities' reluctance towards patents continued to diminish during the 1960s and during the 1970s, mainly as a result of the continued expansion of universities' research operations and their exposure to new commercialisation opportunities in biomedicine.[195] Today, all research universities have a patent policy. In fact, a majority of universities now use the term 'intellectual property policy'[196], which reflects the expansive view of the types of research results and other creative works which today are covered by university policy.[197] Contemporary policies are much more detailed in substance than their earlier brethren, typically stipulating the objectives of the policy, the scope of application (including the types of research results that are covered as well as who it applies to), defining ownership rights and duties, including rights to use the research results and rights to the revenue generated, as well as establishing the procedural and administrative processes and institutions which are necessary for the implementation of the policy.[198]

In contrast to earlier policies, today, there are virtually no normative differences between universities' intellectual property policies. This is astonishing when one considers that there are notable differences in terms of universities' organisational structure, their funding structure and differences in the way universities relate to their respective regional and cultural environments. Universities' earlier mentioned tendency to pattern their respective policies after policies of peer institutions was reinforced by the passage of the BDA, licensing and commercialisation success stories of peer institutions, and last but not least, by the legal insecurities which emerged in the aftermath of *Stanford v. Roche*. These events have prompted many universities to copy the solutions that their peer institutions developed rather than developing their own unique solution based on the respective universities' characteristics and priorities. While in the 1990s and 2000s a few universities still stood out with their

195 See supra 2. B. I.

196 Others have added a 'copyright policy' to the 'patent policy', see e. g. Stanford.

197 As universities attempt to expand their claim on intellectual property, they have to be careful not to tip the balance. This shows a recent debate at Ohio State University where the university attempted to change their policy to the effect that it would read that 'all rights, title and interests in intellectual property are the sole property of the university'. The backlash which ensued prompted the university to abandon the project, see e. g. Flaherty, 'Scholarly Work' (*Inside Higher Ed*). Going forward the term 'intellectual property policy' and 'patent policy' will be used interchangeably.

198 For a detailed discussion of the typical elements of such policies, see e. g. Luppino (2009) 78 UMKC L. Rev. 367, 371–387.

specific approach to the ownership of university inventions, today – with the exception of one university[199] – all universities adhere to the 'standard' of university ownership.[200]

In regard to universities' scope of ownership claims two main observations can be made. Firstly, while the exact scope of the claimed research results differs slightly, most universities seek ownership over patentable research results and generally exclude copyrightable research results from such claims.[201] Secondly, university ownership will typically be implicated if research results are developed by one or more of its faculty, staff, or students,[202] and if such research results have been developed by the inventor(s) in the pursuit of university responsibilities or with the use of 'substantial resources' (including externally funded grants and contracts).[203] While universities use slightly differing terms to refer to the threshold of resource-use which triggers university ownership, most policies do not qualify what constitutes 'substantial resources'.[204]

---

199 University of Wisconsin-Madison, see infra n. 210–213/III and accompanying discussion.

200 See e. g. Chew (1992) 1 Wis. L. Rev. 259, 282–283, referring to: 1) the University of Wisconsin and Stanford University, which both provided that faculty should own university inventions; 2) the University of Minnesota, which only claimed ownership of inventions arising out of sponsored research; and 3) Harvard University, which only claimed ownership of inventions 'primarily concerned with medical diagnostics-therapeutics or public health', ibid. 283.

201 There are two exceptions to this: 1) Many universities will claim ownership of copyright protected software; 2) Universities will often claim ownership of copyrights in 'institutional works', see e. g. Stanford University, which defines 'institutional works' as works 'that are supported by a specific allocation of university funds or that are created at the direction of the university for a specific university purpose', see Stanford Copyright Policy, Research Policy Handbook 9.2.B (hereinafter Stanford Policy). From a practical point of view, the separation between patentable inventions, which the university will claim, and copyrightable works, which the university does not claim, is arbitrary. Under this distinction the same research project will yield one output (the patentable invention) which will be owned by the university and another (e. g. a publication) which will be owned by the authors. Faculty are typically opposed to the distinction on the basis that it puts researchers whose research produces patentable results at a disadvantage compared to researchers who produce copyrightable works, see AAUP (2014) Bulletin AAUP 38, 46.

202 For a detailed analysis of universities' treatment of undergraduate inventions, see infra 7.A.I.3.

203 See e. g. Stanford Policy 9.1.A(1): 'in the course of their university responsibilities or with more than incidental use of university resources'; Cornell University Policy 1.5; Harvard University Statement of Policy in Regard to Intellectual Property I.C (hereinafter Harvard University Policy).

204 See e. g. University of Pennsylvania: 'substantial use of university resource', Patent and Tangible Research Property Policies and Procedures Article 2.0; Arizona State University, University of Arizona, and Northern Arizona University: 'significant use of […] university resources', Arizona Board of Regents, Intellectual Property Policy 6–908 § A.1.a(2); Stanford: 'more than incidental use of university resources', Stanford Policy 9.1.A(1); MIT: 'significant use of funds or facilities', MIT Intellectual Property Policy 13.1.2(3); University of Michigan: 'direct or indirect support of funds administered by the university', University of Michigan Technology Transfer Policy II.A (hereinafter Michigan Policy); Johns Hopkins University: 'university support', Johns Hopkins University Intellectual Property Policy IV.A.–B.; Virginia

The consequence of the application of these policies is that university-developed inventions – unless they were directly sponsored by industry[205] – will be owned by the university. Considering universities' initial hands-off attitude towards patenting, this is a surprising reality. The BDA was crucial in this development: It encouraged universities to patent and commercialise federally funded inventions and it secured – at least in universities' perception – universities' ownership rights to such inventions.[206] But on top of that, after the adoption of the BDA universities increasingly felt legitimated to claim ownership of non-federally funded inventions as well. Indeed, TTOs generally assumed that the university owned all patentable inventions.[207]

The *Stanford* decision confirmed that the BDA does not secure ownership rights to federally funded inventions (let alone to non-federally funded inventions) and that the contractual enforceability is an issue separate to the BDA. It underscored that inventions may be assigned under contract law but that care needed to be taken in choosing the right language for such assignments to be effective.[208] The decision generally took universities by surprise and triggered the most recent surge of changes to universities' patent policies. It prompted universities not only to adopt the 'do hereby assign'-language, which the *Stanford* court discussed, but also prompted universities to extend their ownership claims to all university inventions in their policies. Some universities additionally chose to have faculty sign pre-invention assignement agreements to ensure effective assignment of researchers' inventions.[209]

The one university that today still stands out in terms of its approach to ownership is the University of Wisconsin-Madison. As a general rule, the university does not claim ownership in university-generated inventions.[210] Researchers have an obligation to report all inventions made while carrying out university duties, using university funding, or using university premises, supplies, or

Tech: use of 'university resources', Virginia Tech Policy 13000 2.3.A.1 (hereinafter Virginia Tech Policy).

205 Such inventions have always been exempted from the application of universities' patent policies, see supra 7.A.I.1.

206 See supra 5.E.

207 A majority even believed this to be the case for copyrightable work resulting from university research, see Thursby and others (2001) 26 J. Tech. Transfer 59, 61.

208 See supra 5.D.III.

209 See e.g. Stanford University, University of Pittsburgh, University of Texas System, University of Virginia (UVA); UVA's Patent Agreement and Assignment reads: 'I acknowledge my acceptance of the university of Virginia Patent Policy, and do hereby assign to the rector and visitors of the University of Virginia all of my ownership, right, title and interest in any discovery or invention that is the product of my university research, including without limitation any patent and other intellectual property rights arising under US or any other law, whether I acquired those rights before signing this agreement or acquire them in the future.'

210 University of Wisconsin-Madison Intellectual Property Policies and Procedures for University Research II, University of Wisconsin System, Administrative Policy 346 6.B.I–III (hereinafter UW System Policy).

equipment.[211] If federal funds are involved in a research project, the university may choose to take title in the invention, or it may not, at which point the inventor may petition the funding agency for the rights to pursue patent protection of the invention.[212] If the university concludes that there are no federal funds or any other contractual obligation attached to the invention, inventors are 'free to dispose of their interest in the invention in the manner of their choosing', including assigning the invention to the university's intellectual property management organisation.[213]

Several universities provide that an inventor may have ownership rights granted back to him under certain circumstances. This provision is probably inspired by the BDA, which allows an inventor to petition the federal agency to retain ownership rights to the invention if the university and the government do not elect to retain title to the invention.[214] The specifics of such provisions vary, but inventors generally have to proactively request a release from their university for all inventions, regardless of source of funding of the invention.[215] The decision will, in most cases, depend on a university's obligation to third party sponsors, but universities generally do not specify what (other) factors may influence the outcome of their decision. Some universities may also only grant back a license instead of complete ownership rights to the inventor.[216] The granting back of ownership rights may also come with strings attached, such as a reservation by the university to use the invention,[217] or to provide consideration to the university by reimbursing invention-related expenses and sharing future royalty income.[218]

All universities provide to the inventor a share of royalty income or other proceeds received from the licensing or sale of the invention. This is mandated by the BDA and serves as an incentive for inventors to disclose their inventions.[219] But today, there is still no uniformity in terms of the percentage the inventor will receive.[220] Universities also have started to introduce sliding scales,

[211] UW System Policy 6.A.

[212] Ibid. 6.B.I.

[213] Ibid. 6.B.I–III.

[214] 35 USC § 202(d).

[215] See e. g. University of California Policy III.B; Virginia Tech Policy 2.3.C; MIT Guide to the Ownership, Distribution and Commercial Development of MIT Technology (2018) 2.4. A notable exception is the University of Texas System, which provides that if the university does not assert ownership interest in an invention, the inventor should be notified of the release of ownership rights to him within 20 business days after the decision is made, The University of Texas System, Rule 90101: Intellectual Property Section 11(2).

[216] See e. g. Michigan Policy VI.

[217] See e. g. University of California Policy III.B(2).

[218] See e. g. University of Michigan Policy VI.C: 'recovery of any out-of-pocket university expenses, plus 15 % of royalties, equity, or other value received by the inventor(s) through subsequent use, licensing, or further assignment of the intellectual property'.

[219] 35 USC § 202(c)(7)(B).

[220] At most universities the share is somewhere between 30 %–50 %; see e. g. MIT Policy 4.8(A): share is 30 %; Virginia Tech Policy 2.3.D: share is 50 %.

according to which an inventor's share will be reduced depending on the threshold the proceeds reach.[221] Finally, some universities have added other complexities to these provisions, including how invention-related university expenses will be subtracted from eventual income.[222]

3 The Treatment of Student Inventions

The question of the ownership of student-generated inventions confronts universities with a multitude of legal issues.[223] What makes ownership claims of student-generated inventions tricky is that – unlike ownership claims of faculty-inventions which are rooted in the traditional employee-employer relationship – the relationship between most students and the university is not based on employment. Traditionally, universities simply extended the application of their intellectual property policies to students. This was usually not problematic as the students who were typically involved in research projects were graduate students working as research assistants. Such students would likely be considered employees of the university for the purpose of such research projects and be bound by the intellectual property policy like other employees.[224] In more recent years, however, as part of universities' entrepreneurial paradigm to educa-

221 See e. g. Michigan Policy VB: up to USD 200'000 the inventor receives 50 %, over USD 200'000 only 30 %.

222 See e. g. MIT Policy 4.8(A)1–3, detailing that 15 % administrative fee and out-of-pocket costs not reimbursed by licensees will be deducted from gross royalty income; also see Michigan Policy VB.

223 For a good overview of the legal issues, see Duval-Couetil and others (2014) 30 Int'l J. Eng. Educ. 60, 62. Although publications on the topic are limited, for a general discussion on undergraduate research and potential intellectual property rights issues, see e. g. Nordheden and Hoeflich (1999) 42 IEEE Trans. on Educ. 233; Silvernagel and others (2009) 12 J. of Entrep. Educ. 13; Barrow and others (2014) 2 Tech. Transfer Pract. Manual 1.

224 Like in the case of faculty members, appointment letters for graduate students will generally refer to the university handbook or the general administrative policies of the university to which the graduate students will be bound, see *Chou v. University of Chicago* 1357. Also see supra 4. D. III. Whether students should be considered employees of the respective university is a controversial issue, which ultimately depends on the facts of the case. Historically, there has been a reluctance by courts to consider students to be employees if they were 'primarily engaged in educational or training activities', see Capano and others (1991) 18 J. C. & U. L. 105, 115. Also see Patel (1995) 71 Ind. L. J. 482, 502, concluding that students will not be classified as employees; Smith (1997) 1 Va. J. Law & Tech. 1, 8, suggesting that graduate research assistants could also be considered employees of the professor who they conduct the research for. A 2004 ruling by the National Labor Relations Board (NLRB) held that graduate assistants were not employees of the university. The NLRB based its ruling on the fact that the relationship between graduate assistants and the university was an academic and not an economic one and on the fact that students received academic credit for the performance of their duties, see *Brown University*, 342 NLRB 483 (2004). Similarly, a 2014 ruling on graduate student assistants' right to organise found that 'graduate-students assistants' principal time commitment […] was focused on obtaining a degree and, thus, being a student'. However, in a more recent ruling, the NLRB went back to its original position that student assistants are employees, see *Columbia University*, 364 NLRB 90 (2016).

tion, undergraduate students have increasingly become involved in research.[225] But in contrast to graduate students, most undergraduate students are not employed by the university. Extending the application of existing intellectual property policies to undergraduate students, and thereby claiming ownership of undergraduate inventions, is therefore problematic.

From a policy point of view, there are two competing schools of thoughts on whether universities ought to claim ownership of undergraduate inventions. The prevailing one is that the undergraduate intellectual property policy should reflect the faculty and graduate student policy; because if they differ, undergraduate students might have a different motivation than faculty and graduate students regarding the research. The other school of thought is that universities which claim ownership of undergraduate inventions might stifle students' creativity.[226]

While there may be moral reservations to claiming ownership of undergraduate inventions,[227] the probably biggest concern regarding undergraduate students is the enforceability of university policies which claim (partial) ownership of undergraduate inventions. If a university extends their policy to undergraduate students, the contractual assignment of the respective inventions is likely not going to be effective. For a contract to be legally binding there needs to be sufficient consideration.[228] While (continuous) employment and the payment of wages will likely be considered enough consideration for a legal transfer of inventions generated by faculty and graduate students, in most cases, consideration is missing if undergraduate students conduct research as part of their education: There is no employment contract, students do not get paid for the research, nor is there any other consideration which universities award to undergraduate students in return for a transfer of ownership.

---

225 Factors which contributed to the shift are: 1) Agencies such as the NSF and non-profit organisations and foundations such as the Howard Hughes Medical Institute (HHMI) actively encourage undergraduate research. Such initiatives assume that undergraduate research experiences will attract gifted undergraduate students to graduate study, particularly in the STEM (Science, Technology, Engineering, Mathematics) fields; 2) Undergraduate research is an attractive way for faculty to recruit undergraduates to graduate studies; 3) Generally, undergraduate research is relied upon for its instructional value: Studies indicate that students' learning experience is enhanced by practical and active 'student cantered' learning; 4) There may also be financial considerations at play: Undergraduate students normally do not require tuition waivers but conduct research for credit. In some instances, the lab or supervisor may even be awarded additional resources to accommodate undergraduates. As such, undergraduate research can be lucrative as it can increase the labour force without necessarily increasing the respective costs, see Nordheden and Hoeflich (1999) 42 IEEE Trans. on Educ. 233, 234.

226 Silvernagel and others (2009) 12 J. of Entrep. Educ. 13, 17.

227 Claiming ownership of undergraduate inventions can be problematic from an educational point of view. In doing so, universities may hamper students' general academic curiosity not only by removing the potential incentive function of patents but by exposing them to an institutional spirit that is in conflict with the very entrepreneurial spirit many universities attempt to foster.

228 See supra 4. D. II.

Finally, while there is authority supporting the institutional practice of transferring ownership of inventions to the university as part of the overall employment contract, this practice cannot be applied analogously to undergraduate students. Yet, it is what many universities do: Undergraduate students accept an institutions' intellectual property policy as part of the general admission process (along with agreeing to other institutional policies such as harassment, discrimination, honor code etc.). But most of the time, students will not be aware, nor will they be made aware, that by accepting the offer of admission they are also agreeing to these policies and are thus signing away the rights to future inventions.[229]

Universities' increasing awareness of the legal and procedural challenges with undergraduate inventions (including the realisation that TTOs might not be able to handle the additional invention disclosures),[230] has prompted many universities to step back from overly broad ownership claims regarding undergraduate inventions over the past few years.[231] Nevertheless, most universities still claim ownership of at least some undergraduate-generated inventions.[232]

---

[229] Conversations with students enrolled in the authors' classes in 2014–2017.

[230] TTO Board of Directors (n. 467/II).

[231] See e. g. University of Minnesota: 'The university shall be the sole owner of all rights, titles, and interests (including intellectual property rights) in and to technology […] created by individuals, including employees, students […]', University of Minnesota, Board of Regents Policy (2007 as amended in 2014) V1; versus the changed policy that reads: 'This policy shall not apply to technology created […] (by) students to fulfil a university course requirement unless: 1) the development of the technology was funded […] by an external sponsor; 2) the technology was an improvement of an invention in which the university holds the intellectual property rights; 3) a university faculty member or other university employee was a co-inventor of the technology; or 4) substantial university resources were used to develop or reduce the technology to practice.', University of Minnesota, Board of Regents Policy (2007 as amended in 2015) II.4.

[232] More specifically, universities' policies typically follow one of two approaches: 1) undergraduate intellectual property is owned by students unless: a) funding is received through the university (including external contracts); b) the technology was an improvement of a university-patented invention, c) a faculty member or employee of the university was a co-inventor of the invention; d) students used 'substantial resources'; and/or d) students are employed by the university (e. g. Virginia Tech); or 2) unless undergraduate students are employed by the university, all intellectual property is owned by the students (e. g. University of Michigan). While universities' approach differed substantially up to five years ago, today most research universities' policies fall under the second approach. Establishing when the use of a resource (such as libraries, computers, lab space, materials or even advice of faculty members) would be considered 'substantial' may often prove as tricky as with faculty inventions, see supra n. 203–204/III and accompanying discussion. For instance, Virginia Tech changed its policy from the use of 'at least USD 10'000' to 'any resource typically not available to the public' in 2011 and its policy also applied to undergraduates. This seemingly small change had a lot of impact: While under the old policy undergraduate student inventions would typically not have been affected, with the 2011 policy they were. 'Any resources typically not available to the public' meant, for instance, that if a student received advice from a professor or if a student worked in the library on a computer provided by the university, the intellectual property clause was triggered.

II Universities' Lack of Strategic Commitment to the Protection of the Public Interest

1 Picking Favourites: Universities' Implementation of the BDA

The comparison between early and contemporary patent policies illustrates the fundamental shift which has taken place in regard to universities' attitude towards patents. There are two striking differences. Firstly, today universities claim ownership of *all* university-generated inventions, thereby suggesting that ownership is essential to the dissemination of university research and an effective technology transfer practice. Secondly, patents are considered the default transfer channel if an invention is patentable and has commercial potential. Other considerations to determine whether to patent or – perhaps more importantly – whether not to patent, are generally not mentioned. In other words, the commercialisation argument for the use of patents is the argument which has prevailed.

As mentioned above, universities have become accustomed to base the justification of their broad ownership claims and their patent involvement on the BDA. Surprisingly, this has not changed after *Stanford v. Roche*. An illustration of this phenomenon is the introduction of the 'Patent and Innovation Policy' of Northwestern University which reads: 'The patent and invention policy [...] largely stems from the Bayh-Dole Act [...], which was enacted largely to stimulate economic and entrepreneurial activity by promoting the commercialization of inventions stemming from federally funded research.'

But what is even more surprising is that universities have traditionally ignored and continue to ignore other important aspects of the BDA. After all, the Act does not only promote the use and commercialisation of federally funded inventions but also stresses the importance of the protection of the public interest and the broad dissemination of research results.[233] To this effect, the BDA preamble emphasises that: 1) inventions should only be used 'in a manner to promote free competition and enterprise without unduly encumbering future research and discovery'; 2) 'commercialisation and public availability of inventions' should be promoted; and 3) it needs to be ensured 'that the government obtains sufficient rights' in order to 'protect the public against non-use or unreasonable use of inventions'.[234]

Unfortunately, these three objectives have largely been disregarded by universities. Universities' patent policies may reference the importance of the public interest, but the strategic commitment and technology transfer practices to honour it, as will be discussed below, are usually not in place.[235] The backbone

[233] Also see supra 5. C. I.

[234] USC 35 § 200.

[235] See e. g. Harvard Policy Introduction: 'Harvard University has had a long history of benefiting the public through its research programs.'; Virginia Tech Policy 1.0: 'Publicly

of universities' patent policies and outlined processes is the determination of the ownership of patentable research results coupled with the patent protection and commercialisation of the same. Other transfer channels, including publications, are typically only mentioned on the side and as they relate to copyrightable works, which – as a general rule – universities do not claim. Hesitancy towards patents or making a profit therefrom is absent. To the contrary, many universities outline elaborate calculations and sliding scales of how royalties need to be shared, suggesting that the making of a profit is not only a welcome surprise but an institutional priority.[236]

Certainly, many of the above-discussed problems that the wide-spread use of patents has introduced to the academic research mission are at least in part attributable to a (failed) policy assumption underlying the BDA: It appears that it was simply underestimated how much universities would take to patenting. But while the BDA may have encouraged – and to a certain extent legitimated the use of patents – the blame should also be directed at universities themselves for disregarding their public role and the BDA's objectives, for being increasingly motivated by their own financial interests, and for mismanaging their patent rights. Indeed, the arguably biggest challenge the BDA has created for universities is not the challenge of obtaining or enforcing patents for university inventions but of how to responsibly manage university inventions and other university research.

This includes the very important but completely neglected task of defining a coherent intellectual property strategy. Importantly, and in contrast to for-profit businesses in industry, such a strategy should take into account the question of how the public would best benefit from university research. While in the early days of universities' involvement with patents universities seemed to have been much more aware of their public role and were afraid of being associated with industry, today universities enjoy the idea of being industry-friendly.[237] In this new realty, commercialisation activities have become an end in itself according to which universities compete with other universities, attempting to obtain as many patents as possible and negotiate the highest revenues in licenses.[238]

In the following sub-sections, discussion will thus turn on evaluating how universities have changed their strategic position from 'neutral arbiters of the truth'[239] to commercial business actors and how this shift has shaped univer-

(state) supported universities have the multiple missions of teaching, research, support of the public interest and fostering of economic development. […] The University's mission includes dissemination of IPs (sic) in the most efficient and effective manner possible.'

236 See supra n. 211/III and accompanying discussion.

237 Also see e. g. de Larena (2006) 43 Hous. L. Rev. 1373, 1385.

238 Also see e. g. Dreyfuss (2004) 46 Ariz. L. Rev. 457, 464, stating that universities regard their technology transfer as 'the academic equivalent of their football teams: even if the offices aren't winning, there is cachet in fielding them'.

239 The Economist, 'Bayhing for Blood' (*Economist*).

sities' technology transfer practices. More specifically, emphasis will be placed on the following three aspects: 1) universities' institutional imperative of patenting, 2) universities' focus on maximising licensing income instead of maximising the social benefit of their research, and 3) the marginalisation of professors and researchers in universities' technology transfer practices.

2 The Institutional Imperative of Patenting

The traditional university technology transfer process follows the linear innovation model which was discussed above:[240] A researcher discovers an invention in the pursuit of his research activities, the researcher is obligated to disclose to the university his invention, the TTO evaluates the invention and assesses whether a patent application should be filed, the TTO then files a patent application and searches for potential licensees which will develop the invention further and bring it to the market. The process will be followed as long as the invention is considered to have commercial potential. By design the process will generally disregard the nature of the invention, its level of development, the industry in which commercialisation might be sought, and the desirability of a patent vis-à-vis other transfer channels. In other words, the typical technology transfer process does generally not consider whether patenting is necessary for the commercial development, whether it might inhibit future research, whether it is considered important in the industry where commercialisation is sought, or simply how an invention should be shared in order to maximise its benefit to the public. As such, universities' practices create a heavy bias towards patenting all patentable research.

The obvious explanation for this patenting imperative is that most universities' technology transfer practices (including TTOs) were established in response to the BDA.[241] Since the BDA's logic centres on ownership and is biased towards the use of patents, the focus on ownership and the patent-bias were translated into universities' intellectual property polices and technology transfer practices.[242]

The BDA's 'heavy bias' towards patents has been criticised, predominately for disregarding the availability of other transfer channels.[243] While the criticism is legitimate in so far as the BDA's language is not clear enough regard-

---

240 See supra 2. B. II. 2.

241 See e. g. de Larena (2006) 43 Hous. L. Rev. 1373, 1412, pointing out that there were only 25 active technology transfer offices at the time when BDA was enacted, 25 years later there were 3'300.

242 See supra n. 414/II and accompanying discussion.

243 See e. g. Rai and Eisenberg (2003) 66 L. & Contemp. Probs. 289, 303, criticising the BDA for creating a bias towards patenting as it lets anyone involved in the research (i. e. university, federal agency, inventor) who thinks the invention should be patented prevail over anyone who believes research results should be in the public domain.

ing the importance of other transfer channels and the protection of the scientific commons, nothing in the BDA actually requires universities to favour patents above other transfer channels. Universities are free to choose to retain title to and pursue patent protection of federally funded inventions, and they are certainly also free to claim ownership and pursue patent protection of non-federally funded inventions.

In other words, the patent bias which is inherent in universities' technology transfer practices is as much associable with universities' lack of strategic commitment to broad dissemination and the protection of the scientific commons as it is with the BDA's bias towards patents. This commitment should come naturally to universities which historically not only showed care for the protection of the scientific commons but also always depended on it – and still do. Unfortunately, it looks like that increasingly universities will only be concerned with the honouring of the scientific commons in instances where it is relevant for their own research.[244]

In holding on to the ownership and patent-centred technology transfer practices, universities have not only ignored the BDA's above-mentioned larger objectives, but they also have ignored more recent calls by federal agencies, non-profit organisations, and scholars for universities to ensure the broad dissemination of federally supported research results. Accordingly, federal agencies and the National Research Council (NRC) have encouraged universities to consider the necessity of patents and to negotiate non-exclusive licenses where possible.[245] Federal agencies concern for the broad dissemination of federally funded research is also illustrated by the different strategies the NIH has employed outside the BDA to ensure wide access to federally funded research and to encourage universities (and other grantees) to use patents and exclusive licenses only moderately.[246]

3 Maximising Licensing Revenue Instead of the Public Benefit

There are two likely explanations for why universities continue to hold on to their 'traditional' patent-centred technology transfer practices. Firstly, the traditional approach is simpler in its implementation than processes which incor-

---

[244] See supra 6.A.III.3; also see e.g. R. Nelson (2004) 33 Research Policy 455, 467.

[245] See NIH (2004) 69 FR 223; the NRC supported the NIH's conclusions: 'The committee endorses these NIH policies, in particular the principles that patent recipients should analyse whether further research, development, and private investment are needed to realise the usefulness of their research results and that proprietary or exclusive means of dissemination should be pursued only when there is a compelling need. Also, whenever possible, licenses should be limited to relatively narrow and specific commercial application rather than as blanket exclusive licenses for uses that cannot be anticipated at the moment.', NRC, *Genomic and Proteomic Research* (2006) 138.

[246] See Rai and Eisenberg (2001) Proc. Conf. on Pub. Domain 157, 170–172; R. Nelson (2004) 33 Research Policy 455, 460–470.

porate differing paths and outcomes. Traditional technology transfer practices follow a linear, predictable formula: from invention disclosure, to provisional, national, and international patent applications, to licensing conversations and negotiations. Deviations from this process will result in complexities which will be difficult and ultimately costly to implement. TTO staff would need to dedicate more time to every invention disclosure, including spending time with inventors to understand the invention's context, potential and application, and it would also require TTO staff to be adequately trained and knowledgeable of the fields they are responsible for. Secondly, the possibility of generating additional income through technology transfer efforts has become a central focus of universities. As federal and state funding has continued to decrease over the past decades, universities have started to depend on alternative ways of generating additional income, commercialisation being one of them.[247]

While universities have been enthusiastic about their commercialisation enterprise, in the 40 years since the passage of the BDA, most universities have not been able to generate any income from these activities. Most TTOs' struggle to find licensees for the bulk of their patents to the point where less than half of active licenses normally do not produce any income at all.[248] TTOs are often also underfinanced.[249] Despite this meek bottom line, TTOs seem to be continuously motivated by the 'patent lottery effect'[250] and the potential of a 'blockbuster patent'.[251] Indeed, while TTOs often pursue multiple (sometimes even contradicting)[252] objectives, most TTO's consider the generation of licensing income to be more important than other objectives, such as faculty service, keeping individual faculty members happy,[253] technology commercialisation, economic development, fostering industry collaborations, and patent and licensing rankings.[254]

---

247 See supra 1.C.I.

248 See supra 6.A.II.

249 See e.g. Swamidass and Vulasa (2009) 34 J. Tech. Transfer 343, 350–351.

250 For a detailed discussion of the 'patent lottery effect', see Crouch (2008) 16 Geo. Mason L. Rev. 141, 141, suggesting that patents are similar to lottery tickets: While enough patents will allow the generation of some licensing income, only few are highly valuable. This low probability of winning a large jackpot is similar to a lottery; also making a reference to the lottery effect in intellectual property that was originally discussed by *Frederic M. Scherer*, ibid. 149 n. 39. Also see Lemley (2016) 95 Tex. L. Rev. 1, 40–41.

251 See e.g. Valdivia, *University Start-ups* (2013) 11, discussing how unlikely it is to discover a blockbuster invention; de Larena (2006) 43 Hous. L. Rev. 1373, 1381–1382.

252 See infra n. 428–430/III and accompanying discussion.

253 Despite the small budget of USD 250'000, staff of Virginia Tech's TTO confirmed that on occasion they will apply for a patent as a favour to professors, see TTO Board of Directors (n. 467/II). Also see de Larena (2006) 43 Hous. L. Rev. 1373, 1422.

254 See e.g. Mowery and others, *Ivory Tower* (2004) 189; Abrams and others (2009) 17 Research Mgmt. Rev. 1, 20–22; Thursby and others (2001) 26 J. Tech. Transfer 65; Markman and others (2005) 20 J. Bus. Ventur. 241, 249–251, 253–254, noting that TTOs consider licensing for cash to be the predominant objective.

Universities' financial focus is illustrated by several practices which universities have developed over the years. For instance, universities will obtain patents even if they are not necessary for the commercialisation of the invention in question.[255] In fact, some of these patents have been the most successful in the history of university licensing.[256] While the use of patents in such instances is against the spirit of the BDA, it is not the use of patents per se which is the problem but universities' practice of negotiating exclusive or restrictive licenses. Exclusive licenses may be especially damaging if an invention could be widely used (such as a research tool) or in the case of an early-stage invention which needs considerable development in order to be useful.[257]

Exclusive licenses are usually not necessary to facilitate the transfer of a technology if an invention is 'ready to use' out of the research laboratory.[258] But university inventions often are not the 'ready to use' but the 'embryonic' kind and, as such, are often several steps away from being commercially marketable.[259] The assumption therefore is that exclusivity is needed in order to attract investment for the further development of such an early-stage invention. This is indeed the practice which most universities follow.[260] But the reality is more nuanced than this: Firms often seem to be willing to accept non-exclusive licenses, also for embryonic inventions, especially if the patent is of high quality.[261] Moreover, at least part of the reason why universities have taken to exclusive licenses is not because they are necessary in order to commercialise a

[255] See e. g. Rai and Eisenberg (2003) 66 L. & Contemp. Probs. 289, 300.

[256] See e. g. Eisenberg and Cook-Deegan (2018) 147 Daedalus 76, 78; one prominent example is the 'Axel patents' on methods to insert foreign proteins into eukaryotic cells, from which Columbia University collected around USD 790 million licensing fees. NIH (which funded the research and owned it since it was pre-BDA) only assigned ownership to Columbia under the condition that it would 'use all reasonable effort to bring the (Axel patents) to the commercial market through licensing on a non-exclusive, royalty-free, or reasonable royalty basis' and would refrain from 'repressive' licensing practices, see Leaf, 'Unintended Consequences' (*Fortune*). Although Columbia had already collected USD 600 million during the original duration of the patent, it secretly filed a 'continuation application' in 1995, which covered advances made in the interim and which related to the original patent (a practice which has since been removed from US patent law). By delaying the application, Columbia ensured that it maximised the return on the research results, ibid. Also see Colaianni and Cook-Deegan (2009) 87 Milbank Q. 683. Another example are the three Cohen-Boyer patents on basic recombinant DNA techniques which yielded around USD 255 million to Stanford and University of California, see NRC, *Intellectual Property Rights and Research Tools* (1997) 40–42.

[257] Also see R. Nelson (2004) 33 Research Policy 455, 468.

[258] Colyvas and others (2002) 48 Mgmt. Sci. 61, 65–66.

[259] See supra n. 7/III; also see e. g. R. Nelson (2004) 33 Research Policy 455, 463; Mowery and Ziedonis (2015) 44 Research Policy 50, 60.

[260] TTO Board of Directors (n. 467/II); also see e. g. Lemley (2008) 18 Fordham Intell. Prop. Media & Ent. L. J. 610, 616–617; Mowery and Ziedonis (2015) 44 Research Policy 50, 60.

[261] The Cohen-Boyer patents are an often-cited example for a technology which yielded a great return but that was licensed unrestrictedly, see supra n. 129/III. Also see e. g. Colyvas and others (2002) 48 Mgmt. Sci. 61, 65.

given invention but because they tend to yield bigger returns than non-exclusive licenses.[262]

Ironically, it is exactly for embryonic technologies that the costs of exclusivity and the detriment to the public are greatest. There are two reasons for this: Firstly, the task of assessing whether an embryonic invention is capable of future commercial success is extremely demanding.[263] There are obvious information asymmetries among the parties involved in the licensing process which pose significant challenges to the effectiveness of the process. In this process, the TTO is often the least knowledgeable actor that lacks the (tacit) knowledge which makes a technology truly attractive to a potential licensee.[264] This knowledge is normally tied to the inventor – he is the most likely to have or develop an understanding of how an invention might be useful in a context outside of the research laboratory. Unfortunately, however, as will be detailed in the next subsection, the inventor is often not closely involved in the licensing process. The problem is exacerbated by the common practice of requiring inventors to disclose patentable inventions immediately upon discovery. In doing so, the decision to patent is moved further upstream, increasing the tendency that TTOs have to assess early stage inventions.

Secondly, it is equally difficult trying to identify a suitable industry partner which has the willingness and the capability needed to successfully develop the research further and possibly commercialise it.[265] While exclusivity may generate more revenue for the university in the short term, the TTO may bet on the 'wrong horse' and get stuck with a partner which is not willing or able to bring the invention to successful commercialisation.[266] This will hurt the university and the public in the long run. Indeed, the licensee may not even be interested

[262] See e. g. Bok, *Universities in the Marketplace* (2009) 120.

[263] See Jensen and Thursby (2001) 91 Am. Econ. Rev. 240, 240–241. Early filing of a patent application is typically recommended and is also encouraged by the law. But because there is often only little technical and market information on inventions available, early filing may not always be the sensible thing to do, see e. g. Cotropia (2009) 61 Hastings L. J. 65, 69.

[264] Dasgupta and David (1994) 23 Research Policy 487, 517; Kenney and Patton (2009) 38 Research Policy 1407, 1419.

[265] See e. g. Colyvas and others (2002) 48 Mgmt. Sci. 61, 66.

[266] TTO Review (n. 288/III): A promising water capturing invention was exclusively licensed to the licensee who appeared most attractive to the TTO staff in charge of the negotiations. A three-year development phase was agreed upon, but within a year the licensee stopped paying. Due to an administrative oversight the professor-inventors were not notified until many months after the licensee had stopped paying so that the professors continued to share information and new discoveries with the licensee. To date the future of the development of the invention is uncertain due to the university's inability to induce the licensee to pay or to help formulate an alternative strategy for the development of the invention. Also see e. g. Mowery and others, *Ivory Tower* (2004), detailing the case of a promising Columbia drug named 'Xalatan' (an eyedrop solution to treat glaucoma) the development of which did not proceed in a timely fashion despite the fact that a licensee was found and an exclusive licensee signed.

in the successful development of the invention but may simply hold or even obstruct the technology.[267]

Another practice which TTOs increasingly rely on to optimise their financial returns is the standard use of provisional patent applications.[268] By design, the law of provisional patents encourages to file early, which aggravates the above discussed problem of having to assess inventions early.[269] Provisional applications allow TTOs to protect university inventions from (unwanted) immanent disclosure. To this effect, researchers are generally told not to present at a conference or submit a paper until a provisional patent application has been filed.[270] Provisional applications also give TTOs a window of opportunity within which they may find a licensee and thus a way to finance the cost of patenting the invention.[271] It is not difficult to imagine that this strategy does not put universities in a comfortable position from which to negotiate with potential licensees. But more often than not, TTOs are willing to sacrifice the potential of longer term and more substantial benefits for immediate but comparatively small financial rewards.

Where universities have integrated provisional patent applications in their practices, they may feel inclined not to spend much time and money on the drafting of the provisional applications. After all, many provisional applications will not be converted into a non-provisional application, and spending time and money on drafting a non-provisional application may not seem justified. In an effort to keep costs low, TTOs therefore may file provisional patents themselves.[272] But attempting to save money on provisional patent applications

---

[267] TTO Board of Directors (n. 467/II); also see de Larena (2006) 43 Hous. L. Rev. 1373, 1383. Universities often include 'best effort' or 'due diligence' clauses in agreements to ensure the licensee's commitment to develop the invention. However, such clauses are difficult to enforce and their legal effect is uncertain, see e. g. Goldberg (2000) 44 St. Louis U. L. J. 1465.

[268] Provisional patents have been introduced in the US in 1995. A provisional patent application will not be examined by the USPTO and can be converted into a non-provisional application within 12 months of the filing date. The provisional application establishes an application's filing date, meaning that once the provisional is converted into a non-provisional, the patent application is considered filed as of the date of the provisional application, see 35 USC § 111 (b); Cotropia (2009) 61 Hastings L. J. 65, 77; Migliorini (2007) 89 J. Pat. & Tradem. Off. Soc'y 437, 438–441.

[269] Cotropia (2009) 61 Hastings L. J. 65, 77.

[270] TTO Board of Directors (n. 467/II); TTO Review (n. 288/III); also see Leaf, 'Unintended Consequences' (*Fortune*); McManis and Noh (2011) Wash. U. St. Louis Legal Stud. 1, 25, suggesting that provisional patents may well have affected significant change in university patenting behaviour, as early literature on provisional patents recommended that applicants immediately file on conception of the invention rather than after an actual reduction to practice.

[271] TTO Review (n. 288/III); also see e. g. Lemley (2008) 18 Fordham Intell. Prop. Media & Ent. L. J. 610, 616–617. The cost of filing provisional patents is comparatively low for universities at USD 140, see USPTO, 'Fee Schedule' (*USPTO*). Universities are considered 'small entities' and thus qualify for reduced fees, see 37 CFR § 1.27; 35 USC § 41(h)(1).

[272] TTO Board of Directors (n. 467/II).

is not advisable. A poorly written provisional patent application will result in a weak (if not useless) non-provisional patent application and issuing patent, as claims in the non-provisional application must be supported by the claims filed in the provisional patent application.[273] Thus, TTOs' common practice of simply attaching a coversheet to an abstract or conference presentation will not yield a strong issuing patent.

Universities' focus on maximising licensing revenue instead of maximising the social benefit of their research has also become apparent in the way in which universities enforce and litigate their patents. For instance, universities may seek broad patent rights for early-stage academic research in order to be able to sue firms which later develop products not disclosed by the patent application.[274] But even if universities do not employ patents in such strategic ways, many universities are ever more willing to enforce their patents in litigation.[275] In fact, they often will do so even if the firm they litigate has a successful commercial product which is unrelated to the patent the university holds.[276] The many accounts where universities have used their patents to collect enormous amounts in damage awards and out-of-court settlements has prompted commentators to refer to universities as patent trolls.[277]

The desire to generate revenue at all costs seems to be a short-sighted strategy which may backfire in the long run as universities attempt to collaborate with industry and rely on industry funding as their other income sources dwindle. Universities' aggressive licensing attitude and litigatious behaviour may induce mistrust and frustration on the part of industry and may deter industry partners from seeking collaborations with such contentious institutions.[278] It is almost ironic that – concerned about their reputation – more recently universities have

[273] See e. g. Guinn, 'Provisional Applications' (*IP Watchdog*).

[274] See Eisenberg and Cook-Deegan (2018) 147 Daedalus 76, 80–82, detailing two such lawsuits: *Regents of the University of California v. Eli Lilly* 119 F. 3d 1559 (Fed. Cir. 1997) and *University of Rochester v. G.* D. Searle & Co., Inc., 358 F.3d 916 (Fed. Cir. 2004). The authors illustrate the Federal Circuit's critical stance on this practice and that it voiced concern that broad patents hinder the progress of science and the commercialisation of university research, Eisenberg and Cook-Deegan (2018) 147 Daedalus 76, 82.

[275] See e. g. Rooksby (2011) 10 J. Marshall Rev. Intell. Prop. L. 623, 638; Chung, 'Schools that Sue' (*Reuters*).

[276] Eisenberg and Cook-Deegan (2008) 147 Daedalus 76, 82.

[277] See e. g. *Carnegie Mellon v. Marvell Technology Group* 807 F. 3d 1283 (Fed. Cir. 2015), where Marvell was ordered to pay USD 278 million in damages; *Convolve and MIT v. Compaq and* Seagate (Fed. Cir. 2013). *Mark Lemley* was the first to raise the question whether universities are the new patent trolls, see Lemley (2008) 18 Fordham Intell. Prop. Media & Ent. L. J. 610, 612. Also see e. g. Lee, 'Patent Trolls' (*Washington Post*).

[278] Indeed, there is the 'belief on the part of industry (80 %) that universities are exercising their intellectual property rights too aggressively', see Siegel and others (2003) 32 Research Policy 27, 43. Also see TTO Review (n. 288/III); Link and others (2018) 34 Issues Sci. Tech. 33.

begun to outsource their patent enforcement to patent assertion entities (PAE) more commonly referred to as patent trolls.[279]

Universities' business attitude is particularly contestable when one considers universities' special status as non-profit and often public institutions. As non-profit institutions, universities are exempt from federal income taxation on income derived from research results, including licensing income.[280] Universities also do not pay state and local property tax on laboratory spaces and buildings.[281] The rationale for not taxing private and public universities is that their educational purposes of teaching, research, and public service are considered to be 'critical to the well-being of (a) democratic society'.[282] This made sense in a world where universities predominately were concerned with their traditional missions, but the same policy is difficult to justify in a world where universities are increasingly motivated by commercial interests and financial gain.[283]

At the very least, there is a discrepancy between universities' role (and the public perception of universities' role) as stewards of the public interest and universities' financially motivated business behaviours. The latter is often not in the best interest of society and, in context of federally funded research, conflicts with universities' responsibility under the BDA. Universities' selective commitment to the BDA is also illustrated by universities' poor record of complying with their duty to report to the federal government the patents that they obtained from federally funded inventions.[284] Perhaps even more troublingly, there is a long history of misuse of federal funds by universities – ranging from falsifying research results to double billing federal agencies.[285] This is why it seems important to hold universities accountable for the manner in which they manage their research results beyond the existing oversight from federal agencies, as will be discussed in the final section of this chapter.

4 Marginalising University Professors and Researchers

While university researchers are crucial to the academic enterprise and a successful technology transfer process, the interests of the TTO and researchers are

[279] See e.g. Katz, 'Universities Have Turned over Hundreds of Patents to Patent Trolls' (*Medium*). *Katz* found that Intellectual Venture's (a US based patent troll and one of top-five owners of US patents) portfolio of over 30'000 patents included 500 patents from universities.

[280] See supra 1.C.II; also see Blumberg (1996) 145 U. Pa. L. Rev. 89, 92.

[281] Ibid. 91–92.

[282] AAU, 'Tax Exemption for Universities and Colleges' (*AAU*).

[283] See e.g. Blumberg (1996) 145 U. Pa. L. Rev. 89, 92–93, predicting that 'the tax exemption for licensing and royalty income derived from such activity may be called into question. It is well settled that an otherwise-exempt organization that engages in an 'unrelated trade or business' must pay income tax on its 'unrelated income'.

[284] See supra 5.C.III.4.

[285] See de Larena (2006) 43 Hous. L. Rev. 1373, 1402–1411, for a detailed account of some of these misuses.

often misaligned.[286] The first important step in the technology transfer process is the disclosure. In fact, the whole technology transfer system rests on the assumption that researchers will disclose their inventions. To give researchers an incentive to disclose their inventions, the BDA mandates universities to share a percentage of income derived from inventions with inventors.[287] But despite the incentive, an astonishingly high amount of faculty inventors does not disclose or otherwise obstructs their institution's technology transfer processes.[288]

There are different ways in which faculty may do this: they may simply not disclose an invention; they may publish the research prior to disclosure; they may establish a firm in order for the invention to be developed under the firm and in order to circumvent the disclosure requirement; or they may minimally disclose the invention or minimally cooperate in the technology transfer process.[289] The reasons for such behaviours vary: Often faculty care more about funding than patent rights and are willing to forfeit rights to inventions for funding.[290] In other cases, researchers may not actually recognise when an invention is patentable.[291] Researchers also may not have an incentive to disclose their research due to previous frustrating experiences or due to bad examples which they witnessed from colleagues.[292] Finally, they may simply not want to spend time away from their research.[293]

Moreover, faculty often are confronted with a trade-off which boils down to basic business considerations: If a researcher manages to attract a firm with-

---

[286] See e. g. Dasgupta and David (1994) 23 Research Policy 487, 517.

[287] See 35 USC § 202(c)(7)(B); 37 CFR 401.14(f)(2). Disclosure is typically also mandated by universities' patent policies.

[288] The author led the external review of Virginia Tech's TTO in spring 2017. A total of 46 interviews were conducted: Researchers with a significant number of disclosures and/or a licensing history from each college, key-administrators, and all staff of the TTO were interviewed. Several interviewees stated that it was an open secret that the university's disclosure provision would often be bypassed (cited as 'TTO Review'). This is also confirmed by larger scale studies, see e. g. Markman and others (2008) 55 IEEE Trans. on Eng. Mgmt. 29, 33–35. In their study, they assessed a total of 23'394 faculty members, 3'200 of which were awarded patents between 1989 and 2003. Of these 3'200 inventors, 1'348 (over 42 %) bypassed their institutions at least one time and more than 33 % inventions developed in university laboratories were appropriated privately. Also see Jensen and others (2003) 21 Int'l J. Ind. Org. 1271, 1272, indicating that many TTO directors believe that substantially less than half of faculty inventions with commercial potential are disclosed to their office.

[289] TTO Review (n. 288/III); Kenney and Patton (2009) 38 Research Policy 1407, 1414.

[290] See infra n. 294–295/III.

[291] TTO Review (n. 288/III); Villasenor (2012). This is also suggested by the new 2018 BDA Rule, which stipulates that universities ought to educate their researchers on basic patenting requirements and elements of the patenting process, see 37 CFR § 401.14(f)(2).

[292] Faculty may be frustrated in cases where they disclosed several inventions and the TTO decided not to pursue applications for them. Some faculty also have a desire to establish a company and consider the TTO as not helpful or knowledgeable in this pursuit, see TTO Review (n. 288/III). Also see e. g. Owen-Smith and Powell (2001) 26 J. Tech. Transfer 99, 112.

[293] TTO Review (n. 288/III); also see Jensen and others (2003) 21 Int'l J. Ind. Org. 1271, 1272; de Larena (2006) 43 Hous. L. Rev. 1373, 1376–1377.

out involving the TTO, a bigger payout may be the result. Whether a researcher will disclose their invention thus often also depends on whether there is an existing collaboration with a firm and whether there have been external contributions made to the research project in question.[294] If a strong enough connection with a firm exists, faculty may sell or license their inventions directly to this firm. Finally, whether a researcher follows his institutions' technology transfer processes may often also depend on the seniority and character of the researcher.[295]

Whatever the reasons may be for faculty to bypass their institution's policy, the reality is that many faculty do and as a result a high percentage of inventions will be appropriated privately.[296] Universities will thus only own inventions if inventors choose to adhere to the respective policy and to disclose their invention. This means that who ultimately will own a particular university invention is often not as much determined by a university's patent policy as it is by considerations which ultimately lie in the hand of the respective inventor. For this reason alone, universities should ensure to tailor their technology transfer processes to their researchers.

But researchers are important to the technology transfer process beyond the disclosure. They are also critical to a successful patent application process. Unless researchers work closely with TTO staff and patent attorneys, the quality of the ensuing patent may negatively be affected. Researchers' close participation and input is also crucial in the identification of and negotiation with potential licensees. In many instances, TTOs are rather passive in their approach to licensing.[297] They may try to find suitable licensees by cold calling which seldom yields the desired result. Moreover, in doing so, TTOs risk drawing attention to research which may potentially infringe on existing patents.[298] Ultimately, TTOs often rely heavily on faculty to identify or even connect them with possible industry contacts.[299] Once a potential licensee is identified, researchers' know-how will also be crucial during this step, as researchers are the ones most familiar with the science or technology at hand. They are in the best position to identify or develop an understanding of how their work might be applied

[294] TTO Review (n. 288/III); also see Crespi and others (2010) 19 Econ. Innov. New Tech. 627, 629–631.

[295] Ibid.

[296] Also see Markman and others (2008) 55 IEEE Trans. on Eng. Mgmt. 29, 33–35; Kenney and Patton (2009) 38 Research Policy 1407, 1414.

[297] TTO Board of Directors (n. 467/II); also see e. g. de Larena (2006) 43 Hous. L. Rev. 1373, 1413–1414.

[298] TTO Board of Directors (n. 467/II).

[299] Ibid.; TTO Review (n. 288/III); also see Thursby and others (2001) 26 J. Tech. Transfer 62–63, stating that in their study 58 % of respondents listed inventor contacts as useful for marketing and suggesting that the number could be as high as 75 % as from the answers it was not always clear whether 'personal contacts' referred to their own or faculty contacts; de Larena (2006) 43 Hous. L. Rev. 1373, 1413–1414.

in a context outside their laboratory.[300] Finally, the successful commercialisation often depends on researchers' cooperation with the licensee firm, especially where inventions are embryonic.[301]

But despite the crucial role faculty play, the technology transfer processes are often not centred on them but on the TTOs and their administrators instead. They are the ones making the important decisions, for instance, whether a certain invention disclosure has potential and should be patented and whether a licensing deal should be pursued or not. It is them – and not professors and researchers – who have come to dominate the voice of universities in patent policy debates.[302] In many ways, universities' technology transfer efforts can be considered the figurative tail wagging the dog: Rather than the TTO providing a service to professors it appears to be the professors' duty to provide the TTO with the information it needs to do its job.[303]

It is not without challenge to successfully get faculty to collaborate in the process and to adhere to the policy. Attempts to deter faculty from bypassing institutional policies by monitoring them or limiting interactions with industry may backfire and are thus not advisable. However, there are better ways of inducing researchers' participation, for instance, by increasing their share of royalty income or by giving them other non-pecuniary incentives.[304] Universities should also invest in fostering a culture of trust, thereby inducing faculty to work within the limits of institutional norms.[305]

But beyond this, universities should attempt to design the technology transfer process with the inventor in mind. This includes locating the TTO on campus, perhaps even having TTO staff work on site with researchers and research laboratories. Universities also should invest in educating researchers on the basics of patent law and the technology transfer process and ensure that their

300 TTO Board of Directors (n. 467/II); TTO Review (n. 288/III); also see e. g. Dasgupta and David (1994) 23 Research Policy 487, 517.

301 TTO Board of Directors (n. 467/II); TTO Review (n. 288/III); also see e. g. Jensen and Thursby (2001) 91 Am. Econ. Rev. 240, 243, 255; Thursby and others (2001) 26 J. Tech. Transfer 62.

302 Universities undertake many efforts to give even more power to university and technology transfer administrators. Accordingly, universities have sought to expand their patent rights by lobbying Congress to change the patent laws in their favour, see Eisenberg and Cook-Deegan (2018) 147 Daedalus 76, 84–86; detailing universities' efforts in context of the CREATE Act of 2004 and the AIA of 2011 – in both cases universities managed to influence changes that would make it easier for them to obtain and enforce patents, see ibid.

303 This is illustrated by e. g. Dasgupta and David (1994) 23 Research Policy 487, 517, detailing what the ultimate consequence of a focus on technology transfer activities by universities means in regard to the relationship between the institution and the faculty members.

304 Markman and others (2008) 55 IEEE Trans. on Eng. Mgmt. 29, 35; Kenney and Patton (2009) 38 Research Policy 1407, 1413; Lach and Schankerman (2008) 39 RAND J. Econ. 403, 427; Friedman and Silberman (2003) 28 J. Tech. Transfer 17, 26; Owen-Smith and Powell (2001) 26 J. Tech. Transfer 99, 113.

305 See e. g. Markman and others (2008) 55 IEEE Trans. on Eng. Mgmt. 29, 29–30.

disclosure forms and general paperwork are user-friendly. Finally, universities should include inventors in the decision making process regarding the commercial potential, the desirably of patent protection, and potential licensing options of the respective invention. Indeed, there is indication that one of the most important factors which favourably influences commercialisation successes are technology transfer practices which engage inventors.[306]

B Who Should Own University Inventions?

I Comparing Government, Inventor, and University Ownership

The BDA, universities' patent policies, and technology transfer practices, all centre on university ownership. This raises the question to what extent ownership really influences the dissemination of university research results and the efficiency and efficacy of technology transfer. A considerable amount of literature has analysed this question pre- and post-BDA and has suggested that it does matter whether ownership vests in the inventor, the government, or the university.[307] In these discussions, focus is typically placed on whether a given approach would increase universities' commercialisation outcomes. In other words, models under which patent and licensing numbers may be maximised are typically preferred, suggesting that greatest benefit from university research is derived for society if such research is developed into commercially marketable products.

But, as mentioned above, commercialisation may not always be in society's best interest.[308] The question of who should own university inventions should thus not be narrowly focused on which model most likely yields the greatest commercialisation numbers but should consider who is most likely to act with the public interest in mind and is most likely to protect the scientific commons. A brief comparison of the different ownership models will follow and will include economic as well as historic, philosophical, and social considerations.

The discussion will consider 'public funding' in a broad sense and thus not only focus on university research which is financed through the receipt of federal grants. Contrary to common perception, most public and private universities depend on governmental support beyond the receipt of federal grants and state support for public institutions. Accordingly, public and private universities' budgets heavily depend on federal student loans, tuition tax credits, and

306 Agrawal (2006) 27 Strateg. Mgmt. J. 63, 77.

307 See supra n. 361–362/II and n. 32/III and accompanying discussions respectively; also see e. g. Geuna and Rossi (2011) 40 Research Policy 1068; Crespi and others (2010) 19 Econ. Innov. New Tech. 627; Kenney and Patton (2011) 40 Research Policy 1100.

308 See supra 6. B.

on substantial tax subsidies (on endowments, buildings, and income).[309] For the purpose of the following discussion it is this broader notion of 'public funding' which needs to be borne in mind.

1 Government Ownership

Government ownership of federally funded inventions never was adopted as a unified federal policy in the US. The so-called 'title policy' first appeared as early as 1933 and increasingly became popular in the 1960s and the early 1970s in many federal agencies.[310]

The dominant justification for government ownership is an economic one. It is congruent with the justification for employer ownership of employee-inventions: Since the government provides the funding, it also should own the inventions which result from the funding. Indeed, this was the core argument of the advocates of the title policy who were in favour of government ownership of federally funded research.[311] From the point of view of society, government ownership is beneficial as the government is the most likely stakeholder to honour and protect the public interest and the least likely to be motivated by financial and self-serving interests.

There are two big challenges with government ownership: Firstly, government's organisational and work culture – which in tendency is bureaucratic and slow-moving – is distinct to the academic culture and the culture in industry. This would make it challenging for government agencies to collaborate with industry, find suitable licensees, and connect inventors with industry. Secondly, federal agencies are physically and geographically removed from universities. This would not easily allow federal agencies to closely work with universities and inventors and to establish efficient processes. Researchers could feel alienated and, as a result, would bypass and obstruct the technology transfer process.[312] After all, smooth processes and close collaboration between technology transfer officers and inventors are essential for an efficient and effective technology transfer operation.

Indeed, the government agencies' inability to establish efficient processes, to closely collaborate with universities and researchers, and their difficulty in generating interest in industry for university inventions were among the main reasons for the introduction of the BDA.[313]

---

309 See supra 1. C. II. 2.

310 See supra 5. B. I.

311 See supra n. 301–303/II accompanying discussion.

312 An issue that also can arise in the current setting if the TTO is situated in an off-campus location, see TTO Review (n. 288/III).

313 See supra 5. B.

2 Inventor Ownership

As noted above, in the US in the early years of universities' involvement with patents, inventor ownership was the norm and several universities continued to adhere to the inventor ownership model up until the 1960s.[314] Often inventor ownership did not only cover federally funded inventions but also university-supported research. In Europe, during the better part of the 20th century, especially Scandinavian and German-speaking countries adhered to inventor ownership as well.[315] The so-called 'professor's privilege' was generally restricted to inventions which were derived from publicly funded research.[316] As the term suggests, the professor's privilege was often formulated as an exception to existing employee-invention legislation in the respective countries.[317]

The probably strongest justification for inventor ownership is based on natural law and assumes that the inventor has a natural right in his own idea. The invention is thus considered an extension of the inventor's personality which society is morally obligated to recognise and protect.[318] Based on this argument, it would make sense for faculty to own and control the fate of their inventions. Not surprisingly, faculty normally support this view, often out of a conviction that inventions should not be treated differently to copyrightable works.[319]

Professors' right to their inventions may also be justified on the grounds that they should be rewarded for their inventive activity and their contribution to society. Similarly, inventor ownership may create an incentive for professors to develop inventions in the first place and, as such, may increase universitas' overall inventive productivity.[320] These latter two justifications sit uncomfortably with the traditional notion of a professor who is not motivated by economic goals and who believes that financially driven incentives would 'render sterile the soil of human intellect'.[321] This traditional notion expects the professor to conduct research for the pure love of discovery. According to this reasoning, inventions would neither be considered a reward nor an incentive but a mere by-product of research activities.

The reward and incentive justifications are also flawed in the context of publicly funded research. In theory, publicly funded research addresses the same incentive problem as patents do. Using patents as an additional incentive, results in the overlaying of two institutions which are considered alternatives to

314 See supra 7.A.I.1.

315 See e.g. Pettersson (2018) 56 Minerva 381, 396.

316 See e.g. Patrick van Eecke and others, *Monitoring and Analysis* (2007) 45.

317 See Pettersson (2018) 396; see infra 7.B.II.

318 See supra 2.A.III.

319 See supra 4.B.

320 See supra 2.A.III; also see e.g. Chew (1992) 1 Wis. L. Rev. 259, 309–310; Kulkarni (1995) 47 Hastings L.J. 221, 250–252.

321 Bok, *Universities in the Marketplace* (2009) 140, quoting the mathematician *Norbert Wiener*.

each other.[322] In other words, from a theoretical point of view, it is questionable whether an additional incentive is required if research is already incentivised through other means. Nevertheless, from a practical point of view, and in a reality where universities continue to move towards entrepreneurial activities, professors' motivations may be changing too. Evidently, the argument that inventor ownership may attract and help retain (especially entrepreneurially minded) faculty gains ever more traction.[323] Seen from this perspective, inventor ownership would present an additional perk which universities could use in negotiations with faculty members.

Inventor ownership has been proposed by several scholars as a solution to the problems presented by the current university ownership model.[324] These proposals often refer to the arguably most compelling argument for inventor ownership, namely that it leaves the decision about patenting and commercialisation to the person who is most knowledgeable of the invention, its potential application, and of potential licensees. The flipside is that patenting outcomes may be negatively influenced by a researcher's lack of financial resources and his potential inability to effectively negotiate with licensees.

But beyond efficiency, inventor ownership raises the general question whether faculty are able to adequately protect the public interest. Accordingly, faculty may be driven by financial and otherwise self-serving goals. This potentially could be mitigated by having inventors pay a share of their licensing income to their university.[325] But aside from financial motives, assessing how an invention should be disseminated in a way which maximises its benefits to society, and (where necessary) dealing with the tasks of pursuing patent protection and finding a suitable licensee, may not fall in the skillset of many academics or, at the very least, could potentially distract faculty from their research and teaching responsibilities.

3 University Ownership

Universities in the US and in most European countries, including the UK, France, Denmark, Austria, Germany, Finland, Switzerland, and Norway adhere to some type of university ownership.[326] Several countries have abolished the professor's privilege only more recently in favour of university ownership. Spe-

[322] See supra n. 306–312/I and accompanying discussion.

[323] TTO Review (n. 288/III); also see e. g. Chew (1992) 1 Wis. L. Rev. 259, 284–285; Kulkarni (1995) 47 Hastings L. J. 221, 224.

[324] See e. g. Kenney and Patton (2009) 38 Research Policy 1407, 1414, 1419; Clements (2008) 49 Idea 469, 496–498; Chew (1992) 1 Wis. L. Rev. 259, 311; Greenbaum and Scott (2010) 15 Sci. Tech. Soc. 55, 68–69, proposing an 'opt-in' model that would allow faculty to choose to retain ownership within a window of two to six months following disclosure.

[325] See e. g. Kenney and Patton (2009) 38 Research Policy 1407, 1415.

[326] See e. g. van Eecke and others, *Monitoring and Analysis* (2007) 44–49; Hvide and Jones (2018) 108 Am. Econ. Rev. 1860.

cial mention deserves Italy, which adopted the professor's privilege in 2001 and essentially reverted back to university ownership in 2005 by only maintaining the professor's privilege for inventions derived from research which is not externally funded.[327] Today, Sweden is the only European country which still adheres to the professor's privilege.[328]

The most common justifications for university ownership are the (perceived) weaknesses of alternative ownership models, i. e. the inventor and government ownership model. As such, they are generally economically motivated and based on the conviction that university inventions are under-used and under-exploited if they are owned by the government or the inventor.[329] The university is in the better position to successfully pursue patent protection and commercialisation for two reasons: Firstly, universities maintain a closer relationship with inventors than government agencies. Secondly, universities are better equipped to pursue patent protection than inventors due to more available financial resources and technology transfer and industry expertise. University ownership and the prospect of earning royalties may also give universities an incentive to identify commercially promising research.[330]

Similarly to government ownership, university ownership may also be justified based on the analogy of industry taking ownership of employee inventions. Of importance here is that universities provide the context within which researchers conduct their work and provide (at least partially) the necessary resources. This is at the same time the weak point of university ownership: Faculty typically define and conduct their research in a self-directed way and are immune from supervision and control in a way that employees in industry are not. University administrators do not have the discretion and supervisory authority that industry leadership has over their employees and their work. Giving university administrators the authority over the disposition of faculty research sits uncomfortably with the essence of the academic freedom and production.[331]

But university ownership not only seems justified due to universities' advantageous position compared to the government and inventors as regards the patenting and commercialisation of inventions. Perhaps most importantly, due to universities' historic role as stewards of the public interest, universities seem optimally positioned to assess how a given invention should be disseminated in a manner which maximises the benefit to society. Indeed, this was one of

327 Sterzi and others (2019) 28 Ind. Corp. Change 309, 312.

328 Åstebro and others (2018) ILR Rev. 1096.

329 See e. g. NRC, *University Intellectual Property* (2011) 61, concluding that university ownership of inventions from publicly funded research 'is unquestionably more effective' than government ownership.

330 Bok, *Universities in the Marketplace* (2009) 141, pointing out that this was Congress' main argument for university ownership.

331 To this effect, see AAUP (2014) Bulletin AAUP 38, 47.

the main arguments of the proponents of the BDA for university ownership.[332] While nobody could have foreseen that universities would be progressively motivated by the potential financial returns of patenting activities and would thus neglect the protection of the public interest, this does not in itself negate the arguments for university ownership. In other words, university ownership may still be the optimal and most viable solution, but universities need to be redirected to the protection of the public interest and the scientific commons.

II The Influential Concept of University Ownership

Since the 1980 adoption of the BDA in the US, governments around the world have also moved from government or inventor ownership models to a university ownership model or have considered such a change.[333] Policy goals were often similar if not identical to the policy goals underlying the BDA, namely, to encourage the patenting and commercialisation of university inventions.[334]

In the following discussion, Germany and Switzerland will be analysed and compared to the US experience in order to gain insights to what extent ownership of university research influences technology transfer efforts. While a considerable amount of literature has analysed these efforts in both countries, the following sub-sections merely attempt to give a broad overview. Germany and Switzerland are chosen as examples for two reasons. Firstly, their respective economies repeatedly have been considered amongst the most innovative in the world.[335] Secondly, both countries have developed their own unique perspective on university ownership. Germany abolished the professor's privilege in 2002 and operates essentially under a hybrid model. Conversely, Swiss universities have always adhered to a moderate form of university ownership.

1 Germany

In Germany, ownership rights in an invention originate with the Inventor. But like in the US, ownership rights may be transferred to someone else, by contractual agreement or if an employer claims an employee-invention (*einseitige Inanspruchnahme*)[336] under the German law on employee-inventions (*Arbeitnehmererfindergesetz, ArbnErfG*).[337] In fact, an employer does not need to explicitly claim the rights. As long as he will not release them back to the inventor within four months after disclosure, the rights will be transferred to the employ-

---

332 See supra 5. B. III.

333 See supra n. 25/III accompanying text.

334 See e. g. van Eecke and others, *Monitoring and Analysis* (2007) 20.

335 On the 2020 Bloomberg Innovation Index Germany ranks 1st, Switzerland ranks 4th, see Jamrisko and Lu, 'Most Innovative Nation' (*Bloomberg*).

336 §§ 6(1) and 7(1) ArbnErfG.

337 § 6(1) Patent Act (*Patentgesetz*, PatG); § 15 PatG.

er automatically.[338] Of course, this presupposes that the employee-inventor is under an obligation to immediately disclose his invention to the employer.[339]

Prior to 2002, professors were exempt from the obligation of disclosing inventions to their employers under the ArbnErfG.[340] Inventions developed by professors or university researchers were considered to be 'free inventions' (*freie Erfindungen*) under the ArbnErfG that – in contrast to 'service inventions' (*Diensterfindungen*) – belonged to the inventor.[341] It was researchers' decision whether or not to purse patent protection for a specific invention, but researchers also bore the financial and the administrative burden of such a decision. Researchers were often neither willing to bear the financial risk nor to engage with the bureaucratic and time-intensive effort which patenting necessitated and often only pursued patent protection if it was required due to an agreement with a third party funder or collaborator.[342] The inability to successfully translate research results from universities and research institutes into technological and commercial application had been coined the 'European paradox'.[343] Germany was considered to suffer from this paradox as – despite its exceptional scientific research enterprise – it lagged behind the US in terms of university patenting and commercialisation activities.[344]

In response to this weak commercialisation performance, the German ministry of education and research (BMBF) launched the so-called 'exploitation offensive' (*Verwertungsoffensive*), at the core of which was the abolition of professor's privilege. In BMBF's view, professor's privilege was responsible that the 'considerable innovation potential' present at universities was underused to the detriment of the German economy.[345] The apparent success of US universities with generating income from university patents, supported the view that the professor's privilege was detrimental to an effective exploitation of university research.[346]

Under the new ArbnErfG, professors are under an obligation to disclose inventions to the employer two months before publication, unless the inventor has no intention of publishing the research.[347] In contrast to the US, in most cases

---

338 § 6(2) ArbnErfG; see Krasser, in *Hochschulrecht* (2016) 832, 844.

339 § 5(1) ArbnErfG.

340 § 42 ArbnErfG.

341 § 4(1) and (2) ArbnErfG.

342 Krasser, in *Hochschulrecht* (2016) 832, 847; Cuntz and others (2012) Studien zum deutschen Innovationssystem 5; Grimm and Jaenicke (2012) 37 J. Tech. Transfer 454, 456.

343 European Commission, *Third European Report* (2003) 430.

344 See e. g. Czarnitzki and others (2015) 15–007 ZEW 4.

345 BMBF, *Knowledge Creates Markets* (2001) 3–5.

346 Ibid. 3: 'Lower royalties at German higher education institutions in comparison e. g. to American universities are an indicator of deficits in professional exploitation.'; BLK, *Jahresbericht 2000* (2001) 49, quoting that only 1,8 % of national patent applications stemmed from university research; Cuntz and others (2012) Studien zum deutschen Innovationssystem 6.

347 § 42(1) and (2) ArbnErfG; it is a professor's right to decide when or even whether the

the state government and not the university is the employer of professors and researchers.[348] Disclosures will still have to be made to the university as the university is entitled to represent and act for the government for the purposes of the provisions under the ArbnErfG.[349] The authority of the university to act on behalf of the government extends to interactions with the patent office and to negotiations with potential licensees. This also means that the government and not the university holds the rights to the patent applications, the issued patents, and the claims to licensing contracts.[350] Strictly speaking, then, Germany does *not* adhere to university ownership, as is generally referred to in the literature,[351] but to employer ownership. In contrast to the US, where universities may elect to own title to federally funded inventions and other European countries, where ownership is directly transferred to the university, in Germany the university will never own title to inventions.

The scope of inventions which the university may claim under the ArbnErfG is a topic of some controversy.[352] As mentioned above, the ArbnErfG distinguishes between free inventions and service inventions. Inventions which arise from research which forms part of a professor's responsibilities are considered to be service inventions. The decisive factor is not whether it was in the researchers' discretion to define the area and scope of the research, but whether he was obligated to conduct the research. If he was and an invention results, the invention is considered to be a service invention.[353] If an invention is developed outside of a professor's responsibilities, the invention will be considered a free invention as long as it was not developed based on research and knowledge gained from university duties.[354]

If the university chooses to file a patent application, it has to do so within four months of the disclosure of the invention.[355] If no patent application is filed within this time frame, the professor is at liberty to publish the research results without further notice to the university.[356] If the university pursues patent pro-

---

results of research projects should be published, see e. g. Trimborn, *Arbeitnehmererfindungsrecht* (2013) 27.

[348] This is different in the case of private universities; however, they are typically small and more applied in focus.

[349] Krasser, in *Hochschulrecht* (2016) 832, 849.

[350] Ibid.

[351] See e. g. von Proff and others (2012) 19 Ind. Innov. 23, 25; Czarnitzki and others (2015) 15–007 ZEW 24, 'Among these countries is Germany, where a Bayh–Dole-like intellectual property rights regime for university inventions was adopted in 2002. […] the new legislation allocates intellectual property rights on academic inventions to the universities.'

[352] See Krasser, in *Hochschulrecht* (2016) 832, 850–852.

[353] See ibid. 850; Bergmann, *Erfindungen von Hochschulbeschäfitgen* (2006) 49–58; but contrast with Bartenbach and Hellebrand (2002) Mitt. 165, 167.

[354] Krasser, in *Hochschulrecht* (2016) 832, 851–852.

[355] § 6 ArbnErfG.

[356] Trimborn, *Arbeitnehmererfindungsrecht* (2013) 27.

tection, researchers receive a non-exclusive license to use the invention in the context of their research and teaching activities.[357] Finally, they are also entitled to 30% of the gross income which is generated by the commercial exploitation of the invention.[358]

The second piece of the BMBF's exploitation offensive was the creation of a professional patent and exploitation infrastructure in Germany.[359] The abolition of the professor's privilege was complemented by federal subsidies which would allow the establishment of a network of patent exploitation agencies (*Patentverwertungsagenturen*, PVA). From the US perspective, PVAs are unique as they are federal TTOs that operate on a regional level (typically a *Bundesland* or a part thereof) and assist all institutions of higher education in that region with patenting and commercialisation issues.[360] It was not the goal for PVA's to replace universities' TTOs but to supplement them by providing researchers across Germany with professional expertise on matters of patents and commercialisation.[361] Specifically, PVAs were meant to provide a one-stop-shop which would facilitate the process of commercialisation for researchers, thereby giving researchers an incentive to patent and commercialise their inventions.[362]

The transition from the old to the new regime proved challenging. It was especially difficult to overcome researchers' and universities' resistance towards the newly established PVAs.[363] Over the last decade, PVAs' outputs have improved: Patent applications filed, licenses negotiated, and income generated have grown in numbers.[364] Despite this, PVAs do not break even and the number of university-invented patents has decreased (compared to the number of university-owned patents which have increased).[365] This suggests that the amended ArbnErfG did not encourage more patent activity but merely shifted assignment patterns away from inventors and firms toward universities.[366] Indeed, the new ArbnErfG appears to have especially affected researchers who

---

[357] § 42(3) ArbnErfG.

[358] § 42(4) ArbnErfG; Trimborn, *Arbeitnehmererfindungsrecht* (2013) 28.

[359] BMBF, *Knowledge Creates Markets* (2001) 3.

[360] See ibid. 3; Grimm and Jaenicke (2012) 37 J. Tech. Transfer 454, 456.

[361] BMBF, *Knowledge Creates Markets* (2001) 4.

[362] Grimm (2011) 12 Int'l J. Entrepreneurship Small Bus. 459, 461; BMBF, *Knowledge Creates Markets* (2001) 4–5.

[363] See e. g. Sellenthin (2009) 34 J. Tech. Transfer 603, 605.

[364] Cuntz and others (2012) Studien zum deutschen Innovationssystem 9.

[365] 'University-owned patents' refers to patents that are invented by university researchers and are owned by the university. 'University-invented patents' are patents that are invented by university researchers but are owned by inventors or by third parties, such as firms in industry. 'University patents' is referred to when talking about the sum of university-owned and university-invented patents; see Cuntz and others (2012) Studien zum deutschen Innovationssystem 10, 16–18; von Proff and others (2012) 19 Ind. Innov. 23, 25; Czarnitzki and others (2015) 15-007 ZEW 24; Cunningham and others (2019) J. Tech. Transfer 1451, 1467.

[366] See von Proff and others (2012) 19 Ind. Innov. 23, 41–42.

had prior patenting experience and connections with industry: For these researchers patenting activities decreased substantially.[367]

These numbers suggest the sobering conclusion that the reform of ArbnErfG did not achieve its goal. However, there are factors outside the law change which may have contributed to these developments. A substantial decrease of university patenting was registered already in 2000, thus, before the introduction of the new ArbnErfG in 2002.[368] It was noted that during the 1990s there was an increased expectation for universities to patent their inventions. What may have happened is that due to this pressure, universities essentially patented-away their research pipeline to the point that not as many patentable inventions were left by the time the new ArbnErfG was introduced.[369] Other factors which are being discussed as having at least contributed to the overall decline are the end of the new economy boom, a general decrease in biotechnology inventions (related to uncertainties and changes in the law), an increased emphasis on publications in academic performance evaluations, and a shrinking of the academic job market.[370]

A thorough analysis of these factors would go beyond the reach of this section. What can be observed, however, is that even if these factors contributed to a decline, it seems counterintuitive that especially experienced researchers with industry exposure have been discouraged to patent and engage in commercialisation activities by the new ArbnErfG. Taking into account the literature, the opposite should have happened for the following two reasons. Firstly, researchers who have gained previous experience with patenting normally are more likely to patent again and often patent actively.[371] Secondly, it has been shown that researchers who can draw on a comparatively good support infrastructure typically patent more actively than researchers without such a supportive infrastructure.[372] Applied to Germany, if one were to adopt the view that PVA's improved professors technology transfer infrastructure as was intended, especially experienced professors should have been induced to patent again and more actively due to these changes.

It will be difficult to conclusively establish why commercialisation numbers have developed the way they did at German universities. Nevertheless, there are additional factors which may have influenced this development and which

367 Schmoch, *Patentanmeldungen* (2007) 7; Czarnitzki and others (2015) 15–007 ZEW 24.

368 Schmoch, *Patentanmeldungen* (2007) 5; Czarnitzki and others (2015) 15–007 ZEW 26.

369 Schmoch, *Patentanmeldungen* (2007) 7.

370 See e. g. Schmoch, *Patentanmeldungen* (2007) 5–9; Czarnitzki and others (2015) 15–007 ZEW 14–15; von Ledebur (2008) 88 WD 604, 606–607.

371 See e. g. Sellenthin (2009) 34 J. Tech. Transfer 603, 618; Walter and others (2016) 45 Research Policy 533, 536.

372 See e. g. Sellenthin (2009) 34 J. Tech. Transfer 603, 618; Walter and others (2016) 45 Research Policy 533, 536.

have generally not received a lot of consideration in the literature. They will be discussed below.[373]

2 Switzerland

In the last decade, university technology transfer numbers in Switzerland reflect a positive picture: Invention disclosures, patent applications, and licensing income have continuously increased over the years.[374] This is so, despite the fact that Switzerland joined institutional technology transfer relatively late.[375] In comparison to other universities, several Swiss universities also fare well: ETH Zurich, EPF Lausanne, and University of Zurich are among the top 25 Swiss patent applicants at the EPO.[376] Finally, Switzerland's potential for innovation looks also comparatively promising: In 2018, as in other years, Switzerland had the most patent applications per inhabitants.[377]

Switzerland is an interesting case because it is one of the few countries in Europe which did not change its ownership model. Switzerland never adhered to the professor's privilege but always to a 'moderate' university ownership model.[378] Like in the US and in Germany, policy discussions on technology transfer in Switzerland have generally focused on the importance of patents and have ignored that Swiss firms especially value informal channels of transfer, such as personal contacts, publications, conferences, and a wide spectrum of education-related activities.[379]

Unlike the US or Germany, Switzerland does not have a federal policy or law stipulating the ownership of university inventions. On the contrary, Swiss law on ownership of employee inventions (which includes university-employees) is fragmented. There are two reasons for this. The first one is that Swiss law distinguishes between inventions generated in the private sector and ones generated in the public sector. Like in the US and Germany, in Switzerland, the right to an invention vests in the inventor and is derived from the constitutionally protected right to one's property.[380] The so-called 'creator principle' is based on natural law and stipulates that the creator is the original owner of his creation.[381] In certain exceptional instances, the law will stipulate deviations from

---

373 See infra 7. B. III.

374 See SWITT, 'Reports' (2020).

375 SWITT reports only date back to 2008. Also see NZZ, 'Selbstbedienungsladen' (*NZZ*).

376 IPI, 'EPO Report' (*IPI*).

377 Ibid.; Switzerland filed 956 applications per million inhabitants, the Netherlands 416, Denmark 411, Sweden 403, and Germany 332, see EPO, 'Annual Report 2018' (*EPO*).

378 Moderate because Switzerland never had a federal Act which mandated university ownership.

379 See e. g. Foray, in *Universities* (2007) 56.

380 Decision of the Swiss Federal Court BGE 126 III 129ff. E. 8a.

381 This also applies to copyright law – i. e. in contrast to 'work made for hire' under US law where the ownership in the work vests directly in the employee.

this principle, such as in the context of employment relationships. Private employment relationships and inventions resulting from them are regulated under the Code of Obligations (*Obligationenrecht*, OR).[382] Conversely, employment relationships in the public sector are regulated by the Act on the Personnel of the Federal Government (*Bundespersonalgesetz*)[383] and by cantonal and municipal regulations. Here, institutions which are financed publicly may enact their own intellectual property regulations, as will be discussed below.[384]

The second reason is that the law of ownership of employee inventions is shaped by the landscape of higher education and Swiss federalism. There are three types of public universities in Switzerland: cantonal universities, federal technical universities (ETH Zürich and EPF Lausanne), and universities of applied sciences. The different types of universities are entirely or jointly funded by the federal and/or cantonal governments and, as such, are public institutions of federal or cantonal law. This means that principally the legislative power in regard to universities' affairs is with the federal or the cantonal sovereign respectively.

At the same time, the Swiss Constitution establishes the autonomy of universities, which allows universities to determine matters regarding academic freedom (freedom of research and freedom of teaching).[385] Encouraged by the Federal Act on the Promotion of Research and Innovation (*Bundesgesetz über die Förderung der Forschung und der Innovation,* FIFG)[386] and the Federal Act on Funding and Coordination of the Swiss Higher Education Sector (*Bundesgesetz über die Förderung der Hochschulen und die Koordination im schweizerischen Hochschulbereich,* HFKG),[387] which may require universities to address protection and ownership of intellectual property developed with federal funding, universities amended existing or adopted new regulations which generally assign the ownership of university inventios to the institution.[388]

Thus, despite the absence of a federal act to this effect, in Switzerland inventions are normally also owned by universities. The scope of inventions claimed is similar to that in Germany: Most universities distinguish between inventions which are created while pursuing professional responsibilities and

---

382 *Obligationenrecht, Fünfter Teil Bundesgesetz betreffend die Ergänzung des Schweizerischen Zivilgesetzbuches* 1911 (RS 220).

383 *Bundespersonalgesetz* 2000 (RS 172.220.1).

384 Benhamou and Rieder, in *Employees' Intellectual Property Rights* (2015) 367, 368–369.

385 § 63a *Bundesverfassung*.

386 2012 RS 420.1, specifically § 27 FIFG.

387 2011 RS 414.20, specifically § 66 HFKG.

388 See e. g. § 2 and 36 ETH Act (*Bundesgesetz über die Eidgenössischen Technischen Hochschulen*); ETH Regulation (*Verordnung des ETH-Rates über die Immaterialgüter im ETH-Bereich und die Beteiligung an Unternehmungen*); § 12a University Act of the Canton of Zurich (*Universitätsgesetz Zürich*); § 10a (University Act of the Canton of Friborug (*Universitätsgesetz Fribourg*).

will be owned by the university, and inventions which are developed outside a researcher's professional responsibilities and will generally be owned by the inventor.[389] Professors in Switzerland are also entitled to a share of licensing income. However, there are notable differences between different universities in terms of the share inventors are entitled to, the share the research group or department will receive, and how patent-related costs and other administrative expenses will be handled.[390]

III Reframing the Question of Ownership of University Inventions

Extensive literature has been published on the ownership policy changes and their impact on university technology transfer efforts in Europe.[391] A similar picture to the one in the US emerges in Europe: While there are scholars which point to the success of university ownership,[392] many studies present evidence to the contrary and attribute negative patent numbers to the move away from the professor's privilege.[393] Indeed, the ownership-related policy changes have been associated with a decrease or stagnation of certain metrics of university patenting and decreases in start-up rates by academics in Germany, Finland, Norway, and Denmark.[394] In countries where patenting was well established when the change was introduced, such as in Germany, university-owned patents increased but university-invented patents decreased. The increase of university-

389 See e.g. § 36 ETH Act; § 1 Regulation University of Bern (*Weisungen der Universitätsleitung zur wirtschaftlichen Verwertung von immateriellen Arbeitsergebnissen der Universität Bern*).

390 Most universities award one third of the total of the royalty income to inventors, however, the basis upon which this is calculated differs, see e.g. ETH Zürich and EPF Lausanne which generally award one third to inventors, but the university share may exceed two thirds if the development of the invention was exceptionally expensive, if an inventor did not contribute to the process of commercialisation, or if the licensing income generated is exceptionally high, see § 7 ETH Regulation. At the University of Fribourg 50 % of the licensing income will go towards patenting expenses and the inventor is only entitled to one third of the remaining 50 %, see § 8 Regulation University of Fribourg (*Richtlinien zu Erfindungen, dem Schutz des geistigen Eigentums, Patenten und gewerblichen Beziehungen im Forschungsbereich, Universität Fribourg*).

391 See e.g. van Eecke and others, *Monitoring and Analysis* (2007); Sellenthin (2009) 34 J. Tech. Transfer 603; Cuntz and others (2012) Studien zum deutschen Innovationssystem; Grimm and Jaenicke (2012) 37 J. Tech. Transfer 454; Czarnitzki and others (2015) 15–007 ZEW; von Proff and others (2012) 19 Ind. Innov. 23; Krause, *Hochschulerfindungen* (2017); Åstebro and others (2018) ILR Rev. 1096; Hvide and Jones (2018) 108 Am. Econ. Rev. 1860; Sterzi and others (2019) 28 Ind. Corp. Change 309.

392 See e.g. Krause, *Hochschulerfindungen* (2017).

393 See supra n. 324/III and accompanying discussion, also see e.g. Czarnitzki and others (2015) 15–007 ZEW 27.

394 See e.g. Lissoni and others (2008) 17 Research Eval. 87, 100; Jacobsson and others (2013) 42 Research Policy 874, 883; Åstebro and others (2018) ILR Rev. 1096, 1097; Geuna and Rossi (2011) 40 Research Policy 1068, 1073.

owned patents thus often occurred at the expense of university-invented patents which are owned by inventors and businesses.[395]

Switzerland is an exception as Swiss universities' patenting and licensing numbers have continuously increased in the past decade on all accounts. The positive performance could certainly be attributed to the university ownership model. However, there might be other factors which could have influenced this positive performance. Accordingly, the positive numbers could be a reflection of a still full university research pipeline since Switzerland has not been active as long as other countries in the technology transfer realm.[396] Or they could be a reflection of the fact that universities' ownership policy remained unchanged. While attempting to isolate the factors which were ultimately responsible for the technology transfer numbers in Switzerland would go beyond the scope of this section, a conclusion that nevertheless seems to emerge from the larger context of the US, the German, and the Swiss examples is that the technology transfer performance is likely determined by institutional, cultural, and legal factors which go beyond the ownership of university inventions.

Considering more closely the amendment to the ArbnErfG in Germany, two observations stand out. Firstly, up until 2002 professors in Germany were potentially entitled to the total share of income derived from a patent. Under the amended ArbnErfG, they are only entitled to a share of 30%. This is generous compared to inventors in industry, but it is a substantial reduction to the situation before 2002. While there are different reasons why researchers engage in patenting and commercialisation activities (such as access to external funding for research projects, societal impact of an invention, reputation etc.),[397] it has been shown that incentives form an important part of the equation. Pecuniary incentives such as royalty shares or intrinsic ones such as support for research laboratories have been shown to encourage faculty to disclose their invention to the university and thus often have a positive effect on the licensing income a university generates.[398] It could well be that German professors' patenting outputs were negatively affected by the reduction of a previously existing incentive (the reduced licensing income share).

Secondly, although the amended ArbnErfG on the surface seems to produce a similar result to the BDA, at its core the result is very different. The BDA substantially improved professors' ability to control their federally funded inventions: By shifting control over inventions from federal agencies to universities, professors were moved closer to their inventions and professors were more included in aspects of the technology transfer process than they were before the

395 See e. g. Geuna and Rossi (2011) 40 Research Policy 1068, 1073; also see supra n. 365–367/III and accompanying discussion.

396 See supra n. 74–75/III and accompanying discussion.

397 See e. g. van Dongen and others (2017) 8 Eur. J. L. & Tech. 1, 4.

398 See supra n. 304/III and accompanying text.

BDA. After all, the conviction that universities would be in a better position than the federal government to engage with inventors in the commercialisation process was one of the key arguments of the supporters of the BDA and of university ownership.[399]

Conversely, the amended ArbnErfG did the opposite: It moved German professors further away from their inventions. Not only did professors lose ownership over their inventions, but they also lost the ability to be meaningfully engaged in the technology transfer process since it is now the PVA (and not the university's TTO) which generally carries the responsibility of administering the patenting and commercialisation process.[400] Indeed, removing control over the invention from the professors was the core premise of the amendment to the ArbnErfG.[401]

Yet, it appears that the level of control a researcher has over an invention may determine to what degree researchers participate in the technology transfer process. In other words, the level of control may serve as an incentive to researchers to engage in the technology transfer process.[402] The BDA improved US professors' level of control while the amended ArbnErfG reduced the level of control. The realisation is that these are not absolute but relative measures of control, the determination of which is based on a comparison of the respective levels of control which were present before and after the respective change in the law.

Control is also reflected by the structure of the higher education system and universities' autonomy relative to the government. German universities have generally less autonomy from the government than universities in the US. German professors are typically civil servants, i. e. government employees and as such are less self-directed than their US colleagues. Indeed, in the US starting as early as the rank of assistant professor, faculty have extensive autonomy in terms of defining a research agenda, developing course offerings, and strategies of how to raise external funding. Due to this, in tendency, US professors have to be more entrepreneurially minded and willing to handle a multitude of administrative tasks on a daily basis. It could well be that US professors were therefore better able to deal with the additional (often bureaucratic) workload the BDA required them to do. By the same token, German professors may have been more negatively affected by the demands of the new ArbnErfG.

In conclusion, analyses which narrowly compare ownership models of university inventions are inconclusive in application as they ignore the larger institutional, cultural, and legal context within which researchers and universities

---

399 See supra 5. B. III.

400 See e. g. Grimm (2011) 12 Int'l J. Entrepreneurship Small Bus. 459, 461–462.

401 See 7. B. II. 1.

402 See e. g. Halilem and others (2017) 46 Research Policy 1487, suggesting that in an environment which exercises a high level of control over inventions, researchers' level of participation in commercialisation activities is negatively affected.

operate. Emulations of another country's ownership model may not only hinder the very outcome they try to promote but may hurt the university and the scientific commons as crucial institutions of western societies in the long run.[403] What ought to happen, instead, is to understand the institutional, cultural, and legal framework within which universities operate. Focus should be placed on preserving and strengthening academic freedom and, with it, on researchers control over their research results.

Control is ultimately a reflection of the Institutional, cultural, and legal framework the university is embedded in and is not exclusively determined by ownership. The autonomy of universities, their ability to determine the processes and institutions needed in order to fulfil their missions and conduct (basic) research, is of essence. This includes ensuring that universities are financially supported in key aspects of their research endeavours. For universities it means to commit to the protection of the scientific commons, to actively engage their researchers in their technology transfer efforts where this is an institutional priority, and to embrace a broad notion of dissemination which includes transversal connections between university and industry.[404]

C The Need for a Multi-tiered Approach to the Management of University Research

I Restoring the Balance: Committing to the Protection of the Public Interest

Universities are essential to society far beyond the production of inventions which can be patented and commercialised. It is reasonable to assume that universities will continue to produce the majority of knowledge and research which society will depend on in the future.[405] However, universities' commitment to the protection of the public interest and the scientific commons over the past few decades has slowly faded. There is a fundamental disconnect between universities' more newly developed business-attitudes and the traditional university missions of research, teaching, and service. Due to this conflict, universities are continuously torn between their public role as the producer of knowledge and private interests which are driven by universities' new business identify.

The law of intellectual property (including patent law) has always been about balance: Providing strong enough protection in order to encourage people

[403] Also see David (2005) 04–27 SIEPR 8; Pavitt (2001) 10 Ind. Corp. Change 761, 775; Jacobsson and others (2013) 42 Research Policy 874, 881–883.

[404] Also see David (2005) 04–27 SIEPR 8, 12–13; S. Bieri and Lehner (2014) CREMA 1, 18–20.

[405] See e. g. R. Nelson (2004) 33 Research Policy 455, 467.

to create and innovate, while at the same time allowing access to these creations by society in a way that ensures optimal social benefit. Likewise, the BDA attempted to achieve this balance by not only promoting the protection and commercialisation of federally funded research but by including provisions which ensure the public availability and efficient use of such research.

But, unfortunately, universities' interpretation of the BDA has skewed the balance too far away from the public. As noted above, by focusing on commercialisation, universities' technology transfer practices often marginalise other (often more successful) channels of transfer. In order to restore the equilibrium, universities ought to re-commit to the protection of the public interest and to treating university research as a public good. Focus should shift back from protection to broad dissemination and open access, ensuring that a majority of university research remains in the scientific commons.

This work suggests a three-pronged approach to restore the balance in favour of the public interest. The first step starts with an amendment of the BDA to include provisions which clearly accentuate the importance of broad dissemination of federally funded research in a way that maximises the social benefit derived from it. As a second step, universities should formulate an intellectual property strategy which reflects universities' institutional strengths, characteristics, and priorities and which acknowledges the commitment to the scientific commons and to the protection of the public interest. As a final step, universities should be held accountable by the respective state authorities for how inventions and other university research is managed.

II Amending the Bayh-Dole Act

While the BDA's objectives reference the importance of broad dissemination and public availability of sponsored research, its biggest weakness is its lack of an effective enforcement mechanism which holds universities (and other funding recipients) accountable to the objectives stipulated by the Act. The BDA does not give federal agencies discretion to direct or even oversee how federally funded research is used or disseminated. An agency may only make stipulations to the funding agreement in four instances: 1) if the recipient of the federal funds is not based in the US; 2) in the 'exceptional circumstances' when an agency determines that 'restriction or elimination of the right to retain title' to a specific invention will better promote the objectives of the Act; 3) based on reasons related to foreign intelligence or counter-intelligence; or 4) if the funding agreement relates to one of the Department of Energy's naval nuclear propulsion or weapons programs.[406]

[406] 35 USC § 202(a)(i)–(iv).

To direct universities' use and dissemination of federally funded research only 2) would apply, but making a declaration of 'exceptional circumstances' is cumbersome and time-consuming.[407] Indeed, so much so that the NIH has regularly attempted to find approaches outside the BDA in order to ensure broad dissemination of sponsored research results.[408] The other option the federal government has to control the use and dissemination of funded research are to exercise the statutory march-in rights whereby agencies may require the licensing of a federally funded invention in specific situations, such as to 'alleviate public health or safety needs'.[409] But, unfortunately, the march-in provision proves cumbersome to the extent that no agency has ever made use of it.[410]

At the time when the BDA was passed, universities only occasionally engaged in patenting activities and federal agencies were typically hostile towards patenting. Leaving complete discretion to universities and other funding recipients seemed probably like a sensible solution.[411] In today's reality, however, which has brought to light universities' appetite for patenting and commercialisation, leaving complete discretion to universities to determine how federally funded inventions should be used and disseminated seems no longer the optimal path. Instead, it is important to reorient universities to alternative modes of transfer and recommit them to the protection of the public interest.

In its objectives the BDA calls for the use of inventions 'in a manner to promote free competition and enterprise without unduly encumbering future research and discovery'.[412] Exclusive licenses will generally not promote free competition due to their exclusive nature and for the same reason they will also make follow-on research difficult, if not impossible. Yet, it has been universities standard practice to negotiate exclusive licences.[413] Different scholars have advocated that university inventions should be placed in the public domain and proposed the mandatory use of non-exclusive licensing.[414] These solutions focus on making university research inventions accessible to society by either ensuring

---

407 Every time a funding agency determines such an 'exceptional circumstance' it needs to file the determination, including an 'analysis justifying the determination', with the Commerce Department (which has the authority to implement the BDA), see 35 USC § 202(b)(1). Also see e. g. Rai and Eisenberg (2001) Proc. Conf. on Pub. Domain 157, 165.

408 For a detailed description of these approaches, see Rai and Eisenberg (2001) Proc. Conf. on Pub. Domain 157, 169–173.

409 See supra n. 161/III and accompanying text.

410 See supra 5. C. III. 2.

411 Also see Rai and Eisenberg (2001) Proc. Conf. on Pub. Domain 157, 162.

412 35 USC § 200.

413 See supra 7. A. II. 3.

414 See e. g. Benkler (2004) 305 Science 1110; Dasgupta and David (1994) 23 Research Policy 487, 518; R. Nelson (2004) 33 Research Policy 455, 469; Kenney and Patton (2009) 38 Research Policy 1407, 1419; Lemley (2008) 18 Fordham Intell. Prop. Media & Ent. L. J. 610, 611–612, referring to the Cohen-Boyer patent of which non-exclusive licensees were offered to all comers. This had the effect that – while raising the cost of practicing biotechnology – no one was stopped from entering the market; Mowery and others, *Ivory Tower* (2004) 191;

that no one can own them (i. e. placing them in the public domain) or by employing patents and licensing them unrestrictedly. One solution proposes that universities should voluntarily agree not to use exclusive licensing and to commit to broad dissemination.[415] It is questionable whether this might work as universities already seem to be aware of the issue with exclusive licenses, but they are clearly not willing to voluntary give up the ability to use them. Others propose to enhance the legal authority of federal agencies in order to mitigate the problem.[416]

What is proposed here is neither to rely on universities' insight and voluntary commitment nor bestow federal agencies with more power, which they may not be able to use effectively or simply use to increase administrative control over universities.[417] Instead, the BDA should be rephrased in manner which accentuates the importance of broad dissemination of federally funded inventions via the public domain and the use of non-exclusive licenses.[418]

Currently, the Act is not explicit enough. Broad dissemination is certainly implied in the wording 'promote free competition', 'without duly encumbering future research and discovery', promoting 'public availability' and 'protect the public against non-use or unreasonable use of inventions', and it is obvious that none of the above can be achieved by the general use of exclusive licenses and some other practices that universities have started to rely on. But the Act does not explicitly discourage the use of exclusive licenses nor specifically mention broad dissemination via the public domain and non-exclusive licenses. The phrasing should thus be changed to specifically state that broad dissemination via the public domain and non-exclusive licenses should be the default and that exclusive licenses should only be used in exceptional circumstances, where there is a compelling need for them.

Unfortunately, the most recent revision to the Bayh-Dole Rule, which the Department of Commerce issued in 2018, is a step in the wrong direction: Rather than reaffirming the importance of universities' commitment to the public interest, the amendment added new reporting obligations and tightened compliance deadlines, thereby increasing administrative complexities and universities' bureaucratic workload under the BDA.

Aside from the removal of the time period during which the government may request title of an untimely disclosed or elected invention,[419] universities

---

Nelson (2001) 18; AAUP (2014) Bulletin AAUP 38, 50, de Larena (2006) 43 Hous. L. Rev. 1373, 1383.

415 See e. g. Bok, *Universities in the Marketplace* (2009) 142; NRC, *University Intellectual Property* (2011) 4, 10.

416 See e. g. Rai and Eisenberg (2001) Proc. Conf. on Pub. Domain 157, 173; Bok, *Universities in the Marketplace* (2009) 142; NRC, *University Intellectual Property* (2011) 10–11; also see 8. C. IV.

417 See infra n. 419–425 and accompanying discussion; also see infra 7. C. IV.

418 Also see R. Nelson (2004) 33 Research Policy 455, 469.

419 See supra 5. C. III. 4.

(and other contractors) now need to notify funding agencies 60 days (instead of 30 days) before abandoning a patent application or if they choose not to take certain administrative steps required in the patenting process.[420] If provisional patent applications are filed for federally funded inventions, the provisional application must now be converted to a non-provisional application within 10 months instead of the 12 months which is the general time-frame for conversions.[421] An extension to 12 months may be requested but the agency has 60 days to deny it.[422]

The new regulation changes will apply to all new federal funding contracts which have been entered into after May 2018, to preexisting contracts which are amended, and if the respective agency chooses to introduce the new rule.[423] It is not difficult to imagine that the application of two sets of rules to government contracts, and the need to thus keep track of the federal grants which fall under the old rule and the ones which were amended or awarded after the revision and will fall under the new rule, will lead to new but unnecessary administrative complexities.[424] The fact that TTOs typically operate separately from offices which are in charge of dealing with government contracts at universities only exacerbates the problem.[425]

III The Need for Universities to Become Strategic

1 The Formulation of an Intellectual Property Strategy

It is common advice that companies should formulate an intellectual property strategy and especially companies which engage in patenting activities. The same applies to universities.[426] In fact, the formulation of an intellectual property strategy is of even greater importance to universities for two reasons: Firstly, in contrast to companies, universities' missions are usually not reduced to generating a profit.[427] Secondly, the different areas in which a university conducts research and potential inventions arise are typically far greater than in a private firm. A university's intellectual property strategy should thus be more refined than to simply attempt to patent anything which is disclosed and has commercial potential. (Albeit that is not a good strategy for a company either.)

---

420 37 CFR § 401.14(f)(3).

421 37 CFR § 401.14(c)(3).

422 37 CFR § 401.14(c)(5).

423 NIST, 'Bayh-Dole Act FAQs' (*NIST*).

424 See e. g. Gardner and Haidner, 'Practical Advice' (*Quarles & Brady*).

425 For a detailed overview of the changes to the Bayh-Dole Rule, see e. g. Gardner and Haidner, 'Practical Advice' (*Quarles & Brady*); Bailey, 'Avoiding Loss of Title to Inventions' (*Fenwick*).

426 Also see Gollin, *Intellectual Property Strategies* (2008) 137; Palfrey, *Intellectual Property Strategy* (2011) 3.

427 See e. g. Palfrey, *Intellectual Property Strategy* (2011) 109–111.

But universities typically do not have an intellectual property strategy. Most have an intellectual property policy, and while it may reference strategic goals, such as the protection of the public interest, in most instances, intellectual property policies lack comprehensive strategic guidance for all aspects of the technology transfer process and institutions. In fact, frequently, it is not even clear why a university engages in patent activities. The lack of this strategic focus will have a detrimental impact on other parts of the institutional operation, such as the TTO. As a result, a TTOs objectives may be misaligned with or even contradictory to other institutional priorities. For instance, a TTO may have the objectives of 'maximising revenue', 'holding costs down' with the 'goal of eventual self-sufficiency'.[428] On top of this, TTO staff may be required to ensure that their 'customers" (i. e. researchers') needs are met.[429] While these objectives may be sensible on their own merit, they are contradictory and therefore impossible to achieve.[430]

In the literature, the importance of the strategic aspect of universities' technology transfer practices and intellectual property management has received only minimal attention. The few studies which do address the issue confirm the importance of a focused mission for TTOs.[431] TTOs which have the single objective of maximising licensing income typically perform better than TTOs which follow multiple objectives.[432] This book proposes the need for universities to formulate a comprehensive intellectual property strategy which goes beyond a focused objective for TTOs. While the focus of the discussion will be placed on patents, the intellectual property strategy should include all aspects of an institutions' intellectual property portfolio.

As a first step, a university thus needs to develop an appreciation of what its intellectual property portfolio consists of. The intellectual property portfolio of a university consists of the totality of the knowledge and know-how of researchers, administrators, students, and staff and thus includes all types of intellectual creations (including a description of the university brand[433]).[434] An important aspect of this step is to develop a clear understanding of the composition of the

---

[428] TTO Review (n. 288/III).

[429] Ibid.

[430] Ibid., TTO staff confirming that they prioritise between their objectives of keeping costs down (through limiting patent claims, filing provisional patents by themselves, choosing cheaper intellectual property attorneys, not filing international patent applications etc.) while at the same time attempting to keep faculty members happy.

[431] See e. g. NRC, *University Intellectual Property* (2011) 4; Friedman and Silberman (2003) 28 J. Tech. Transfer 17, 29; Agrawal (2006) 27 Strateg. Mgmt. J. 63, 77; Phan and Siegel (2006) 2 Found. Trends Entrep. 77.

[432] Friedman and Silberman (2003) 28 J. Tech. Transfer 17, 29.

[433] On the importance of brands in the context of US universities, see S. Bieri and Lehner (2014) CREMA 1, 10.

[434] Palfrey, *Intellectual Property Strategy* (2011) 3.

institution's research portfolio and its research strengths.[435] In this process, universities should also take stock of invention disclosures, patented inventions, licensing contracts, licensing income, and collaborations with industry. For instance, there might be a specific department or lab which disproportionally contributes to a university's licensing income.[436] The information and data which is collected in this manner should form the basis upon which the intellectual property strategy is formulated. Finally, it is important that once stock of all assets has been taken, the intellectual property portfolio needs to be managed. In other words, owning an intellectual property portfolio is not a passive task but an ongoing, dynamic task which involves keeping track of the institutions' intellectual property as it evolves and assessing how to share and use it on a continuous basis.[437]

As a second step, a university needs to understand its available resources to manage the intellectual property portfolio.[438] If a university decides to engage in technology transfer efforts, the TTO's objective needs to be clearly formulated and matched with the necessary resources. Universities may do so for different reasons, such as for the generation of additional income, as a service to faculty, or for reputational reasons – because it may be expected by their alumni and donors or because they aspire to participate in patent rankings. Whatever the objective may be, the university needs to make enough resources available so that the objective may be achieved realistically. This may seem obvious, yet, it is where many technology transfer efforts struggle. Indeed, most TTO lack the necessary financial resources and adequately trained and qualified staff to reach their objectives.[439]

2 To Share or Not to Share

One of the most important aspects a university should consider is how to disseminate its intellectual property assets. Put differently, the university intellectual property strategy should account for the fact that intellectual property (in-

[435] This should take into account universities' 'discovery themes', 'destination areas', 'focus themes' i. e. areas of expertise in research and teaching that universities are actively defining and growing in order to solve complex problem, see e. g. Virginia Tech www.provost.vt.edu/destination_areas.html.; Ohio State University https://discovery.osu.edu.

[436] TTO Review (n. 288/III); where it became apparent that one lab (in fact one professor) was responsible for over 50% of the TTO's licensing income. Nevertheless, the TTO was not set-up with staff trained in the specific field nor was the university administration aware of the financial importance of this lab to the generation of licensing income. Indeed, the professor acknowledged his struggles of receiving adequate financial and administrative support and that – once he retired in a few years – there would be no one to succeed him.

[437] Palfrey, *Intellectual Property Strategy* (2011).

[438] Also see Gollin, *Intellectual Property Strategies* (2008) 137.

[439] See e. g. Owen-Smith and Powell (2001) 26 J. Tech. Transfer 99; Swamidass and Vulasa (2009) 34 J. Tech. Transfer 350; Siegel and others (2004) 21 J. Eng. Tech. Mgmt. 115, 135.

cluding patents) may be used on a spectrum ranging from excluding others from the use, allowing limited use, to open access.[440] In terms of patentable research, most universities generally use a strategy of limited exclusion. In other words, patents will be obtained in order for them to be licensed and generate revenue. Ever more universities also choose the path of full exclusion, where they employ patents to file infringement lawsuits or engage PAEs to enforce patent rights.[441] While universities are familiar with open access when it comes to most copyrightable works, it is typically not a strategic choice for inventions – whether it is through placing them in the public domain or through patenting them but licensing them broadly.

There are several reasons why universities should consider open access as an important aspect of intellectual property strategy. Some may object to open access on the basis that it seemingly results in an unfair advantage to businesses which may use a technology without having to pay for it. In reality, open access may foster competition and spur innovation to the benefit of society. There are several examples of private companies which have given free access to their patent portfolios in an effort to spur innovation.[442] Moreover, history has shown that without open access to some new technologies, certain follow-on research would not have been possible the way it occurred.[443]

A strategy of open access may also directly benefit a universities' research endeavours. In fact, studies have found that a comparatively high percentage of entrepreneurial efforts by faculty occur outside the 'formal university intellectual property system'.[444] These efforts are thus not based on disclosed and patented inventions but on research which is shared openly. Universities could benefit on several levels by supporting such activities and by actively choosing to disseminate certain knowledge without any restrictions. For one, it could help create a spirit of trust which is essential to a universities' successful technology transfer enterprise.[445]

But it may also positively influence university-industry collaborations. Firms have increasingly voiced concern over universities' aggressive pursuit of intellectual property protection.[446] In contrast to universities, which typically perceive licensing to be the most important output of their technology transfer operations, firms are generally more interested in informal modes of transfer and value personal relationships over contractual ones.[447] Indeed, they may

---

440 For a detailed explanation of the choices available in terms of 'sharing' a company's intellectual property, see Palfrey, *Intellectual Property Strategy* (2011) 89–108.

441 See supra accompanying discussion to n. 274–279/III.

442 An often-discussed example is Tesla, see e. g. Maynard, 'Elon Musk' (*Forbes*).

443 See supra n. 125–132/III and accompanying discussion.

444 Fini and others (2010) 39 Research Policy 1060, 1067.

445 See supra 7.A.II.4.

446 See supra 7.A.II.3.

447 See supra 6.A.I.

often only engage with universities in patent negotiations because of universities' persistence.[448] If a university is interested in industry collaboration in a specific field, the sensible strategy may thus be to share research results openly and to actively foster connections and interactions between faculty and industry.

This is not to suggest that open access is a viable strategy for all university research. Instead, it is proposed that universities should be strategic in how they employ intellectual property protection. Ultimately, the intellectual property strategy should reflect what a university creates, and with whom it intends to share its research results and for what purpose, thereby mirroring a university's strengths, characteristics, institutional goals and objectives.

One of the key aspects in this process is for universities to realise that owning patentable research does not equate to patenting and licensing it. In other words, alternative transfer channels to patenting and licensing should not only be chosen as an afterthought, i. e. if patent (or other intellectual property) protection is not available or possible. Instead, universities ought to proactively define how their research results should be disseminated. Based on the above-discussed understanding a university needs to develop regarding its research strengths, its relationship with industry, and its institutional objectives and priorities, areas ought to be defined in which research results should generally be left unpatented and areas in which patent protection ought to be pursued. Patent protection might be aspired in specific fields with the hope of generating income or with the purpose of ensuring quality control and access to a large pool of licensees. But where patents are considered, the strategy also ought to factor in industry preferences and thus generally only opt for patents in fields where industry values patents as a transfer vehicle, such as is generally the case for pharmaceutical compounds, for instance.

Finally, a strategy would have to be formulated in regard to other intellectual property assets, such as certain teaching materials for instance: Perhaps a university might choose to offer certain lecture materials, including certain videos, for free online.[449]

The intellectual property strategy should also be consistent with other university policies, such as the policy on promotion and tenure. Often there is a disconnect between universities' ambition to do well in their commercialisation enterprise and the faculty promotion and reward structure.[450] In institutions where academic and commercial rewards are linked, frustration with the tech-

[448] TTO Review (n. 288/III); Siegel and others (2004) 21 J. Eng. Tech. Mgmt. 115, 135–136; Fini and others (2010) 39 Research Policy 1060, 1067; Gulbrandsen and Smeby (2005) 34 Research Policy 932.

[449] See Palfrey, *Intellectual Property Strategy* (2011) 117–119, for a detailed discussion on different dissemination strategies for universities related to teaching materials.

[450] TTO Board of Directors (n. 467/II); also see Siegel and others (2004) 21 J. Eng. Tech. Mgmt. 115, 136.

nology transfer process may be overcome.[451] Thus, where a university engages in patent activities, faculty should be rewarded for achieving milestones, such as disclosures, patent applications, negotiations with industry and so forth.

It should also be accounted for that such milestones may have a different meaning to different faculty groups. For instance, junior faculty may pursue patents milestones, including provisional patent applications, as a 'trophy' – something to include in the tenure dossier. It may not even matter whether a patent will be issued and a licensing contract negotiated, as long as they can tick off an additional item on the tenure list. By the same token, other, especially tenured faculty, may attach less meaning to the same milestones and are therefore often more likely to negotiate away the rights to patents for the benefit of obtaining industry grants.[452] For them the receipt of a substantial grant may translate into a decreased teaching load or may provide them with additional resources for their research laboratory or additional summer salary which may be of greater value than other rewards. Finally, for more entrepreneurially minded senior faculty in applied fields patents may often be very important in their pursuit to establish their own company.[453]

3 Implementing the Strategy: One Size Does not Fit All

The implementation of the intellectual property strategy will naturally require that technology transfer processes and institutions such as the intellectual property policy and the TTO are formulated and organised in a way which reflects the strategy. While many papers have suggested alternative ways of organising TTOs and associated processes,[454] the details will not be discussed here, nor will it be attempted to suggest how specifically a TTO should be organised. What will be stressed, however, is that the TTO's organisation and processes should reflect the intellectual property strategy, which naturally implies that industry-specific needs should be reflected in the way processes are designed and in the background and training of the respective technology transfer professionals.

Where patenting and commercialisation efforts are an institutional priority, universities should also invest in educating faculty and students in the basics of patent law and technology transfer processes. Studies have shown that faculty frequently lack the most basic knowledge about intellectual property protection.[455] In fact, the revised Bayh-Dole Rule requires universities to educate

---

[451] See Owen-Smith and Powell (2001) 26 J. Tech. Transfer 99, 113.

[452] TTO Review (n. 288/III).

[453] Ibid.

[454] See e. g. Kenney and Patton, in *Knowledge Perspectives* (2012) 255; Siegel and others (2004) 21 J. Eng. Tech. Mgmt. 115, 136; Swamidass and Vulasa (2009) 34 J. Tech. Transfer 358.

[455] See e. g. Villasenor (2012).

their researchers on basic patenting requirements and elements of the patenting process.[456]

In this process, it is not only important to outline to researchers the details of the technology transfer process but instead to design processes which centre on the workflow of researchers.[457] This could entail situating the TTO in a central location where TTO staff and other technology transfer resources are easily accessible for researchers. Universities might also want to consider having patent professionals work directly on site, i. e. with faculty, research laboratories, and departments in fields where patenting and licensing is an institutional priority. This is a model which corporations are increasingly implementing, based on the realisation that a multitude of translational issues arise if patent professionals are located and organised in separate units to researchers and inventors.[458]

Ultimately, if the intellectual property strategy is formulated and implemented in the above-described manner, universities will end up with unique, institution-specific technology transfer practices. In other words, the chief advantage of this top-down solution of formulating an intellectual property strategy and then systematically breaking it down to the whole technology transfer operation is that – in contrast to universities' current technology transfer practices – it does not result in a one-size-fits-all approach to technology transfer. Instead, universities will end up with an intellectual property policy, a TTO, and general technology transfer practices which are unique and which are tailored to the respective universities' research strength and its objectives and priorities. This is also how this proposal differs to many other scholars' solutions who generally propose a specific approach for all universities or for certain types of inventions (such as the proposal to switch to inventor ownership, to place federally funded inventions into the public domain, or to establish a federal technology transfer centre which serves all universities).[459]

IV Last but not Least: Regulatory Oversight

Aside from the changes to the BDA and the need for universities to approach their involvement with patents and the management of their research on a strategic level, the third and final piece in recommitting universities to the public good is regulatory oversight. Universities need to be held accountable for the

---

[456] 37 CFR § 401.14(f).

[457] TTO Review (n. 288/III), in which faculty members expressed frustration that the technology transfer process is not clear, that information is not available online, that it is difficult to reach TTO staff, and that they often feel their time is wasted. Also see AAUP (2014) Bulletin AAUP 38, 43.

[458] Conversation with legal counsel of Siemens in July 2017.

[459] See e. g. Kenney and Patton (2012); R. Eisenberg (1996) 82 Va. L. Rev. 1663, 1727; de Larena (2006) 43 Hous. L. Rev. 1373, 1437–1444.

way they manage not only federally funded inventions and patents but research results in general.[460]

The accountability of universities has become a topic of increasing importance in the past few decades.[461] The challenge is to strike the right balance between preserving universities' autonomy in order for them to stay sufficiently safe from external pressures while remaining responsive enough to society's needs.[462] Put differently, too much autonomy might prompt universities to be unresponsive to society's needs, and too much accountability might destroy the academic spirit.[463] In regard to the protection of the public interest, it appears that the balance has been skewed too far in the direction of universities' autonomy. Since the adoption of the BDA, universities have been able to operate their patenting and commercialisation efforts in a self-directed manner. They freely defined priorities and objectives and have increasingly neglected the broader societal demands and some of the key objectives which the BDA stipulated. Universities should be held accountable if they do not operate their technology transfer efforts in the interest of the public.

In contrast to what other scholars have proposed, namely, to increase oversight of the federal government and thus of federal agencies, it is proposed that the respective state governments should assume the oversight of universities in this regard. State governments are more suitable than the federal government for several reasons. Firstly, the above-mentioned proposals generally focus on federally funded research and the BDA, thereby ignoring the larger context of financial support from state and federal government which public and private universities receive. In other words, universities should not only be held accountable for how they disseminate federally funded research and manage inventions resulting from federally funded research, but they also ought to be held responsible for the way they disseminate and manage research outputs in general. Secondly, states have always provided the legal framework within which public and private universities have operated.[464] Ensuring that the academy stays responsive to the protection of the public interest falls in the purview of state governments.[465] Thirdly, state governments are better suited to define standards and measures which reflect the individual states' strengths and needs.

---

460 Excluded from this should generally be research that is financed with industry funding, which – by design of the current technology transfer practice – it already is: Industry contracts are typically dealt with by a separate office to the TTO and include intellectual property provisions that will typically give joint or full ownership of intellectual property that result from the research project to the respective firm.

461 See supra 1. C. II. 2.

462 Burke, in *Achieving Accountability* (2005) 1, 5.

463 Berdahl (1990) 15 Stud. in High. Educ. 169, 172; Burke, in *Achieving Accountability* (2005) 1, 5.

464 McGuinness, in *American Higher Education* (2011) 139, 141.

465 See supra 1. C. II. 2.

This may help to produce competition between different states and the respective universities.

This solution would require states to amend or implement respective state laws which define universities' obligation regarding the dissemination of research results, the management of patents and other intellectual property, and the commitment to the scientific commons and the protection of the public interest. Some states do already address aspects of this in their respective state regulations, but most states only require universities to adopt an intellectual property policy with or without other specified but limited standards.

For instance, the Virginia Code states that '(t)he boards of visitors of state-supported institutions of higher education [...] shall adopt policies regarding the ownership, protection, assignment, and use of intellectual property.'[466] The Code, however, is silent on the specific objective such a policy should fulfil. It is merely stipulated that employees of state supported institutions of higher education 'as a condition of employment shall be bound by the patent and copyright policies of the institution employing them.'[467] Other states' statutes are more specific in terms of the content that universities' intellectual property policies need to address. Accordingly, they may stipulate how universities should use income derived from patent activities,[468] or they address how potential royalty income ought to be shared between the universities and inventors.[469] Some states codes are completely silent on the topic of intellectual property or inventions produced in higher education institutions[470] or have removed the respective provisions.[471]

The most comprehensive state law has been passed in Texas and stipulates that institutions of higher education need to have an intellectual property policy which addresses certain minimum standards, including 'royalty participation by inventors and the institution',[472] and that 'the commissioner of higher educa-

---

466 Virginia Code § 23–4.3 A.

467 Virginia Code § 23–4.3 B.

468 See e. g. West Virginia Code: 'Encourage(s) the development of patentable inventions by members of the faculty [...] of the university' and provides that a share of the income should go to both the university and the faculty member. It also stipulates that the university may only use the income 'for the furtherance of a university program of general scientific research, through payments for personal services, for the purchase of equipment and supplies, and for other expenses necessarily incident to such a program', see West Virginia Code § 18–11–24.

469 See e. g. the Connecticut Code stipulates that faculty inventors shall be entitled to at least 20% of the net proceeds, see Connecticut Code § 10a–98c. Also see e. g. Ohio State Code § 2345.14., providing that faculty members shall have no rights to interests from inventions unless stipulated by the board of trustees of the respective college or university.

470 See e. g. Minnesota Statutes, which was a pioneer in dialling back employer's rights insofar as under Minnesota law employers are prohibited from requiring assignment of inventions unrelated to the employee's work or the employer's business.

471 See e. g. North Dakota.

472 Texas Code, subchapter O.

tion shall establish procedures for the monitoring of this policy of the state'.[473] If institutions do not comply with these standards, they 'shall not receive funds under any state-run competitive research or advanced technology funding programs'.[474]

Using the Texas state law as an example, states could expand it to include other standards according to which universities' performance will be assessed, such as the broad dissemination of research results via the public domain and non-exclusive licenses in certain specified areas. The Texas Code illustrates the two important aspects which should be included in order for the respective state law to be effective. Firstly, states ought to define how universities should be measured and what would constitute acceptable performance. Secondly, the outcomes and performance measures should be clearly communicated not only to universities themselves but to the public. In general, what seems most important is that officials of the state government and university administrators work together closely in an effort to define what a suitable balance might look like between universities' commitment to the protection of the public interest and their autonomy to actively pursue commercialisation of university research.

473 Texas Code, subchapter O, Section c.
474 Texas Code, subchapter O, Section d.

Conclusion

US research universities evolved towards the end of the 19th century and were greatly influenced by the ideals of the German university. What distinguished them from earlier institutions of higher education in America, was their commitment to original inquiry, academic freedom and a general focus on the generation and dissemination of practical and useful knowledge. It is this focus that would make it inevitable that research universities not only would develop inventions but that they eventually would need to address whether to protect these inventions and thus would need to define how to engage with patents.

Fuelled by expansive investment in research by the federal government, especially during the era after World War II, research universities continued to evolve and grow into their position of world prominence throughout the 20th century. But despite their vital role to society and the US economy, research universities' financial stability has been increasingly jeopardised. Over the past few decades, the decline of federal and state support and the deterioration of universities' endowments have compelled universities to seek alternative ways to generate income. The patenting and licensing of university inventions and other entrepreneurial activities is one way through which universities have attempted to close their existing financial shortfall.

Historically, research universities objected to an engagement with patents. On a practical level, inventions were believed to be the private property of faculty and patents hence the private concern of the respective faculty member. On a more strategic level, an involvement with patents was considered inconsistent with the academic mission and its commitment to open science. Moreover, it was feared that the appearance of profiting at the expense of the public would undermine public trust and support of academia.

In spite of this critical attitude towards patents, during the first quarter of the 20th century, a few research universities explored the value of patents. The conviction emerged that under certain circumstances inventions needed to be protected in order to attract possible investors who would bring the respective invention to the market. This commercialisation argument for the use of patents has evolved into the key justification for universities' patent involvement today. Two additional arguments were also frequently raised to justify the use of patents, both of which illustrate that the debate over introducing patents to academia has always raised concerns as to the protection of the public interest.

Firstly, the use of patents was also considered permissible where they were necessary to control the development and future use of the invention and secondly, where they were employed to prevent the wrongful appropriation of a developed invention.

While more universities followed suit and increasingly also introduced and refined patent policies, many of them remained reluctant towards the use of patents well into the 1960s. As a result, some universities forbade or restricted the patenting of health-related research and most universities refrained from directly managing university patents, choosing instead to outsource the management to a separate legal entity. But, most significantly, patents were not considered a standard solution to the dissemination of university research. Instead, they were only employed as needed, on a case by case basis.

Progressively, these last reservations towards patents were dropped as well, and since the adoption of the 1980 Bayh-Dole Act (BDA), more and more universities consider patents a standard solution to their technology transfer efforts and engage in a hands-on management of patents and licences. Today, all research universities in the US pursue patents and the number of university patents issued and licenses negotiated has continuously increased.

The ownership of university inventions forms a central component of universities' patenting efforts. Research universities have their faculty and researchers assign inventions to them by way of pre-invention agreement. This approach to the ownership of university inventions was originally inspired by the solution developed by employers in industry to the problem of employee-inventions in the early 20th century. The reason for this contractual solution is that – unlike laws of other major industrialised jurisdictions – the US Patent Act does not address how the ownership of employee-inventions should be determined. The general premise of the Patent Act holds that an invention initially vests in its inventor.

There is a common law doctrine which changes or limits this presumption of ownership under certain circumstances. Where an inventor is hired to work on something specific and an invention results, the invention will be owned by the employer. Additionally, where an inventor develops an invention using the employer's resources but was not hired to invent the invention, the employer will be awarded a royalty-free, non-exclusive license to the invention. Due to the common law doctrine's limited scope and employers' increasing awareness of the value associated with employee-inventions, employers have become accustomed to require their employees to assign inventions by contract on the outset of employment.

Universities did not typically rely on the common law doctrine. From the beginning of their involvement with patents, several research universities – and especially land-grant universities – imitated the industry approach and had faculty assign ownership of their inventions to the university. Moreover, after the adoption of the BDA, many universities came to rely on the BDA for their ownership claims of federally funded inventions. It was understood that the Act reordered the priority of ownership rights in federally funded inventions and vested ownership of such inventions in universities. Indeed, many institutions even assumed that the university owned all patentable research.

When the BDA was adopted, it had two main objectives: the first one was to establish a unified federal patent policy; the second one was to encourage the use and commercialisation of federally funded inventions through patents for the benefit of the public. Central to this second objective was the assumption that university ownership (rather than ownership of the government or private contractors) – coupled with patenting – was essential to the successful commercialisation of federally funded inventions. The BDA thus allowed universities (and other federal contractors) to retain title to federally funded inventions. However, it did not re-order the priority of ownership rights in federally funded inventions as universities had become accustomed to believing.

This was clarified in the landmark Supreme Court decision of *Stanford v. Roche* in 2011. The court confirmed that the BDA did not vest federally funded inventions in universities and that, in order to secure ownership rights to federally funded inventions, universities needed to have inventors assign them to the university by way of contract. As a response to the decision, universities changed their patent policies, and today, faculty and researchers generally have to assign all their inventions to their university – regardless of the funding source. The only exception to this comprehensive ownership claim are industry-sponsored inventions, the ownership of which is normally stipulated in separate contractual agreements between the university and the industry sponsor.

The BDA succeeded in achieving the first of its two objectives: the establishment of a unified federal patent policy. But it is difficult to conclusively establish whether the BDA was also successful at encouraging the use and commercialisation of federally funded inventions through patents for the benefit of the public. Universities patent and license more than they did before the adoption of the BDA. But what is not clear is to what extent other factors, such as a general pro-patent environment, the emergence and growth of lucrative biomedicine and biotechnology, and a simple desire by universities to earn revenue with patents, aided this overall growth.

Most importantly, there is an increasing indication that universities' focus on patents negatively impacts their research mission and their role as stewards of the public interest. There is evidence that patenting may negatively weigh on researchers' publication behaviour: from researchers delaying or even foregoing publication, to introducing a higher degree of secrecy and influencing the scope and direction of research projects – the commercial flavour patents have introduced into the university is at odds with traditional norms of academic production. On a more general level, the continuous push to patent and commercialise university research has the worrisome effect of emptying the 'research pipeline'. As a consequence, the very foundation upon which universities' research enterprise is built is being eroded.

The erosion of the research pipeline, and with it the erosion of universities' special function as producers of knowledge and of the value of university research as a public good, is not necessarily intrinsic to the BDA. The BDA is explicit about the importance of the protection of the research enterprise, the broad dissemination, and the public availability of federally funded inventions. But it is these important objectives of the BDA which universities have overlooked in their quest to grow their commercialisation undertaking and generate additional income.

This lack of universities' commitment to the protection of the public interest is reflected in how universities' technology transfer practices typically operate. Firstly, universities technology transfer practices are based on an institutional imperative of patenting. They disregard the availability of other transfer channels. Secondly, universities have grown comfortable with maximising licensing revenue instead of maximising the social benefit of their research. This is demonstrated by universities' standard use of exclusive licenses and by their increasingly litigious behaviour. Thirdly, universities generally fail to centre their technology transfer practices around their researchers – who are the backbone of universities' research enterprise. This does not mean that ownership should necessarily be left with inventors, but – as a comparison with the respective ownership regimes in Germany and Switzerland suggests – it appears crucial that inventors are included in the technology transfer processes and that they have some level of control over their inventions.

In order to re-orient research universities to the protection of the public interest, a three-pronged approach is proposed. Firstly, the BDA should be amended to include provisions which clearly accentuate the importance of alternative channels of dissemination, including the public domain and the use of non-exclusive licenses. Secondly, universities should refrain from using patents as a default solution for their technology transfer efforts and should avoid copying other institutions' approaches to technology transfer. Instead, universities ought to develop an intellectual property strategy which encompasses the dissemination of all research (and other intellectual property assets) and reflects the respective institution's research strengths, characteristics, and institutional priorities. Finally, state governments should hold universities accountable for the way that they manage their patents and other research outputs.

Bibliography

Abrams, David S. and Wagner, R. Polk, 'Poisoning the next Apple – the America Invents Act and Individual Inventors' (2013) 65 Stanford Law Review 517

Abrams, Irene, Grace Leung, and Ashley J. Stevens, 'How Are US Technology Transfer Offices Tasked and Motivated: Is It All About the Money?' (2009) 17 Research Management Review 1

Agrawal, Ajay, 'Engaging the Inventor: Exploring Licensing Strategies for University Inventions and the Role of Latent Knowledge' (2006) 27 Strategic Management Journal 63

Agrawal, Ajay, and Rebecca Henderson, 'Putting Patents in Context: Exploring Knowledge Transfer from MIT' (2002) 48 Management Science 44

American Academy of Arts and Sciences, *Public Research Universities – Recommitting to Lincoln's Vision: An Educational Compact for the 21st Century* (American Academy of Arts and Sciences 2017)

American Association for the Advancement of Science (AAAS), *The Protection by Patents of Scientific Discoveries, Report of the Committee on Patents, Copyrights and Trade Marks* (Science Press 1934)

American Association of University Professors (AAUP), '1915 Declaration of Principles on Academic Freedom and Academic Tenure' in Louis Joughin (ed.), *Academic Freedom and Tenure: A Handbook of the Association of University Professors* (University of Wisconsin Press 1967) 291

–, 'Defending the Freedom to Innovate: Faculty Intellectual Property Rights after Stanford v. Roche' (2014) Bulletin of the AAUP 38

–, 'Statement on Intellectual Property' (2014) Bulletin of the AAUP 35

Apple, Rima D., *Vitamania: Vitamins in American Culture* (Rutgers University Press 1996)

Asche, Matthias and Stefan Gerber, 'Universität' in Friedrich Jaeger (ed.), *Enzyklopädie der Neuzeit Online* (Metzlersche Verlagsbuchhandlung und Carl Ernst Poeschel Verlag GmbH 2012)

Armitage, Robert A., 'Understanding the America Invents Act and Its Implications for Patenting' (2012) 40 AIPLA Quarterly Journal 1

Arno, Peter S. and Michael H. Davis, 'Why Don't We Enforce Existing Drug Price Controls – The Unrecognized and Unenforced Reasonable Pricing Requirements Imposed upon Patents Deriving in Whole or in Part from Federally Funded Research' (2000) 75 Tulane Law Review 631

Arrow, Kenneth, 'Economic Welfare and the Allocation of Resources for Invention' in National Bureau of Economic Research (ed.), *The Rate and Direction of Inventive Activity: Economic and Social Factors* (Princeton University Press 1962) 609

Association of American Universities (AAU) 'Tax Exemption for Universities and Colleges – Internal Revenue Code Section 501 (c)(3) and Section 115' (*AAU*, 2014)

<www.aau.edu/sites/default/files/AAU%20Files/Key%20Issues/Taxation%20%26%20Finance/Tax-Exempt-Status-of-Universities-FINAL.pdf> accessed 1 November 2021

Association of University Technology Managers (AUTM), 'Driving the Innovation Economy: Academic Technology Transfer in Numbers' (*AUTM,* 20 June 2017) <https://autm.net/AUTM/media/Surveys-Tools/Documents/AUTM_FY2017_Infographic.pdf> accessed 1 November 2021

–, '2020 US Licensing Activity Survey' (*AUTM*, 4 August 2021) <https://autm.net/AUTM/media/SurveyReportsPDF/FY20-US-Licensing-Survey-FNL.pdf> accessed 1 November 2021

Association of American Universities (AAU), American Association for the Advancement of Science, American Council on Education, Association of American Medical Colleges, Association of Independent Research Institutes, Association of Public and Landgrant Universities, Association of University Technology Managers, Council on Governmental Relations, 'Brief of Amicus Curiae Supporting Petitioner' (2011) *Board of Trustees of the Leland Stanford Junior University v. Roche Molecular Systems*, No. 09–1159

Åstebro, Thomas, Serguey Braguinsky, Pontus Braunerhjelm, and Anders Broström, 'Academic Entrepreneurship: The Bayh-Dole Act versus the Professor's Privilege' (2018) 72 ILR Review 1094

Azoulay, Pierre, Waverly Ding, and Toby Stuart, 'The Impact of Academic Patenting on the Rate, Quality and Direction of (Public) Research Output' (2009) 57 Journal of Industrial Economics 637

Backs, Sabrina and Christian Stummer, 'Akademische Patente und ihre Auswirkungen auf Forschung, Lehre und Administration an Universitäten' (2015) 65 Management Review Quarterly 35

Bagley, Margo A., 'Academic Discourse and Propriety Rights: Putting Patents in Their Proper Place' (2005) 47 Boston College Law Review 217

Bailey, Pinar, 'Avoiding Loss of Title to Inventions Made Under Federal Funding as New Bayh-Dole Requirements Affect Patent Rights' (*Fenwick*, 16 August 2019) <www.fenwick.com/insights/publications/avoiding-loss-of-title-to-inventions-made-under-federal-funding-as-new-bayh-dole-requirements-affect-patent-rights> accessed 1 November 2021

Barrow, Abigail, La Royce Batchelor, Alex Breger, Nathalie Duval-Couetil, Latanya Scott, Jeffrey Skinner, and Phyl Speser, 'Managing Student Intellectual Property Issues at Institutions of Higher Education: An AUTM Primer' (2014) 2 Technology Transfer Practice Manual 1

Bartenbach, Kurt and Ortwin Hellebrand, 'Zur Abschaffung des Hochschullehrerprivilegs – Auswirkungen auf den Abschluss von Forschungsaufträgen' (2002) 1 Mitteilungen der Deutschen Patentanwälte 165

Bartow, Ann, 'Inventors of the World, Unite – a Call for Collective Action by Employee-Inventors' (1997) 37 Santa Clara Law Review 673

Bator, Francis M., 'The Anatomy of Market Failure' (1958) 72 Quarterly Journal of Economics 351

Becker, Amanda, 'Patent Reform Measure Ignited Fierce Lobbying Effort' (*Washington Post*, 27 March 2011) <www.washingtonpost.com/capital_business/2011/03/25/AFzD9VkB_story.html> accessed 1 November 2021

Begley, Sharon, 'As Revenue Falls, a Pioneer of Cancer Gene Testing Slams Rivals with Overblown Claims' (*Stat News*, 29 November 2016) < https://www.statnews.com/2016/11/29/brca-cancer-myriad-genetic-tests/> accessed 1 November 2021

Bekkers, Rudi and Isabel Maria Bodas Freitas, 'Analysing Knowledge Transfer Channels between Universities and Industry: To What Degree Do Sectors Also Matter?' (2008) 37 Research Policy 1837

Benderly, Beryl Lieff, 'Who Counts as an Inventor? The Answer Could Be Worth Millions' (Science, 2 August 2017) <https://www.science.org/content/article/who-counts-inventor-answer-could-be-worth-millions> accessed 1 November 2021

Benhamou, Yaniv and Cyrill Rieder, 'Employees' Intellectual Property Rights in Switzerland' in Sanna Wolk and Kacper Szkalej, *Employees' Intellectual Property Rights* (Wolters Kluwer 2015) 367

Benkler, Yochai, 'Commons-based Strategies and the Problems of Patents' (2004) 305 Science 1110

Berdahl, Robert, 'Academic Freedom, Autonomy and Accountability in British Universities' (1990) 15 Studies in Higher Education 169

Bergmann, Andrea, *Erfindungen von Hochschulbeschäftigten nach der Reform von § 42 ArbNErfG* (Carl Heymanns Verlag 2006)

Bessen, James and Michael James Meurer, *Patent Failure: How Judges, Bureaucrats, and Lawyers Put Innovators at Risk* (Princeton University Press 2008)

Bieri, Anna-Marion, 'Patents' in Frederick F. Wherry and Juliet B. Schor (eds.), *The SAGE Encyclopedia of Economics and Society* (Sage Publishing 2015)

Bieri, Stephan, 'Die richtigen Dinge tun – Universitäre Praxis im Wettbewerb' in Helmut J Schmidt (ed.), *Engagement gehört zum Lebenssinn – Gedenkschrift Klaus Landfried* (Universität Kaiserslautern 2017) 161

Bieri, Stephan and Franz Lehner, 'The US Research University – Systemic Limits of a Model' (2014) Center for Research in Economics, Management and the Arts (CREMA) 1

Bix, Brian, *Contract Law: Rules, Theory, and Context* (Cambridge University Press 2012)

Blumberg, Peter D., 'From 'Publish or Perish' to 'Profit or Perish': Revenues from University Technology Transfer and the § 501 (c)(3) Tax Exemption' (1996) 145 University of Pennsylvania Law Review 89

Blumenthal, David, Eric G. Campbell, Melissa S. Anderson, Nancyanne Causino, and Karen Seashore Louis, 'Withholding Research Results in Academic Life Science: Evidence from a National Survey of Faculty' (1997) 277 JAMA 1224

Boettiger, Sara and Alan B. Bennett, 'Bayh-Dole: If We Knew Then What We Know Now' (2006) 24 Nature Biotechnology 320

Bok, Derek, *Beyond the Ivory Tower: Social Responsibilities of the Modern University* (Harvard University Press 1982)

–, 'The Benefits and Costs of Commercialization of the Academy' In Donald G Stein (ed.), *Buying in or Selling out – the Commercialization of American Research Universities* (Rutgers 2004) 32

–, *Universities in the Marketplace: The Commercialization of Higher Education* (Princeton University Press 2009)

Boldrin, Michele and David K. Levine, 'The Case Against Patents' (2013) 27 Journal of Economic Perspectives 3

Bracher, Hans, *Entstehung und Bedeutung des Schweizerischen Patentwesens* (Paul Haupt 1923)
Bremer, Howard W., 'The First Two Decades of the Bayh-Dole Act as Public Policy' (Presentation to the National Association of State Universities and Land Grant Colleges, Washington DC, 11 November 2001) <https://ipmall.law.unh.edu/sites/default/files/BAYHDOLE/4_PREPPED_FILES/2001.11.11_The_First_Two_Decades_of_the_BayhDole_Act_as_Public_Policy_by_Howard_W._BrBremer_COPY.pdf> accessed 1 November 2021
Broad, William J., 'Patent Bill Returns Bright Idea to Inventor' (1979) 205 Science 473
Brooks, Jack and Toby Moffett: 'Views of Representatives Jack Brooks and Toby Moffett on BDA', House Report No. 96–1307 (*Knowledge Ecology International*, 23 September 1980) <https://keionline.org/bayh-dole/jack-brooks-toby-moffett> accessed 1 November 2021
Browning, Christopher Grafflin Jr., 'The Souring of Sweet Acidophilus Milk: Speck v. North Carolina Dairy Foundation and the Rights of University Faculty to Their Inventive Ideas' (1985) 63 North Carolina Law Review 1248
Brubacher, John and Willis Rudy, *Higher Education in Transition: A History of American Colleges and Universities* (4th ed., Routledge 1997)
Bugbee, Bruce Willis, *Genesis of American Patent and Copyright Law* (Public Affairs Press 1967)
Bund-Länder-Kommission für Bildungsplanung und Forschungsförderung (BLK), *BLK Jahresbericht* 2000 (BLK 2001)
Bundesministerium für Bildung und Forschung (BMBF), *Knowledge Creates Markets – Action Scheme of the German Government* (BMBF 2001)
Burk, Dan L., 'Law and Economics of Intellectual Property: In Search of First Principles' (2012) 8 Annual Review of Law and Social Science 397
Burke, Joseph C., 'The Many Faces of Accountability' in Joseph C Burke (ed.), *Achieving Accountability in Higher Education: Balancing Public, Academic, and Market Demands* (Jossey-Bass 2005) 1
–, *Achieving Accountability in Higher Education: Balancing Public, Academic, and Market Demands* (Jossey-Bass 2005)
Burlingame, Roger, *Inventors behind the Inventor* (Harcourt, Brace & Company 1947)
Bush, Vannevar, 'Science – The Endless Frontier' (1945) 48 Transactions of the Kansas Academy of Science 231
Cahan, David, 'The Institutional Revolution in German Physics, 1865–1914' (1985) 15 Historical Studies in the Physical Sciences 1
Capano, Kathleen M., Cheryl A. Hoey, and Claudia M. Zuch, 'In Re Cronyn: Can Student Theses Bar Patent Applications' (1991) 18 Journal of College and University Law 105
Carnegie Foundation for the Advancement of Teaching, *The Control of the Campus: A Report on the Governance of Higher Education* (Princeton University Press 1982)
The Carnegie Classification of Institutions of Higher Education, 'Standard Listings, Doctoral Universities: Very High Research Activity' (*Carnegie Classifications*) <https://carnegieclassifications.iu.edu/lookup/srp.php?clq=%7B%22basic2005_ids%22%3A%2215%22%7D&start_page=standard.php&backurl=standard.php&limit=0,50> accessed 1 November 2021
Casper, Steven, 'The Spill-over Theory Reversed: The Impact of Regional Economies on the Commercialization of University Science' (2013) 42 Research Policy 1313.

Caulfield, Timothy, Robert M. Cook-Deegan, F. Scott Kieff, and John P. Walsh, 'Evidence and Anecdotes: An Analysis of Human Gene Patenting Controversies' (2000) 24 Nature Biotechnology 1091

Charle, Christophe, 'Patterns' in Walter Rüegg (ed.), *A History of the University in Europe, Volume 2* (Oxford University Press 2004) 33

Cherensky, Steven, 'A Penny for Their Thoughts: Employee-Inventors, Preinvntion Assignment Agreements, Property, and Personhood' (1993) 81 California Law Review 595

Chew, Pat K., 'Faculty Generated Inventions: Who Owns the Golden Egg' (1992) 1 Wisconsin Law Review 259

Chisum, Donald S., 'The Allocation of Jurisdiction between State and Federal Courts in Patent Litigation' (1971) 46 Washington Law Review 633

Chung, Andrew, 'Schools that Sue: Why More Universities File Patent Law Suits' (*Reuters*, 15 September 2015) <www.reuters.com/article/university-patents-idUSL1N11G2C820150915> accessed 1 November 2021

Clark, Burton, *Places of Inquiry: Research and Advanced Education in Modern Universities* (University of California Press 1995)

Clements, James D., 'Improving Bayh-Dole: A Case for Inventor Ownership of Federally Sponsored Research Patents' (2008) 49 Idea 469

Cohen, Seth A., 'To Innovate or Not to Innovate, That Is the Question: The Functions, Failures, and Foibles of the Reward Function Theory of Patent Law in Relation to Computer Software Platforms' (1998–1999) 5 Michigan Telecommunications and Technology Law Review 1

Cohen, Wesley M., 'Fifty Years of Empirical Studies of Innovative Activity and Performance' in Bronwyn H. Hall and Nathan Rosenberg (eds.), *Handbook of the Economics of Innovation, Volume 1* (Elsevier 2010)

Cohen, Wesley M., Richard R. Nelson, and John P. Walsh, 'Links and Impacts: The Influence of Public Research on Industrial R&D' (2002) 48 Management Science 1

Colaianni, Alessandra and Robert Cook-Deegan, 'Columbia University's Axel Patents: Technology Transfer and Implications for the Bayh-Dole Act' (2009) 87 Milbank Quarterly 683

Colyvas, Jeannette A., 'From Divergent Meanings to Common Practices: The Early Institutionalization of Technology Transfer in the Life Sciences at Stanford University' (2007) 36 Research Policy 456

Colyvas, Jeannette A., Michael Crow, Annetine Gelijns, Roberto Mazzoleni, Richard R. Nelson, Nathan Rosenberg, and Bhaven N. Sampat, 'How Do University Inventions Get Into Practice?' (2002) 48 Management Science 61

Cotropia, Christopher, 'The Individual Inventor Motif in the Age of the Patent Troll' (2009) 12 Yale Journal of Law and Technology 52

–, 'The Folly of Early Filing in Patent Law' (2009) 61 Hastings Law Journal 65

Cottrell, Frederick Gardner, 'The Research Corporation – an Experiment in Public Administration of Patent Rights' (1912) Journal of Industrial and Engineering Chemistry 864

–, 'Patent Experience of the Research Corporation' (1932) 26 Transactions of the American Institute of Chemical Engineers 222

Crespi, Gustavo A., Aldo Geuna, Önder Nomaler, and Bart Verspagen, 'University IPRs and Knowledge Transfer: Is University Ownership More Efficient?' (2010) 19 Economics of Innovation and New Technology 627

Crespi, Gustavo A., Pablo D'Este, Roberto Fontana, and Aldo Geuna, 'The Impact of Academic Patenting on University Research and its Transfer' (2011) 40 Research Policy 55

Crosson, Patricia H., *Public Service in Higher Education: Practices and Priorities* (Association for the Study of Higher Education 1983)

Crouch, Dennis, 'The Patent Lottery: Exploiting Behavioral Economics for the Common Good' (2008) 16 George Mason Law Review 141

–, 'Supreme Court: Inventors Can Retain Rights Even for Federally Funded Inventions' (*Patently-O*, 6 June 2011) <https://patentlyo.com/patent/2011/06/stanford-v-roche-563-u-s-____-2011-in-a-split-decision-the-supreme-court-has-ruled-that-a-federally-funded-contractor.html> accessed 1 November 2021

–, 'AIA Shifts USPTO Focus from Inventors to Patent Owners' (*Patently-O*, 4 August 2012) <https://patentlyo.com/patent/2012/08/aia-shifts-usptos-focus-from-inventors-to-patent-owners.html> accessed 1 November 2021

–, 'Independent Inventors' (*Patently-O*, 7 June 2015) <https://patentlyo.com/patent/2015/06/independent-inventors.html> accessed 1 November 2021

Cunningham, James A., Erik E. Lehmann, Matthias Menter, and Nikolaus Seitz, 'The Impact of University Focused Technology Transfer Policies on Regional Innovation and Entrepreneurship' (2019) 44 Journal of Technology Transfer 1451

Cuntz, Alexander, Helge Dauchert, Petra Meurer, and Annika Philipps, 'Hochschulpatente zehn Jahre nach Abschaffung des Hochschullehrerprivilegs' (2012) Studien zum Deutschen Innovationssystem No. 13–2012, Expertenkommission Forschung und Innovation

Cutaia, Alfonso and Ranjana Kadle, 'Micro-Entity Status for Institutions of Higher Education' (*Hudgson Russ*, 12 November 2013) <www.hodgsonruss.com/newsroom-publications-MicroEntityStatusforHigherEducation.html> accessed 1 November 2021

Czarnitzki, Dirk, Thorsten Doherr, Katrin Hussinger, Paula Schliessler, and Andrew A. Toole, 'Individual versus Institutional Ownership of University-discovered Inventions' (2015) 15–007 ZEW Centre for European Economic Research Discussion Paper

Dasgupta, Partha and Paul A. David, 'Toward a New Economics of Science' (1994) 23 Research Policy 487

David, Paul A., 'Intellectual Property Institutions and the Panda's Thumb: Patents, Copyrights, and Trade Secrets in Economic Theory and History' in Mitchel B. Wallerstein, Mary Ellen Mogee and Roberta A. Schoen (eds.), *Global Dimensions of Intellectual Property Rights in Science and Technology* (National Academy Press 1993) 19

–, 'Innovation and Universities' Role in Commercializing Research Results: Second Thoughts about the Bayh-Dole Experiment' (2005) 04–27 Stanford Institute for Economic Policy Research Discussion Paper 1

David, Paul A. and Bronwyn H. Hall, 'Property and the Pursuit of Knowledge: IPR Issues Affecting Scientific Research' (2006) 35 Research Policy 767

Decker, Ryan, John Haltiwanger, Ron Jarmin, and Javier Miranda, 'The Role of Entrepreneurship in US Job Creation and Economic Dynamism' (2014) 28 Journal of Economic Perspectives 3

Delanty, Gerard, *Challenging Knowledge: The University in the Knowledge Society* (Open University Press 2001)

Demsetz, Harold, 'Toward a Theory of Property Rights' (1967) 57 American Economic Review 347

Derzko, Natalie M., 'In Search of a Compromised Solution to the Problem Arising from Patenting Biomedical Research Tools' (2003) 20 Santa Clara Computer & High Technology Law Journal 347

van Dongen, Peter, Alfredo Yergos, Robert Tijssen, and Eric Claassen, 'The Relationships between University IP Regimes, Scientists' Motivations and their Engagement with Research Commercialisation in Europe' (2017) 8 European Journal of Law and Technology 1

Dölemeyer, Barbara and Diethelm Klippel, 'Der Beitrag der Deutschen Rechtswissenschaft zur Theorie des gewerblichen Rechtschutzes und Urheberrechts' in *Gewerblicher Rechtsschutz und Urheberrecht. Festschrift zum hundertjährigen Bestehen der Deutschen Vereinigung für gewerblichen Rechtsschutz und Urheberrecht und ihrer Zeitschrift* (VCH 1991) 185

Dratler, Jay, 'Incentives for People: The Forgotten Purpose of the Patent System' (1979) 16 Harvard Journal of Legislation 129

Dreyfuss, Rochelle, 'Collaborative Research: Conflicts on Authorship, Ownership, and Accountability' (2000) 53 Vanderbilt Law Review 1159

–, Varying the Course in Patenting Genetic Material: A Counter-Proposal to Richard Epstein's Steady Course' (2003) 59 NYU Law School Public Law Research Paper 1

–, 'Protecting the Public Domain of Science: Has the Time for an Experimental Use Defense Arrived' (2004) 46 Arizona Law Review 457

Ducor, Philippe, 'Coauthorship and Coinventorship' (2000) 289 Science 873

Duderstadt, James J. and Farris W. Womack, *Beyond the Crossroads – the Future of the Public University in America* (Johns Hopkins University Press 2004)

Dutton, Harold I., *The Patent System and Inventive Activity* (Manchester University Press 1984)

Duval-Couetil, Nathalie, Jessamine Pilcher, Phil Weilerstein, and Chad Gotch, 'Undergraduate Involvement in Intellectual Property Protection at Universities: Views from Technology Transfer Professionals' (2014) 30 International Journal of Engineering Education 60

Eaton, Khyle, '2019 USPTO Patent Statistics: Breaking the Trend' (*ANAQUA*, 11 February 2020) <www.anaqua.com/2019-uspto-patent-statistics-breaking-trend/> accessed 1 November 2021

Eaton, William W., 'Patent Problem: Who Owns the Rights?' (1967) 45 Harvard Business Review 101

Ebersole, John, 'Going Private: Why Public Institutions Are Considering Crossing Over' (*EvoLLLution*, 3 November 2014) <https://evolllution.com/opinions/private-public-institutions-crossing-part-1/> accessed 1 November 2021

The Economist, 'Bayhing for Blood or Doling out Cash?' (*Economist*, 24 December 2005) <www.economist.com/science-and-technology/2005/12/20/bayhing-for-blood-or-doling-out-cash> accessed 1 November 2021

–, 'Opinion: Innovation's Golden Goose' (*Economist*, 14 December 2002) <www.economist.com/technology-quarterly/2002/12/14/innovations-golden-goose> accessed 1 November 2021

van Eecke, Patrick, Jeanne Kelly, Peter Bolger, and Maarten Truyens, *Monitoring and Analysis of Technology Transfer and Intellectual Property Regimes and their Use* (European Commission 2007)

Ehrenberg, Ronald G., 'The Perfect Storm and the Privatization of Public Higher Education' (2006) 38 Change: The Magazine of Higher Learning 46

Eisenberg, Melvin Aron, 'Principles of Consideration' (1982) 67 Cornell Law Review 640

Eisenberg, Rebecca S., 'Patents and the Progress of Science: Exclusive Rights and Experimental Use' (1989) 56 University of Chicago Law Review 1017

–, 'Public Research and Private Development: Patents and Technology Transfer in Government-Sponsored Reserach' (1996) 82 Virginia Law Review 1663

–, 'Patent Swords and Shield' (2003) 299 Science 1018

–, 'Noncompliance, Nonenforcement, Nonproblem – Rethinking the Anticommons in Biomedical Research' (2008) 45 Houston Law Review, 1059

Eisenberg, Rebecca S. and Robert Cook-Deegan, 'Universities: The Fallen Angels of Bayh-Dole?' (2018) 147 Daedalus 76

Eskridge, Nancy K., 'Dole Blasts HEW for 'Stonewalling' Patent Applications' (1978) 28 BioScience 605

D'Este, Pablo and Pari Patel, 'University-industry Linkages in the UK: What are the Factors Underlying the Variety of Interactions with Industry?' (2007) 36 Research Policy 1295

Etzkowitz, Henry, 'The Evolution of the Entrepreneurial University' (2004) 1 International Journal of Technology and Globalisation 64

European Commission, *Third European Report on Science & Technology Indicators* (European Commission 2003)

European Patent Office (EPO), 'Annual Report 2018, European Patent Applications Filed with the EPO' (*EPO*, 21 January 2019) <https://epo.org/about-us/annual-reports-statistics/annual-report/2018/statistics/patent-applications.html#tab6> accessed 1 November 2021

Fallon, Daniel, *The German University. A Heroic Ideal in Conflict with the Modern World* (Colorado Associated University Press 1980)

Feltz, James, 'UCLA's Effort to Patent a Costly Prostate Cancer Drug in India Hurts the Poor, Critics Say' (*Los Angeles Times*, 22 October 2017) <www.latimes.com/business/la-fi-ucla-cancer-drug-20171022-story.html> accessed 1 November 2021

Fichte, Johann Gottlieb, *Deduzierter Plan einer zu Berlin zu errichtenden höhern Lehranstalt* (Humboldt-Universität zu Berlin 1807)

Fini, Riccardo, Nicola Lacetera, and Scott Shane, 'Inside or Outside the IP System? Business Creation in Academia' (2010) 39 Research Policy 1060

Fisch, Christian O., Tobias M. Hassel, Philipp G. Sandner, and Joern H. Block, 'University Patenting: A Comparison of 300 Leading Universities Worldwide' (2015) 40 The Journal of Technology Transfer 318

Fisher, William, 'Theories of Intellectual Property', in Stephen R. Munzer (ed.), *New Essays in the Legal and Political Theory of Property* (Cambridge University Press 2001) 168

Fisk, Catherine L., 'Removing the 'Fuel of Interest' from the 'Fire of Genius': Law and the Employee-Inventor, 1830–1930' (1998) 65 The University of Chicago Law Review 1127

Flaherty, Colleen, 'Rights to Scholarly Work' (*Inside Higher Ed*, 26 March 2015) <www.insidehighered.com/news/2015/03/26/ohio-state-faculty-object-draft-intellectual-property-policy> accessed 1 November 2021

Foner, Philip S. (ed.), *Basic Writings of Thomas Jefferson* (Willey Book 1944)

Foray, Dominique, 'University-Industry Knowledge Transfer in Switzerland', in Shahid Yusuf and Kaoru Nabeshima (eds.) *How Universities Promote Economic Growth, Directions in Development* (World Bank 2007)

Friedman, Joseph and Jonathan Silberman, 'University Technology Transfer: Do Incentives, Management, and Location Matter?' (2003) 28 Journal of Technology Transfer 17

Frischmann, Brett, 'Innovation and Institutions: Rethinking the Economics of US Science and Technology Policy' (1999) 24 Vermont Law Review 347

Fromer, Jeanne C., 'Patent Disclosure' (2009) 94 Iowa Law Review 539

Gardner, Stephen J. and Ameera Haider, 'Practical Advice Regarding Changes to Bayh-Dole Act Obligations' (*Quarles & Brady*, 6 September 2018) <www.quarles.com/publications/practical-advice-regarding-changes-to-bayh-dole-act-obligations/> accessed 1 November 2021

Gattari, Patrick G., 'Determining Inventorship for US Patent Applications' (2005) 17 Intellectual Property & Technology Law Journal 16

Geiger, Roger L., *To Advance Knowledge: The Growth of American Research Universities, 1900–1940* (Oxford University Press 1986)

Geuna, Aldo and Lionel J. J. Nesta, 'University Patenting and its Effects on Academic Research: The Emerging European Evidence' (2006) 35 Research Policy 790

Geuna, Aldo and Federica Rossi, 'Changes to University IPR Regulations in Europe and the Impact on Academic Patenting' (2011) 40 Research Policy 1068

Ginsberg, Benjamin, *The Fall of the Faculty* (Oxford University Press 2011)

Godin, Benoît, 'The Linear Model of Innovation: The Historical Construction of an Analytical Framework' (2006) 31 Science, Technology, & Human Values 639

Gold, Richard E. and Julia Carbone, 'Myriad Genetics: In the Eye of the Policy Storm' (2010) 12 Genetics in Medicine 39

Goldberg, Victor P., 'In Search of Best Efforts: Reinterpreting Bloor v. Falstaff' (2000) 44 Saint Louis University Law Journal 1465

Goldhammer, Michael, *Geistiges Eigentum und Eigentumstheorie* (Mohr Siebeck 2012)

Gollin, Michael A., *Driving Innovation – Intellectual Property Strategies for a Dynamic World* (Cambridge University Press 2008)

Gotkin, Joel Matthew, *The United States Bayh-Dole Act and Its Effect on University Technology Transfer: An Assessment of the Successes and Shortfalls of the Act's Provisions, Its Future as Interpreted by the Stanford v. Roche Case, and Its International Implications* (Nomos 2012)

Grady, Mark F. and Jay I. Alexander, 'Patent Law and Rent Dissipation' (1992) 78 Virginia Law Review 305

Graham, Hugh Davis and Nancy Diamond, *The Rise of American Research Universities – Elites and Challengers in the Postwar Era* (Johns Hopkins University Press 1997)

Granstrand, Ove, 'Innovation and Intellectual Property Rights', in Jan Fagerberg, David C. Mowery, and Richard R. Nelson (eds.), *Oxford Handbook of Innovation* (Oxford University Press 2005) 266

Greenbaum, Dov and Christopher Scott, 'Hochschullehrerprivileg – a Modern Incarnation of the Professor's Privilege to Promote University to Industry Technology Transfer' (2010) 15 Science, Technology and Society 55

Grelon, André, 'The Training and Career Structures of Engineers in France', in Robert Fox and Anna Guagnini (eds.), *Education, Technology and Industrial Performance in Europe, 1850–1939* (Cambridge University Press 1993) 42

Grimaldi, Rosa, Martin Kenney, Donald S. Siegel, and Mike Wright, '30 Years after Bayh–Dole: Reassessing Academic Entrepreneurship' (2011) 40 Research Policy 1045

Grimm, Heike, 'The Diffusion of Bayh-Dole to Germany: Did New Public Policy Facilitate University Patenting and Commercialisation?' (2011) 12 International Journal of Entrepreneurship and Small Business 459

Grimm, Heike and Johannes Jaenicke, 'What Drives Patenting and Commerzialisation Activity at East German Universities? The Role of New Public Policy, Institutional Environment and Individual Prior Knowledge' (2012) 37 Journal of Technology Transfer 454

Guinn, Gene, 'Provisional Applications: The Good, the Bad and the Ugly' (*IP Watchdog*, 20 January 2018) <www.ipwatchdog.com/2018/01/20/provisional-applications-good-bad-ugly/id=92623/> accessed 1 November 2021

Gulbrandsen, Magnus and Jens-Christian Smeby, 'Industry Funding and University Professors' Research Performance' (2005) 34 Research Policy 932

Gullette, Robert L., 'State Legislation Governing Ownership Rights in Inventions under Employee Invention Agreements' (1980) 62 Journal of the Patent Office Society 732

Hagelin, Ted, *Technology Innovation Law and Practice: Cases and Materials* (LexisNexis 2011)

–, 'The Unintended Consequences of Stanford v. Roche' (2011) 39 AIPLA Quarterly Journal 335

Halilem, Norrin, Nabil Amara, Julia Olmos-Peñuela, and Muhammad Mohiuddin, 'To Own or not to Own? – A Multilevel Analysis of Intellectual Property Right Policies' on Academic Entrepreneurship' (2017) 46 Research Policy 1479

Harbridge House Inc., *Government Patent Policy Study: Final Report* (US Government Printing Office 1968)

Hardin, Garrett, 'The Tragedy of the Commons' (1968) 162 Science 1243

Heller, Michael A. and Rebbeca S. Eisenberg, 'Can Patents Deter Innovation? The Anticommons in Biomedical Research' (1998) 280 Science 698

Hemel, Daniel J. and Lisa Larrimore Ouellette, 'Bayh–Dole Beyond Borders' (2017) 4 Journal of Law and the Biosciences 282

Henig, Robin Marantz, 'To Market, to Market … New Patent Policy Bill Gathers Congressional Support' (1979) 29 BioScience 281

Henry, Matthew D. and John L. Turner, 'The Court of Appeals for the Federal Circuit's Impact on Patent Litigation' (2006) 35 Journal of Legal Studies 85

Hershovitz, Marc, 'Unhitching the Trailer Clause: The Rights of Inventive Employees and Their Employers' (1995) 3 Journal of Intellectual Property Law 187

Hill, Thomas A., 'Origin and Development of Letters Patent for Invention' (1923) 6 Journal of the Patent Office Society 405

Höflechner, Walter, 'Humboldt in Europa? – Zugleich ein Kommentar zu Teil II' in Rainer Christoph Schwinges (ed.), *Humboldt international: der Export des Deutschen Universitätsmodells im 19. und 20. Jahrhundert* (Schwabe & Co. Verlag 2001) 263

Hovell, William P., 'Patent Ownership: An Employer's Rights to His Employee's Invention' (1982) 58 Notre Dame Law Review 863

Howell, Parker A., 'Whose Invention Is It Anyway? Employee Invention-Assignment Agreements and Their Limits' (2012) 8 Washington Journal of Law, Technology & Arts 80

Hudak, John, 'Congress in 2019: Why the First Branch Should Bring Back Earmarks' (*Brookings*, 27 December 2018) <www.brookings.edu/blog/fixgov/2018/12/27/congress-in-2019-why-the-first-branch-should-bring-back-earmarks/> accessed 1 Novmeber 2021

Hughes, Justin, 'The Philosophie of Intellectual Property' (1988) 77 Georgetown Law Journal 287

von Humboldt, Wilhelm, *Über die innere und äussere Organisation der höheren wissenschaftlichen Anstalten in Berlin* (Humboldt Universität 1810/2010)

Hunter, Dan, *Intellectual Property – the Oxford Introduction to US Law* (Oxford University Press 2012)

Hvide, Hans K. and Benjamin F. Jones, 'University Innovation and the Professor's Privilege' (2018) 108 American Economic Review 1860

IP Advocate Foundation, 'University Inventions that changed the world (*IP Advocate Foundation*, 2019) <http://ipadvocatefoundation.org/pdfs/Uni%20Inventions%20Changed%20the%20World.pdf> accessed 1 November 2021

Jacobsson, Staffan, Åsa Lindholm-Dahlstrand, and Lennart Elg, 'Is the Commercialization of European Academic R&D Weak? A Critical Assessment of a Dominant Belief and Associated Policy Responses' (2013) 42 Research Policy 874.

Jamrisko, Michelle and Wei Lu, 'Germany Breaks Korea's Six-Year Streak as Most Innovative Nation' (*Bloomberg*, 16 January 2020) <www.bloomberg.com/news/articles/2020-01-18/germany-breaks-korea-s-six-year-streak-as-most-innovative-nation> accessed 1 November 2021

Janis, Mark D., 'Patent Abolitionism' (2002) 17 Berkeley Technology Law Journal 899

Januta, Andrea, 'Entrepreneur 101: To Nurture Job Growth US Universities Seed Start-Ups' (*Reuters*, 10 May 2018) <www.reuters.com/article/us-world-work-collegestartups-idUSKBN1IB18B> accessed 1 November 2021

Jensen, Richard A. and Marie C. Thursby, 'Proofs and Prototypes for Sale: The Licensing of University Inventions' (2001) 91 American Economic Review 240

Jensen, Richard A., Jerry G. Thursby, and Marie C. Thursby, 'Disclosure and Licensing of University Inventions: 'The Best we Can Do with the S**t we Get to Work with'' (2003) 21 International Journal of Industrial Organization 1271

Jeremy, David J., *Transatlantic Industrial Revolution: The Diffusion of Textile Technologies Between Britain and America, 1770–1830s* (MIT Press 1981)

–, *Technology and Power in the Early American Cotton Industry: James Montgomery, the Second Edition of His 'Cotton Manufacture' (1840) and the Justitia Controversy about Relative Power Costs* (American Philosophical Society 1990)

Jongbloed, Ben, Jürgen Enders, and Carlo Salerno, 'Higher Education and Its Communities: Interconnections, Interdependencies and a Research Agenda' (2008) 56 Higher Education Research 303

Jordan, Carey C. and Iona Kaiser, 'United States: Working With Inventors Post-AIA: Managing Inventor Challenges And Preventing Common Mistakes' (*Mondaq*, 16 April 2014) <www.mondaq.com/unitedstates/patent/307594/working-with-inventors-post-aia-managing-inventor-challenges-and-preventing-common-mistakes> accessed 1 November 2021

Kapczynski, Amy, Samantha Chaifetz, Zachary Katz, and Yochai Benkler, 'Addressing Global Health Inequities: An Open Licensing Approach for University Innovations' (2005) 20 Berkley Technology Law Journal 1031

Kaplin, William A. and Barbara A. Lee, *The Law of Higher Education: A Comprehensive Guide to Legal Implications of Administrative Decision Making* (4th edn., Josey-Bass 2006)

Kappos, David, *Memorandum in Opposition re Motion for Preliminary Injunction* (*USPTO*, 30 August 2012) www.plainsite.org/dockets/n7xt700r/florida-middle-district-court/madstad-engineering-inc-et-al-v-us-patent-and-trademark-/

Katz, Michael L. and Janusz A. Ordover, 'R&D Cooperation and Competition' (1990) Brookings Papers on Micoreconomics 137

Katz, Yarden, 'Universities Have Turned over Hundreds of Patents to Patent Trolls' (*Medium*, 13 October 2016) <https://yarden.github.io/publication/iv_patents_universities/> accessed 1 November 2021

Kaufer, Erich, *The Economics of the Patent System* (Routledge 1989)

Keck, Otto, 'The National System for Technical Innovation in Germany' in Richard R. Nelson (ed.), *National Innovation Systems – A Comparative Analysis* (Oxford University Press 1993) 115

Kenney, Martin and Donald Patton, 'Reconsidering the Bayh-Dole Act and the Current University Invention Ownership Model' (2009) 38 Research Policy 1407

–, 'Does Inventor Ownership Encourage University Research-Derived Entrepreneurship? A Six University Comparison' (2011) 40 Research Policy 1100

–, 'Bayh-Dole and Alternative University Technology Transfer Regimes', in Dimitris G. Assimakopoulos, Elias G. Carayannis and Rafiq Dossani (eds.), *Knowledge Perspectives of New Product Development* (Springer 2012)

Kerr, Clark, *The Uses of the University* (Harvard University Press 1963)

Kitch, Edmund W., 'The Nature and Function of the Patent System' (1977) 20 Journal of Law and Economics 265

Kline, Stephen and Nathan Rosenberg, 'An Overview of Innovation', in Ralph Landau and Nathan Rosenberg (eds.), *The Positive Sum Strategy – Harnessing Technology for Economic Growth* (National Academy Press 1986) 275

Klippel, Diethelm, 'Historische Wurzeln und Funktionen von Immaterialgüter- und Persönlichkeitsrechten im 19. Jahrhundert' (1982) 4 Zeitschrift für neue Rechtsgeschichte 132

–, 'Geistiges Eigentum, Privileg und Naturrecht in rechtshistorischer Perspektive' (2015) 7 Zeitschrift für Geistiges Eigentum 49

Knapp, Charles L., Nathan M. Crystal, and Harry G. Prince, *Problems in Contract Law: Cases and Materials* (Aspen Publishers 2019)

Kneller, Robert, 'Technology Transfer: A Review for Biomedical Researchers' (2001) 7 Clinical Cancer Research 761

Krasser, Rudolf, 'Erfindungsrecht des wissenschaftlichen Personals' In Michael Hartmer and Hubert Detmer (eds.), *Hochschulrecht: ein Handbuch für die Praxis* (CF Müller 2016) 832

Krause, Michael, *Erfolg patentierter Hochschulerfindungen* (Carl Heymanns Verlag 2017)

Kulkarni, Sunil R., 'All Professors Create Equally: Why Faculty Should Have Complete Control Over Intellectual Property Rights in their Creations' (1995) 47 Hastings Law Journal 221

Lach, Saul and Mark Schankerman, 'Incentives and Invention in Universities' (2008) 39 RAND Journal of Economics 403

LaFrance, Mary, 'Nevada's Employee Inventions Statute: Novel Nonobivous and Patently Wrong' (2003) Nevada Law Journal 88

Lamoreaux, Naomi R. and Kenneth L. Sokoloff, 'Long-Term Change in the Organization of Inventive Activity' (1996) 93 Proceedings of the National Academy of Sciences of the United States of America 12686

Lander, Eric S. and Eric E. Schmidt, 'America's 'Miracle Machine' is in Desperate Need of, well, a Miracle' (*Washington Post*, 5 May 2017) <www.washingtonpost.com/opinions/americas-miracle-machine-is-in-desperate-need-of-well-a-miracle/2017/05/05/daafbe6a-30e7-11e7-9534-00e4656c22aa_story.html> accessed 1 November 2021

Landes, William M. and Richard A. Posner, *The Economic Structure of Intellectual Property Law* (Harvard University Press 2003)

Laredo, Philippe, 'Revisiting the Third Mission of Universities: Toward a Renewed Categorization of University Activities?' (2007) 20 Higher Education Policy 441

de Larena, Lorelei Ritchie, 'The Price of Progress: Are Universities Adding to the Cost' (2006) 43 Houston Law Review 137

Leaf, Clifton, 'The Law of Unintended Consequences' (*Fortune*, 19 September 2005) <https://archive.fortune.com/magazines/fortune/fortune_archive/2005/09/19/8272884/index.htm> accessed 1 November 2021

von Ledebur, Sidonia, 'Warum gehen die Patentanmeldungen aus Hochschulen zurück?' (2008) 88 Wirtschaftsdienst 604

Lee, Timothy, 'Patent Trolls Have a Surprising Alley: Universities' (*Washington Post*, 30 November 2013) <https://www.washingtonpost.com/news/the-switch/wp/2013/11/30/patent-trolls-have-a-surprising-ally-universities/>
accessed 1 November 2021

Lee, Yong S., "Technology Transfer' and the Research University: A Search for the Boundaries of University-Industry Collaboration' (1996) 25 Research Policy 843

Lee, Yong S. and Gaertner, Richard, 'Translating Academic Research to Technological Innovation' in Yong S. Lee (ed.), *Technology Transfer and Public Policy* (Quroum Books 1997) 110

Lemley, Mark A., 'Ex Ante Versus Ex Post Justifications for Intellectual Property' (2004) 71 University of Chicago Law Review 129

–, 'Patenting Nanotechnology' (2005) 58 Stanford Law Review 601

–, 'Are Universities Patent Trolls' (2008) 18 Fordham Intellectual Property Media & Entertainment Law Journal 610

–, 'The Myth of the Sole Inventor' (2012) 110 Michigan Law Review 709

–, 'Faith-based Intellectual Property' (2015) 62 UCLA Law Review 1328

–, 'The Surprising Resilience of the Patent System' (2016) 95 Texas Law Review 1

Letwin, William L., 'The English Common Law Concerning Monopolies' (1954) 21 University of Chicago Law Review 355

Levin, Richard C., Alvin K. Klevorick, Richard R. Nelson, Sidney G. Winter, Richard Gilbert, and Zvi Griliches, 'Appropriating the Returns from Industrial R&D' (1987) Brookings Papers on Economic Activity 783

Levy, Daniel, 'Private versus Public Financing of Higher Education: U. S. Policy in Comparative Perspective' (1982) 11 Higher Education 607

Link, Albert N., Robert S. Danziger, and John T. Scott, 'Is the Bayh-Dole Act Stifling Biomedical Innovation?' (2018) 34 Issues in Science and Technology 33

Lissoni, Francesco, Patrick Lierena, Maureen McKelvey, and Bulat Sanditov, 'Academic Patenting in Europe: New Evidence from the KEINS Database' (2008) 17 Research Evaluation 87

Lissoni, Francesco, Fabio Montobbio, and Lorenzo Zirulia, 'Inventorship and Authorship as Attribution Rights: An Enquiry into the Economics of Scientific Credit' (2013) 95 Journal of Economic Behavior & Organization 49

Litan, Robert E., Lesa Mitchell, and E. J. Reedy, 'The University as Innovator: Bumps in the Road' (2007) 23 Issues in Science and Technology 57

Lobel, Orly, 'Opinion: My Ideas, My Boss's Property' (*New York Times*, 14 April 2014) <www.nytimes.com/2014/04/14/opinion/my-ideas-my-bosss-property.html> accessed 1 November 2021

Locke, John, *Two Treatises of Government* (McMaster University Archive of the History of Economic Thought 1999)

Locke, Scott D., 'Patent Litigation over Federally Funded Inventions and the Consequences of Failing to Comply with Bayh-Dole' (2003) 8 Virginia Journal of Law & Technology 1

Lohr, Steve, 'Inventor Challenges a Sweeping Revision in Patent Law' (*New York Times*, 27 August 2012) <www.nytimes.com/2012/08/27/technology/mark-stadnyk-challenges-sweeping-revision-in-patent-law.html> accessed 1 November 2021

Loise, Vicki and Ashley J. Stevens, 'The Bayh-Dole Act Turns 30' (2010) 52 Science Translational Medicine 185

Lubar, Steven, 'New, Useful, and Nonobvious' (1990) 6 American Heritage of Invention and Technology 8

Lucas, Christopher J., *American Higher Education – A History* (2nd edn., Palgrave Macmillan 2006)

Lundvall, Bengt-Ake, 'Innovation as an Interactive Process: From User-Producer Interaction to the National System of Innovation' in Giovanni Dosi (ed.), *Technical Change and Economic Theory* (Pinter 1988) 349

Luppino, Anthony J., 'Fixing a Hole: Eliminating Ownership Uncertainties to Facilitate University-Generated Innovation' (2009) 78 University of Missouri Law Review 367

Lutz, Karl B., 'Patents and Science – a Clarification of the Patent Clause of the US Constitution' (1949) 18 George Washington Law Review 50

Machi, Peter, 'What's Mine Is Yours: Navigating Ownership Rights in Academia' in Nadya Reingand (ed.), *Intellectual Property in Academia: A Practical Guide for Scientists and Engineers* (CRC Press 2011) 235

Machlup, Fritz, *An Economic Review of the Patent System* (US Government Pringing Office 1958)

Machlup, Fritz and Penrose, Edith Tilton, 'The Patent Controversy in the Nineteenth Century' (1950) 10 The Journal of Economic History 1

Mächtel, Florian, *Das Patentrecht im Krieg* (Mohr Siebeck 2009)

MacLeod, Christine, *Inventing the Industrial Revolution: The English Patent System, 1660–1800* (Cambridge University Press 1988)

Manegold, Karl-Heinz, *Universität, Technische Hochschule und Industrie – Ein Beitrag zur Emanzipation der Technik im 19. Jahrhundert under besonderer Berücksichtigung der Bestrebungen Felix Kleins* (Dunker & Humblot 1970)

Mansfield, Edwin, 'Patents and Innovation: An Empirical Study' (1986) 32 Management Science 173

–, 'Academic Research and Industrial Innovation' (1991) 20 Research Policy 1

–, 'Academic Research and Industrial Innovation: An Update of Empirical Findings' (1998) 26 Research Policy 773

Markman, Gideon D., Peter T. Gianiodis, and Phillip H. Phan, 'Full-Time Faculty or Part-Time Entrepreneurs' (2008) 55 IEEE Transactions on Engineering Management 29

Markman, Gideon D., Phillip H. Phan, David B. Balkin, and Peter T. Gianiodis, 'Entrepreneurship and University-based Technology Transfer' (2005) 20 Journal of Business Venturing 241

Matal, Joe, 'A Guide to the Legislative History of the America Invents Act: Part I of II' (2011) 21 The Federal Circuit Bar Journal 435

Maynard, Micheline, 'Tesla's Elon Musk: Take our Patents, They're Yours' (*Forbes*, 12 June 2014) <www.forbes.com/sites/michelinemaynard/2014/06/12/teslas-elon-musk-take-our-patents-theyre-yours/?sh=2e3a8ac053f6> accessed 1 November 2021

McGarey, Barbara and Annette Levey, 'Patents, Products, and Public Health: An Analysis of the CellPro March-in Petition' (1999) 14 Berkeley Technology Law Journal 1095

McGuinness, Aims C., 'The States and Higher Education' in Philip G. Altbach, Patricia J. Gumport, and Robert O. Berdahl (eds.), *American Higher Education in the Twenty-first Century: Social, Political, and Economic Challenges* (Johns Hopkins University Press 2011) 139

McKusick, Vincent Lee, 'A Study of Patent Policies in Educational Institutions, Giving Specific Attention to the Massachusetts Institute of Technology' (1948) 245 Journal of the Franklin Institute 193

McLendon, Michael K., 'State Governance Reform of Higher Education: Patterns, Trends, and Theories of the Public Policy Process' in *Higher Education: Handbook of Theory and Research* (Springer 2003) 57

McManis, Charles R. and Sucheol Noh, 'The Impact of the Bayh-Dole Act on Genetic R&D: Evaluating the Arguments and Empirical Evidence' (2011) Washington University in St. Louis Legal Studies Research Paper 1,

Merges, Robert P., 'Intellectual Property Rights and Bargaining Breakdown: The Case of Blocking Patents' (1994) 62 Tennesse Law Review 75

–, 'The Law and Economics of Employee Inventions' (1999) 13 Harvard Journal of Law & Technology 1

–, 'One Hundred Years of Solicitude: Intellectual Property Law, 1900–2000' (2000) 88 California Law Review 2187

–, *Justifying Intellectual Property* (Harvard University Press 2011)

Merges, Robert P., Peter S. Menell, and Mark A. Lemley, *Intellectual Property in the New Technological Age* (5th edn., Wolters Kluwer 2012)

Merrill, Dave, Blacki Migliozzi, and Susan Decker, 'Billions at Stake in University Patent Fight' (*Bloomberg*, 24 May 2016) <www.bloomberg.com/graphics/2016-university-patents/> accessed 1 November 2021

Meurer, Michael J., 'Inventors, Entrepreneurs, and Intellectual Property Law' (2008) 45 Houston Law Review 1201

Migliorini, Robert A., 'Twelve Years Later: Provisional Patent Application Filing Revisited' (2007) 89 Journal of the Patent & Trademark Office Society 437

Morand, Pierre-André, 'Les Lois Cantonales Relatives aux Brevets', in Institut für Gewerblichen Rechtschutz (ed.), *Kernprobleme des Patentrechts. Festschrift zum einhundertjährigen Bestehen des eidgenössischen Patentgesetzes* (Stämpfli 1988) 3

Moraw, Peter, *Kleine Geschichte der Universität Giessen* (2nd edn., Verlag der Ferber'schen Universitätsbuchhandlung Giessen 1990)

Moser, Petra, 'Patents and Innovation: Evidence from Economic History' (2013) 27 Journal of Economic Perspectives 23

Mowery, David C., Richard R. Nelson, Bhaven N. Sampat, and Arvids A. Ziedonis, 'The Growth of Patenting and Licensing by US Universities: An Assessment of the Effects of the Bayh-Dole Act of 1980' (2001) 30 Research Policy 99

–, *Ivory Tower and Industrial Innovation: University-Industry Technology Transfer Before and After the Bayh-Dole Act* (Stanford University Press 2004)

Mowery, David C, and Bhavan N. Sampat, 'University Patents and Patent Policy Debates in the USA, 1925–1980' (2001) 10 Industrial and Corporate Change 781

–, 'Universities in National Innovation Systems' in Jan Fagerberg, David C. Mowery, and Richard R. Nelson (eds.), *Oxford Handbook of Innovation* (Oxford University Press 2005) 210

–, 'The Bayh-Dole Act of 1980 and University-industry Technology Transfer: A Model for Other OECD Governments?' (2005) 30 Journal of Technology Transfer 233

Mowery, David C. and Arvids A. Ziedonis, 'Markets versus Spillovers in Outflows of University Research' (2015) 44 Research Policy 50

Mumper, Michael, Lawrence E. Gladieux, Jacqueline E. King, and Melanie E. Corrigan, 'The Federal Government and Higher Education' in Philip G. Altbach, Patricia J. Gumport, and Robert O. Berdahl (eds.), *American Higher Education in the Twenty-first Century: Social, Political, and Economic Challenges* (Johns Hopkins University Press 2011) 113

Murane, John D. and Jamar W. Tyndale, 'Stanford v. Roche: Should the Supreme Court Dismiss Certiorari as Improvidently Granted?' (*Intellectual Property Today*, 1 April 2011) <www.venable.com/wp-content/uploads/Murnane_Tyndale4.pdf> accessed 1 November 2021

Murray, Fiona and Scott Stern, 'When Ideas are not Free: The Impact of Patents on Scientific Research' (2006) 7 Innovation Policy and the Economy 33

Mutnick, Ally and Caitlin Emma, 'House Democrats Eye New Earmarks Plan – Spooking Endangered Freshmen' (*Politico*, 24 January 2020) <www.politico.com/news/2020/01/24/freshmen-democrats-earmarks-plan-103836> accessed 1 November 2021

Narea, Nicole, 'Startup 101: More Universities Are Tring to Figure out How to Teach Entrepreneurship' (*Forbes*, 29 July 2015) <www.forbes.com/sites/nicolenarea/2015/07/29/startup-101-more-universities-are-trying-to-figure-out-how-to-teach-entrepreneurship/> accessed 1 November 2021

Nash, Ralph C. and Leonard Rawicz, *Intellectual Property in Government Contracts* (6th edn., CCH 2008)

Nash-Hoff, Michele, 'Has the America Invents Act Been Benefical or Harmful? – Changing US Patent System to 'First to File' Creates Expensive Dilemma for Small Inventors' (*IndustryWeek*, 18 February 2015) <www.industryweek.com/innovation/intellectual-property/article/22008085/has-the-america-invents-act-been-beneficial-or-harmful> accessed 1 November 2021

National Center for Education Statistics (NCES), 'Digest of Education Statistics, Table 105.50 Number of educational institutions 1980–81 through 2016–17' (*NCES*) <https://nces.ed.gov/programs/digest/d18/tables/dt18_105.50.asp?current=yes> accessed 1 November 2021

–, 'Digest of Education Statistics, Table 105.10. Projected number of participants in educational institutions Fall 2018' (*NCES*) <https://nces.ed.gov/programs/digest/d18/tables/dt18_105.10.asp?current=yes> accessed 1 November 2021

National Institute of Health (NIH), 'Principles and Guidelines for Recipients of NIH Research Grants and Contracts on Obtaining and Disseminating Biomedical Research Resources' (1999) 64 FR 72090

–, 'Best Practices for the Licensing of Genomic Inventions' (2004) 69 FR 223

National Institute of Standards and Technology (NIST), 'US Department of Commerce, Technology Partnerships Office, Bayh-Dole Act FAQs' (*NIST*, 12 August 2021) <https://www.nist.gov/tpo/bayh-dole/bayh-dole-regulations-faqs> accessed 1 November 2021

National Public Radio (NPR), 'Are Public Universities Still Public?' (*NPR*, 21 June 2012) <www.npr.org/2012/06/21/155524647/are-public-universities-still-public> accessed 1 November 2021

National Research Council (NRC), *Intellectual Property Rights and Research Tools in Molecular Biology: Summary of a Workshop Held at the National Academy of Sciences* (National Academies Press 1997)

–, *Reaping the Benefits of Genomic and Proteomic Research: Intellectual Property Rights, Innovation, and Public Health* (National Academies Press 2006)

–, *Managing University Intellectual Property in the Public Interest* (National Academies Press 2011)

–, *Research Universities and the Future of America – Ten Breakthrough Actions Vital to Our Nation's Prosperity and Security* (2012)

National Science Board, *Diminishing Funding and Rising Expectations: Trends and Challenges for Public Research Universities, A Companion to Science and Engineering Indicators 2012* (*NSF*) <https://nsf.gov/nsb/sei/companion2/files/nsb1245.pdf> accessed 1 November 2021

National Science Foundation, 'Federal Funds Survey, Detailed Historical Tables, FYs 1951–97' (*NCSES Web Archive*) <https://wayback.archive-it.org/5902/20150629143710/http://www.nsf.gov/statistics/fedfnd45/hist45/pdf/sum.pdf> accessed 1 November 2021

–, 'Higher Education Research Expenditures (HERD), 'Table 10: Federally Financed Higher Education R&D Expenditures, FYs 2009–18' (*NSF*) <https://ncsesdata.nsf.gov/herd/2018/html/herd18-dt-tab010.html> accessed 1 November 2021

Nedeva, Maria, 'New Tricks and Old Dogs? The 'Third Mission' and the Re-Production of the University' (2006) 66 Geographies of Knowledge, Geometrics of Power: Framing the Future of Higher Education 85

Nelson, Andrew J., 'Putting University Research in Context: Assessing Alternative Measures of Production and Diffusion at Stanford' (2012) 41 Research Policy 678

Nelson, Richard R., 'The Simple Economics of Basic Research' (1959) 67 Journal of Political Economy 297

–, 'Observations on the Post-Bayh-Dole Rise of Patenting at American Universities' (2001) 26 Journal of Technology Transfer 13

–, 'The Market Economy, and the Scientific Commons' (2004) 33 Research Policy 455

Neue Zürcher Zeitung (NZZ), 'Selbstbedienungsladen oder Wirtschaftspartner' (*NZZ*, 3 September 2004) <www.nzz.ch/article9TBWQ-1.301687?reduced=true> accessed 1 November 2021

Neumeyer, Fredrik and John C. Stedman, *The Employed Inventor in the United States* (MIT Press 1971)

Newman, Frank, *Choosing Quality: Reducing Conflict Between the State and the University* (Education Commission of the States 1987)

Newman, Frank, Lara Couturier, and Jamie Scurry, *The Future of Higher Education: Rhetoric, Reality, and the Risks of the Market* (John Wiley & Sons 2010)

Nordheden, Karen J. and Michael Hoeflich, 'Undergraduate Research and Intellectual Property Rights' (1999) 42 IEEE Transactions on Education 233

Note, 'The Disclosure Function of the Patent System (Or Lack Thereof)' (2005) 118 Harvard Law Review 2007

O'Brien, William, 'March-in Rights under the Bayh-Dole Act: The NIH's Paper Tiger' (2013) 43 Seton Hall Law Review 1403

O'Connor, Sean M., 'The Aftermath of Stanford v. Roche: Which Law of Assignments Governs?' (2011) 6 Intellectual Property Journal 29

Okuley, John J., 'Resolution of Inventorship Disputes: Avoiding Litigation Through Early Evaluation' (2003) 18 Ohio State Journal on Dispute Resolution 915

Organisation for Economic Co-operation and Development (OECD), *Knowledge Management in the Learning Society* (OECD 2000)

Ornstein, Charles and Katie Thomas, 'What These Medical Journals Don't Reveal: Top Doctors' Ties to Industry' (*New York Times*, 8 December 2018) <www.nytimes.com/2018/12/08/health/medical-journals-conflicts-of-interest.html> accessed 1 November 2021

Overly, Steven, 'How Ford Turned Thousands of Employees into Inventors – The Washington Post' (*Washington Post*, 14 December 2016) <www.washingtonpost.com/news/innovations/wp/2016/12/14/how-ford-turned-thousands-of-employees-into-inventors/> accessed 1 November 2021

Owen-Smith, Jason, *Research Universities and the Public Good: Discovery for a Uncertain Future* (Stanford University Press 2018)

Owen-Smith, Jason and Walter W. Powell, 'To Patent or Not: Faculty Decisions and Institutional Success at Technology Transfer' (2001) 26 Journal of Technology Transfer 99

Paletschek, Sylvia, 'Verbreitete sich ein 'Humobldt'sches Modell' an den Deutschen Universitäten im 19. Jahrhundert?' in Rainer C. Schwinges (ed.), *Humboldt international: der Export des Deutschen Universitätsmodells im 19. und 20. Jahrhundert* (Schwabe & Co. Verlag 2001) 75

Palfrey, John, *Intellectual Property Strategy* (MIT Press 2011)

Palmer, Archie M., 'University Patent Policies' (1934) 16 Journal of the Patent Office Society 96

–, *University Patent Policies and Practices* (National Academy of Sciences, NRC 1952)

–, *Nonprofit Research and Patent Management in the United States* (National Academy of Sciences, NRC 1955)

–, *Patents and Nonprofit Research: A Study Prepared for the Subcommittee on Patents, Trademarks, and Copyrights of the US Senate Committee on the Judiciary* (US Government Printing Office 1957)

–, *University Research and Patent Policies, Practices, and Procedures* (National Academy of Sciences, NRC 1962)

Parker, Henrik D., 'Reform for Rights of Employed Inventors' (1984) 57 California Law Review 603

Patel, Sandip H., 'Graduate Students' Ownership and Attribution Rights in Intellectual Property' (1995) 71 Indiana Law Journal 482

Paulus, Paul B. and Bernard A. Nijstad, 'Group Creativity: An Introduction' in Paul B. Paulus and Bernard A. Nijstad (eds.), *Group Creativity – Innovation through Collaboration* (Oxford University Press 2003) 1

Pavitt, Keith, 'What Makes Basic Research Economically Useful?' (1991) 20 Research Policy 109

–, 'Public Policies to Support Basic Research: What Can the Rest of the World Learn from US Theory and Practice? (And What they Should not Learn)' (2001) 10 Industrial and Corporate Change 761

Peberdy, Morag and Alain Strowel, 'Employee's Rights to Compensation for Inventions – a European Perspective' (2009) Cross-border Life Sciences Handbook 63

Penman, Jennifer and Fran Quigley, 'Better Late Than Never: How the US Government Can and Should Use Bayh-Dole March-In Rights to Respond to the Medicines Access Crisis' (2017) 54 Willamette Law Review 171

Perkin, Harold, 'History of Universities' in James J. Forest and Philip G. Altbach (eds.), *International Handbook of Higher Education* (Springer 2007) 159

Perkmann, Markus, Valentina Tartari, Maureen McKelvey, Erkko Autio, Anders Broström, Pablo D'Este, and Riccardo Fini, 'Academic Engagement and Commercialisation: A Review of the Literature on University–industry Relations' (2013) 42 Research Policy 423

Pettersson, Ingemar, 'The Nomos of the University: Introducing the Professor's Privilege in 1940s Sweden' (2018) 56 Minerva 56 381,

Phan, Philip H. and Donald S. Siegel, 'The Effectiveness of University Technology Transfer' (2006) 2 Foundations and Trends® in Entrepreneurship 77

Pisegna-Cook, Evelyn, 'Ownership Rights of Employee Inventions: The Role of Preinvention Assignment Agreements and State Statutes' (1994) 2 University of Baltimore Intellectual Property Law Journal 163

Popp Berman, Elizabeth, 'Why Did Universities Start Patenting? Institution-Building and the Road to the Bayh-Dole Act' (2008) 38 Social Studies of Science 835

President Kennedy, John F., *Memorandum and Statement of Government Patent Policy*, 28 Federal Register 10943–46 (10 October 1963)

President Nixon, Richard M., *Memorandum and Statement of Government Patent Policy*, 36 Federal Register 16886 (23 August 1971)

President Obama, Barack, 'Transcript: Obama on Debt Deal' (*Washington Post*, 2 August 2011) <www.washingtonpost.com/politics/2011/08/02/gIQADiGvpI_story.html> accessed 1 November 2021

von Proff, Sidonia, Guido Buenstorf, and Martin Hummel, 'University Patenting in Germany before and after 2002: What Role Did the Professors' Privilege Play?' (2012) 19 Industry and Innovation 23

Pulsinelli, Gary, 'Share and Share Alike: Increasing Access to Government-Funded Inventions under the Bayh-Dole Act' (2005) 7 Minnesota Journal of Law, Science & Technology 393

Rabban, David M., 'A Functional Analysis of 'Individual' and 'Institutional' Academic Freedom Under the First Amendment' (1990) 53 Law and Contemporary Problems 227

Rafferty, Matthew, 'The Bayh–Dole Act and University R&D' (2008) 37 Research Policy 29

Rai, Arti K., and Rebecca S. Eisenberg, 'The Public and the Private in Biopharmaceutical Research' (2001) Proceedings of the Conference on the Public Domain 157
Rai, Arti K. and Rebecca S. Eisenberg, 'Bayh-Dole reform and the progress of biomedicine' (2003) 66 Law and Contemporary Problems 289
Reder, Margo E., 'Board of Trustees v. Roche Molecular Systems, Inc: Negotiating the Web of Comepeting Ownership Claims to Inventions Arising from Government-Funded Academic-Industry Collaboration' (2011) 44 Business Law Review 211
Reichman, Jerome H., 'Overlapping Proprietary Rights' (1992) 51 Columbia-VLA Journal of Law & Arts 51
Riesenfeld, Stefan A., 'Patent Protection and Atomic Energy Legislation' (1958) 46 California Law Review 40
Roessner, David, Jennifer Bond, Sumiye Okubo, and Mark Planting, 'The Economic Impact of Licensed Commercialized Inventions Originating in University Research' (2013) 42 Research Policy 23
Rooklidge, William C. and W. Gerard von Hoffmann, III, 'Reduction to Practice, Experimental Use, and the 'On Sale' and 'Public Use' Bars to Patentability' (1988) 63 St. John's Law Review 1
Rooksby, Jacob H., 'University Initiation of Patent Infringement Litigation' (2011) 10 John Marshall Review of Intellectual Property Law 623
Roose-Snyder, Beirne and Megan K. Doyle, 'The Global Health Licensing Program: A New Model for Humanitarian Licensing at the University Level' (2009) 35 American Journal of Law & Medicine 281
Rosenberg, Nathan and Richard R. Nelson, 'American Universities and Technical Advance in Industry' (1994) 23 Research Policy 323
Rowe, Elizabeth A., 'The Experimental Use Exception to Patent Infringement: Do Universities Deserve Special Treatment?' (2005) 57 Hastings Law Journal 921
Rudolph, Frederick, *American College and University: A History* (University of Georgia Press 1991)
Salter, Ammon J. and Ben R. Martin, 'The Economic Benefits of Publicly Funded Basic Research: A Critical Review' (2001) 30 Research Policy 509
Sampat, Bhaven N., David C. Mowery, and Arvids A. Ziedonis, 'Changes in University Patent Quality after the Bayh-Dole Act: A Re-examination' (2003) 21 International Journal of Industrial Organization 1371
Sampat, Bhaven N., 'Patenting and US Academic Research in the 20th Century: The World before and after Bayh-Dole' (2006) 35 Research Policy 772
Sandrik, Karen E., 'Formal but Forgiving: A New Approach to Patent Assignments' (2014) 66 Rutgers Law Review 299
Schacht, Wendy H., *The Bayh-Dole Act: Selected Issues in Patent Policy and the Commercialization of Technology* (Congressional Research Service 2010)
Schechter, Roger E. and John R. Thomas, *Principles of Patent Law* (Thomson West 2004)
Schelsky, Helmut, *Einsamkeit und Freiheit-Idee und Gestalt der Deutschen Universität und ihrer Reformen* (Rowholt 1963)
Schiff, Eric, *Industrialization Without National Patents: The Netherlands, 1860–1912; Switzerland, 1850–1907* (Princeton University Press 1971)
Schleiermacher, Friedrich, *Gelegentliche Gedanken über Universitäten in Deutschem Sinn* (1808)
Schlesinger, Divya, 'UCLA Students Protest University Patent Claim On Prostate Cancer Treatment' (*Health Policy,* 13 March 2019) <www.healthpolicy-watch.org/ucla-

students-protest-university-patent-claim-on-prostrate-cancer-treatment/> accessed 1 November 2021

Schmidt, Alexander K., *Erfinderprinzip und Erfinderpersönlichkeitsrecht im Deutschen Patentrecht von 1877 bis 1936* (Mohr Siebeck 2009)

Schmidtlein, Frank A. and Robert O. Berdahl, 'Autonomy and Accountability: Who Controls Academe', in Philip G. Altbach, Patricia J. Gumport, and Robert O. Berdahl (eds.), *American Higher Education in the Twenty-first Century: Social, Political, and Economic Challenges* (Johns Hopkins University Press 2011) 69

Schmoch, Ulrich, *Patentanmeldungen aus Deutschen Hochschulen, Analysen im Rahmen der jährlichen Berichterstattung zur Technologischen Leistungsfähigkeit Deutschlands, Studien zum Deutschen Innovationssystem* (Fraunhofer-Institut für System- und Innovationsforschung 2007)

Schumpeter, Joseph A., *Theorie der wirtschaftlichen Entwicklung* (von Duncker & Humbolt 1912)

Schwinges, Rainer C. (ed.), *Humboldt international: der Export des Deutschen Universitätsmodells im 19. und 20. Jahrhundert* (Schwabe & Co. Verlag 2001)

– 'Einführung' in Rainer C. Schwinges (ed.), *Humboldt international: der Export des Deutschen Universitätsmodells im 19. und 20. Jahrhundert* (Schwabe & Co. Verlag 2001) 1

Scotchmer, Suzanne, 'Standing on the Shoulders of Giants: Cumulative Research and the Patent Law' (1991) 5 Journal of Economic Perspectives 29

Scott, Myrtle M., 'Intellectual Property Rights: A Ticking Time Bomb in Academia' (1998) 84 Academe 22

Sellenthin, Mark O., 'Technology Transfer Offices and University Patenting in Sweden and Germany' (2009) 34 Journal of Technology Transfer 603

Seltzer, Rick, 'Endowment Returns Slow; Survey Offers Peek at Spending' (*Inside Higher Ed,* 31 January 2019) <www.insidehighered.com/news/2019/01/31/college-endowments-returned-82-percent-2018-annual-survey-adds-some-insight-how> accessed 1 November 2021

Seymore, Sean B., 'My Patent, Your Patent, or Our Patent? Inventorship Disputes within Academic Research Groups' (2006) 16 Albany Law Journal of Science & Technology 125

Shane, Scott, 'Patents Granted to Small Entities in Decline' (Small Business Trends, 20 January 2016) <https://smallbiztrends.com/2010/07/how-smart-is-the-average-entrepreneur.html> accessed 1 November 2021

–, 'Encouraging University Entrepreneurship? The Effect of the Bayh-Dole Act on University Patenting in the United States' (2004) 19 Journal of Business Venturing 127

Siegel, Donald S., David A. Waldman, Leanne E. Atwater, and Albert N. Link, 'Toward a Model of the Effective Transfer of Scientific Knowledge from Academicians to Practitioners: Qualitative Evidence from the Commercialisation of University Technologies' (2004) 21 Journal of Engineering and Technology Management 115

Siegel, Donald S., David A. Waldman, and Albert Link, 'Assessing the Impact of Organizational Practices on the Relative Productivity of University Technology Transfer Offices: An Exploratory Study (2003) 32 Research Policy 27

Siepmann, Thomas J., 'The Global Exportation of the US Bayh-Dole Act' (2004) 30 University Dayton Law Review 209

Silvernagel, Craig, Richard R. Schultz, Steven B. Moser, and Marie Aune, 'Student-generated Intellectual Property: Perceptions of Ownership by Faculty and Students' (2009) 12 Journal of Entrepreneurship Education 13

Singh, Jasjit and Fleming Lee, 'Lone Inventors as Sources of Breakthroughs: Myth or Reality?' (2010) 56 Management Science 41

Slaughter, Sheila and Larry L. Leslie, *Academic Capitalism – Politics, Policies, and the Entrepreneurial University* (Johns Hopkins University Press 1997)

van Slyke, Paul C. and Mark M. Friedman, 'Employer's Right to Inventions and Patents of Its Officers, Directors and Employees' (1990) 18 AIPLA Quarterly Journal 127

Smith, G. Kenneth, 'Faculty And Graduate Student Generated Inventions: Is University Ownership A Legal Certainty?' (1997) 1 Virginia Journal of Law and Technology 1

So, Anthony D., Bhaven N. Sampat, Arti K. Rai, Robert Cook-Deegan, Jerome H. Reichman, Robert Weissman, and Amy Kapczynski, 'Is Bayh–Dole Good for Developing Countries? Lessons from the U. S. Experience' (2008) 6 PLoS Biology 2078

Spinello, Richard A. and Herman T. Tavani, 'Intellectual Property Rights: From Theory to Practical Implementation' in Richard A. Spinello and Herman T. Tavani (eds.) *Intellectual Property Rights in a Networked World: Theory and Practice* (IGI Global 2005) 1

Stedman, John C., 'Rights and Responsibilities of the Employed Inventor' (1970) 45 Indiana Law Journal 254

–, 'The Employed Inventor, the Public Interest, and Horse and Buggy Law in the Space Age' (1970) 45 New York University Law Review 1

Steffens, Henrich, 'Über die Idee der Universitäten, Vorlesungen 1809' in Eduard Spranger (ed.), *Fichte, Schleiermacher, Steffens – Über das Wesen der Universität* (Verlag der Dürr'schen Buchhandlung 1910) 205

Sterzi, Valerio, Michele Pezzoni, and Francesco Lissoni, 'Patent Management by Universities: Evidence from Italian Academic Inventions' (2019) 28 Industrial and Corporate Change 309

Stierle, Martin, *Das nicht-praktizierte Patent* (Mohr Siebeck 2018)

Stiglitz, Joseph E., 'Knowledge as a Global Public Good' in Inge Kaul, Isabelle Grunberg, and Marc Stern (eds.), *Global Public Goods: International Cooperation in the 21st Century* (Oxford University Press 1999) 308

Stokols, Daniel, Kara L. Hall, Brandie K. Taylor, and Richard P. Moser, 'The Science of Team Science. Overview of the Field and Introduction to the Supplement' (2008) 35 American Journal of Preventive Medicine 77

Strandburg, Katherine J., 'What Does the Public Get – Experimental Use and the Patent Bargain' (2004) Wisconsin Law Review 81

Straus, Joseph, Henrik Holzapfel, and Matthias Lindenmeir, *Genetic Inventions and Patent Law, an Emperical Survey of Selected German R&D Institutions* (Verlag Median Design 2004)

Supreme Court of the United States, '*Board of Trustees of Leland Stanford Junior Univ. v. Roche Molecular Systems, Inc.*, Oral Argument Audio Transcript' (*SCOTUS*, 28 February 2011) <www.supremecourt.gov/oral_arguments/argument_transcripts/2010/09-1159.pdf> accessed 1 November 2021

Sutton, John, 'Employment Contracts' in Warren D. Niederhauser and E. Gerald Meyer (eds.), *Legal Rights of Chemists and Engineers* (American Chemical Society 1977) 45

Swamidass, Paul M. and Venubabu Vulasa, 'Why University Inventions Rarely Produce Income? Bottlenecks in University Technology Transfer' (2009) 34 Journal of Technology Transfer 343

Swiss Federal Instiute of Intellectual Property (IPI), 'EPO Report – Switzerland has the most Patent Applications per Inhabitants' (*IPI*, 12 March 2019) <www.ige.ch/en/services/newsroom/news/news-details/epo-report-switzerland-has-the-most-patent-applications-per-inhabitant> accessed 1 November 2021

Swiss Technology Transfer Association (SWITT), 'Annual Swiss Technology Transfer Reports' (*SWITT*, 2020) <https://switt.ch/swittreport> accessed 1 November 2021

Takenaka, Toshiko, 'Serious Flaw of Employee Invention Ownership under the Bayh-Dole Act in Stanford v. Roche: Finding the Missing Piece of the Puzzle in the German Employee Invention Act' (2011) 44 Texas Intellectual Property Law Journal 281

Tavani, Herman T., 'Locke, Intellectual Property Rights, and the Information Commons' (2005) 7 Ethics and Information Technology 87

Thomas, John R., *The Leahy-Smith America Invents Act: Innovation Issues* (Congressional Research Service 2014)

Thursby, Jerry G. and Marie C. Thursby, 'University Licensing and the Bayh-Dole Act' (2003) 301 Science 1052

Thursby, Jerry G., Richard Jensen, and Marie C. Thursby, 'Objectives, Characteristics and Outcomes of University Licensing: A Survey of Major US Universities' (2001) 26 Journal of Technology Transfer 59

Times Higher Education, 'World University Rankings 2020' (*Times Higher Education*, 2021) <https://timeshighereducation.com/world-university-rankings/2020/world-ranking#!/page/3/length/25/sort_by/rank/sort_order/asc/cols/stats> accessed 1 November 2021

Toole, Andrew A. and Dirk Czarnitzki, 'Commercializing Science: Is There a University 'Brain Drain' From Academic Entrepreneurship?' (2010) 56 Management Science 1599

Treasure, Carolyn, Jerry Avorn, and Aaron Kesselheim, 'What is the Public's Right to Access Medical Discoveries Based on Federally Funded Research?' (2014) 311 Journal of the American Medical Association 907

Trimborn, Michael, *Arbeitnehmererfindungsrecht* (3rd edn., Berliner Wissenschaftsverlag 2013)

US General Accounting Office (GAO), *Problem Areas Affecting Usefulness of Results of Government-Sponsored Research in Medicinal Chemistry: A Report to the Congress* (US Government Printing Office 1968)

–, *Patent Policy: Recent Changes in Federal Law Considered Beneficial* (US Government Printing Office 1987) 3

–, *Technology Transfer: Administration of the Bayh-Dole Act by Research Universities* (GAO 1998) 1

–, *Technology Transfer: Agencies' Rights to Federally Sponsored Biomedical Inventions* (GAO 2003) 5

US Patent and Trademark Office (USPTO), 'Fee Schedule' (*USPTO*, 25 June 2021) <www.uspto.gov/learning-and-resources/fees-and-payment/uspto-fee-schedule#Patent%20Fees> accessed 1 November 2021

–, 'Calendar Year Patent Statistics 2020, Number of Patents Granted as Distributed by Year of Patent Grant' (*USPTO*, 14 October 2021) <www.uspto.gov/web/offices/ac/ido/oeip/taf/topo_20.htm> accessed 14 November 2021

US Senate, *The University and Small Business Patent Procedures Act, Hearings Before the Senate Committee on the Judiciary, 96th Congress, 1st Session* (US Government Printing Office 1979)

Valdivia, Walter D., *University Start-Ups: Critical for Improving Technology Transfer* (Centre for Technology Innovation at Brookings 2013)

Vaughan, Floyd L., *The United States Patent System – Legal and Economic Conflicts in American Patent History* (Greenwood Press Publishers 1977)

Veblen, Thorstein, *The Higher Learning in America: The Annotated Edition: A Memorandum on the Conduct of Universities by Business Men*, edited by Richard F. Teichgraeber III (Johns Hopkins University Press 2015)

Vedder, Richard K., 'Is the University of Virginia Going Private?' (*Minding the Campus*, 12 September 2013) <www.mindingthecampus.org/2013/09/12/is_the_university_of_virginia_/> accessed 1 November 2021

–, 'There Are Really Almost No Truly Private Universities' (*Forbes*, 8 April 2018) <www.forbes.com/sites/richardvedder/2018/04/08/there-are-really-almost-no-truly-private-universities/?sh=254eefa957bc> accessed 1 November 2021

–, *Restoring the Promise: Higher Education in America* (Independent Institute 2019)

Verspagen, Bart, 'University Research, Intellectual Property Rights and European Innovation Systems' (2006) 20 Journal of Economic Surveys 607

Vest, Charles, 'Technological Innovation in the 21th Century' in Luc E. Weber and James J. Duderstadt (eds.), *University Research for Innovation* (Glion Coll 2010) 51

Villasenor, John, 'Intellectual Property Awareness At Universities: Why Ignorance Is Not Bliss' (*Forbes*, 27 November 2012) <www.forbes.com/sites/johnvillasenor/2012/11/27/intellectual-property-awareness-at-universities-why-ignorance-is-not-bliss/?sh=25b467e213ce> accessed 1 November 2021

Walsh, John P., Ashish Arora, and Wesley M. Cohen, 'Effects of Research Tool Patents and Licensing on Biomedical Innovation' in Wesley M. Cohen and Stephen A. Merrill (eds.), *Patents in the Knowledge-based Economy* (National Academies Press 2003) 285

Walsh, John P., Charlene Cho, and Wesley M. Cohen, 'View from the Bench: Patents and Material Transfers' (2005) 309 Science 2002

Walsh, John P., Wesley M. Cohen, and Charlene Cho, 'Where Excludability Matters: Material Versus Intellectual Property in Academic Biomedical Research' (2007) 36 Research Policy 1184

Walter, Sascha G., Arne Schmidt, and Achim Walter, 'Patenting Rationales of Academic Entrepreneurs in Weak and Strong Organizational Regimes' (2016) 45 Research Policy 533

Walterscheid, Edward C., 'The Need for a Uniform Government Patent Policy: The DOE Example' (1990) 3 Harvard Journal Law & Technology 103

–, 'The Early Evolution of the United States Patent Law: Antecedents (Part I)' (1996) 78 Journal of the Patent Office Society 615

Weber, Wolfgang E., *Geschichte der Europäischen Universität* (Kohlhammer 2002)

Weiner, Charles, 'Universities, Professors, and Patents: A Continuing Controversy' (1986) 89 Technology Review 1

–, 'Patenting and Academic Research: Historical Case Studies' (1987) 12 Science, Technology, and Human Values 50

Wright, Bradley C., 'Intellectual Property Employees May Own Key Patents' (2000) The National Law Journal 1

Zemsky, Robert, 'Have we Lost the 'Public' in Higher Education?' (*Chronicle of Higher Education*, 30 May 2003) <www.chronicle.com/article/have-we-lost-the-public-in-higher-education/> accessed 1 November 2021

Zumeta, William M., 'Accountability and the Private Sector: State and Federal Perspective' in Joseph C. Burke (ed.), *Achieving Accountability in Higher Education: Balancing Public, Academic, and Market Demands* (Jossey-Bass 2005) 25

Cases

Alcatel USA, Inc. v. Brown, No. 199–00596–97 (Tex. Dist. Ct. 2002)
Amax Fly Ash Corporation v. United States, 514 F. 2d 1041 (Court of Claims 1975
Arefolov. v. Presidents and Fellows of Harvard College et al, 1:17-cv-10785 (Dist. Ct. MA)
Aronson v. Quick Point Pencil 440 U. S. 257(1979)
Association for Molecular Pathology v. Myriad Genetics, 132 S. Ct. 1794 (S. Ct 2012)
Banks v. Unisys Corp., 228 F.3d 1357 (Fed. Cir. 2000)
Beech Aircraft Corp. v. Edo Corp., 990 F. 2d 1237, 1248 (Fed. Cir. 1993)
Board of Trustees of Leland v. Roche Molecular, 487 F. Supp. 2d 1099 (Dist. Ct. 2007)
Board of Trustees of Leland Stanford v. Roche, 583 F. 3d 832 (Fed. Cir. 2009)
Board of Trustees of the Leland Stanford Junior University v. Roche Molecular Systems, 131 S. Ct. 2188 (S. Ct. 2011)
Burroughs Wellcome Co. v. Barr Laboratories, Inc., 40 F. 3d 1223 (Fed. Cir. 1994)
C. R. Bard, Inc. v. M3 Systems, Inc., 157 F.3d 1340 (Fed. Cir. 1998)
Carnegie Mellon v. Marvell Technology Group 807 F. 3d 1283 (Fed. Cir. 2015),
Chou v. University of Chicago, 254 F. 3d 1347 (Fed. Cir. 2001)
Convolve and MIT v. Compaq and Seagate (Fed. Cir. 2013).
Cubic Corp. v. Marty 185 Cal. App. 3d 438 (CA Ct. of Appeals 1986):
DDB Technologies v. MLB Advanced Media 517 F. 3d 1284 (Fed. Cir. 2008)
Diamond v. Chakrabarty, 447 U. S. 303, 100 S. Ct. 2204, 65 L. Ed. 2d 144 (S. Ct. 1980).
Eldred v. Ashcroft, 537 U. S. 186 (S. Ct. 2003)
Eli Lilly and Co. v. Aradigm Corp., 376 F. 3d 1352 (Fed. Cir. 2004)
Ethicon, Inc. v. United States Surgical Corp., 135 F. 3d 1456 (Fed. Cir. 1998)
Feist Publications, Inc. v. Rural Telephone Service Co., Inc., 499 U. S. 340 (S. Ct. 1991)
FilmTec Corporation v. Allied-Signal Inc. and UOP Inc., 939 F.2d 1568 (1991)
Fina Oil and Chemical Co. v. Ewen, 123 F. 3d 1466 (Fed. Cir. 1997)
Garrett Corporation v. United States, 422 F. 2d 874 (Court of Claims 1970
Gayler v. Wilder, 51 US 477, 493 (S. Ct. 1851)
Golan v. Holder, 565 U. S. (S. Ct. 2012)
Hallmark Personnel of Texas v. Franks, 562 SW 2d 933, 936 (TX Ct. of Civil Appeals 1978)
Hapgood v. Hewitt 119 US 226 (S. Ct. 1886)
Houghton v. United States, 23 F. 2d 386 (Circuit Ct. of Appeals, 4th Circuit 1928).
In re Katz, 687 F. 2d 450 (Ct. of Customs and Patent Appeals 1982)
Ingersoll-Rand Co. v. Ciavatta, 542 A.2d 879 (S.Ct. NJ 1988)
Integra Lifesciences I v. Merck, 545 US 193 (S.Ct. 2005)
Kaplan v. Corcoran, 545 F.2d 1073 (7th Cir. 1976)
Kaplan v. Johnson, 409 F. Supp. 190 (Dist. Ct. ND Ill. 1976)
Kimberly-Clark v. Procter & Gamble, 973 F. 2d 911 (Fed. Cir. 1992)

Madey v. Duke University, 307 F.3d 1351 (Fed. Cir. 2002).
MadStad & Mark Stadnyk v. USPTO, 12-cv-1589 (M. D. Florida 2012)
McClurg v. Kingsland 42 US 202 (S. Ct. 1843)
Meng v. Chu, No. 14–1746 (Fed. Cir. 2016)
Mueller Brass v. Reading Industries, Inc., 325 F. Supp. 1357 (Dist. Ct., ED PA 1972)
New Marshall Engine Co. v. Marshall Engine Co., 223 U. S. 473 (S. Ct. 1912)
Peregrine Semiconductor Crop. v. RF Micro Devices Inc., No. 3:2012cv00911 (D. Ct. SD CA 2014)
Public Citizen v. Sampson, 379 F. Supp. 662 (Dist. Ct. DC 1974)
Reading & Bates Const. Co. v. O'Donnell, 627 SW 2d 239, 243 (TX Ct. of Appeals 1982)
Regents of the University of California v. Eli Lilly 119 F. 3d 1559 (Fed. Cir. 1997
Roberts v. Sears, Roebuck & Co., 697 F. 2d 796 (Ct. of Appeals, 7th Circuit 1983)
Roche Products v. Bolar Pharmaceuticals Co., 733 F. 2d 858 (Fed. Cir. 1984).
Sewall v. Walters, 21 F. 3d 411 (Fed. Cir. 1994)
Shukh v. Seagate Technology LLC, 803 F.3d 659 (Fed. Cir. 2015)
SmithKline Diagnostics, Inc. v. Helena Lab. Corp., 859 F.2d 878 (Fed. Cir. 1988).
Solomons v. United States 137 US 342 (1890)
Speck v. North Carolina Dairy Foundation, 307 SE 2d 785 (NC Ct. of Appeals 1983) (Speck I)
Speck v. North Carolina Dairy Foundation, 319 SE 2d 139 (NC S. Ct. 1984) (Speck II)
Standard Brands, Inc. v. US Partition & Packaging Corp., 199 F. Supp. 161, 176 (Dist. Ct. ED WI 1961)
Standard Parts v. Peck 264 US 52 (1924)
Stark v. Advanced Magnetics, Inc., 119 F. 3d 1551 (Fed. Cir. 1997)
State v. Neal, 12 So. 2d 590 (S. Ct. LA 1943);
StoneEagle Services, Inc. v. Gillman, 746 F. 3d 1059 (Fed. Cir. 2014)
Trovan Ltd. v. Sokymat SA, Irori, 299 F. 3d 1292 (Fed. Cir. 2002)
Trustees of Dartmouth College v. Woodward, 17 U. S. 518 (S. Ct. 1819)
University Patents, Inc. v. Kligman, 762 F. Supp. 1212 (Dist. Ct. 1991)
United States v. Dubilier Condenser Corp., 289 US 178 (S. Ct. 1933)
University of Colorado Foundation v. American Cynamid Company, 196 F.3d 1366 (Fed. Cir. 1999)
University of Pittsburgh v. Hedrick, 573 F.3d 1290 (Fed. Cir. 2009)
University of Rochester v. G. D. Searle & Co., Inc., 358 F.3d 916 (Fed. Cir. 2004
University of Utah v. Max Planck Gesellschaft zur Förderung der Wissenschaft E. V., 734 F.3d 1315 (Fed. Cir. 2013)
Whittemore v. Cutter 29 F. Cas. 1120 (Circuit Court District MA 1813)

Index

Geistiges Eigentum und Wettbewerbsrecht

edited by
Peter Heermann, Diethelm Klippel†,
Ansgar Ohly, and Olaf Sosnitza

In the information age, the significance of intellectual property laws, in particular patent law, copyright law and trademark laws, has increased considerably. At the same time, those dealing with legal issues are facing numerous new questions. Jurisprudence has scarcely been able to keep up with the current turbulent developments, and legal literature continues to be dominated by works which are practically oriented and in which basic issues of legal scholarship are neglected. Whereas general civil law regards property law as its natural sphere of activity, it has to a large extent lost sight of intangible property rights. The goal of *Geistiges Eigentum und Wettbewerbsrecht* is to contribute to an analysis of the law of intellectual property and competition law and in doing so not to lose sight of practical experience. The series accepts habilitations, outstanding dissertations and comparable monographs which deal with patent law, copyright law, trademark law and related fields of the law, in particular the code of standards for advertising practices, antitrust law and personal rights. It focuses on those works which address the basic issues in the law of intellectual property, including their historical, philosophical and economic aspects and thus contribute to a "general part of intellectual property," which presently does not exist. Since the European approximation of laws in intangible property rights and competition law is proceeding very quickly and in addition there are numerous international agreements which have a large impact on these fields of the law, the series also deals with international contexts.

ISSN: 1860-7306
Suggested citation: GEuWR

All available volumes can be found at *www.mohrsiebeck.com/geuwr*

Mohr Siebeck
www.mohrsiebeck.com